S0-AFQ-591

FLORIDA STATE
UNIVERSITY LIBRARIES

SEP 15 1995

TALLAHASSEE, FLORIDA

EAST ASIA
IN TRANSITION

With contributions by leading authorities on the security and political economy of East Asia, this volume examines the implications of the profound strategic and economic transformations in the region since the demise of the Soviet Union ended Cold War polarization and the emergence of new East Asian economic powers transformed regional economic relations. By studying the implications of these strategic and economic transformations for the interests of the great powers and key local powers and for the maintenance of regional stability, the contributors ponder how the changing relations among these states might evolve into a new regional order characterized by extensive stability and cooperation. By so doing, they consider potential sources of instability, including changes in domestic politics and enduring bilateral conflicts of interests, and the importance of developing creative bilateral policies and of maximizing the contribution of multilateral institutions in mitigating the impact of these factors on regional security.

Published with the support of the East-West Center

EAST ASIA IN TRANSITION
Toward a New Regional Order

Robert Gilpin
Richard Betts
Charles Ziegler
Mike Mochizuki
Donald Zagoria

Robert Scalapino
Michael Vatikiotis
Danny Unger
Michael Leifer
Herbert Ellison
Harry Harding

Robert S. Ross
Editor

INSTITUTE OF SOUTHEAST ASIAN STUDIES
Singapore

M.E. Sharpe
Armonk, New York
London, England

DS
511
E15
1995

An East Gate Book

Copyright © 1995 by M. E. Sharpe, Inc.

All rights reserved. No part of this book may be reproduced in any form without written permission from the publisher, M. E. Sharpe, Inc., 80 Business Park Drive, Armonk, New York 10504.

First published in the United States in 1995 by M. E. Sharpe, Inc., 80 Business Park Drive, Armonk, New York 10504.

First published in Singapore in 1995 by the Institute of Southeast Asian Studies, Heng Mui Keng Terrace, Pasir Panjang, Singapore 0511.

Library of Congress Cataloging-in-Publication Data

East Asia in transition : toward a new regional order / Robert S. Ross, editor.
p. cm.
"East gate book."
Includes bibliographical references and index.
ISBN 1–56324–560–4. — ISBN 1–56324–561–2 (pbk.)
1. East Asia—Foreign relations. 2. East Asia—Foreign economic relations. 3. East Asia—Politics and government. I. Ross, Robert S., 1954–
DS511.E15 1995
327.5—dc20
94–23743
CIP

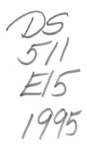 **Institute of Southeast Asian Studies**

The Institute of Southeast Asian Studies was established as an autonomous organization in 1968. It is a regional research centre for scholars and other specialists concerned with modern Southeast Asia, particularly the many-faceted problems of stability and security, economic development, and political and social change.

The Institute is governed by a twenty-two-member Board of Trustees comprising nominees from the Singapore Government, the National University of Singapore, the various Chambers of Commerce, and professional and civic organizations. A ten-man Executive Committee oversees day-to-day operations; it is chaired by the Director, the Institute's chief academic and administrative officer.

ISBN 981-3055-02-2 (soft cover, ISEAS, Singapore)

Printed in the United States of America

The paper used in this publication meets the minimum requirements of American National Standard for Information Sciences— Permanence of Paper for Printed Library Materials, ANSI Z 39.48-1984.

∞

BM (c) 10 9 8 7 6 5 4 3 2 1
BM (p) 10 9 8 7 6 5 4 3 2 1

Contents

Part IV: Toward a New Regional Order

Contributors

Richard K. Betts is professor of political science at Columbia University. He was a Senior Fellow at the Brookings Institution, has taught at Harvard and Johns Hopkins, and worked on the staffs of the Senate Select Committee on Intelligence and the National Security Council. Among his books are *Soldiers, Statesmen, and Cold War Crises*; *The Irony of Vietnam*; *Surprise Attack*; and *Military Readiness*.

Herbert J. Ellison is professor of Russian and East European Studies in the Henry M. Jackson School of International Studies, and in the history department of the University of Washington. He writes on Russian history and foreign policy. He edited and contributed to *The Sino-Soviet Conflict in Global Perspective* (1982), *Soviet Policy Toward Western Europe* (1983), and *Japan and the Pacific Quadrille* (1987).

Robert Gilpin is Dwight D. Eisenhower Professor of International Affairs in the Department of Politics and in the Woodrow Wilson School of International Affairs, Princeton University. He is the author of numerous works on international politics and political economy, including *War and Change in World Politics* (1981) and *The Political Economy of International Relations* (1987).

Harry Harding is dean of the Elliott School of International Affairs, and professor of political science and international affairs at George Washington University. Professor Harding did his undergraduate work at Princeton University, and received his M.A. and Ph.D. in political science from Stanford University in 1974. He has served on the faculties of Swarthmore College and Stanford University, and was a Senior Fellow in the Foreign Policy Studies Program at the Brookings Institution. His major works include *A Fragile Relationship: The United States and China Since 1972* (1992), *China's Second Revolution: Reform After Mao* (1987), and *Organizing China: The Problem of Bureaucracy, 1949–1976* (1981). He is completing a new book on the phenomenon of "Greater China," and an edited volume on China's cooperative international behavior.

Michael Leifer is professor of international relations at the London School of Economics and Political Science where he has been involved in establishing a new research center for the study of the Asian economy, politics and society. His most recent books are *ASEAN and the Security of Southeast Asia* (1990) and *A Dictionary of the Modern Politics of Southeast Asia* (1995).

Mike M. Mochizuki is senior fellow in the Foreign Policy Studies program of the Brookings Institution. Before joining Brookings, he was co-director of the Rand Center for Asia-Pacific Policy and associate professor of international relations at the University of Southern California. He specializes in Japanese domestic politics and foreign policy, U.S.-Japan relations, and East Asian security issues.

Robert S. Ross is associate professor of political science at Boston College and associate-in-research at the John King Fairbank Center for East Asian Research, Harvard University. He is the author of various works on Chinese policy toward East Asia and U.S.-China relations, including *Negotiating Cooperation: The United States and China, 1969–1989* (1995).

Robert A. Scalapino is Robson Research Professor of Government Emeritus, University of California, Berkeley, former director of the Institute of East Asian Studies, and co-editor of the monthly journal *Asian Survey*. He is the author of numerous books and monographs on East Asia and U.S. policies in Asia.

Danny Unger is assistant professor of government at Georgetown University. He works in the areas of international relations theory, comparative and international political economy with geographical emphases on Japan and Thailand. He edited *Japan's Emerging Global Role* and is currently completing four books: *The Politics of Economic Policymaking in Thailand*, *The Politics of Financial Liberalization in Thailand* (co-author), *the Political Economy of the ASEAN Four* (co-author), and *Burden-Sharing in the Persian Gulf War* (co-editor and co-author).

Michael R. J. Vatikiotis spent four years in Indonesia as a correspondent for *Far Eastern Economic Review*. A graduate in Southeast Asian studies, he has a Ph.D. from Oxford University, and is also the author of *Indonesian Politics Under Suharto* (1993). Vatikiotis is currently the Bangkok Bureau Chief of *Far Eastern Economic Review*.

Donald S. Zagoria is a professor of government at Hunter College and an adjunct professor at Columbia University's East Asian Institute. He is the author of three books and more than two hundred articles on East Asian security issues.

Charles E. Ziegler is professor of political science at the University of Louisville, and director of the Council on Foreign Relations, Louisville Committee. He is the author of *Foreign Policy and East Asia* (1993), *Environmental Policy in the U.S.S.R.* (1987), and numerous articles on Soviet/Russian politics. He was a Fulbright Lecture/Research fellow in Korea during 1995.

Preface

This volume is the final product of a five-year collaborative project focusing on the international politics of East Asia. The first half of the project entailed cooperation among Chinese- and Western-trained scholars aimed at understanding U.S.–China–Soviet strategic interactions during the Cold War. A June 1990 conference in Beijing brought together six Chinese and six American scholars to present early drafts of their papers and four senior Chinese scholars and three senior American scholars to act as discussants and advisers. The papers and the ensuing multinational discussion in Beijing stimulated extensive rethinking of the dynamics of Cold War interactions. We learned from one another much new information concerning pivotal Cold War developments, and we debated the continuities and the long-term dynamics of the Cold War tripolarity. This meeting resulted in the publication of a English-language volume containing the papers prepared in English and a Chinese-language volume containing all the papers from this conference.

The collapse of the Soviet Union and the resulting transformation of global and regional politics presented the project with an opportunity to consider the ramifications of this transformation for East Asia and the emerging implications for a stable post–Cold War order. A first conference of paper writers was held at the East-West Center in Honolulu in January 1993. In addition to the paper writers, discussants were invited from each of the countries addressed in the volume. The discussants who attended this conference from both the region and the United States were:

Byung-joon Ahn	Charles Morrison
Ngoc Dao Huy	Michel Oksenberg
Vladimir Ivanov	Akihiko Tanaka
Ji Guoxing	

The contributions of these scholars cannot be overestimated. The opportunity to present their papers to distinguished specialists from the various countries in East Asia played an important part in shaping the authors' understanding of their respective subjects. The chapters in this book reflect the collaborative effort of the participants at this meeting.

On the basis of the valuable assistance the authors received at the January

1993 meeting, they revised their papers and discussed them with one another at a meeting held in August 1993 at the Henry M. Jackson School of International Studies, University of Washington. In addition to the paper writers, participants in this meeting included David Bachman, Charles Morrison, and Michel Oksenberg. We are grateful for their participation in the project and their very helpful contributions to the discussion. Charles Morrison also contributed extensive written comments on all the papers. Once again, on the basis of the comments and suggestions from all the participants at this meeting, the authors revised their papers.

Subsequent to his participation in the meetings at the East-West Center and at the University of Washington, Donald Emmerson found that he could not complete his contribution to the project. We were very fortunate that Michael Vatikiotis was willing to join the project and contribute a first-rate paper on an important subject.

The staff at M. E. Sharpe deserves special recognition. Doug Merwin was a fine and knowledgeable editor, sensitive to the intellectual currents of the East Asia field. Aud Thiessen moved the manuscript through its various stages with welcomed speed and professionalism. Angela Piliouras managed the difficult process of coordinating numerous chapters across numerous continents with admirable grace and much-appreciated patience. It was a pleasure to work with all of them.

Funding for the project was provided by a generous grant from the Collaborative Research Grant Program of the Program of Peace and International Cooperation of the John D. and Catherine T. MacArthur Foundation to the Henry M. Jackson School of International Studies at the University of Washington, when the editor was teaching at the University of Washington. The project also received valuable support from the Program on International Economics and Politics at the East-West Center, which made possible the August 1993 meeting held at the University of Washington.

Introduction: East Asia in Transition

Robert S. Ross

The chapters in this volume all reflect a common concern. The authors recognize the considerable stability in contemporary East Asia. Nevertheless, they also recognize various trends that suggest the potential for significant regional instability that could affect the vital interests of countries throughout the region. The common concern over these countervailing trends stimulated the first efforts to develop this book and forms the basis of the intellectual problems and the analytical perspectives for all of the contributors to this volume.

This concern is based on our understanding of the sources of foreign policy and of change in international politics. Each of us has observed the fundamental transformation of the distribution of power among the great powers in East Asia and believes that this transformation will have a profound and far-reaching impact on the policies of states and on the ability of policymakers both to pursue their countries' respective interests and to maintain regional stability. The origins of this transformation are self-evident—the dissolution of the Soviet Union and the end of the Cold War have destroyed the foundations of the preexisting regional order and the foreign policies of every state in East Asia. In the context of reduced Russian power, the regional polarization and national preoccupation with immediate threats to vital national interests that characterized Cold War East Asia have ended.

Coinciding with the transformation of the regional strategic order, there has also been a transformation of the East Asian economic order. Although this change began earlier than the end of the Cold War and occurred far more gradually, by the end of the 1980s its implications for the region had become fully apparent. Whereas the United States had once been the overwhelmingly dominant economic power in East Asia, by the end of the 1980s its relative role in the regional economy had significantly diminished. No longer could Washington use its economic authority to dictate the form of either its bilateral economic relationships with the East Asian economies or the regional economic order. Similar to the dynamics in the security realm, the relative decline of the influence of a dominant regional economic power has transformed the region's economic order and, ultimately, its strategic order.

By the beginning of the 1990s, the strategic and economic orders of East Asia in no way resembled those of the Cold War era. This book reflects the authors' concern for the implications of these changes for the region. But the authors also have a common normative concern for thinking through the potential sources of a new regional order characterized by stability and prosperity. Thus, this volume is more than a description of the forces of change and the responses of key actors. It also explores and analyzes what the states can do, individually and collectively, to promote peaceful change and the emergence in post-transition East Asia of relationships that serve the security and economic interests of the individual states, while not eliciting counterproductive and destabilizing responses from their counterparts. The authors are concerned about the sources of change and the elements of future stability.

The Transformation of the East Asian Strategic Order

The collapse of Soviet power has been of paramount importance to the international relations of East Asia. Nonetheless, this change is only one of the many complex and changing aspects of the East Asian international order that, together, contribute to regionwide apprehension over the future of the region. Coinciding with the collapse of the Soviet Union and the emergence of a smaller, less powerful, and internally chaotic Russia have been fundamental changes in the capabilities of all the great powers in East Asia.

The transformation of Japan's regional role has been fundamental to the ongoing transformation in East Asia. By the end of the Cold War, Japan had become an economic power surpassing any European country in economic authority and rivaling the United States for economic influence in East Asia. Moreover, Japanese economic growth and technology development have contributed to moderate yet sustained growth in military capabilities, suggesting for the first time since World War II that Tokyo can develop the capabilities to be a regional political power and even a military power. Its defense budget and its relatively modern naval forces are already the second largest in the world.

Simultaneously with the rise of Japanese economic power and political potential, as the Cold War has ended, the region has also experienced the maturation of China's post-Mao economic reforms and the growing potential of China as a far more capable regional power. The combination of ongoing rapid economic growth, increasing technological sophistication, and expanding defense spending will inevitably give rise to increased Chinese military and economic power and, thus, a change in the regional balance of power. Given the rapid transformation of Chinese capabilities and the potential for domestic instability, there is also widespread concern as to how China's objectives will develop as its capabilities improve.

With the rising regional authority of Japan and China, there is considerable uncertainty about America's role in post–Cold War East Asia, despite its current status as "the world's only superpower." Given America's relatively benign threat environment and its distance from East Asia, it has a considerable range of choice regarding its presence in the region. At a minimum, given developments in Japan and China, the United States will play a less preponderant role in this region than in the past. But it may also draw down its military forces to such an extent that its regional presence will decline, significantly so that its role in the regional balance will be merely equal to that of the other regional powers. It might even withdraw sufficiently that it will play only a minor role in the regional balance.

Finally, Russia remains an East Asian power. It may be considerable weaker than the former Soviet Union, and its political system and economy may be in a shambles, but it maintains the long-term ability to influence the vital security interests of the other regional powers and to determine the character of the regional balance of power. Its absolute size, its strategic forces, its resources, its location at the nexus of the interests of the world's most powerful countries, and, thus, its mere potential as a great power create considerable uncertainty over its future contribution to the regional order. These factors ensure that Russia will remain a force in the contemporary foreign policy considerations of all of East Asia.

This uncertainty over the changing balance of power among the great powers is a central theme running through each chapter in this volume. Equally significant, however, is the authors' concern for the changing roles of local powers and the implications for regional stability. The local powers played a crucial role in both the outbreak of regional wars and great-power relations throughout the Cold War, and they will play an equally important role in post–Cold War East Asia. This is particularly the case for four key areas—the Korean peninsula, Indonesia, Thailand, and Vietnam.

The continued division of Korea remains a major determinant of the security policies of all the countries of Northeast Asia. A unified Korea under the Seoul government would be more powerful and independent and would also confront a fundamentally different border relationship with China. These changes would radically transform the security considerations and foreign policies both of the Korean successor state and of its great-power neighbors. Moreover, the very process of unification—whether it is peaceful or violent—will affect regional stability. But even in the absence of unification, the potential for instability remains high. The ongoing possibility of a nuclear-armed Pyongyang magnifies the importance of the Korean peninsula for regional stability, especially in the midst of a North Korean succession crisis and social instability. However, a nuclear-armed unified Korea would also complicate questions of regional stability and the foreign policies of the powers.

During the early years of the Cold War, Indonesia played an important destabilizing role in Southeast Asia, and during the latter half of the Cold War, it made a vital contribution to the development of stability in the region and the development of the Association of Southeast Asian Nations (ASEAN). Indonesia's size and its growing economic and military capability suggest that it will play an increasingly influential role in the post–Cold War regional order. Jakarta's policies toward its immediate neighbors could determine whether or not ASEAN continues to contribute to regional stability and how Indonesia's neighbors align themselves toward the regional powers. Similarly, Jakarta's posture toward China and Vietnam could determine both countries' stake in regional order and their corresponding interests in stability.

Thailand's role in Southeast Asia has been transformed since the end of the Cold War. Whereas it had consistently been an aligned country seeking protection against Vietnamese power in Indochina, it now finds itself with an economy that is more prosperous than the economies of the Indochinese countries and the prospect of establishing an influential economic and political role throughout the area, including in Burma. Moreover, its much-improved security position and the significant importance of Japanese investment in its developing economy suggest that Bangkok may well develop substantial foreign policy flexibility and that it will not merely accommodate itself to Chinese strategic power on mainland Southeast Asia. Given Thailand's sensitive position on mainland Southeast Asia, how Bangkok uses this flexibility will affect the policies of the regional powers and contribute to the character of the post–Cold War regional order and the prospects for stability.

Whereas Thailand is experiencing greater international maneuverability in post–Cold War East Asia, Vietnam finds itself in its most passive strategic position since World War II. Lacking a great-power partner with which to offset Chinese power on its northern border, having lost its strategic presence throughout Indochina after its withdrawal from Cambodia, and confronting a war-devastated economy requiring its full attention, Hanoi has no choice but to accommodate itself to Chinese power and acknowledge Chinese leadership in Indochina. This transformation affects the security considerations of the entire region. Nonetheless, it is also clear that the Vietnamese leadership is not content with this situation. Not only is Hanoi determined to modernize its economy, but it also will take advantage of any opportunity to extricate itself from Chinese power. Vietnamese policies toward the great powers played a fundamental role in the development of East Asian Cold War instability, and they are likely to continue to be influential in the post–Cold War era.

The strategic changes in East Asia in the aftermath of the Cold War have been profound. The strategic roles of both the regional powers and the most influential local powers have been radically altered by the end of the U.S.–Soviet bipolar struggle, by the subsequent emergence of a truly multipolar environment, and by the fundamentally altered foreign policy objectives of the key regional actors. The result is a strategic order in transition toward an uncertain future.

The Transformation of the East Asian Economic Order

Accompanying the transformation of the East Asian strategic order has been the less dramatic and more gradual, but nonetheless profoundly important, transformation of the regional economic order. The changes that have taken place in regional economic relations have affected the regional trade order and the regionwide patterns of direct foreign investment. They have also given rise to more states characterized by economic stability and prosperity. These changes have affected the economic interests of the regional states, the distribution of economic power throughout the region, and the international political order of East Asia.

The entire region has been affected by the significant changes in the international trading order. Where there was once a global system basically characterized by a single set of nondiscriminatory trade rules, there are now regional economic groups based on particularistic rules encouraging intraregional trade through preferential treatment of the exports of the member countries. But coinciding with this trend in North America and Europe has been the continued dependence of the economic health of East Asian countries on exports to these regions; the preponderance of the trade of countries situated within East Asia continues to take place with countries outside the region. The North American Free Trade Agreement (NAFTA) only exacerbates local concerns over trade flows, insofar as it suggests that the United States market, the traditional market for much of East Asia's exports, may become increasingly dominated by exports from Canada and Mexico. Until the East Asian economies find substitute markets for their manufactured goods, the current trend in the international economic system will continue to be a source of considerable economic insecurity.

The prospect of reduced access to the American market for East Asian economies has been accompanied by a relative reduction in annual U.S. investments in East Asia. Whereas U.S. investment in East Asia had been the dominant source of hard currency and investment capital for the East Asian economies throughout much of the Cold War, by the 1970s Japan had begun to assume much of America's role as the dominant regional economic power, as it became the primary source of new investment capital and, in the 1980s, the principal external source of industrialization in Indonesia, Thailand, and Malaysia. The region, thus, faces the prospect that the United States will play an increasingly reduced role in regional trade and investment. The economic implications of this transition are unsettling, if only because the region flourished in the context of American economic preeminence. But there are also political implications. In the context of U.S. ambivalence over its strategic role in the region and the associated anxiety throughout the region, declining U.S. economic interests in East Asia could well exacerbate the trend toward U.S. political and strategic disengagement from the region and create additional regionwide uncertainty over the emerging political order.

The relative decline in America's economic presence has been accompanied by the growing regional economic importance of Japan, especially as a source of investment capital for the entire region. In addition to its role in the Indonesian, Thai, and Malaysian economies, Japan has been an important economic partner of South Korea, it has been a primary external source of Chinese investment capital, and its role in the Indochinese economies is likely to increase as economic reforms in these countries continue to deepen. The implications of this are twofold. First, accompanying the export of Japanese capital has been the Japanese strategy of export-led economic development. The implications of this by-product of Japanese investment remain uncertain. Although the export-led strategy has been a major force behind regional prosperity, it has also been a major source of trade friction between recently developed economies and the mature economies in Europe and North America. Thus, trade friction involving East Asian countries may well increase as more countries in the region encounter the difficulties in economic relations with North America and Europe that Japan has met. The first stages of this trend have already aggravated regional anxieties over the uncertainties of post–Cold War East Asia.

Second, the political impact of Japan's growing economic role is also unclear. The expansion of Japan's regional economic presence will inevitably give Japan greater influence on the security and foreign policies of its neighbors. Attitudes toward Japan vary throughout the region, ranging from deep suspicion to welcome embrace. How Japan exercises its expanded economic influence and the reaction of Japan's neighbors to its expanded regional authority will be crucial determinants of the post–Cold War political environment in East Asia.

Japan already rivals the United States as a major regional economic power. But just as the regional strategic order is becoming multipolar, East Asia has also become economically far more complex. Not only has the Chinese economy been growing at a phenomenal rate, but South Korea, Taiwan, and Singapore have also all achieved high per-capita GNP figures. These developments could well have positive implications—China could provide an expanding market, enabling the sustained growth of the local economies, and the development of South Korean, Taiwan, and Singaporean capital for foreign investment may augur reduced regional dependence on Japanese direct foreign investment and development loans. On the other hand, regional dependence on the Chinese market could lead to political anxiety over the corresponding expansion of Chinese political power, and the dispersion of economic power could undermine the concentration of economic authority necessary to create a stable economic order founded on regionwide adherence to common rules of behavior. As in strategic affairs, the transition toward an economic order characterized by greater distribution of economic power across the region could create considerable uncertainty concerning the prospects both for continued economic growth and for political alignments. Under such circumstances, national policy responses could aggravate preexisting sources of economic instability in East Asia.

The Challenge of the Transition

The authors share a concern for the implications of the economic and strategic transitions taking place in East Asia. But they also share an interest in trying to understand how this troubling transition might lead to a new regional order characterized by security in both strategic and economic affairs and to opportunities for the countries to develop relationships conducive to relatively minimal tension and maximal cooperation. The authors' approach to both regionwide issues and the roles of individual countries considers how current dynamics can be channeled into relatively constructive directions.

Thus, the volume reflects both the authors' concern for the implications of change in economic and strategic power relations in the region and their refusal to draw fatalistic conclusions from these circumstances. The authors are "realists" insofar as their analysis reflects their considerable apprehension over the implications of shifting power relations for the prospects of maintaining peaceful international relations. Contemporary political and economic developments in East Asia seem to fit the classic description of the central propositions of realist thought regarding uneven rates of growth and their implications for differential growth of power, stability among great powers, and the probability of general war. Such transitions can generate considerable instability, and just such a transition seems to be taking place in East Asia in the aftermath of the Cold War. The authors approach contemporary East Asia with this analytical perspective, and they are concerned by the regional trends it suggests.

On the other hand, the authors are dissatisfied with the inability of realism to offer only costly and perhaps unnecessary and even counterproductive recommendations for ways in which the implications of uneven rates of change for international stability might be mitigated by decision makers necessarily preoccupied with furthering their respective countries's national interests. The authors are unwilling to reconcile themselves to the conclusion drawn from realist analysis that international politics can generate only policies that prescribe security maximization and lead to heightened instability and, thus, preclude an alternative future of regionwide stability. While recognizing the realist dilemma faced by the countries in an evolving and uncertain East Asia, they are compelled by this lack of alternatives to adopt a nonrealist approach in order to consider the implications of various policy directions for regionwide trends.

Thus, the chapters that address the roles of the great and local powers in the emerging East Asian order consider how each nation perceives the implications of the transition in East Asia for its own national interests. For the most part, these national concerns are taken as givens, reflecting the countries' apprehensions over how changing power relations will affect their particular national security interests. In this respect, the authors observe that decision makers throughout East Asia are making security assessments primarily based on their neighbors' changing capabilities rather than on their intentions, an important but less stable indicator of the potential for hostility and insecurity. They further recognize that national policies throughout the region will inevitably reflect these changing capabilities and the shifting regional balance of power. In this respect, the authors remain wedded to realist perspectives on the sources of state behavior.

The authors depart from the fatalism of realism insofar as the volume reflects their appreciation that alternative policies can often provide equally well for a country's security but have fundamentally different implications for its counterparts' security and, thus, for international stability. On the one hand, the authors acknowledge that unintentional and spiraling conflict is often the consequence of the anarchy of international politics—in the pursuit of national security, states may adopt policies that unintentionally undermine the security of their counterparts. In such circumstances, spiraling conflict and heightened insecurity result from the defensive aspirations of the protagonists. On the other hand, the authors also believe that such unintended consequences can often be mitigated by appropriate policy choices.

Despite the uncertainty in East Asia over the emerging regional order and apprehension over uneven rates of change, the region truly remains in transition—alignments have yet to gel and policies remain in flux. Most important, the nations of East Asia have not settled on foreign policies driven by erroneous worst-case analyses of their counterparts' intentions. Thus far, the spiraling conflict often associated with the anarchy of international politics has been avoided, as the states throughout the region are also waiting to see what emerges from the transition. There thus remains considerable opportunity for policymakers to develop creative policies aimed at maximizing the possibility that the outcome of this transition will be an East Asian international order conducive to both the security of the countries of the region and the resolution of conflicts of vital national interests by methods short of unnecessary and unintentional spiraling economic protectionism, arms races, and war.

Thus, the volume has an overtly normative objective—it tries to point to ways in which East Asian policymakers can provide for their countries' security while avoiding unintended and unnecessary spiraling conflict with their neighbors. The authors analyze the security concerns of the individual states and the policies they have thus far adopted in response. But they also try to go further—they consider how these countries can respond to these concerns without eliciting counterproductive policies from the target countries. They also consider the role that other countries can play in promoting the development of such policy choices. Stability will require efforts on the part of all the countries in East Asia.

In weighing the potential for the development of a stable post–Cold War order, the authors consider both potential impediments to and facilitators of cooperation. A potential obstacle to the development of regional stability is domestic instability. Nearly all of the countries in East Asia are undergoing some form of fundamental change in their political, economic, or social systems, or some combination thereof. In such circumstances, should domestic considerations come to dominate the policy agenda of the national elites, foreign policy could well become hostage to parochial domestic objectives, so that foreign policies could become less subtle and more amenable to compromise. The result could be domestic-driven and unintended heightened regional instability.

The challenge of domestic instability is particularly pronounced in the former and current Leninist countries of Russia, China, Vietnam, and North Korea, where the multifaceted transformations that are currently underway or that will inevitably occur are the most dramatic and potentially destabilizing in East Asia. Such domestic instability may well promote excessive nationalism and international belligerence and, thus, heightened regional tension. On the other hand, the authors recognize that these same domestic dilemmas can create opportunities for political change conducive to regional stability. To the extent that democratic societies tend to develop more cooperative relations among each other, the emergence of democratic institutions in Russia, no matter how tentative and fragile, and the prospect that the development of market economies in China and Vietnam will promote political liberalization suggest that domestic change could also promote foreign policies supportive of regional stability. How elites in each of these countries respond to the pressures for and from reform policies and how they manage their political successions within an unstable domestic environment and an uncertain international environment may well determine the security of their neighbors and the stability of the region. Domestic change in each of these countries warrants special consideration.

But there are also multilateral developments in East Asia that could facilitate regional cooperation. Should current trends continue, policymakers may well be able to take advantage of multilateral institutions to promote the reduction of regional tensions and the development of a stable East Asian order. Although the contributors to this volume recognize that multilateral institutions may influence only the margins of policy and that this is particularly the case where security policy is concerned, they also believe that the importance of regional stability requires policymakers to utilize every instrument of diplomacy and that even marginal influences, when they complement the influence of other policies, can significantly affect national interests and contribute to regional stability. Confidence-building measures, for example, may be supplemental, but they are not necessarily irrelevant.

Moreover, there is reason to believe that East Asia is particularly well prepared to develop such institutions. The independent initiative of local powers created the Association of Southeast Asian Nations (ASEAN), which has become one of the world's most established multilateral institutions. In 1991, all of the governments in the region agreed to establish the forum for Asia Pacific Economic Cooperation (APEC), an institution that has the potential to develop a role in ameliorating economic tension. And in 1993, the ASEAN Regional Forum (ARF) was established as a regionwide forum for security issues. This recent history suggests that the region may be able to use multilateral institutions to help manage the difficulties inherent in the post–Cold War transition in East Asia.

Thus, the volume gives extensive consideration to the role that existing and potential multilateral institutions can play in promoting the emergence of a stable post–Cold War regional order. Consideration is given to how such institutions might best be organized in order to address particular security concerns. Thus, in addition to an analysis of the value of such institutions per se, individual chapters consider the abilities of specific institutions to address specific conflicts and, thus, evaluate the benefits of issue-specific institutions and subregional specific institutions.

East Asia is experiencing greater stability than at any time since the Second World War. Nonetheless, neither the history of nations nor contemporary regional dynamics suggest that this reprieve from escalated conflict and war can be taken for granted. It is the hope of the authors in this volume that an understanding of the forces of change and of the policies of key nations will make it possible to use the present opportunity to help sustain and even consolidate the current trend of international cooperation in East Asia.

Part I:
Economic and Political Change in East Asia

1

Economic Change and the Challenge of Uncertainty

Robert Gilpin

Recent developments are transforming the international political economy in significant ways and thus causing new uncertainties for national economies throughout the world. Among the recent changes are the end of the Cold War, the slowdown of global economic growth (particularly in the United States and Western Europe), and increased tensions between Western and Asian models of capitalism. These political and economic changes have raised uncertainties with respect to the openness of the trading system, the adequacy of the rules governing the international economy, and the prospects for economic conflict. These recent changes and their potential effects are especially important for the East Asian economies. In the first part of this article, I shall address the recent changes and their particular significance for East Asia. In a subsequent section, I shall discuss longer-term trends and changes that are making the stability of the global economy more precarious.

The collapse of the Soviet Union and the end of the Cold War are the most dramatic and far-reaching of these recent developments. While many of the long-term results of these developments cannot yet be determined, it is clear that a shift in national priorities is taking place in the United States and other countries. Throughout the Cold War, American leaders generally placed American security interests above American economic interests. With the end of the Cold War and the advent of the Clinton administration, American priorities are being revised, and much greater emphasis is being placed on American economic interests. The implications for Asia of this reorientation of American policy, however, are uncertain. On a positive note, Secretary of State Warren Christopher has stated that Asia represents "a primacy of opportunity" for American business.[1] The United States has become an active member of the Asia Pacific Economic Cooperation (APEC) forum and now supports multilateral approaches to Asian issues. Yet the goals of this remodeled American policy toward East Asia continue to be a mystery. Despite the new multilateral emphasis, the policy shift has meant intensified unilateral American pressures on Japan to open its economy to American goods and direct investment. Furthermore, with the decline of the Soviet threat, Japan has greater freedom of action; its resentment of American demands has increased, and, for the first time, Japan is actively encouraging other Asian countries to resist American pressures. The result is an intensification of economic and political tensions across the Pacific.

Another notable development causing economic uncertainty is the slowdown of global economic growth, especially within the Western economies. In fact, with the exception of the Reagan years, the West has been in a recession since the surge in oil prices in 1973. The economic excesses of the Reagan years, moreover, left a huge legacy of debt and asset losses that have further burdened the Western economies and greatly limited their capacity to pursue Keynesian expansionary economic policies. In addition, the economic consequences of German reunification have slowed European and American growth. At the same time, the collapse of Japan's bubble economy has significantly lowered Japan's rate of economic growth and accentuated Japan's trade surplus, which set a record of about $150 billion in 1993. In fact, both Western Europe and the United States have huge trade imbalances with the East Asian economies. The high levels of Western unemployment and the contrast between a stagnant West and a dynamic East have intensified demands for trade protection against Japan and East Asia. These political demands have also led the Clinton administration to put strong pressure on Japan to stimulate its economy because it is the only major economy capable of responding to a sustained economic stimulus. The Clinton administration believes that stimulation of that economy would reduce Japan's overall trade surplus and would increase Japanese demand for foreign goods, thereby reducing American unemployment. American pressure for greater Japanese economic leadership and Japanese resistance to this pressure have increased economic frictions.

In addition to the above-mentioned developments, another cause of economic uncertainty is the increased conflict between different national models of political economy. Throughout most of the postwar era, the economic interdependence of national economies was actually at a low level. Beginning in the 1970s and accelerating in the late 1980s, however, the integration of the global economy increased significantly, especially in the areas of finance, industrial production, and services. Greater interdependence in services and other sectors has meant that national differences in governmental regulatory mechanisms and private business practices have become increasingly important barriers to international commerce. The intensification of economic integration among national economies in recent years has brought to the fore problems posed by disparate models of national capitalism with vastly different economic policies and domestic business practices. These differences have become particularly significant in Western interactions with Japan and, to a lesser extent, with other East Asian economies. The national differences among Western and Asian capitalism are important factors in the movement of Western countries away from economic multilateralism toward trade protection and economic regionalism.

Although recent developments are having a profound impact on the entire global economy, the consequences for the East Asian economies, including Japan, China, and the smaller economies of East and Southeast Asia, are especially significant. The distinctive characteristics of these economies and their peculiar position in the global economy make them particularly vulnerable to the potential spread of trade protection and economic regionalism. For example, they fear that the North American Free Trade Agreement (NAFTA) may divert American imports and investment away from the developing countries of East Asia. Growing concerns within these countries over their vulnerability to significant changes in American and Western European economic policies is a factor in the efforts of Malaysian prime minister Mahathir Mohamad to establish an East Asian economic organization to counter the threat of North American and Western European protectionism. An assessment of the distinctive features of the East Asian economies is fundamental to an appreciation of the possible significance of these recent developments for East Asia.

The Distinctive Characteristics of the East Asian Economies

The East Asian region has become the most dynamic economic region in the contemporary world. The growth rate of almost every economy in the region exceeds that of the United States and the countries of the European Community.[2] In recent years, as Mike Mochizuki demonstrates in his contribution to this volume, trade and investment flows within the region have grown enormously. In fact, the economic importance of the region has increased so much that the global economic balance has shifted noticeably away from the North Atlantic economies toward East Asia; this trend will almost certainly continue. ASEAN, for example, has become the fourth largest trading partner of the United States.[3] Although many still argue about the geographical boundaries of the region, one can certainly conclude on the basis of these developments that a distinct and significant East Asian economy is emerging.

Despite its economic vitality, however, East Asia continues to be highly dependent and vulnerable. The region is more integrated into the larger global world economy than it is separated from it. While it is possible that a more or less exclusive regional trading bloc centered on Japan may be emerging, a number of econometric studies support the position that the evidence is, in the words of Jeffrey Frankel, "not so clear."[4] Although intraregional trade has increased substantially in recent years, it is still far smaller than the trade within the European Community, and it is not increasing as much as might be expected in view of the national economic growth rates. The East Asian economies, including Japan itself, continue to be highly dependent upon the American and other external markets. This dependence, especially of the smaller economies, is likely to continue for many years. Nonetheless, one can still speak of a distinctive East Asian regional economy in terms of economic behavior and the emerging pattern of regional integration. Several distinctive features of the East Asian economies set them apart from the Western economies and contribute importantly to growing economic friction between the East Asian and Western economies:

1. The increasing importance of Japan and the Japanese model of political economy in the economic development strategies of the economies in the region.[5] The Japanese model has at least several important components that distinguish it from the American and, to a lesser extent, European economic models: the crucial role of the state in guiding economic development, an industrial structure based on powerful corporate groupings (*keiretsu*), the primacy of producer over consumer interests, an extraordinarily high savings rate, a highly skilled labor force, and a reliance on export-led growth. While the Japanese model of political economy has proven enormously successful, some Western critics argue that this model gives Asian competitors an unfair advantage in economic competition and, by its nature, limits the access of Western firms to the rapidly growing East Asian markets.

2. The internationalization of Japanese industrial policy—that is, the effort of powerful Japanese corporate groups backed by the Japanese government to create a regional division of labor, or what Mochizuki calls "network capitalism," managed by Japanese corporations and centered on the Japanese economy. Through the trade and investment policies of Japanese firms and the official development assistance of the Japanese government, the East Asian economies are becoming part of a Japanese-led regional industrial system. These economies are increasingly being integrated as subcontractors and component suppliers into a Japanese industrial and financial core. For Japan, with its appreciating currency and the decreasing competitiveness of its traditional industries, the regional economies, with their inexpensive, skilled labor forces are a source of manufactured products for the Japanese market, and also constitute export platforms for Japanese subsidiaries to third markets, especially the United States. Although Japanese trade, investment, and technology are a major benefit to the economic development of the region, many Western observers worry about the formation of a new Japanese-led "East Asian co-prosperity sphere" from which the West will be excluded.[6]

3. The aggressive development strategies based on export-led growth that, with the strong encouragement of Japan, the East and Southeast Asian economies are pursuing, following Japan's lead. For these economies, this so-called flying geese pattern generally means exporting to the United States rather than to Japan itself, even though exports of manufactured products to Japan by Japanese subsidiaries in the region are increasing. Underlying the outstanding success of this outward-oriented strategy has been an extraordinarily high savings rate and a skilled, low-wage labor force in many East Asian economies. The region's em-

phasis on savings and investment is an important factor accounting for the region's overall large trade surplus with the low-saving United States. In a demand-deficit world economy, however, the pursuit of this export strategy not only causes irritation in the West, but also may not be feasible in the long term; at least in the case of Japan, this situation cannot continue. Moreover, the concentration of Asian exports in a few sectors, such as textiles and consumer electronics components, has led to Western charges that these economies are pursuing adversarial trade strategies designed to increase certain manufacturing exports.

In addition to the uncertainties raised by the vulnerability of the region to Western trade protection, a number of uncertainties are indigenous to the region itself. While the East and Southeast Asian economies benefit from Japanese trade and investment, one may question the possible long-term consequences of the flying geese strategy. For example, will it create local and regional economies capable of sustained, independent development, or merely appendages of the Japanese economy? Is the strategy leading to a regional division of labor among complementary economies, or is it causing the regional economies to develop in ways that will force them to compete for the same market niches? Is an Asian export-oriented economy that will be more and more difficult to integrate into the larger global economy being created? Most certainly, the development prospects of the newly industrializing countries (NICs) will be limited if the Japanese market continues to be largely closed to the manufactured exports of non-Japanese firms and if Japan, as regional economic leaders charge, tries to confine the rest of Asia to the lesser value-added phases of the manufacturing processes and severely limits the access of regional economies to Japanese technology. Furthermore, the region is extraordinarily dependent on a huge and growing volume of energy from the unstable Middle East. And, of course, there is the question of the role that the United States will eventually choose to play in the region.

Among the most important unanswered questions is China's role in the region. In recent years, China's rate of economic growth has been astounding. As China has grown, its economic presence in the region and in the world economy more generally has greatly increased.[7] As a result, the increasingly intertwined economies of mainland China, Hong Kong, and Taiwan are becoming an important economic force in the region. But of still greater importance, Chinese military capabilities have continued to expand, and, with the declining military importance of Russia and the United States in East Asia, China looms as a dominant and unpredictable regional military power. Whether China can continue its rapid growth and how it ultimately chooses to exercise its expanding economic and military power are of crucial importance to the world, but especially to East Asia.

Despite these long-term worrisome considerations, the possibilities of an East Asian economic bloc are remote. Although Japanese firms are leading the region's industrial and financial integration, Japan has no interest, at least at the moment, in creating an exclusive regional bloc. As Japanese government officials generally acknowledge, the East Asian market is much too small an export market for the Japanese economy. Although APEC is of growing importance in creating a regional identity, it is primarily a political forum rather than a nascent regional economic entity; also, it is noteworthy that the United States has recently become more active as a member. Moreover, in a world in which economic bargaining over export shares and managed trade are of increasing importance, East Asia, because of its greater diversity and lack of political unity, is still not a match for the other major economic powers. For these reasons, East Asia, in contrast to both the European Community and North America, has not moved very far in the direction of creating a regional economic or political entity. In brief, East Asia's dependent and vulnerable position in the global economy continues to be of greater importance than the movement toward a regional economic and political identity.

Changes and Uncertainties in the Larger Global Economy

Thus far, I have emphasized those changes and uncertainties that are especially pertinent to the Asian region and its ties to the global economy. In the rest of this article, I shall stress longer-term global economic developments and their possible significance for the East Asian region. These global changes have introduced new elements of uncertainty that are spilling over to East Asia. There is an asymmetry between the security issues discussed in Richard Betts's contribution to this volume on Asian security and the economic matters discussed in this piece. Whereas the security arena is and always has been separated into distinct European and Asian theaters, Asia is very much a part of the larger global economy. In fact, a growing inability to isolate a nation or a region from global market forces increases uncertainty and instability. Both national and regional economies are constantly awash with destabilizing market forces. Efforts in Western Europe, North America, and East Asia to integrate regional economies and coordinate economic policies, and thus to create stable regional economies in a turbulent world economy, are, at least in part, a response to this situation. For this reason, we must turn to global developments and their significance for East Asia. The place to begin such a discussion, however, is with the nature of the postwar global economy, and in particular the so-called Bretton Woods system. As I shall argue below, much of the uncertainty in the contemporary international economy is due to the fact that the Bretton Woods norms and institutions have not kept pace with the changing nature of the international political economy.

The Postwar Bretton Woods System

The Bretton Woods system, established in 1944, had several important features. The first was the crucial role of the United States in the functioning of the system. The United States exercised considerable leadership in the construction and management of the system itself. The United States, in cooperation with Great Britain, laid down the rules that would govern international economic affairs for the next half century. These rules, with several important exceptions, reflected the American commitment to a liberal economic order, that is, one based on multilateralism, the Most Favored Nation principle, and the principle of national treatment. These basic precepts were embodied in such international institutions as the International Monetary Fund (IMF) and the General Agreement on Tariffs and Trade (GATT), which continue, at least formally, to govern the international economic system. Throughout the postwar era, the United States, despite occasional backsliding, has taken the lead in promoting the successive and successful rounds of tariff reductions and the movement toward an open, multilateral global economy.

Several features and assumptions of the Bretton Woods system are worth noting. It was assumed at the time of its founding that the domestic and international economic realms were largely independent of each other; national economies were regarded essentially as "black boxes" connected by exchange rates. In such a compartmentalized world economy, national economies were not highly interdependent, as they are today, and structural differences among national systems of political economy were not very important. Also, trade, finance, and other areas of economic policy and activity were generally isolated from one another; financial movements, for example, did not significantly affect exchange rates and therefore did not have a major impact on trade flows. It was believed that comparative advantage was provided by nature rather than the result of deliberate state and corporate policies, as may be the case today with most high-tech industries. The basic task of the norms governing international commerce was to proscribe certain types of behavior; these rules told nations what they could not do, not what they must do. The proscriptions were directed primarily at formal barriers to commerce, not at domestic practices or informal barriers, such as government regulations and corporate structures that might restrict imports.

Moreover, the fundamental purpose of GATT and its rules was to govern the exchanges of products and commodities. Services, foreign investment, and intellectual property rights were left outside the rules of GATT. The norms of GATT were formulated for a world in which international trade was not greatly affected by foreign direct investment or by foreign production by multinational corporations. The role of international financial flows and technology transfers, which would transform the global economy in the 1970s and 1980s, was unanticipated, and thus no rules were developed to govern such flows. Today, financial and other services have become one of the most rapidly expanding aspects of international commerce; this is also an area in which the United States has an overall surplus. Yet, because services and their regulation are so much at the heart of the contemporary economy, developing countries in particular invoke the infant industry argument and strongly resist opening their service sectors to the outside.

Still other important economic issues were intentionally ignored; for example, at the insistence of the United States, agriculture was largely excluded from GATT rules. Another exception to GATT principles was the question of free-trade areas. For many years, this exception was of minor significance. However, today the increasing importance of the European Community and possibly other regional arrangements poses serious problems for the multilateral trading system. Another issue left unresolved was whether deficit or surplus countries have the primary responsibility for resolving global balance of payments problems; this issue is at the heart of the American-Japanese debate over which nation has the greater responsibility for decreasing the trade imbalance. In brief, the economic activities and economic problems that are of increasing concern in bilateral and multinational negotiations in the 1990s are precisely the ones that were not covered by the original GATT framework. These issues will need to be resolved by the World Trade Organization that will be established with the ratification of the Uruguay Round of GATT negotiations.

Contemporary Changes in the System

Almost every one of the defining features of the postwar Bretton Woods system has changed, is changing, or is being challenged as the system generally is becoming outdated in the highly interdependent and truly global economy of the 1990s. Opinions differ, however, on the significance of this development. While one observer opines that the world economy has entered the Second Golden Age of Capitalism with the end of the East-West conflict, other observers are much less sanguine and fear that without greater international leadership, the emerging global economy will break down into feuding regional blocs. Many believe that renovated international institutions and increased cooperation among the United States, Western Europe, and Japan will be required if the global economy is to function well and overcome the challenges ahead. Our task at the moment, however, is to understand the changes taking place and the challenges that they pose.

In addition to the more recent developments mentioned at the beginning of this article, the global economy is changing and becoming more uncertain as a result of a number of long-term developments. One major change, whose importance has already been mentioned, is the massive redistribution of world economic power away from the United States and the Atlantic economies toward Japan and the Pacific. The consequences of this redistribution of power are profound. The United States is no longer able or willing to exercise its prior leadership role in the areas of money, trade, and finance. At this time, the leadership role, such as it is, has largely passed to the so-called G-7 nations. Indeed, a G-2 composed of Japan and the United States has played a vital role in governing the world monetary system. Germany is playing a greater leadership role in what may become a European economic bloc, and American and Japanese economic

cooperation, despite its innumerable difficulties, has become another central feature of the contemporary international economy. However, if global economic
uncertainties are to be reduced, the United States, Germany, and Japan, as the
three foremost economic powers, will have to work out a more systematic way to
coordinate their economic policies.

The decline of the American economy relative to other developed and developing economies also means that the United States no longer can perform its
postwar role as the engine of growth for the rest of the world. This shift in the
economic status of the United States and the huge American international debt
mean that the United States must increase its exports if it is to reverse its relative
decline and repay its vast accumulated foreign debt. This change in economic
status requires, in turn, that the other major economies adjust their macroeconomic policies. If global economic demand is to increase, Japan in particular
must shift even more than it has already to a domestic-led growth strategy and
must import more manufactured goods produced by the firms of other nations.

Despite the "success" of the Uruguay Round of GATT negotiations, the task
of continuing trade liberalization has become increasingly difficult. As formal
tariff barriers have fallen as a result of the succession of multilateral GATT
negotiations, they have frequently been replaced by bilateral arrangements and
informal barriers such as so-called voluntary export restraints and local-content
rules. The highly controversial issues of agriculture, services, and foreign direct
investment have now moved to center stage in trade negotiations and, as noted
above, have yet to be resolved. The huge American trade imbalance with Japan
and Japan's low level of manufactured imports have caused the Clinton administration to adopt a policy of what the Japanese quite correctly call managed trade.
The battle against protectionist forces in the United States, Western Europe, and
elsewhere continues.

Problems for the trading system posed by the rapid rise of Japan as an economic power are especially difficult to resolve. Japan is the fourth (and China is
rapidly becoming the fifth) nation in modern history to greatly increase its share
of world exports in a short time period. The other expanding economic powers
were Great Britain early in the nineteenth century, Germany in the latter decades
of that century, and the United States in the early decades of this century. Each
time this phenomenon has occurred, the difficult adjustment problems imposed
on other economies by these trade offensives has given rise to intense economic
competition and political conflict. Similar adjustment problems and intensifying
negative reactions on the part of other economies are occurring in the 1990s as
Japan moves rapidly up the technological ladder. Moreover, despite recent setbacks, Japan's dynamic comparative advantage and the adjustments that this
situation imposes on its competitors are greatly intensified by what many com-
mentators regard as the unique pattern of Japanese trade.

In contrast to other advanced industrialized countries, Japan has tended toward *interindustry* trade rather than *intraindustry* trade. Whereas interindustry

trade involves importing and exporting goods in different economic sectors, such as importing raw materials and exporting manufactured goods, intraindustry trade involves importing and exporting goods in the same sectors, such as importing and exporting different types of automobiles. Japan primarily imports raw materials and a small but growing fraction of the manufactured goods that it consumes. Germany, on the other hand, which has traditionally had an even larger trade surplus than Japan, imports a significant proportion of its consumption of manufactured goods. Although in recent years Japan has imported an increasing fraction of the manufactured goods that it consumes, this trade has tended to be *intrafirm* trade; that is, these imports have been transfers from an overseas subsidiary of a Japanese firm to a Japanese firm located in Japan itself. For example, a substantial fraction of manufactured exports from the United States to Japan are from Japanese subsidiaries in the United States to their parent companies. This unique aspect of Japanese behavior poses a problem for other countries.

As Dennis Encarnation has pointed out, a substantial fraction of world trade is now intrafirm trade.[8] Much of the flow of goods and components into and out of all the major industrialized economies is really intrafirm transfers from one branch of a multinational corporation to another. However, Japan stands apart from the other advanced economies because of its high level of direct investment in other countries compared to the low amount of direct investment of other countries in Japan; in contrast to this asymmetrical situation, American and European firms invest heavily in one another's markets. As a result of the asymmetrical access of Japanese and non-Japanese firms to opportunities to invest in and import into one another's markets, non-Japanese firms find it much more difficult to sell manufactured goods in the Japanese home market. To put the point another way, non-Japanese firms have not had the same access to the Japanese market for their manufactured exports that Japanese firms have had to foreign markets.[9]

A growing number of critics in the United States, Western Europe, and elsewhere now regard Japan's unique trade and investment behavior as adversarial and as prima facie evidence that Japan is a closed economy that does not play by the liberal rules, much less the spirit, of GATT.[10] The strategic objective of Japanese trade policy, these critics charge, is to destroy systematically the high-technology industries of its trading partners. Whatever the truth of these charges, it should be pointed out that one of the major reasons for the successful lowering of trade barriers and the huge expansion of trade among advanced economies in the postwar era has been the predominance of intraindustry over interindustry trade. The prevalence of the former over the latter has meant that economies did not have to fear that the lowering of trade barriers would wipe out whole industrial sectors. As some observers correctly suggest, Japan's unusual trading pattern is at least in part a cause of the movement today away from free trade. The political task of absorbing a dynamic Japan with its unusual trade pattern into the world economy has become a major challenge to the world economic system.

The economic rise of China and its integration into the global economy is another important and more recent challenge. China's share of global trade has increased rapidly over the past few years, and this expansion, especially into ever more sophisticated exports, can be expected to continue at a rapid pace. Yet neither China nor Taiwan is a member of GATT, although both seek membership. In addition to the human rights issue, China's accession is complicated by its lack of a rules-based trading system, making the Chinese economy even more uncertain and opaque than Japan's for outsiders. The growing decentralization of the Chinese economy, with provinces and municipalities handling much of their own economic direction, is another problem. Outsiders, for example, cannot be sure that commitments made by the central government will be enforced at the provincial level. In short, China's entry into the global economy raises a number of unprecedented issues for the international community that are far from being resolved.

Profound changes in the international financial system have also transformed the trading system and the world economy more generally. The deregulation of domestic financial systems, the increased velocity of international financial flows as a result of modern communications, and the sheer scale of these financial flows have all had significant effects. International financial flows now dwarf trade flows; they have become an important determinant of exchange rates, at least in the short run. The immense size of these financial flows can cause exchange rates to fluctuate wildly and can exacerbate trade imbalances, again reinforcing protectionist forces.[11] The size and velocity of these financial and monetary flows also have reduced the autonomy of domestic economic policy. Huge financial flows across national boundaries, for example, can counter or undermine the intended effects of macroeconomic policy. The integration of the traditionally separated national and international economic spheres has thus introduced a new element of instability and uncertainty into the global economic system. Since trade and other areas of economic policy have become highly intertwined, questions are raised about the adequacy of existing GATT norms and the need for greater international economic cooperation.

Yet another development changing the world economy is the globalization or internationalization of industrial production. Although American firms continue to lead in foreign direct investment, they have been joined by Japanese and European corporations, and even corporations from the developing world. As Kenichi Ohmae has observed, these firms realize that they must invest and establish production facilities in all three centers of the world economy if they are to remain competitive.[12] In the 1990s, multinational corporations of all nationalities are increasingly following an investment strategy in which production processes around the world are integrated and rationalized; that is, components produced in one location may be assembled in a second and sold in a third.[13] The loci of production, assembly, and marketing around the world are being largely determined by global corporate strategies. Since corporate strategies are highly dependent upon the economics of location, the existence of trade barriers, and the desire to minimize taxation, investment strategies have become globally rather than nationally based. Needless to say, the activities of multinational corporations in turn have a significant effect upon the distribution of world industry and upon the interests of every nation.

The globalization of industrial production has potentially profound and as yet unappreciated implications for the global economic system. This development means that a substantial proportion of world trade takes place as intrafirm transfers at prices set by the firm and as part of a global corporate strategy. For example, about one-half of American imports are intrafirm transfers.[14] Conventional trade theory does not apply to this growing portion of global trade to any significant degree. As several writers have noted, differential or asymmetric access of national corporations to one another's markets has become a serious source of international friction.[15] Yet, hardly any rules exist to govern this particular type of managed trade. If political conflict is to be avoided, new rules governing foreign direct investment and the behavior of multinational corporations will surely be required. The resolution of this issue will be especially difficult because it deeply divides the developed North from the less developed South.

In addition to these political and economic developments, the technological environment is undergoing a profound transformation. In fact, it would be no exaggeration to suggest that mankind has entered upon a third phase of the Industrial Revolution. Whereas the first phase, in the eighteenth century, was based on new technologies of iron and steam power and the second, in the late nineteenth century, on steel, chemicals, and electricity, the present phase represents a shift to knowledge-intensive industries. The assembly line and specialized, single-purpose equipment of the mass-production era are rapidly being displaced by radically new techniques of industrial production. Service industries based upon the production and processing of information are growing in importance. Revolutionary technologies in bioengineering, electronics, and materials are creating new products and production techniques. As a consequence, the technologies upon which the industrial organization of all the advanced economies has been based for over a century are now becoming anachronistic.

Today, technologies of mass production decreasingly provide a source of growth and employment for the advanced economies of Western Europe, the United States, and Japan. Indeed, the comparative advantage in industries employing mass production is shifting to the developing countries. At the same time, the more advanced economies, with Japan and the United States taking the lead, are restructuring their economies around the computer and the other high-tech industries of the third Industrial Revolution; traditional mass-production techniques are being displaced by the lean and flexible production methods pioneered in Japan. Throughout the world, modern telecommunications are linking the service and manufacturing industries into a highly interdependent global economy. Anxiety about the consequence of these developments has stimulated trade protection and state interventionism with respect to high technology.

International competition in technology is intensifying. The outcome of this competition will determine which nation or nations will be the dominant industrial and technological powers in the decades ahead. While the race has just begun and it is obviously much too soon to predict winners and losers, it is at least certain that the distribution of industrial activities and global wealth is undergoing a decisive shift. It appears to be unlikely, however, that there will be a single predominant technological leader similar to Great Britain in the first or the United States in the second Industrial Revolution.[16] While Japan is likely to be the leader in many of these information-based technologies, leadership in various scientific and technological fields will most probably be shared and spread across a broad front. The scope and magnitude of the present technological revolution are simply too immense for one economy to be dominant in all aspects of contemporary science and industrial technology. A diffusion of technological entrepreneurship will encourage technological trading and corporate alliances within and across national boundaries, with as yet unforeseen consequences for the world economic system. Whatever the outcome, however, the intensified competition is exacerbating economic and technological rivalries and will certainly continue to do so.

The increasing importance of high-tech industries has undercut the assumption of the Bretton Woods trading system that comparative advantage was a given of nature that could not be altered by government policies. Today, although the debate over the effectiveness of industrial policy is unresolved, the experience of Japan and of U.S. defense-related industry supports the contention that in many high-tech industries, comparative advantage is to a significant degree a product of deliberate policy choices by national governments. The fact that comparative advantage can, at least to some extent and under certain circumstances, be intentionally created has encouraged governments to intervene in the market and to pursue sector-specific industrial policies.

These several developments in economics, politics, and technology are transforming the nature of the international economy profoundly and posing new problems for governments. A truly global and transnational economy is replacing the postwar international economy composed of "black box" economies, largely isolated from one another, with their interactions governed by a simple set of proscribing rules. However, the extent of interdependence in trade, finance, and production has become wider and deeper than most societies and political leaders realize. National economies have become so intertwined that domestic economic policies are losing their effectiveness and governments have less capacity to pursue autonomous and independent policies. The overall result is a much more uncertain world than in the past.

In today's more tightly integrated world economy, the differences among capitalist economies have become an increasingly important source of economic conflict. With greater interdependence, what once appeared to be solely domestic actions and national systems of economic regulation necessarily impinge upon the interests of other countries. Thus, a domestic matter such as tax policy or the regulation of monopoly can easily and rapidly become an international one. Some of the more serious obstacles to international commerce, for example, are located in domestic economic institutions and private business practices. The Structural Impediments Initiative (SII) talks between Japan and the United States during the Bush administration were a crude attempt to deal with this problem. The rules and institutions governing the contemporary highly integrated and transnational economy must shift, at least to some extent, from the merely pro-scriptive 1944 Bretton Woods regulations to more prescriptive rules and regulations. Many observers believe, for example, that the ultimate solution to trade conflicts must incorporate "competition policy," that is, what constitutes fair competition, in terms of both governmental policies and private business practice, must be defined in the rules governing international trade. Consideration must be given to determining the amount of harmonization among national economic practices and institutions that is required for a smoothly functioning and highly interdependent global economy.

The greatest economic source of uncertainty, however, is the increasing tension between the opposed tendencies of economic multilateralism and economic regionalism. Economic multilateralism has many manifestations. Integration of national economies into a global and transnational economy is occurring at an astonishing rate in the areas of trade, finance, and production as a world market for goods and services is replacing a world economy composed of generally isolated national markets, domestic financial markets are integrated into a truly global financial system, and the multinational corporation becomes the principal mechanism for the allocation of investment capital and determination of the location of production throughout much of the world. Nevertheless, while this process of globalization and transnational integration is taking place, economic protection and strategic alliances among particular states and corporations are also rapidly expanding. These economic alliances are being used to influence, and, in some cases, to determine, market relations and economic outcomes. In addition, as formal tariffs have come down, informal barriers such as "voluntary" export restraints and quantitative restrictions on imports have replaced them, especially in the United States. On the whole, in the 1990s, a substantial fraction of world trade is managed trade of some kind. Bilateral and regional arrangements such as the North American Free Trade Agreement and the movement toward European integration have grown in extent and significance. In brief, a regionalization of the world economy appears to be occurring simultaneously with the trend toward economic globalization.[17]

For many writers, "economic regionalism" conjures up an image of the 1930s, when the world collapsed in the face of exclusive and antagonistic economic and political blocs, and they therefore reject the idea of a regionalization of the world as either undesirable or impossible. However, others foresee a greater regionalization of the world economy accompanying the postwar movement toward economic multilateralism and trade liberalization without any return to the exclusiveness or antagonisms of the 1930s. As new entities with closer economic ties emerge, they may prove to be merely trading regions rather than economic blocs. Today three quite different processes taking place in Western Europe, North America, and East Asia are indeed resulting in new trading regions.

The movements toward regional integration differ greatly from one another; they range from the highly institutionalized movement toward economic and political integration in Western Europe to the less institutionalized and nonpolitical nature of East Asian integration. The Western European movement toward regional integration has been moving faster than the others, has the potential of creating the largest market, and is most likely to result in an at least partially closed market. Indeed, the crucial importance of European integration has led some observers to posit a world economy composed of "the European Community and all the rest."[18] The rapid growth of intra-European trade and the powerful tendency toward European protectionism suggest that the extent of economic regionalism in the world will be decided by the Europeans.

The predominant interpretation in the United States (especially among professional economists) of these contradictory developments emphasizes the process of global integration over the parallel development of economic regionalism. Some argue that in the postwar era we have witnessed and are continuing to observe a linear and essentially irreversible movement toward global interdependence. Inexorable economic and technological forces are said to be driving the economies of the world to ever-higher levels of economic integration. According to this position, economic regionalism is essentially an attempt to overcome the problems of uncertainty in a turbulent world economy, and the several movements toward regional economies are merely stepping-stones to a multilateral world economy.[19] It is argued that this overall process of economic integration and globalization is sometimes limited by irrational forces and those threatened interests that respond to the forces of economic integration with appeals to economic nationalism and demands for economic protectionism. In time, however, the inherent logic of economic efficiency will prevail, and nations will move in the direction of increased globalization. As C. Fred Bergsten has put it, although "virtually all countries on occasion attempt to resist these external pressures . . . efforts to resist the forces of market globalization can succeed only partially and for limited periods of time."[20] Thus, nations, try as they might, cannot ultimately escape the inexorable forces of global unification.

A second interpretation, put forth in particular by some so-called revisionist critics of Japanese economic policies, is that, with the end of the Cold War, the international economy is rapidly fragmenting into antagonistic regional economic blocs centered on the three dominant economic powers.[21] Some adherents of this position believe that the East-West military conflict is being replaced by a world in which economic conflict becomes the functional equivalent of military conflict. Proponents of this position emphasize the fact that as formal tariffs have come down, informal barriers have become more important. To support their position, these individuals note that in the 1980s the share of American imports covered by quantitative restrictions increased from 5 to 18 percent. Western Europe has been particularly active in forging nontariff barriers, especially against Japanese goods. Although Japanese formal tariffs have come down, many informal barriers have continued. Bilateral trading arrangements are rapidly spreading. Today, the rules of GATT may cover as little as 5 to 7 percent of global economic activities.[22] As a consequence of these and other developments, this position argues, it is highly probable that economic competition among the three economic regions will degenerate into political conflict.

A third interpretation, which I share, is that what is taking place today in the international political economy is a dialectical process. Both economic globalization and economic regionalism are taking place simultaneously. These two developments are in fact complementary and responsive to each other. They reflect a world in which states want the absolute benefits of a global economy at the same time that they are seeking to increase their own relative gains through economic protection, the formation of regional arrangements, and managed trade. We are not witnessing a linear process in which the forces of economic integration will triumph decisively over the forces of economic nationalism; indeed, political boundaries will continue to have economic significance. But it is also not inevitable that regional blocs will lead to a breakdown and fragmentation of the world economy, and thence to political conflict. The balance and the stability of the balance between the global and the regional emphases have yet to be decided.

Conclusion

The process of global economic integration has greatly outpaced the development of the political and institutional capacity within the international community to control and manage it. This fact has caused uncertainty for all economies, yet the East Asian economies must deal with special problems, such as those posed by Japanese economic expansionism and the potentially threatening presence of a powerful China. The fundamental differences between the Asian and Western models of political economy also raise uncertainties regarding the Western response to Asian economic success. But the most important economic uncertainties lie outside the region and cannot be substantially reduced until the problems of creating a more stable global economic order are resolved.

In 1968, Richard Cooper, in his influential book *The Economics of Interdependence,* alerted us to the problems and complexities posed by an increasingly integrated world economy. The world, he wrote, was becoming increasingly interdependent in trade, investment, and money.[23] But the political will and the institutions necessary to manage this highly interdependent world economy, Cooper pointed out, did not yet exist. If the international community did not generate the will and the institutions to govern a more interdependent world economy, he warned, economic interdependence would degenerate into national rivalries. The required solution, he argued, was either some sort of world government or, more realistically, a greater international coordination of the economic policies of the major industrial powers.

Nearly three decades later, Cooper's challenge still confronts us. Efforts to coordinate policies among the major economic powers have been initiated. Yet the political challenge of managing the world economy has become even more difficult. When Cooper wrote, the subtitle of his book, *Economic Policy in the Atlantic Community,* anticipated a much more unified and homogeneous world economy than the truly global economy of the post–Cold War world. In the absence of a global solution, regional solutions have become more attractive. Thus, while Cooper's admonition that there should be a great increase in political cooperation at the global level has become more relevant, achievement of that goal has become ever more elusive.

Notes

1. *The Economist,* July 31, 1993, p. 13.
2. Ibid.
3. Ibid., p. 32.
4. Jeffrey A. Frankel, "Is a Yen Bloc Forming in the Pacific?" in Richard O'Brien, ed., *Finance and the International Economy: No. 5, The AMEX Bank Review Prize Essays in Memory of Robert Marjolin* (New York: Oxford University Press for The AMEX Bank Review, 1991), p. 5.
5. On Japan's increasingly important role in the region, the reader should consult Mochizuki in this volume and Charles E. Morrison, "Japan's Roles in East Asia," *Business and the Contemporary World,* vol. 5, no. 2 (Spring 1993).
6. American foreign direct investment (FDI) in the region still exceeds that of Japan. American FDI is primarily in energy and electronics. Its integrating effects are far less than those of Japanese FDI.
7. Nicholas R. Lardy, "China's Growing Economic Role in Asia," in *The Future of China, NBR Analysis,* vol. 3, no. 3 (1992), p. 1.
8. Dennis J. Encarnation, *Rivals beyond Trade: America versus Japan in Global Competition* (Ithaca, NY: Cornell University Press, 1992).
9. Ibid.
10. The term "adversarial trade" was first used to characterize Japanese trade policy by Peter Drucker.
11. Jagdish Bhagwati, *Protectionism* (Cambridge, MA: The MIT Press, 1988).
12. Kenichi Ohmae, *Triad Power: The Coming Shape of Global Competition* (New York: Free Press, 1985).
13. Richard E. Caves, *Multinational Enterprise and Economic Analysis* (New York: Cambridge University Press, 1982).

14. Paul R. Krugman and Maurice Obstfeld, *International Economics: Theory and Practice* (Glenview, IL: Scott, Foresman and Company, 1988), p. 160.

15. Encarnation, *Rivals beyond Trade*; Sylvia Ostry, *Governments and Corporations in a Shrinking World: Trade and Innovation Policies in the United States, Europe and Japan* (New York: Council on Foreign Relations, 1990).

16. Angus Maddison, *Phases of Capitalist Development* (New York: Oxford University Press, 1982).

17. Survey of World Trade, *The Economist,* September 22, 1990, p. 6.

18. This observation has been made by Lawrence B. Krause and Mark Sundberg in "Inter-Relationship between the World and Pacific Economic Performance" (unpublished), revised February 1990.

19. Peter Drysdale, *International Economic Pluralism: Economic Policy in East Asia and the Pacific* (New York: Columbia University Press, 1988).

20. C. Fred Bergsten, *America in the World Economy: A Strategy for the 1990s* (Washington, DC: Institute for International Economics, 1988), p. 60.

21. Adherents of this position include Lester Thurow, Chalmers Johnson, and Edward Luttwak.

22. Bergsten, *America in the World Economy*, p. 72.

23. Richard N. Cooper, *The Economics of Interdependence: Economic Policy in the Atlantic Community* (New York: McGraw-Hill, 1968).

2

Wealth, Power, and Conflict: East Asia after the Cold War

Richard K. Betts

East Asia is becoming a more important region at the same time that it is becoming less stable as an arena of great-power interaction. This is a bad combination and precisely the opposite of the situation in Western Europe. This contrast is also not entirely obvious. Superficially, the region appears fairly peaceful at present, but the security order that will replace the Cold War framework is not yet clear.[1]

During the Cold War, strategic competition in East Asia was driven by the titanic global struggle between Washington and Moscow.[2] The Soviet collapse makes the answers to some basic questions less obvious than they once seemed. Is it now in the interest of international order for China to succeed in economic liberalization and become prosperous? or for Japan to become a "normal" state, developing a ratio of military to economic power comparable to that of other large, rich countries? or for Korea to unify? or for Taiwan to democratize? or for Vietnam to remain poor? The answers depend on more fundamental questions: How will the distribution of power in the region evolve, and does it matter? Is it important to have a balance of power in East Asia—a distribution of national capabilities that is not obviously hierarchical[3]—or do booming economies and liberalizing polities make traditional strategic calculations obsolete?

Far more than during the Cold War, when strategic debate became routinized and focused on a familiar menu of issues, these questions force analysis back to first principles about the causes of war and peace. Two broad traditions dominate thinking on this subject: realism and liberalism.[4] Realism has been dominant in academic theory, liberalism in American politics, and the two are intertwined in all Western debates about foreign affairs. Assumptions about cause and effect in most arguments are derived, often unconsciously, from these philosophies. Un-

A different version of this chapter appeared as an article in *International Security*, vol. 18, no. 3 (Winter 1991/92).

less the underlying logic is examined rather than assumed, proponents of the different philosophies often argue past each other when making policy proposals because they take their premises for granted.

As is true of the relation between any general theory and specific cases, hardly anyone's views fit snugly within either paradigm. Policymakers also have no interest in endless scholastic debates about them. Making theoretical distinctions explicit, however, is the first step in clarifying the competition of logical frameworks to replace the Cold War frame of reference.[5] The implications of realist and liberal assumptions are not simple, because there are contradictions within the schools and consistencies between them. This essay outlines how different combinations of assumptions about the causes of war and peace produce different conclusions about which economic, political, and military developments in East Asia would be desirable or dangerous. My own position tilts toward realism, but is syncretic in significant ways indicated along the way.

Assumptions: Power, Values, and Peace

Realists believe that wars are awful but natural, and that states are subject to natural selection. Wars happen because there is nothing to prevent them when countries would rather defend conflicting claims than relinquish them. Without any supranational enforcer, states are the ultimate judges of their own rights and enforcers of their own interests, material or moral, as they see them. Power determines whose claims prevail, so peace must flow from a distribution of power that convinces states that the costs of enforcing or resisting claims exceed the gains.[6]

Classic liberalism sees wars as unnatural, occurring because states fail to recognize their common interest in efficient market exchange or because glory-seeking rulers are unconstrained by the will of their subjects, who bear the costs of combat. Peace can emerge from the spread of understanding that liberal norms make the potential for material gain from cooperation greater than that from wasteful conflict. Ideas, once properly recognized and buttressed by law, enlightened custom, and institutions to foster cooperation, exert a power of their own.[7]

Within the realist school, all agree that the distribution of national power is the most important concern of policy,[8] but there is no agreement about *which* distribution is most stable. There are three structural alternatives: multipolarity, bipolarity, and unipolarity. Classical balance-of-power theorists tend to favor the first,[9] "neorealists" the second,[10] and some others the third.[11] This lack of consensus, as well as the various ambiguities about which strategies produce certain results, makes realism quite indeterminate; it is much clearer about what the general problem is than about what the particular solutions should be.

Within the liberal school, there are three main variants. One emphasizes that economic liberty—free markets and trade, division of labor according to comparative advantage, and interdependence—makes countries avoid war in order to maximize material gain.[12] Another sees political liberty as the source of states' confidence in one another's benign intentions; in the past two centuries, constitutional democracies have virtually never fought one another.[13] The third, "neoliberal institutionalism," focuses on the role of international organizations, informal as well as formal, in cultivating norms of cooperative behavior.[14] Whereas realism is inadequate as a guide to policy because it is indeterminate, the distinction between the first variant of the liberal paradigm and the second and third poses a potential problem. Whatever its impact on inclinations toward war or peace may be, economic liberalism generates power, by virtue of its dynamic impact on national development. Therefore, if political liberalism or neoliberal institutional liberalism turn out to be more the source of peaceful behavior than economic liberalism, economic liberalism could turn out to promote realists' worst nightmares about the dangers of an imbalance of power if it is decoupled from the other two variants of liberalism—as it could well be in East Asia.

All these variations within the contending schools complicate the prescriptions we might infer. There is no simple correlation between the two paradigms and the propensity to use force.[15] But on one vital point, the relative importance of national power and ideological values, the basic dichotomy remains relevant to strategy. Realists part company with liberals on the priority of maintaining a favorable material power position—conceived in terms of military and economic capability relative to those of other countries[16]—for its own sake. Liberals, in turn, are more reluctant to subordinate international law, political justice, or absolute prosperity to strategic competition and economic autonomy. Nurturing national power is unobjectionable only so long as it does not impair international cooperation. On the use of force beyond the direct defense of one's own homeland, realists are most inclined to it when the balance of power is at stake, liberals when moral values are at stake. These differences should be highlighted for two reasons.

First, the question of what objectives a state should shed blood for, and on behalf of whom, is the most essential aspect of security policy. In the United States—the one superpower remaining on the world scene—that issue was contentious enough during the second half of the Cold War, after fighting two hot wars in East Asia. Now, with the passing of the global threats of Soviet national power and transnational communist ideology, there is no consensus whatever on this question, especially in regard to Asia.

Second, if realism is relevant, it is likely to animate policy in many East Asian capitals more readily than in Washington. There it faces an uphill battle in the policy arena because its logic is not automatically compelling to Americans. The Cold War was won without proving which of the two general paradigms was correct, since victory correlated with both the assertion of Western power and the adversary's acceptance of Western ideals. Realism can explain why Gorbachev and his crew decided that glasnost and perestroika were necessary, but not why they blithely gave away the Soviet empire in 1989 without a murmur. Liberal logic is deeply rooted in American society (which is why laissez-faire liberals in the United States are called conservatives).[17] Realism is not; it is an acquired taste, offensive to many Americans when stated baldly, uncloaked in righteousness. The perspective of American policymakers, in turn, is disproportionately significant for assessing the prospects for East Asian international order. This is because the United States is now the only global power, and since the withdrawal of the European colonial powers long ago, it has been the only power from outside the region that remains involved in its politico-military interactions.

The American affinity for liberal assumptions was not a problem during the Cold War because at many points throughout that period, officials in the West and Japan did not have to choose between the imperatives of power and values. The communist threat, like the fascist threat before it, combined military power with antiliberal ideology, allowing conservative realism's focus on might and liberal idealism's focus on right to converge in a militant policy. It would not otherwise have been as easy for the United States to play power politics so enthusiastically in the half century after Pearl Harbor.[18]

Winning the Cold War could not help but confirm liberal optimism about the natural progress of history toward peace. An axiomatic liberal consensus is riskier now, however, because without a clear adversary like the USSR, it will not complement concern with military power and strategic activism as easily as before. Now the conceptual choices associated with the two main paradigms point more often in divergent directions. Nowhere is this more true than in Asia.

World Power, Regional Power, and Strategic Interests

The worldwide structure of power no longer governs the regional structure of power, as it did during the Cold War. Global unipolarity[19] now coincides with regional multipolarity. No country but the United States can project large amounts of military force at all points in the world, but this unique capacity is fractionated by multiple commitments in different regions. Although the United States is in a military class by itself, in many cases it cannot act independently, but needs the cooperation of allies to supply bases (such as Saudi Arabia for the Gulf War, or Japan and South Korea in East Asia). Without the challenge of another superpower to contend with, moreover, U.S. military forces are shrinking and are likely to level off well below the baseline of the Cold War.[20]

The divergence in trends illustrates the self-liquidating character of unipolarity. In East Asia, in contrast to the United States, militaries are growing (Table 2.1). China especially has boosted its defense budget since the late 1980s. It is buying weapons at a fast clip, seeking naval facilities closer to the Malacca Straits, and developing rapid-deployment units.[21] This activity is not in itself evidence of malign intent, since China's defense spending was depressed in the 1980s, and most countries increase defense spending as their economies grow.

Table 2.1

Recent Defense Budget Trends: Great Powers and Middle Powers in East Asia

	1990	1991	1992	1993	1994	% 1990–94
United States	291.4	272.95	270.9	258.7	261.7	−10.2
USSR	116.7	—	—	—	—	—
Russia	—	107.0	N.A.	N.A.	77.0	−28.0[a]
Japan	28.73	32.68	35.94	39.71	42.1	+46.5
China (PRC)[b]	6.06	6.11	6.71	7.31	6.7	+10.6
Taiwan	8.69	9.29	10.29[c]	10.45	11.13	+30.0
South Korea	10.62	10.77	11.19	12.06	14.0	+31.8
North Korea[c]	5.23	2.36	2.06	2.19	2.3	−56.0
Vietnam[c]	N.A.	1.87	1.75	N.A.	0.435	−76.7[d]
Indonesia	1.45	1.55	1.77	1.95	2.3	+58.6
Australia	7.01	7.06	6.94	6.96	6.9	−11.0

Sources: The Military Balance 1990–1991 (London: International Institute for Strategic Studies [IISS], 1990), p. 17; *The Military Balance 1991–1992* (London: IISS, 1991), pp. 19, 150, 157, 164, 169, 180; *The Military Balance 1992–1993* (London: IISS, 1992), pp. 18, 141, 145, 148, 150, 152, 153, 161, 164; *The Military Balance 1993–1994* (London: IISS, 1993), pp. 20, 98, 152, 156, 157, 159,161, 168, 171; *The Military Balance 1994–1995* (London: IISS, 1994), pp. 22, 167, 170, 174, 176, 178, 180, 189, 192, 285.

*Notes:*Figures in current U.S. $ billions, except as noted below. Figures are for defense budgets, which indicate intended level of effort and for which more recent data are available, rather than defense expenditures. NB: Data do not correct for exchange rate fluctuations, hence exaggerate some changes; for example, change for Japan calculated in yen is only 19.5%

[a]1991–94, figures in constant 1993 $.

[b]Estimated actual *expenditures* much higher: $27.4 billion for 1993.

[c]Estimates.

[d]1991–94.

As for Japan, it "alone among the rich countries . . . is still increasing its defense spending in real terms."[22]

The situation in East Asia is similarly diverse in other dimensions of power. Economically, no other country approaches the United States in global leverage, but this is not true within East Asia. Here too, the difference between being Number One in the world in terms of gross national product (GNP), domestic markets, or other indices does not translate into local dominance. Politically, the demise of Marxism-Leninism leaves Western liberalism without any powerful transnational ideological competition.[23] Democracy has not surged as far in East Asia, however, as in some other regions.[24]

The change from worldwide bipolarity to unipolarity makes the global dimen-

Table 2.2

One Decade of Shifting Power Potential

	NATO Europe	East Asia	All Europe	All Asia
GNP (billions of 1989 U.S. dollars)				
1979	3,728	2,516	7,427	2,716
1989	4,610	4,117	9,032	4,454
% change	23.7	63.6	21.6	64.0
Per capita GNP (1989 U.S. dollars)				
1979	11,480	1,656	9,400	1,128
1989	13,410	2,349	10,720	1,557
% change	16.8	41.8	14.0	38.0
Population (millions)				
1979	324.7	1,519.0	790.2	2,406.2
1989	343.8	1,752.4	842.8	2,859.0
% change	5.9	15.4	6.7	18.8

Source: ACDA, *World Military Expenditures and Arms Transfers 1990* (Washington, D.C.: GPO, November 1991), pp. 48, 50.
Note: "All Asia" is East and South Asia.

sion of strategic competition irrelevant. U.S. strategy no longer contends with the prospect of a multifront global war or an epochal struggle over which of two universalist value systems will dominate the world. If the United States intervenes somewhere now, it cannot be because of a derivative interest affecting the worldwide balance with another superpower, but because of an intrinsic interest in the place itself.[25]

Attention to military problems in East Asia declined during the second half of the Cold War, following U.S. withdrawal from Vietnam and reconciliation with China. (It is ironic how seldom anyone ever notes that the United States spent almost 60,000 American lives, hundreds of thousands of Indochinese lives, and several hundred billion of today's dollars fighting the Vietnam War in no small part to contain China regionally,[26] only to turn on a dime and embrace China in order to contain the USSR globally.) At the same time as the downshift in military activism, however, global stakes were moving in the opposite direction, as trans-Pacific trade was outstripping that across the Atlantic. By the early 1990s, two-way trade between the United States and East Asia was well over $300 billion, a third more than with Europe.[27] (For Asia as a whole, the difference is even greater.)

Thus, in terms of the material stakes of most interest to hardheaded strategic realists, the population and growing wealth of East Asia (see Table 2.2) should have boosted it over Europe on the list of superpower priorities some time ago.

That did not happen for several reasons, including inertia and, perhaps, a wee whiff of unconscious racism. Another reason was political affinity. The United States and Western Europe were a set of fraternal, stable democracies. In East Asia such ideological bonds have been rare.

Other explanations for the lower military priority of Asia were less inconsistent with balance-of-power criteria. Material stakes do not automatically dictate levels of military effort. Geographic conditions made the cost of deterrence for the West much higher in Europe than in East Asia in terms of treasure, though it proved much lower in terms of blood. At least half of the cumulative peacetime defense expenditures of the United States (including most of the strategic nuclear force) could be fairly attributed to the European commitment,[28] although it was in East Asia that the United States fought two long, nasty wars after 1945. The conventional Soviet military threat was more manageable in Asia than in Europe. In the Atlantic theater, the challenge was to block an armored advance over land to the English Channel that could extend communist control over Germany, France, and the rest of the continent, taking a large portion of the world's industrial power into Moscow's orbit. In East Asia, Japan was the only modern industrial power for most of the Cold War, and it was protected, as England had been against Napoleon and Hitler, by a buffer of water. China alone was a major state directly threatened by Soviet invasion. The People's Republic was only an ally of convenience for the United States, and only a tacit one at that. The country's strategic depth also made its complete conquest less likely.

For whatever reasons, East Asia's importance as an objective strategic interest, as a stake on the global board, seldom paralleled its profile in global military policy after 1945. More military effort was invested in the region during the first half of the Cold War, when it was less important than Europe, than during the second half, when it was becoming more important. Except in the 1960s, however, when the U.S. military commitment was excessive (the Vietnam War), the levels of effort by the superpowers were not out of line with the threats to the stakes. Will this remain true if, as was argued at the outset, the stakes in East Asia are rising while the region's stability is declining?

The higher stakes are matters of arithmetic. East Asia has about a third of the world's population, a growing share of total world economic product, and the largest portion of world trade. But what will be the source of conflict that will imply a military corollary to the economic stakes? Is there now a natural balance in the region, so that no local state can dominate even if the United States does not act to maintain equilibrium? The evidence of instability is less straightforward than the stakes. In one sense, stability in the region has never been so good. For more than a century East Asia has been an international subsystem in which up to five great powers have interacted, and at the moment they all have decent relations with one another. But of the six dyadic relationships among the current four great powers (U.S.–Japan, U.S.–China, U.S.–Russia, Japan–China, Japan–Russia, Russia–China), none has been consistently stable and friendly, and all

Table 2.3

Selected Comparisons of Military Forces in East Asia, 1992[a]

	Ground force divisions	Main battle tanks	Combat aircraft	Principal surface combatants	Submarines
United States[b]	4	N.A.[c]	278	110	61
Russia[d]	53	9,800	1,320	54	86
Japan	13	1,210	564	64	17
China	101+	7,500–8,000	5,850	54	46
Taiwan	22+	459+	518	33	4
South Korea	24+	1,800	470	38	4
North Korea	30+	3,000	732	3+	26
Vietnam	73+	1,300	185	7+	—

Source: International Institute for Strategic Studies, *The Military Balance, 1992–1993* (London: Brassey's/IISS, Autumn 1992), pp. 27, 100, 145–47, 150–54, 161–62, and enclosed map.

[a]Excludes independent brigades/regiments/battalions, light tanks, patrol/coastal combatant ships; "+" after numbers indicates high ratios of such units to ones tabulated. Tabulations do not indicate relative combat power, due to qualitative disparities and asymmetries in untabulated capabilities.

[b]Pacific Command (PACOM).

[c]No number given for PACOM; 15,629 MBT in total U.S. inventory.

[d]Siberian, Transbaykal, and Far East Military Districts.

Note: Tabulations do not indicate relative combat power, because of qualitative disparities and asymmetries in untabulated capabilities.

have eventuated in combat at some point in this century. Today there is only one scene of contention where all the great powers' interests intersect (Korea); elsewhere they cooperate or compete in various combinations. Moreover, the regional countries have become actors on the world scene and are no longer just acted upon. This reduces the leverage of the outside great powers. Finally, as the end of the Cold War takes rising middle powers such as South Korea and Taiwan out of the arena of superpower competition, more countries develop the capacity to maneuver and complicate relations.[29]

The most important local countries remain the great powers, China, Japan, and Russia. When the Cold War subsumed strategic competition in East Asia, the first two were not independent strategic actors (except in the decade between the Sino-Soviet split and the Sino-American rapprochement); without the Soviet threat, it is hard to see why China and Japan should not become more independent. This does not mean that the great powers cannot avoid direct conflict and feel content to secure defense of their interests with minimal military means, even if economic nationalism prevails. As James Kurth suggested in the waning days of the Cold War:

> If a Pacific Basin international system based upon the concepts of international mercantilism and finite deterrence were to come into being. . . the United

States would no longer be the core country in the Pacific region . . . without the U.S. open market and the U.S. Seventh Fleet, the United States would be of little importance to Asia and the Pacific. Japan and China would become the core countries.[30]

This would keep external powers like the United States out of war in the area as well as a liberal system would, but it would keep them out of liberal economic relations as well. It is also unlikely that "finite deterrence" could mean anything but nuclear armament for all the players. The only other countries that could recreate a superpower-sized threat early in the twenty-first century, in any case, are the other great powers of East Asia: Russia, China, and Japan.

Power Centers and Instabilities

The future roles of China and Japan highlight how critical the choice of a realist or liberal model of international relations is, because some developments will look desirable in terms of one and disastrous in terms of the other. By the assumptions of the liberal model, the main problem is to promote liberalization—especially political and economic liberalization in China, and free trade among all. Liberalization in one sphere reinforces the other; as countries become more prosperous, they are more likely to become democratic. Thus it is in the security interest of countries to help one another become rich, even if that widens differences in national capability. If political and economic liberty become universal, peace will be secure, and differences in national power will be beside the point. Commercial competition should displace military competition. The economic development and expanding trade that characterize Asia point to opportunities for mutual profit throughout the region. National competitions for power waste resources, at best, or generate conflicts artificially, at worst.

For realists, ideology is barely relevant. Political fraternity will wilt under other pressures, and differences in power will resolve conflicts of interest. Or even if the pacifying effect of political liberalism is accepted, there is the problem that market efficiency may operate within authoritarian polities, yielding material strength without ideological discipline. For realists, it is not in a country's strategic interest for others to get rich unless they can be counted on to remain militarily weak or diplomatically allied. To realists, liberal theory overestimates the value states place on absolute as opposed to relative gains:

> For the United States, which future is preferable: one in which the U.S. economy grows at 25 percent over the next decade, while the Japanese economy grows at 75 percent, or one in which the U.S. grows at only 10 percent while that of Japan grows 10.3 percent? Robert Reich . . . posed that choice in 1990 in a series of meetings with graduate students, U.S. corporate executives, investment bankers, citizens of Massachusetts, senior State Department officials, and professional economists. A majority of every group, with one exception, expressed a preference for the latter outcome. The economists

unanimously chose the former, and ... were surprised that other Americans would voluntarily forgo fifteen percentage points of economic growth in the interest of hampering the progress of one of America's principal trade and financial partners.[31]

It is good that a country other than one's own has impressive military power as long as it is bonded to one's own country by the imperative to cooperate against a common threat. Otherwise, its friendship depends on the vicissitudes of international developments, and wealth that is convertible into military power makes it a potential threat. By liberal logic, other countries are more dangerous if they are lean and hungry than if they are fat and happy. Realists worry that prosperity may just make them muscular and ambitious.

Prospects for China and Japan thus have radically different implications for stability, depending on which models of the causes of war and peace are superimposed on the future. Those prospects have been obscured until recently because analysts have tended to consider the two countries' power in terms of how they lined up in the global conflict with Moscow, and to see them as junior partners. Reconciliation with China, which turned the tables on the superpowers and made the Soviets confront the strategic planning problem of a two-front war, as the United States had earlier, allowed Washington to remain one of the two principal powers in the area even as it withdrew a huge chunk of the forces it had deployed in the area between 1950 and 1972. By the end of the Cold War, only about 17 percent of U.S. military manpower was allocated to Asia, only about 6 percent was deployed forward in the region, and 70 percent of those deployed forward were in Japan and Korea.[32]

Now both Russia and the United States are less dominant in the region. Russia is preoccupied with internal transformation, and its power is drastically reduced from that of the Soviet Union. As a group of sober Russian strategic analysts put it:

Having retained more than four-fifths of the territory of the USSR, Russia nonetheless accounts for slightly over one-half of the population. It controls (taking into consideration production decline) less than one-half of the Soviet gross national product for 1990. In terms of most parameters ... Russia has become a middle-sized country. In Europe this is the equivalent of France, Great Britain, and Italy; in Asia, of India, and Indonesia.[33]

To the extent that Russian foreign policy focuses on Asia, it is much less on East Asia than on Central Asia and the multiple disorders on the country's southern borders.[34] In the near future, Russia's weakened condition facilitates more cooperation with China (by reducing the threat that Beijing might worry about) at the same time that it enhances incentives for it. For example, Russian civilian products are not competitive internationally, and the country's only industrial comparative advantage is in weapons manufacture, but these products are frozen out of the Western market, and the West is trying to prevent either Moscow or

Beijing from selling more arms elsewhere.[35] In the longer term, if Russia solves its problems, balance of power concerns should bring back at least modest tension between the two great powers of mainland Asia.[36] Moscow will inevitably be a strategic heavyweight in the region, especially when and if its own economic and political situation stabilizes, but its clout is unlikely to grow as fast as Beijing's or Tokyo's.

The United States remains formally committed to a strategic role in the Pacific, but its military presence has again been attenuated as the flag has come down from Philippine bases, land- and sea-based tactical nuclear weapons have been removed, and defense budget cuts have trimmed the size of the forces regularly stationed elsewhere in the neighborhood. U.S. political rhetoric minimizes change, but military movement highlights it. There is an important difference on this point between Northeast and Southeast Asia. American deployments in Korea may last for a long time, and those in Japan would be the last to go. The U.S. military role in the northern area has not shifted from substance to symbol, but in the southern part of the region it shifted clearly in that direction after 1973. Whether this matters brings us back to the opposing implications of the liberal and realist models.

Two potential changes would most focus attention on the U.S. role in regional stability. These would be China's achievement of a high level of economic development (close to Taiwan's or South Korea's) and Japan's development of a normal amount of military power (a share of national product allocated to the military comparable to the share in other wealthy countries). For those guided by liberal theories of the causes of war and peace, such outcomes would be desirable at best and harmless at worst; for those concerned with the balance of power, either one should be disturbing.

Even by the conventional economic measurements that kept estimates low, China has grown at an impressive pace since embracing the market. According to the most authoritative U.S. figures, real GNP grew at an average rate of about 7 percent from 1988 to 1991, and at a whopping average rate of about 13 percent from 1992 to 1994; industrial output grew at an average rate of about 16 percent from 1988 to 1994.[37] If we take more recent IMF calculations based on purchasing power parity rather than exchange rates (see below), the results look dramatic.[38] *The Economist,* which makes the case that most official statistics for China are meaningless, claims that the average GNP growth rate has been nearly 9 percent for fourteen years, and that China's true output is already at least a quarter of the United States'. China's marginal savings rate is also among the highest in the region.[39]

It is not inevitable that anything close to recent average rates will continue indefinitely, but if they do, the long-term prospects for the balance of power—global as well as regional—are staggering. Consider the implications of Table 2.4, based on the most conservative estimates of China's recent economic performance. If the country ever achieved a per capita GNP just one-fourth that of the United States (about South Korea's ratio today), it would have a total GNP

Table 2.4

Prosperity and Power Potential

	China	South Korea	Japan	United States
Per capita GNP ($)	1,327.0	6,430.0	27,300.0	22,550.0
(% of U.S.)	(5.9)	(28.5)	(121.1)	
Total GNP ($ billions)	1,528.0	280.9	3,386.0	5,695.0
(% of U.S.)	(26.8)	(4.9)	(59.5)	
Population (millions)	1,151.5	43.7	124.0	252.5
(% of U.S.)	(456.0)	(17.3)	(49.1)	
Percentage of U.S. per capita GNP needed to equal total U.S. GNP	22.0	582.7	201.9	

Source: U.S. Arms Control and Disarmament Agency, World Military Expenditures and Arms Transfers 1990 (Washington, D.C.: U.S. Government Printing Office, November 1991), pp. 58, 68, 69, 85.

Note: This compilation uses 1989 figures because the most recent official World Bank data publicly available at this writing[a] go only one year later, are incommensurable (listing per capita income in terms of GNP and national income in GDP), and understate the size of the Chinese economy even more than the above data, citing $370 per capita GNP for 1990. (See analysis in "China: The Titan Stirs," *The Economist*, Nov. 28, 1992, pp. 3–5. More realistic data would show much less current disparity between China and the United States, reinforcing the argument in the text of this paper).

[a]World Bank, *World Development Report 1992: Development and the Environment* (New York: Oxford University Press, 1992), pp. 218–223. U.S. government estimates report World Bank figures in 1991 and do not offer figures for China in 1992; see *The World Factbook 1992* (Washington, D.C.: Central Intelligence Agency, n.d.).

greater than that of the United States. That in itself is a limited indicator, since it would not equate to comparable disposable income, but it would still be an epochal change in the distribution of world power. By the same token, Japan's smaller population mitigates the implications of its per capita income. Japan would need double the American level to exceed the absolute U.S. GNP.[40] Similarly, the prospect of Russia's economic development poses less of a threat to the balance of power than does China's. Even by the conservative estimates, the prospect of China as an economic superpower is not remote; if the IMF calculations are to be believed, that eventuality is much closer. By those numbers, China's economy is four times larger than previously estimated, and became the third largest in the world years ago.[41]

With only a bit of bad luck in the evolution of political conflict between China and the West, such rapid economic development would make either the old Soviet military threat or the more recent trade frictions with Japan seem a comparatively modest challenge. More than a bit of good luck will be needed to avoid clashing with China politically. This is true according to either set of assumptions about international relations, realist or liberal. For realists, Chinese power was not a problem for Asia in the second half of the Cold War because the USSR was pinning it down. With that constraint reduced, the only alternatives will be to accept Chinese hegemony in the region or to balance Chinese power. The latter course need not and should not mean a new Cold War in Asia, but it does imply cautious moves toward containment without confrontation—polite containment, which need not preclude decent relations. This is feasible because China has not manifested aggressive intent, at least not as clearly as the Soviet Union appeared to be doing in the late 1940s, so there is no need to mobilize explicit alliances in opposition.

Diplomatic discussion should be about equilibrium rather than containment, a loaded term. If containment in fact is infeasible or undesirable, then realists will have to learn to live with Beijing in Asia as other countries have learned to live with the U.S. colossus in the Western Hemisphere,[42] or hope for the division of Chinese power through the breakup of the country. Disintegration is hardly a fanciful prospect; overcoming disunity has been a historic Chinese problem, and a violent one for much of this century, and the current uneven development in the country increases centrifugal strains.[43] And there is reason to believe that disintegration would not pose at least as many dangers as cohesion; consider the results the last time China fell apart.

The other theoretical approach does not make the question less vexing unless we assume that Chinese politics joins the End of History. Liberal theory is nonchalant about power imbalances only in regard to liberal polities or economies, so unless China embraces democracy and free trade, it may, for internal and ideological reasons, evince all the nasty vices in foreign policy that realism ascribes to imperatives imposed by the international system. But the liberal solution for pacifying international relations—liberal ideology—is precisely what present Chinese leaders perceive as a direct security threat to their regime.

So should we want China to get rich or not? For liberals, the answer is yes, since a quarter of the world's people would be relieved from poverty and because economic growth should make democratization more likely, which in turn should prevent war between Beijing and other democracies. For realists, the answer should be no, since a rich China (like a fully armed Japan) would overturn any balance of power. But what can be done about it anyway? No outside power has tremendous leverage on Beijing after the Cold War. Active efforts to keep China poor or to break it up are hard to imagine, and would be counterproductive by aggravating antagonism. Realists at best can passively hope for Chinese economic misfortune. Otherwise, we had better hope that liberal theory about the causes of peace pans out, so that what is good for China turns out to be good for everyone. As with all too many of the problems of security in East Asia, we may begin with a realist diagnosis but be forced into banking on liberal solutions simply because the costs of controlling the balance of power may be too high.

Normal Development as a Threat

As for Japan, its democracy ostensibly eliminates grounds for anxiety from one of the liberal perspectives, but limitations on the openness of trade still leave the country as a problem for either liberalism or realism. The main reason that recent trade frictions between Tokyo and Washington have not become a security problem as well as an economic one is that Japan is an unevenly developed great power. Cold War bipolarity obscured the discrepancies among the country's economic, military, and political weights. The situation grew increasingly anomalous as Japan grew richer; it can only seem even more peculiar as the end of the Cold War finishes sinking into everyone's consciousness.

The United States may continue to provide the security guarantee that allowed Japan to remain militarily limited, but the reason to do so will steadily become less obvious as time goes on and the residue of the Cold War strategic mentality dissipates. Or, even with attenuated American protection, Japan might dispense with advanced military power of its own if the threat that it worried about during the Cold War—the USSR—is not replaced by some other. Without U.S.–Russian military domination of Asia, however, can China avoid becoming such a threat? The old reasons that Tokyo's political and military roles should remain incommensurate with the country's wealth were peculiar. While it is not at all inevitable that the country will turn away from this peculiarity—it is deeply rooted in the postwar aversion to militarism—there is no reason to assume that new circumstances will not push Tokyo toward more normal great-power status. If Japan's economic, political, and military roles were to come into balance, strategic relations would be revolutionized in East Asia and beyond.

After emphasizing the potential danger that China poses for a balance of power, it might seem that realists should want full Japanese armament so that Tokyo could balance Beijing. Unless a bipolar contest between the two Asian great powers emerges as the only alternative to Chinese primacy, however, this is not the case. Despite the unbalanced nature of Japan's power, its lopsided economic clout already makes it a hefty great power in a multipolar balance. If Japan suddenly starts spending two to three times as much on defense and acquires nuclear weapons, it will be a dominating rather than a balancing power within the region. The only good reason to want Japan as a superpower to balance China would be if that were to become the only alternative to a multipolar balance, that is, if Russia and the United States ceased to provide strategic counterweights.

Yet some outside Japan still want the country to improve its military and contribute forces to enterprises like the 1991 war against Iraq. American critics especially berate Tokyo for "only" shelling out money, rather than lives, for the Persian Gulf War, and argue, "The key question Americans should ask themselves is: 'How long are we prepared to be loyal allies of Japan and act as volunteer Hessians serving Japanese interests, without demanding genuine military reciprocity?' "[44] They are right about the question but wrong about the answer, which should be, "As long as possible." There is nothing significant in the post–Cold War U.S. defense budget for the defense of Japanese interests that would not be there anyway for other purposes. Once Tokyo starts spending blood as well as treasure to support international order, it will justifiably become interested in much more control over that order.

If classic realists made Japanese foreign policy, they would want a full measure of national power, since the country's security is hostage to integration in markets that it does not control, but realists in other capitals contemplating the balance of power should have no interest in making Japan stronger than it already is. At present, Japan's foreign policy stance bears similarities to what would have been called liberal isolationism in an earlier era; it is based on the logic of "civilian power."[45] Realists anywhere but in Tokyo should encourage that stance, not disparage it. Nor should they let theoretical dogmatism preclude taking advantage of exceptions that all great theories have; there is no need to assume that international pressures inevitably dictate that Japanese leaders become military realists. After all, if Moscow could trade in a realist foreign policy for a liberal one, there is no reason that Tokyo has to do the reverse, or that it must do so sooner rather than later.

The notion that it would be better for Japan to be a regular military power is strategic old thinking, the echo of concerns about burden sharing in the global conflict with communism. When containing Soviet power was a difficult and expensive mission, getting Japan to share the burden made sense. Since the burden has been lifted, however, so has the guarantee that Japanese security interests can never diverge from those of other great powers. Thinking about Japan as a replacement for the Soviet threat to keep American strategists gainfully employed would be compulsive realism, and perhaps the prevalent trepidations of other Asian nations about Japanese power are a bit hysterical. (After Tokyo's precedent-breaking decision to send troops for the UN mission in Cambodia, Singapore's Lee Kuan Yew was reported to have said that encouraging Japan to engage in peacekeeping was like offering a drink to a recovering alcoholic.) But even if a more heavily armed Japan would behave as meekly as it did when it was an American strategic dependency, it is hard to see why such a change would buttress regional stability rather than shake it, unless Washington withdraws from the region and relies on Tokyo as its proxy.

Neoliberal institutionalist logic, which emphasizes the self-reinforcing dynamics of integrative activities, makes a reasonable case for encouraging a normal role for Japan. Promoting Japanese military participation in multilateral peacekeeping would especially make sense if the alternative were Japanese remilitarization outside such a framework. As Jack Snyder suggests in response to the Lee Kuan Yew line, social drinking is all right; it's drinking alone that we should worry about. But there is as yet no appreciable impulse to remilitarization from within Japan. Multilateral military integration should be the fallback position, not the current objective. A growing political role for Japan could be encouraged and accommodated within nonmilitary international institutions.[46] Why not postpone Japan's development of normal power until the Japanese press for it themselves?

The argument for Japanese military power actually makes more sense in terms of liberalism, or in terms of economic nationalism divorced from military considerations. In one view, the Japanese got an international commercial edge by allocating to civilian investment the 5 to 8 percent of GNP that was the difference in Japanese and American defense allocations throughout the Cold War. If one believes that only economic power is important, one could want the Japanese to spend more on military forces in order to level the economic playing field. Since its long-standing alliance with Washington and its democratic political system prevent Japan from becoming a military threat to other democracies, by this reasoning, it can hardly be worse for Tokyo to divert resources to military power than for other countries.[47]

In absolute terms, Japan's defense budget already ranks high: between third and sixth in the world in recent years (and even second, after the Soviet collapse and high exchange rates).[48] This makes the disproportion in spending all the more significant. Japan has been spending relatively less on military power than any other major state—less than a sixth of the proportional effort of the Cold War superpowers, and between a fifth and a third of the rates of Britain, Germany, France, China, and India (Table 2.5). While the Western powers' military efforts are now declining, however, Tokyo's is not. Japan's capacity in high technology also suggests that it would have a comparative advantage over most other countries in fielding a modern force if it focused on that goal.

For a realist, a normally armed Japan, unless it is pinned down by a powerful common enemy, is a potential threat. It would be the strongest military power in Asia, and the second-ranking one in the world. The fact that Japan is democratic, in this view, does not bar it from conflict with other democracies[49] (not to mention that some observers doubt whether Japan really is or will remain a democracy in Western terms).[50] To keep Tokyo a unidimensional superpower, however, the United States would have to avoid provoking the Japanese in the economic sphere and avoid making them feel fully responsible for their own fate. All that cuts against arm twisting over bilateral trade issues, pressure made more likely by U.S. domestic politics. Can American political leaders convince voters either that unfair Japanese trade practices are a myth or, if not, that they should "coddle" the Japanese because some academic theory implies that otherwise they might have to fight them again? Here liberal theory could rescue realism if arguments for free trade in U.S. domestic politics helped reduce diplomatic friction with Tokyo.

If Japan's power does develop fully, political friction with other Asian countries—most significantly China—would grow more than with Washington.[51] When Tokyo had an independent military policy during the past century, it was

Table 2.5

Relative Levels of Military Effort by Major States: Military Expenditures as Percentage of GNP

	1965	1970	1975	1980	1985	1990
United States	7.6	7.9	5.9	5.5	6.6	5.5
USSR	15.7	14.2	13.7	13.0	12.5	11.0
China	6.8	7.7	13.2	9.8	6.7	3.7
UK	5.9	4.8	4.9	5.0	5.3	4.1
France	5.2	4.1	3.8	4.0	4.1	3.6
W. Germany	4.3	3.3	3.6	3.3	3.2	2.8
India	3.7	3.1	3.2	3.4	3.8	3.0
Japan	1.0	0.8	0.9	0.9	1.0	1.0

Sources: For 1965–70, ACDA, *World Military Expenditures and Arms Transfers, 1965–1974* (Washington, D.C.: U.S. Government Printing Office, n.d.), pp. 24, 28, 29, 32, 34, 46, 50; for 1975–85, ACDA, *World Military Expendutures and Arms Transfers, 1990* (Washington, D.C.: U.S. Government Printing Office, November 1991), pp. 58, 62, 63, 67, 68, 85; for 1990, ACDA, *World Military Expenditures and Arms Transfers, 1991–92* (Washington, D.C.: U.S. Government Printing Office, March 1994), pp. 58, 62, 63, 68, 81, 85.

Note: Data for USSR and China are soft; many other sources estimate higher figures for USSR.

driven by China. All three of Japan's wars (1894–95, 1904–5, 1931–45) originated in disputes related to China. The whole question of balance between these two countries has been a nonissue since 1945 because of the Washington–Tokyo alliance, and stability in Asia has depended on the lack of strategic competition between China and Japan.[52]

Asymmetries would make it hard to estimate the balance of conventional military capability in such a competition. China is more of a continental power, reliant on ground forces and quantity of weaponry, whereas Japan is more of a maritime power, reliant on naval and air forces and quality of technology. Confusion about which one had a military edge could be especially destabilizing. Rough parity is more conducive to miscalculation and decisions to gamble on a resort to force than is clear hierarchy.[53]

For Japan to be a big-league player, it would have to have nuclear weapons. Neorealists like Kenneth Waltz are happy with that prospect because they see nuclear deterrence as stabilizing, and believe that it makes anxieties about conventional military balance beside the point.[54] If that is convincing, balance of power theorists can simply endorse nuclear proliferation as the solution to security dilemmas in Asia, and let the United States pack up its strategic bags and come home. It is not clear, though, how many statesmen have the courage of Waltz's convictions.

Chinese–Japanese bipolarity would be a problem for liberal theory as well if

China does not liberalize, since those who tout the separate peace among democracies recognize that they fight frequently and with alacrity against non-democracies. The Chinese elite have also not accepted the positive-sum logic of free trade, but remain mercantilist and zero-sum in outlook.[55] "China's leaders encounter great difficulty in accepting the fact that state sovereignty has been overtaken by an era of interdependence in which national boundaries are highly permeable."[56]

By realist criteria, a China and a Japan unleashed from Cold War discipline cannot help but become problems. Japan is powerful by virtue of its prosperity, which in turn depends on penetrating foreign markets, which creates political friction with competitors. Because of its bigness and its central location in regional geography, China evokes the structural theory of the German Problem; even without evil designs, the country's search for security will abrade the security of surrounding countries. Geographically, the "Middle Kingdom" is close to virtually everyone in East Asia. It is also the strategic pivot between the otherwise distinct subregions of Northeast and Southeast Asia. Individually, countries on the mainland cannot hope to deter or defeat China in any bilateral test of strength; collectively, they could not help but worry China if they were to seem united in hostility.

If China becomes highly developed economically, the problem will change. In this case, Asia would be stable but unhappy, because a rich China would be the clear hegemonic power in the region (like the United States in the Western Hemisphere) and perhaps the world. If China remains economically limited—while the American and Russian recession from the area proceeds further and Japan normalizes the balance among its roles—then Japan will be the dominant power in Asia.

The United States and Stability in East Asia

For these reasons, and because of Japan's desire to avoid becoming a normal great power, many governments in East Asia dread the prospect of American withdrawal. If a symbolic U.S. presence suffices—and some spokesmen in Asian capitals imply that it would—there is no reason that the United States cannot remain one of the principal strategic players.[57] It is not probable, however, that a simply symbolic military involvement will suffice outside Korea. There it works because it represents a tripwire.[58] The same presumption cannot exist in Southeast Asia because offshore forces cannot be positioned as a tripwire, because of the legacy of aversion still flowing from the old Indochina War, and because the United States has not cultivated deterrence by indicating its willingness to fight either of the potential threats in the subregion, China or Vietnam.

The time that U.S. commitment would actually matter would be when someone called on it to deter or defend against such a specific challenger. At such a moment, a symbolic role could well be exposed for what it was—a hesitant and weak commitment, accepted within the United States only by unelected elites (and a fraction of them at best). The United States has been in that position, though, ever since 1975. In the 1980s, when Vietnam had an army of 180,000 in Cambodia and clashed with Thai troops several times in border skirmishes, although Washington remained formally committed by the Manila Treaty to defend Thailand, was anyone really confident that the United States would go to war in a big enough way to save the country (meaning combat on the ground) if the Vietnamese moved westward? The pretense served by a token presence and symbolic commitment can continue, but it scarcely matters unless a test comes.

Southeast Asia is the part of East Asia where U.S. military engagement appears to be least likely, although Washington has a disconcerting habit of going to war in places it had not anticipated (for example, Kuwait) or, indeed, in places where officials had publicly indicated they would refrain (Korea in 1950). Southeast Asia is also where diplomacy to improve the balance of power is impeded by visceral American bitterness over the fruitless war there two decades ago. By balance of power criteria, the United States should have repaired relations with Vietnam long ago. Although Vietnam cannot be expected to contain China on its own, there is no strategic reason anymore to keep Hanoi weak. There are, of course, ample emotional reasons,[59] but winning the Cold War should be counted as more important than not winning the Vietnam War. In the new postwar world, the prospect of economic development makes the power potential of Vietnam, with a population of nearly 70 million, more significant than that of any other mainland country in Southeast Asia, with the possible exception of Thailand.

Since Vietnam is no longer an extension of Soviet power and influence, no longer occupies Cambodia, has demobilized half of its huge army, has moved to liberalize its economy and (to a lesser degree) its polity, and faces China on its northern border, it is also far less of a threat to the interests of the United States or its friends in the Association of Southeast Asian Nations (ASEAN) than during the Cold War. This would change in the unlikely event that Hanoi decided to reoccupy Cambodia, but Chinese capacity to punish Vietnamese adventurism is stronger than the reverse. In the bipolar Cold War world, it may have made sense for the United States to want Vietnam to be weak and vulnerable. In the new postwar world, there is no reason to want that unless Chinese dominance is preferred to some measure of balance.

One situation in which limited U.S. military engagement could prove most potent, and U.S. diplomacy most decisive, would be a regional multipolarity in which Washington shifted to playing the role of makeweight or external balancer, as Britain sometimes did on the continent of Europe. That way the United States might be the most important strategic player without having the most potent military force in the region. U.S. deployments, nevertheless, would still have to be substantial rather than symbolic. As time goes on, the rising capabilities of the local states will make the threshold of substantial presence harder for a post–Cold War U.S. defense budget to meet.

It is hard to imagine Washington playing the game of agile external balancer, tilting one way, then another, rather than faithful ally. Such unvarnished realism seems out of liberal character. (Divorced from the criterion of defending democracy, how would the mission be described to American voters and taxpayers—defense of markets? defense of economic competitors?) Despite realist criticism of American legalism and moralism, however, the United States is not totally unaccustomed to dumping friends and embracing bitter enemies for balance of power purposes. Taiwan discovered that in the 1970s. The most delicate question posed by a balancer role is what it would mean for U.S. relations with Japan, since it implies moving away from the Mutual Security Treaty. Washington would have to make an exception; otherwise, the move to balancing would be counterproductive, provoking Tokyo to rearm and act independently. With an exception for the Mutual Security Treaty, the U.S. balancer role would be between China and Russia. That, however, implies an unstable tripolar configuration. Or, playing balancer while still firmly linked with Tokyo could encourage more Russian–Chinese cooperation and reversion toward the bipolar groupings of the early Cold War. If the local powers—especially Japan—move more independently anyway, there may be little choice. Otherwise, facile proposals for an American balancer role overlook too many pitfalls.

Cleavages and Casus Belli

Even those who lack faith in liberal guarantees of peace must consider intentions and interests as well as power in estimating the odds that states will clash. International anarchy and national anxiety about power are necessary but not sufficient conditions for war. Some conflict of interest, some substantive dispute, some casus belli has to enter the equation to provide the impetus to violence.[60] One of the reasons for optimism about peace in Europe is the apparent satisfaction of the great powers with the status quo. Eastern Europe is a mess, but traditional nationalist, ideological, religious, communal, or resource conflicts appear to have been wrung out of the relationships among France, Germany, Britain, Russia, and Italy. And in Asia, no great power is now as revisionist in its aims for the general international order as Japan was before World War II.

East Asia is less beset by traditional casus belli than volatile regions like the Middle East or South Asia. For example, the relative ethnic homogeneity of the major East Asian states reduces the potential for irredentism.[61] Yet there is still an ample pool of festering grievances, with more potential for generating conflict than during the Cold War, when bipolarity helped stifle the escalation of parochial disputes. Endless numbers of scenarios can be dreamed up, and those that are far-fetched provide no useful guidance. But three are worth mentioning to illustrate two simple points. First, the possibilities of miscalculation and escalation are far from remote. Second, in two of the three cases there has been scant evidence that any of the governments involved have been planning seriously for how they would deal with the strategic questions posed by such instabilities.

One example is the discord over who owns the Spratly Islands, in the South China Sea. China claims all of them,[62] in conflict with claims by Vietnam, the Philippines, Malaysia, and Brunei. In one sense this issue is trivial and hard to see as the source of major conflict, since the islands are tiny, barren, and isolated. (There are similar disputes over the Paracel Islands as well.[63]) That insignificance, however, abets miscalculation and unintended provocation. If important amounts of oil or seabed minerals turn up in the area, moreover, greed will compound national honor as a potential source of conflict. The other claimants would probably be unable to contest determined Chinese efforts to occupy the islands. That would leave two alternatives: roll over and accept the Chinese conquest, conceding PRC dominance in the area, or regroup and retaliate on some other issue. It is not fanciful to see another Sino-Vietnamese war or a heating up of the Sino-Japanese dispute over the Senkaku/Diaoyutai Islands in the East China Sea growing out of the Spratly dispute. What if China fights with the Philippines and Vietnam over a couple of the Spratlys, Tokyo reacts by fortifying the Senkakus, and Beijing threatens retaliation if the Japanese do not pull back? If the national security establishments of any of the involved countries have considered what to do in such circumstances, their deliberations have been well hidden.

A second difficult case is a residue of the Cold War, but a potentially different problem in its own right: Korea. This is one of the few places in the world where it is easy to make the case that deterrence has been necessary, effectively achieved, and efficient. In contrast to most cases, where the propensity of an adversary to attack in the absence of a counterthreat is uncertain, it is as obvious as it could ever be that without the U.S. guarantee to Seoul, North Korea would be likely to resort to force. Since the direct attack in 1950, Pyongyang has frequently demonstrated its risk propensity in more consistently reckless provocations than any other government in the world: trying to assassinate the South Korean president (in the 1968 Blue House raid, and again in 1974, when Park Chung Hee's wife was killed in the attempt), seizing the U.S.S. *Pueblo* in 1968, hacking American officers to death in the DMZ tree-cutting incident of 1976, murdering half the South Korean cabinet with a bomb in Rangoon in 1983, feverishly digging infiltration tunnels under the Demilitarized Zone (DMZ), and blowing up KAL Flight 858 in 1987. The presence of American forces has been a permanent and potent reminder of how close Kim Il Song came to absolute disaster when he tried to invade. The deterrent has been efficient, in turn, because it is small and functions primarily as a tripwire.

Today, pessimists worry about a North Korean nuclear weapons program. Would any government be more willing to do wild and crazy things with such weapons than the one that so regularly perpetrates acts like those mentioned above? Optimists, on the other hand, see Korean unification around the corner. That is plausible if the North Korean regime collapses. Whether that happens or not, the problem with the nuclear issue is that no likely outcome can be comfortable for other countries.

North Korea has concluded an agreement to "freeze" its nuclear facilities pending further negotiations, but it is not surrendering any of the physical capacity to manufacture nuclear weapons if it decides to abrogate the agreement. It would have to accept unprecedented and absolutely unlimited inspections to give the West any reason for confidence that its nuclear activities could be fully monitored. Experience with Iraq has made astoundingly clear how much nuclear activity a zealous and secretive government can keep hidden. Yet no government accepts unlimited inspection, which is a virtual abrogation of sovereignty, except in a surrender agreement. The Iraq case also makes clear why preventive attack, however attractive an option it might become, should be written off. Initial confidence that the six-week air war in 1991 had destroyed Iraq's nuclear potential turned out to be terribly wrong. Confidence that buried and hidden facilities in North Korea had been found and eliminated would require not just air attack, but invasion and occupation of the country.

If Korea does unify under Seoul, however, the new government will have powerful incentives of its own for a nuclear deterrent. First, it would be much harder for the United States to maintain its military role in the country once the North Korean threat was gone. Second, the Seoul regime would have new borders with both China and Russia. Third, relations with Japan, always testy, would probably worsen, as Tokyo's apprehensions about the prospect of a stronger Korea grew. Some have speculated that one reason the South Koreans were initially less exercised than Washington about the North Korean nuclear program was that they would not mind inheriting it.

For the third example, suppose democratization continues in Taiwan, as even most realists hope. What if the result is that the Taiwan independence movement overpowers the Kuomintang, and Beijing fulfills its threat to act militarily to prevent secession?[64] Has the U.S. government seriously tried to figure out what it should or would do in such circumstances? The Taiwan Relations Act genuflects to peaceful reunification, but Washington has made no clear commitment about how it would react to military conflict. For liberals, it was not too hard to dump Taipei in the 1970s, when it was an authoritarian regime itself and when its conquest was not imminent, but a democratic Taiwan would be harder to abandon to a repressive Beijing in a moment of crisis. For realists, nothing could seem more within Beijing's legitimate sphere of influence than the island that all sides have so far recognized as part of China. It would seem hard to justify major war and the risk of nuclear escalation to defend Taiwan after virtually all states of consequence on the international scene blithely approved when Washington derecognized the Republic of China government, and in consequence abrogated the treaty guaranteeing its defense.

Pressures in both directions—defending Taiwan or standing aside—would be extreme, because the consequences either way could be catastrophic. At the same time, Beijing could hardly be expected to assume that Washington would intervene, given the evolution of policy since the Shanghai Communiqué; Chinese leaders would have at least as good an excuse to miscalculate as Kim Il Song in June 1950 or Saddam Hussein in August 1990. This is the scariest of the potential crises.

Traditional preoccupation with Europe, the painful memory of the price of indulging ambitious strategic aims in the Vietnam War, and the late Cold War entente with China have all disposed most American strategists against thinking very hard about potential situations such as those mentioned above. Similarly, the residue of Cold War thinking for pessimists, and the euphoria over the advance of liberalism for optimists, make it seem fanciful or demented to worry about balancing the power of Germany, Japan, China, or other Cold War friends. But the Cold War is over, and so is the particular realist calculus that went with it; the pacifying logic of liberal theory does not convince everyone as an alternative; and it is doubtful that East Asia will liberalize enough anyway to make new violence improbable. Thinking harder about nasty scenarios is hardly hysterical.

Prospects

There is only one world power uniquely positioned to play a stabilizing role in East Asia while remaining sufficiently detached and distant to avoid alarming most local states. The United States now has more leverage in more places on more issues than any other state, simply because there is no other comparable pole, as during the Cold War. That fact, in turn, naturally erodes American democracy's inclination to pay significant costs to call the tune in all the regions that it could. It could be a long time, though, before this erosion alters power configurations substantially, or the erosion could be reversed by the emergence of a significant threat.

The problem for policy is that every one of the three basic structural patterns of distribution of power could plausibly evolve. Moreover, realist theory is divided over which should even be preferred. There is also the possibility of a neoliberal solution in which institutionalization of cooperation comes to modify anxiety about relative power and to cause peace, although the plausibility of that outcome varies inversely with the odds that more intense casus belli will develop. The four general possibilities are:

1. *Unipolarity.* This could develop in two opposite ways. In one, the United States would reenter the region in force, on a scale comparable to the 1950s and 1960s, and become the dominant power. In the other, it would withdraw completely, as Britain did from East of Suez a quarter century ago. The latter course is less improbable than the former. In that case, the dominant power would be Japan, in the near term, if it arms more heavily and takes a more active political role, or China, in the long term, if its economic development continues at a high rate. The least likely of the great powers to develop a hegemonic position is Russia, although that could happen if China broke up and Japan remained restrained and nonnuclear while the United States withdrew. Japan's peculiar stra-

tegic passivity, however, has been premised on the Mutual Security Treaty, and so the latter combination of developments is hard to imagine.

Dominance of Asia by a single great power would be uncomfortable for all but the dominant one, but once accomplished, it would dampen the prospects for a major war, for the reasons that Geoffrey Blainey suggests about the stability of hierarchy: "Wars usually end when the fighting nations *agree* on their relative strength and wars usually begin when fighting nations *disagree* on their relative strength."[65] This accords with Robert Gilpin's view that a bipolarity that emerges as a rising power challenges a declining hegemonic state is likely to lead to war,[66] and conflicts with Waltz's argument that bipolarity is stabilizing. It is also a helpful reminder that what is good for stability—that is, strong inhibitions on resort to force—does not necessarily go with what is best for individual countries' independence.

Local states, however, are not likely to allow one of their number to achieve dominance without a fight. Unlike the states of the Western Hemisphere that live with the U.S. colossus, several states in East Asia have the capacity to contest a rising threat. As Arthur Waldron has noted, China's role might not be to dominate the region. Rather, in the process of asserting hegemony, Beijing might stimulate arms races (with Japan, Taiwan, Korea, and others) that it does not win. Such a process, complicated by disagreements about what the structure of the system was (with China considering it hierarchical and others seeing it as multipolar), could be quite volatile.

If the system was insecurely hierarchical and edged toward bipolarity rather than wider balance, it might become more dangerous for the reasons Gilpin suggests in his interpretation of history as a series of hegemonic transitions. Or, if Waltz is correct and the Cold War analogue is more appropriate than the Peloponnesian, bipolarity could make the structure stable. Even the Cold War model is not entirely reassuring, however, since stability in that case did not begin to emerge until 1963, after fifteen years of probing and scary crises over Berlin and Cuba worked out the bounds of strategic interaction.

2. *Bipolarity*. Depending on which countries develop their regional power in all its dimensions, a bipolar configuration could include any two of the four current great powers of the area (United States, Russia, China, Japan). Probably the least dangerous combination would be the two peripheral to the region, the Russians and the Americans, but without a Cold War between them it is hard to see why they would want to invest as much military and political capital in the region as the states that are fully located there. The most probable bipolar pair, and potentially the most antagonistic, is China and Japan. That would probably be the one with the most potential for war among great powers (for example, with Korea as a bone of contention, as it was a century ago) unless the two somehow established a condominium (which I have heard no regional experts argue is probable).

3. *Multipolarity*. This would continue the present situation or some variation with at least three of the major powers in the area: the United States, Russia,

China, and Japan.[67] India could also figure in the balance. As the middle powers develop further, the situation could become more complicated if alignments are fluid. The majority of states might also coalesce against the most troublesome. Except in the unlikely event that Japan's politics and society turned toward militarism again, the great power most likely to feel surrounded and beset would be China.

Multipolarity seems the most likely pattern, if only because it leaves open the widest number of possible combinations. Theory is not consistent on the question of whether multipolarity is more or less stable than the alternatives. Much writing about the classical European balance of power saw multipolarity as most stable in terms of preserving the main actors and preventing major war (although small wars or dismemberment of weak states, especially in the eighteenth century and earlier, was sometimes the price of general equilibrium). Most agree, though, that if multipolarity exists, a balance of five or more powers is more stable than a tripolar configuration, since a shift in alignment by one state can turn the latter upside down without any available redress. Only if India becomes a full player in East Asia would there be five such power centers. That is less likely than the possibility that the United States would drop out and leave a tripolar combination of Russia, China, and Japan. Thus the odds that the particular form of multipolarity that evolves will be stable, combined with the odds that some form of multipolarity will exist, are not reassuring.

There is one potential pattern of multipolarity that would be ideal, and that merges conceptually into the institutionalist option discussed below: a consensual pattern modeled on the nineteenth-century Concert of Europe. This would depend on delicate diplomacy, but it is not out of the question if the great powers are basically satisfied and can resolve minor grievances by compromise and offsetting concessions. While there is disagreement about whether a concert must rest on a balance of power,[68] the two are certainly compatible. While such a system may have some of the self-reinforcing advantages touted by liberal regime theorists, however, there is little evidence that it can survive the emergence of significant conflicts of interest, and thus that it is anywhere near as much a cause of stability as a reflection of it. The Concert of Europe also depended on a fair amount of ideological homogeneity (not yet evident in East Asia), and when this consensus waned, so did the Concert. Moreover, in the Concert of Europe, the principle that big states had the right to set the rules for small ones was more explicit than it could be in today's international climate.[69] Some sort of concert would be desirable in Asia, although no one should depend on it to solve more than modest disputes. In 1991, however, when Gorbachev proposed something like it—a five-power regional security conference of the United States, USSR, China, Japan, and India—the idea proved unpopular because it "smacked most inopportunely of a great-power deal, something that is clearly unpopular in the world right now."[70]

4. *Institutions overriding imbalances?* What stands out so far is the raft of uncertainties about what distribution of power in East Asia is either likely or

desirable. This raises the incentives to look beyond realism for solutions. Neoliberal institutionalism, in linking the logic of self-interested cooperation to the concerns of security policy, offers some other hypothetical possibilities for fostering stability. One hope is that development of regional economic cooperation or integration, for example in ASEAN, will have spillover effects in reducing apprehensions and facilitating confidence in political security (in a sense the reverse of the sequence in Europe, where NATO and security cooperation eased the promotion of European unity in other spheres).

Moves to make a security forum out of the ASEAN Post-Ministerial Conference (including the United States, Japan, Canada, and South Korea) and the establishment of the ASEAN Regional Forum (which includes the four great powers and most of the rest of Asia) are modestly promising, as are the revival of the Five-Power Defense Arrangement, which ties Britain, Australia, and New Zealand to Singapore and Malaysia, and the growth of intelligence cooperation among ASEAN states. Inhibitions against more integration are strong, however,[71] and even if multilateral security organization succeeded in the ASEAN region, that is not the larger part of East Asia.

Other possibilities have been broached. In 1990 Australia and Canada proposed a Conference for Security and Cooperation, and a North Pacific Security Dialogue. Others have proposed utilizing the Asia-Pacific Economic Cooperation (APEC) process to deal with security matters. The Bush administration, preferring continued emphasis on bilateral arrangements, opposed such moves, but the Clinton administration endorsed them.[72] There is scant evidence, however, that favorable attitudes about developing discussion forums extend further, toward more explicit security organization, and some countries have explicitly indicated that they are not interested in agreements for collective action, especially binding defense commitments. The leap from economic multilateralism to multilateral security planning is not yet in sight.[73]

Neoliberal analysis has sometimes emphasized the difficulty of constructing effective multilateral institutions in the absence of hierarchy, when no dominant power bears disproportionate costs in providing collective goods. The United States did that in Asia at the height of the Cold War when it provided the bulk of the resources for the United Nations Command in Korea, undertook the one-sided Mutual Security Treaty with Japan (obliging Washington to defend Tokyo, but not the reverse), and shepherded the Southeast Asia Treaty Organization (SEATO), the broadest alliance in the region. The United States is not about to shoulder such burdens now, nor is any other great power.

The most ambitious institutionalist alternative to relying on a balance of power to keep peace, hypothetically, is a genuine collective security arrangement. The idea was broached in the past in regard to Asia in Soviet and other proposals and became vaguely popular again as a result of the end of the Cold War, but it does not offer much for Asia. First, the fundamental logic of the concept is dubious. It is no accident that collective security schemes have seldom if ever worked elsewhere, and that the situations in which the concept is said to have been validated (NATO's organization for deterrence, or the United Nations' wars for Korea and Kuwait) are ones in which hegemonic or balance of power dynamics operated behind the facade of collective security rhetoric.[74] Second, Asia is behind Europe in the development of integrative organizational forms that could be appropriate foundations. The counterparts to NATO, the Conference on Security and Cooperation in Europe (CSCE), the Western European Union (WEU), or the European Community (EC) that have been evident in Asia have been concentrated in Southeast Asia, just one corner of the huge region. The most significant security analogue, SEATO, is defunct. Third, and most fundamental, there is no consensus on norms or status or supranational order shared by all major states of East Asia.

The profusion of predictions allowed by both general approaches to explaining international relations, realism and liberalism, precludes any wide analytical consensus that could serve as a basis for prescription. This makes it especially reasonable to look for a synthesis of various strands of the basic theories.

The easiest starting point is to assume that liberal solutions of all sorts are desirable as long as they do not conflict with maintaining a stable distribution of power. And since realist theory is divided about which distribution of power is most desirable for stability, it is reasonable to combine preferences on this matter with those recommended by liberal theories. This could yield the following conditional verdicts.

The ideal result would be an even balance of power among five or more states, all of which enjoyed democratic governments and free trade.[75] Short of that, acceptability of patterns of national power should vary more with the incidence of political than of economic liberalism. Empirical support for the pacifying impact of constitutional democracy is somewhat firmer than for the assumption that economic interdependence breeds peace.[76] In a reasonable synthesis of realist and liberal theory, therefore, a country with a liberal economy but an illiberal polity should warrant at least as much concern as the old communist or fascist powers ever did, since it poses the prospect of economic power without political restraint. The possibility of this combination in China's future, together with the country's size, makes it potentially the most problematic great power in the region[77] (as the absence of that combination in Japan makes it presently less worrisome). Gambling that democracy will underwrite peace should be a reasonable risk for reasonable realists, but compounding the wager by gambling that wealth will produce democracy sometime in the future compromises balance of power norms too much.[78] In the Cold War, realism subordinated concern with human rights in China to strategic cooperation against the USSR; after the Cold War, supporting liberal political values in China is compatible with concern about the balance of power.

There could be no reason not to welcome neoliberal institutional developments—they may help and are not likely to hurt—unless they lulled governments into indifference to unbalanced power. That danger is not likely. It is most probable that if such institutions do develop, they will, as in Europe, parallel or emerge from alliances based on common political and strategic interests rather than transcend or subvert them.

Asia's relative importance has been obscured in other great-power capitals by the traditional preoccupation with Europe, the recent preoccupation with the Middle East, and, in the United States, the residue of distaste from the Vietnam War. Emerging questions about balance of power in the East Asian region have been avoided because of liberal faith in the progress of peace and realist habits of mind grounded in the Cold War. Potential casus belli in the area have been overlooked by most because interstate violence in East Asia (except for the Indonesian invasion of East Timor) was driven by now-defunct global bipolarity. These oversights should make Asia the most fertile ground for adjusting and reinventing strategic concepts in the post–Cold War era.

Notes

1. Ambivalence about how the security situation in Asia should be assessed can be found even among seasoned experts. For example: "The United States and Russia have a growing community of interests. . . . China is fully preoccupied with its domestic problems. Japan, an economic superpower, is only beginning to apply that power for political purposes. . . . In sum the risk of a major power conflict in Asia is at its lowest point in this century"; but, "On the political front one worrisome fact emerges. For the first time in the twentieth century, U.S. relations with China and Japan are troubled simultaneously"; and, "given the likely power relationships in East Asia, U.S. policy can proceed with minimal concern about new hostile coalitions"; yet "the current leaders of the People's Republic of China are telling both Russia and Japan that there must be closer cooperation to block a hegemonic America." Robert Scalapino, "The United States and Asia: Future Prospects," *Foreign Affairs*, vol. 70, no. 5 (Winter 1991–92), pp. 26, 32, 36.

2. In the 1960s, Beijing was seen as an independent threat, but otherwise its role in U.S. strategy depended on its relation to Soviet power and transnational Leninism. Washington opposed China in the 1950s largely because of its alliance with the USSR, and courted it in the 1970s and 1980s because of its enmity with the USSR.

3. This is the sense in which I use the term unless otherwise indicated. "Balance of power" is notoriously ambiguous in common usage, referring variously to any distribution of power, a roughly equal (usually multipolar) distribution, international stability or equilibrium, deliberate policies to create or maintain equilibrium, automatic equilibrating tendencies in the international system, and other things. See Ernst Haas, "The Balance of Power: Prescription, Concept, or Propaganda?" *World Politics*, vol. 5, no. 4 (July 1953); Inis L. Claude, Jr., *Power and International Relations* (New York: Random House, 1962), chap. 2; and Martin Wight, "The Balance of Power," in Herbert Butterfield and Martin Wight, eds., *Diplomatic Investigations* (Cambridge, MA: Harvard University Press, 1968).

4. Not all choices fit into this dichotomy, which does not subsume serious alternatives such as Marxism-Leninism. Since it never influenced policymaking in great powers other than the USSR and China, and now exerts scant influence in those or other countries, that alternative is ignored here. For thinking about international conflict, moreover, Marx and Lenin shared many assumptions with the other schools. If classes are substituted for

states, their view of conflict as natural and inevitable is quite similar to realism. Leninist regimes that twisted doctrine to support nationalism had quite realist foreign policies. Pure Marxism, though, believes in progress. When class conflict is resolved with the arrival of communism (the stage of development after socialism), the Marxist view resembles the liberal in its assumption that peace and harmony become natural.

5. Officials typically disdain the notion that theory can inform policy as a naive academic conceit. This view is rooted in practitioners' respect for their own experience; in the misconception that a general argument that does not fit all cases well, or any case perfectly, is self-evidently faulty; and in encounters with foolish academics spouting silly or unintelligible theories. Policymakers usually regard themselves as pragmatists, operating case by case, without theoretical blinders. In reality, experience cannot predict what will happen unless the current case is absolutely identical to one already experienced (which never happens) or unless the policymaker filters experience through a theory. The difference between academics and officials is not reliance on theory, but explicit or unconscious reliance on theory. For a promising effort to link theory and policy, see Alexander George, *Bridging the Gap* (Washington, DC: U.S. Institute of Peace, 1993).

6. Exemplary realists include Thucydides, Niccolo Machiavelli, and Thomas Hobbes, and in the twentieth century, E.H. Carr, Hans Morgenthau, Reinhold Niebuhr, Arnold Wolfers, Kenneth Waltz, and Robert Gilpin. For a representative selection of arguments, see Part 2 of Richard K. Betts, ed., *Conflict after the Cold War* (New York: Macmillan, 1994).

7. Examples in this tradition include Immanuel Kant, Hugo Grotius, Adam Smith, and Richard Cobden, and in the twentieth century, Woodrow Wilson, Joseph Schumpeter, Norman Angell, Hedley Bull, and Robert Keohane. See selections in Parts 3–5 of Betts, ed., *Conflict after the Cold War.* For comparative examinations from varying perspectives, see Charles Beitz, *Political Theory and International Relations* (Princeton, NJ: Princeton University Press, 1979); Joseph S. Nye, Jr., "Neorealism and Neoliberalism," *World Politics*, vol. 40, no. 2 (January 1988); Robert Gilpin with the assistance of Jean M. Gilpin, *The Political Economy of International Relations* (Princeton, NJ: Princeton University Press, 1987), chap. 2.

8. The latest wave, known as neorealism, focuses entirely on the international structure of power. Old realists consider domestic political and psychological factors as important in explaining decisions for war, but they too emphasize the external distribution of state power as the prime concern for policy.

9. The reasoning is that primacy of one state deprives too many others of independence, or is impossible in the absence of a universal empire; bipolarity is unstable because it invites struggle for primacy, miscalculation, and preventive war; and multipolarity (preferably with five or more great powers) allows flexible alignments to redress developing imbalances. See Edward Vose Gulick, *Europe's Classical Balance of Power* (New York: Norton, 1967); F.H. Hinsley, *Power and the Pursuit of Peace* (New York: Cambridge University Press, 1967); Albert Sorel, *Europe under the Old Regime*, Francis H. Herrick, trans. (New York: Harper Torchbooks, 1964); Ludwig Dehio, *The Precarious Balance*, 2d ed. (London: Chatto and Windus, 1962).

10. This view derives inductively from the stability of the U.S.-Soviet balance during the Cold War and deductively from the argument that multipolarity makes alliance solidarity too important and allows crises to escalate too easily when states drag their allies into confrontation. Kenneth N. Waltz, *Theory of International Politics* (Reading, MA: Addison-Wesley, 1979), chap. 8.

11. Geoffrey Blainey, *The Causes of War*, 3d ed. (New York: Free Press, 1988), pp. 109, 112–114; Samuel P. Huntington, "Why International Primacy Matters," *International Security*, vol. 17, no. 4 (Spring 1993).

12. Early expositors of this view were Richard Cobden and the Manchester school in the nineteenth century. For a critique, see Blainey, *Causes of War,* chap. 2. For a balanced recent version of the argument, see Richard Rosecrance, *The Rise of the Trading State: Commerce and Conquest in the Modern World* (New York: Basic Books, 1986).

13. Michael Doyle, "Liberalism and World Politics," *American Political Science Review,* vol. 80, no. 4 (December 1986); and Doyle, "Kant, Liberal Legacies, and Foreign Affairs," Parts 1 and 2, *Philosophy and Public Affairs,* vol. 12, no. 3 (Summer 1983) and no. 4 (Fall 1983).

14. For example, Robert Keohane, *International Institutions and State Power* (Boulder, CO: Westview Press, 1989); and Stephen D. Krasner, ed., *International Regimes* (Ithaca, NY: Cornell University Press, 1983). The institutionalist variant of the liberal approach incorporates significant elements of realist logic.

15. For example, realists Henry Kissinger and Hans Morgenthau split on the Vietnam War, as did liberals Henry Jackson and George McGovern. More recently, proponents of intervention in Bosnia and Somalia were more often liberals than realists.

16. Space constraints preclude full discussion of ambiguities and qualifications in definitions of power, especially nonrealist ones. See David Baldwin, *Paradoxes of Power* (New York: Blackwell, 1989); and Joseph Nye, *Bound to Lead* (New York: Basic Books, 1990).

17. Louis Hartz argues in *The Liberal Tradition in America* (New York: Harcourt, Brace, 1955) that liberalism so infuses American political culture that it is taken for granted, and allows politically significant debates to take place only among schools within liberalism.

18. The exception to the consensus was the decade after the Tet Offensive, when liberals became disillusioned with intervention and argued that interdependence and negotiation rather than military muscle would best serve peace and stability. The debate crested in the Carter administration with the split between the dovish Vance and the hawkish Brzezinski. The split was resolved in the hawks' favor after the invasion of Afghanistan, and the reborn consensus was confirmed with Reagan's election. In 1993, however, the Vance school got its revenge, as Warren Christopher and Anthony Lake, his old lieutenants, took charge of foreign policy. Lake described himself and President Clinton as "neo-Wilsonian," opposed to the "classic balance of power" perspective. Steven A. Holmes, "Choice for National Security Adviser Has a Long-Awaited Chance to Lead," *New York Times,* January 3, 1993, p. 16.

19. Other terms used in place of unipolarity include hegemony, hierarchy, and primacy. These connote more about the amount of control that goes with a dominant power position than I wish to assume at most points in this essay. For an activist view of the implications for U.S. policy, see Charles Krauthammer, "The Unipolar Moment," *Foreign Affairs,* vol. 70, no. 1 (1990–91).

20. For a related view of current power structures, see the discussion of the "uni-multipolar" world in Samuel P. Huntington, "America's Changing Strategic Interests," *Survival,* vol. 33, no. 1 (January/February 1991), p. 6.

21. David Shambaugh, "In Shanghai's Busy Shipyards, a Warning about Chinese Might," *International Herald Tribune,* January 15, 1993, p. 8; Nicholas Kristof, "China Raises Military Budget despite Deficit," *New York Times,* March 17, 1993, p. A9. By some accounts the nominal increase was more than half, but Chinese sources claim that it was only 17.2 percent in 1988–91 when adjusted for inflation. Qimao Chen, "New Approaches in China's Foreign Policy," *Asian Survey,* vol. 33, no. 3 (March 1993), p. 245.

22. "Asia's Arms Race," *The Economist,* February 20, 1993, p. 19.

23. In contrast to most realists, I count ideology as an element of power, rather than just a matter of values, when it contributes to social mobilization, willingness to bear high costs for strategic rivalry, and incentives for alliance between countries. The only candi-

date to replace Marxism-Leninism as a competing global ideology is radical Islam, which hypothetically could coordinate movements in areas as diverse as the Middle East and North Africa, Nigeria, Pakistan, Indonesia, and some of the former Soviet republics of Central Asia, to team up with the regime in Iran. Nothing indicates the probability of successful coordination, however, and such a coalition would also lack the industrial power or geographic cohesion to stand up to Western military force.

24. See Charles E. Morrison, "The Future of Democracy in the Asia-Pacific Region: The Security Implications," in Dora Alves, ed., *Evolving Pacific Basin Strategies* (Washington, DC: National Defense University Press, 1990).

25. On derivative and intrinsic interests, see Richard K. Betts, "Southeast Asia and U.S. Global Strategy," *Orbis*, vol. 29, no. 2 (Summer 1985), pp. 354–62. The difference related to the domino theory. One way of putting it would be to say that the United States committed itself militarily to NATO and the Mutual Security Treaty with Tokyo because it cared about Western Europe and Japan, whereas it committed itself militarily in Korea and Vietnam because it cared about Western Europe and Japan.

26. For example, in 1964–66, when the move to large-scale intervention occurred, China was the focus of official statements on Vietnam between three and five times as often as the Soviet Union. F.M. Kail, *What Washington Said: Administration Rhetoric and the Vietnam War* (New York: Harper Torchbooks, 1973), Appendix.

27. Secretary of Defense Dick Cheney, *Defense Strategy for the 1990s: The Regional Defense Strategy* (Department of Defense, January 1993), p. 21.

28. Fungibility of forces makes any allocation of expenditures to specific regional commitments contestable, but internal planning generated force requirements largely for war in Europe. In the early 1960s planners were directed to develop capabilities for a so-called 2½-war scenario, in which Europe would be only one of the total. The results still allocated about 60 percent of ground force divisions and fighter-attack wings to NATO. William W. Kaufmann, *Planning Conventional Forces, 1950–1980* (Washington, DC: Brookings Institution, 1980), Tables 1 and 2, pp. 6–7. Later, the Nixon Doctrine reduced the criterion to 1½ wars, of which Europe was the one. It was also an open secret that the United States had a "swing" strategy, in which military forces in the Pacific would move to Europe in the event of war there.

29. I owe much of this paragraph to Michel Oksenberg.

30. James R. Kurth, "The Pacific Basin versus the Atlantic Alliance: Two Paradigms of International Relations," *The Annals of the American Academy of Political and Social Sciences,* vol. 505 (September 1989), p. 37.

31. Michael Mastanduno, "Do Relative Gains Matter?" *International Security*, vol. 16, no. 1 (Summer 1991), p. 73.

32. *A Strategic Framework for the Asian Pacific Rim: Looking toward the 21st Century*, Report to Congress (Office of the Assistant Secretary of Defense for International Security Affairs/East Asia Pacific Region, April 1990), p. 5.

33. "Some Theses for the Report of the Foreign and Defense Policy Council," in Foreign Broadcast Information Service, *Central Eurasia,* FBIS-USR-92-115, September 8, 1992, p. 54.

34. See Sergei Karaganov, "Russia and Other Independent Republics in Asia," in *Asia's International Role in the Post–Cold War Era: Part II,* Adelphi Paper No. 276 (London: International Institute for Strategic Studies, April 1993), pp. 27–29.

35. "Instead of being coopted and integrated, the powerful political and economic interests connected with the Russian armaments industry are being pushed in an anti-Western direction. A side effect of these policies will be, of course, a further shift towards relatively indiscriminate arms sales . . . particularly to China." Karaganov, "Russia and Other Independent Republics in Asia," p. 26.

36. "The Chinese factor is encouraging Russia to retain its political reliance on nuclear containment and on strategic alliance with the West." "Some Theses for the Report of the Foreign and Defense Policy Council," p. 57.

37. Central Intelligence Agency, *China's Economy in 1993 and 1994: The Search for a Soft Landing*, EA 94–10016 (n.p.: CIA Directorate of Intelligence, August 1994), p. iii.

38. Nicholas D. Kristof, "China Builds Its Military Muscle, Making Some Neighbors Nervous," *New York Times*, January 11, 1993, p. A8.

39. "China: The Titan Stirs," *The Economist*, November 28, 1992, pp. 3–5; David Shambaugh, "China's Security Policy in the Post-Cold War Era," *Survival*, vol. 34, no. 2 (Summer 1992), p. 101. See also Charles Horner, "China on the Rise," *Commentary*, vol. 94, no. 6 (December 1992).

40. Population itself is not a source of power. Indeed, at present China's population is a source of weakness and will become a greater one if its growth is not curbed. The point is that population makes for power when it is associated with an advanced economy. The United States is not the most powerful country in the world because of its per capita income—several countries rank higher on that index. No matter how efficient Switzerland or Sweden may be, however, they can never be superpowers. Countries with the most power potential in the twenty-first century will be those that *combine* high rankings in productivity, population, and resources; those with the most actual power will be the ones from among that group that marshal the most military power from that potential.

41. Steven Greenhouse, "New Tally of World's Economies Catapults China into Third Place," *New York Times*, May 20, 1993, pp. A1, A8.

42. China might seem less of a problem, since in modern times it has not intervened as often in neighboring countries as the United States has, but it has still used force against neighbors and engaged in coercion a number of times since 1949. Moreover, China lost large amounts of territory in the last century and a half, and, as Michel Oksenberg suggests, nationalism could emerge "as a substitute for Marxism as a unifying ideology." Quoted in Kristof, "China Builds Its Military Muscle," p. A8.

43. Pressures in this direction come from economic warlordism. For example, in 1990, Guangdong province, transferring productive resources from rice to cash crops and industry, sought to import rice from Hunan, which demanded above-market prices. Guangdong tried to circumvent the Hunan government and buy directly from producers. "Hunan put troops on its borders to stop the rice shipments; Guangdong countered with its own mobilization." "Cut along the Dotted Lines," *The Economist*, June 26, 1993, p. 35. In a different view, however, trends in Chinese unity point in the other direction, toward "diaspora economic power," as cooperation among the PRC, Taiwan, Hong Kong, and Singapore builds an "inter-tribal economy" and fosters transgovernmental Chinese economic hegemony. Joel Kotkin, "China Dawn," *Washington Post National Weekly Edition*, October 12–18, 1992, p. 23.

44. Edward Olsen, "Target Japan as America's Economic Foe," *Orbis*, vol. 36, no. 4 (Fall 1992), p. 496.

45. Hanns W. Maull, "Germany and Japan: The New Civilian Powers," *Foreign Affairs*, vol. 69, no. 5 (Winter 1990–91).

46. "For example, of the 150-plus slots allocated to Japan in the United Nations Secretariat, only 88 are now filled." Joseph S. Nye, Jr., "Coping with Japan," *Foreign Policy* no. 89 (Winter 1992–93), p. 109.

47. Chalmers Johnson does not promote Japanese militarization but sees vested interests in traditional U.S. military strategy as partly responsible for failure to confront Tokyo's economic challenge. He wants Americans to "recognize that Japan has replaced the USSR as America's most important foreign policy problem," and sees adaptation blocked by "entrenched interests in the preservation of the system of inequalities that

characterized Japanese-American relations during the 1960s . . . the interests of the defense establishment in the role of America as a hegemon athwart the Pacific, of the diplomatic establishment in Cold War dualism, of . . . the Atlanticists in not having to come to grips with problems for which they do not have the requisite skills." Chalmers Johnson, "Japan: Their Behavior, Our Policy," *National Interest*, no. 17 (Fall 1989), pp. 26–27. If the United States and Japan do become more confrontational economically, however, and at the same time modify the traditional one-sided security relationship, does it not become less improbable that military tension could arise?

48. Unusually high personnel costs help prevent this level of expenditure from providing a comparable amount of combat power at present. One obstacle to Japanese remilitarization is the difficulty of recruitment even at currently low numbers of mobilized manpower.

49. Hisahako Okazaki has called attention to the discomfiting analogy of the seventeenth-century rivalry and war between Britain and the Netherlands, two republics. Cited in Peter J. Katzenstein and Nobuo Okawara, "Japan's National Security: Structures, Norms, and Policies," *International Security*, vol. 17, no. 4 (Spring 1993), p. 91.

50. Karel van Wolferen, *The Enigma of Japanese Power* (New York: Knopf, 1989). For a more benign and carefully researched view, see Gerald Curtis, *The Japanese Way of Politics* (New York: Columbia University Press, 1988). See also Francis Fukuyama and Kong Dan Oh, *The U.S.-Japan Security Relationship after the Cold War*, MR-283-USDP (Santa Monica, CA: Rand Corporation, 1993).

51. Japan's 1987 decision to breach the symbolic ceiling of 1 percent of GNP for defense spending alarmed the Chinese because it seemed inconsistent with the warming of superpower relations, and was interpreted as a demonstrated intent to become a "political power." Jonathan Pollack, "The Sino-Japanese Relationship and East-Asian Security: Patterns and Implications," *China Quarterly* (December 1990), pp. 718–19.

52. Fred C. Iklé and Terumasa Nakanishi, "Japan's Grand Strategy," *Foreign Affairs*, vol. 69, no. 3 (Summer 1990), pp. 84–85. As Michael Chambers points out, this could have been due as much to their own underdeveloped capacity to project power as to Cold War constraint.

53. Blainey, *Causes of War*, chap. 8. If it is clear which power in a confrontation is superior to the other, bargaining leverage should be irresistible, since the weaker one can get nothing from resisting except defeat in war.

54. Kenneth N. Waltz, *The Spread of Nuclear Weapons: More May Be Better*, Adelphi Paper No. 171 (London: International Institute for Strategic Studies, Autumn 1981).

55. Michel Oksenberg, "The China Problem," *Foreign Affairs*, vol. 70, no. 3 (Summer 1991), p. 10.

56. Shambaugh, "China's Security Policy in the Post-Cold War Era," p. 93.

57. For a discussion of alternative U.S. force postures, see James A. Winnefeld, et al., *A New Strategy and Fewer Forces: The Pacific Dimension*, R-4089/2-USDP (Santa Monica, CA: Rand Corporation, 1992).

58. The concept of a tripwire is capsulized in the answer given by General Foch in 1910 to General Wilson's query about the minimum British force that would be useful to the French: "A single British soldier—and we will see to it that he is killed." Quoted in Barbara Tuchman, *The Guns of August* (New York: Dell, 1963), p. 68.

59. The POW/MIA issue can never be satisfactorily resolved because (1) testimony of former U.S. officials in the summer of 1992 and the discovery in Soviet archives of the translation of an apparently incriminating North Vietnamese document, whether genuine or not, invigorated old suspicions, and (2) it is impossible to prove the negative (that is, that Hanoi never held back any prisoners, in any hiding place, for any time after 1973).

60. The fact that intentions as well as capabilities matter is part of the reason that

"balance of threat" theory improves on balance of power theory. See Stephen M. Walt, *The Origins of Alliances* (Ithaca, NY: Cornell University Press, 1987).

61. There are still problems of this sort that are not trivial: divided Mongols and Kazakhs, repressed Tibetans, or communal tensions in smaller states like Malaysia.

62. Beijing and Taipei have overlapping claims, both in the name of one China.

63. See Wayne Bert, "Chinese Policies and U.S. Interests in Southeast Asia," *Asian Survey,* vol. 33, no. 3 (March 1993), p. 327.

64. Taiwan's opposition independence party has protested moves toward rapprochement between Taipei and Beijing (such as high-level talks) and announced in Singapore, "We assert to China and the world: Taiwan is not a part of China." Quoted in Nicholas D. Kristof, "China and Taiwan Have First Talks," *New York Times,* April 28, 1993, p. A8.

65. Blainey, *Causes of War,* p. 122 (emphasis in original).

66. Robert Gilpin, *War and Change in International Politics* (New York: Cambridge University Press, 1981).

67. A hybrid would be a bipolarity of blocs organizing a multipolarity of states, with one alliance led by the continental powers Russia and China, the other by the offshore powers Japan and the United States. This might be fairly stable, given the geographic breakdown, unless smaller states on the continent sought protection from Washington and Tokyo. The relatively even balance of power between the two leading states in each of the blocs could also complicate the functioning of the alliances, making them more similar to the European blocs before 1914 than to those of the Cold War. The vulnerability of the structure to quick realignment could thus make it shaky.

68. See Paul W. Schroeder, "Did the Vienna Settlement Rest on a Balance of Power?"; Enno E. Krahe, "A Bipolar Balance of Power"; Robert Jervis, "A Political Science Perspective on the Balance of Power and the Concert"; and Wolf D. Gruner, "Was There a Reformed Balance of Power System or Cooperative Great Power Hegemony?" all in *American Historical Review,* vol. 97, no. 3 (June 1992).

69. See Richard K. Betts, "Systems for Peace or Causes of War? Collective Security, Arms Control, and the New Europe," *International Security,* vol. 17, no. 1 (Summer 1992), pp. 24, 27–28. For a more favorable view, see Charles and Clifford Kupchan, "Concerts, Collective Security, and the Future of Europe," *International Security,* vol. 16, no. 1 (Summer 1991).

70. V. Golobnin, quoted in William T. Tow, "Northeast Asia and International Security: Transforming Competition to Collaboration," *Australian Journal of International Affairs,* vol. 46, no. 1 (May 1992), p. 15.

71. Richard Stubbs, "Subregional Security Cooperation in ASEAN: Military and Economic Imperatives and Political Obstacles," *Asian Survey,* vol. 32, no. 5 (May 1992), pp. 403–9; Leszek Buszynski, "ASEAN Security Dilemmas," *Survival,* vol. 34, no. 4 (Winter 1992–93), pp. 101–3.

72. Tow, "Northeast Asia and International Security," pp. 14–15, 17–18; Elaine Sciolino, "U.S. to Urge Asia to Build Security," *New York Times,* April 1, 1993, p. A8.

73. David E. Sanger, "Asian Countries, in Shift, Weigh Defense Forum," *New York Times,* May 23, 1993, p. 16; Tow, "Northeast Asia and International Security," p. 18. See also Gerald Segal, "North-East Asia: Common Security or à la Carte?" *International Affairs,* vol. 67, no. 4 (October 1991), pp. 763–65; and David Youtz and Paul Midford, *A Northeast Asian Security Regime: Prospects after the Cold War,* Public Policy Paper No. 5 (New York: Institute for East-West Studies, 1992).

74. For detailed arguments, see Betts, "Systems for Peace or Causes of War?"

75. This could ultimately pose a problem for realist norms if the economic specialization fostered by free trade left some states without the internal means to provide for their

own defense. Fulfilling the rest of the prescription would be worth risking that result; if it began to develop, the prescription could be reassessed.

76. See the compilations in the appendices to Doyle's "Liberalism and World Politics," and Zeev Maoz and Bruce Russett, "Normative and Structural Causes of Democratic Peace, 1946–1986," *American Political Science Review*, vol. 87, no. 3 (September 1993). In a thorough review of theories on the causes of war, Jack Levy concludes that "this absence of war between democratic states comes as close as anything we have to an empirical law of international relations," and that "liberal economic theories are consistent with the absence of wars among democracies but would incorrectly predict a lower overall war involvement for democratic as opposed to nondemocratic states." Levy, "The Causes of War: A Review of Theories and Evidence," in Philip Tetlock et al., eds., *Behavior, Society, and Nuclear War*, vol. 1 (New York: Oxford University Press, 1989), p. 270. For deductive arguments that economic interdependence causes conflict, see Waltz, *Theory of International Politics*, chap. 7. The case most often cited for such arguments is Japan's attempt to achieve autarky by force. See Michael A. Barnhart, *Japan Prepares for Total War: The Search for Economic Security, 1919–1941* (Ithaca, NY: Cornell University Press, 1987). Liberal critics argue that the character of modern interdependence, particularly the transnationalization of production and direct investment, as distinct from interdependence based on trade in raw materials, contradicts realist arguments based on examples such as Japanese imperialism in the 1930s or Western oil dependence in the 1970s. See Rosecrance, *Rise of the Trading State*, pp. 144–50.

77. For a discussion of conditional prospects for democratic reform, see Andrew Nathan, "China's Path from Communism," *Journal of Democracy*, vol. 4, no. 2 (April 1993), which notes at the outset that "in October 1992 Party Secretary Jiang Zemin summarized two of the reasons why the regime has been able to stabilize itself since 1989: economic growth and political repression" (p. 28).

78. Realism suggests, however, that Washington should end economic warfare against Vietnam and encourage that country's development in order to help balance Chinese power and to support tendencies to political liberalization in Hanoi; the double gamble that is too risky in regard to a big country like China is not in regard to a weak one.

Part II:
The Great Powers

3

Russia and East Asia After the Cold War

Charles E. Ziegler

Russia's relations with East Asia have been dramatically transformed over the past decade, reflecting a sea-change in foreign policy that began with Gorbachev's new thinking.[1] These dramatic changes cannot be understood in isolation from domestic political and economic processes that took place within the former Soviet Union, and which continue to influence its successor. Succumbing to the pressures of domestic reform, Soviet leaders conceded first the external and then the internal empire, the latter involving the loss of half its population and one-fourth of its territory. Boris Yeltsin's administration has continued to pursue Gorbachev's conciliatory policies in Asia, but the highly unstable political situation in Russia, coupled with a more assertive posture toward the West, raises serious questions about the future directions of Russian foreign policy. Fundamental disagreements over the basic direction of domestic and foreign policies have yet to be resolved.

The question then arises, will Russia continue to follow a peaceful and accommodating foreign policy, or might the imperialist and threatening policies of the communist era be resurrected at some time in the future? The answer depends on whether one is more convinced by the realist or the liberal paradigm of international relations. From the realist perspective, Soviet abandonment of empire and superpower status is very difficult to explain. The former Soviet Union was obsessed with maintaining control over Eastern Europe, and expanding its power and influence around the globe. Realism, with its emphasis on the national level of analysis, has great difficulty in accounting for the rapid turnaround in foreign policy theory and practice under Gorbachev.

Liberalism, by contrast, assumes that internal factors—type of regime and economic system—are fundamental causal factors influencing a state's propensity toward war or peace. A comparison of former Soviet with current Russian foreign policies would appear to support the liberalist paradigm's assumption that democratic systems are less likely to engage in international conflicts than are authoritarian systems. Economic self-interest and the perceived benefits of acting as a responsible member of the international community make cooperation preferable to confrontation.

The realist school, premised on the assumption that war is a natural state of relations in the international sphere regardless of regime type, would suggest that Russian foreign policy may not over the long term prove significantly different from that of its communist predecessor. According to the realist line of thought, Russia's accommodative stance is more readily explained by its temporarily reduced capabilities than by the collapse of authoritarianism. It follows that Russia may some time in the future revert to imperial great-power behavior, regardless of the type of economic and political structures that emerge.

Earlier research has supported the liberal explanation for change in Soviet East Asian policy; this paradigm continues to have relevance for the Russian Federation.[2] Russia's relations with East Asia have been strongly influenced by internal political and economic circumstances. Democratization, for example, has been the driving force in ending the Cold War in East Asia. However, the long-term future of democracy is still problematic in Russia, and foreign policy has become an issue in the political struggle between liberal reformers and the more conservative and nationalist factions in Russian politics.

Russia's position in the post-Cold War international order has been subject to intense factional debate within Moscow. Bowing to pressure from an increasingly nationalistic foreign policy elite, the Yeltsin government shifted from a very accommodative posture in 1992–93, to a more assertive advocacy of Russian national interests in 1994–95. This move toward the center should be interpreted as a natural process, since early Russian foreign policy probably was not viable over the long term. In any case, the evolution toward a more nationalistic foreign policy stance by many "liberal" politicians does not suggest a consensus has emerged on foreign policy.

Conflicting foreign policy perspectives may be expected to continue and to intensify, and these debates will have major implications for the future directions of Russian foreign policy. The Chechnya fiasco will oblige Russian policy makers to reassess the linkages between domestic and foreign security interests, and the utility of military force in achieving those interests. Some foreign policy elites may be expected to continue to advocate positions more compatible with Western liberal democratic values; others, occasionally subsumed under the Eurasianist school, reflect the more authoritarian perspective of Russia as a traditional great power.

On relations with East Asia, however, there is a surprising degree of consensus across the Russian political spectrum. There is no longer any major security threat from the region, significant opportunities exist for economic cooperation, and political relations are good. Of course problems exist, and Russia now occupies a fairly marginal position in Asia. But the principal areas of disagreement among Russian foreign policy elites encompass relations with the United States,

Western Europe, and Western multilateral institutions, not Asia. For this reason, we may expect a degree of continuity in Russian–East Asian relations not found in Russia's policies toward the West.

The Soviet Union and the Cold War in Asia

Russia's relations with East Asia cannot be understood in isolation from the Soviet experience. Two major points should be emphasized. First, East Asia in Soviet foreign policy priorities was clearly secondary to Europe, for several reasons. Europe had the largest concentration of military forces deployed against the Soviet Union, and hence constituted the greatest security threat to the USSR. The Russians who dominated the Soviet state felt closer geographically and culturally to Europe than to East Asia. From a Marxist perspective Europe was more significant than East Asia since, at least prior to the 1980s, Europe was more economically developed than East Asia. Lastly, personal factors should not be discounted. Former Minister of Foreign Affairs Andrei Gromyko, who served from 1957 to 1985, was distinctly Western in his foreign policy orientation, and East Asian posts in the Soviet foreign affairs ministry (aside from China) were considered less prestigious than European positions.

Second, Soviet leaders, at least until the accession of Mikhail Gorbachev, perceived East Asia far more in terms of threats than opportunities. This was the result of a mentality that conceptualized power almost exclusively in terms of military might. In East Asia, there were only two countries that genuinely threatened Soviet national security—the United States and People's Republic of China. The Brezhnev regime approached the perceived military threat from these two nations from a classic balance of power perspective. When the threat diminished as America's presence in the Pacific declined, Soviet military forces moved to fill the resultant power vacuum. Until Gorbachev's new thinking, there was little appreciation among the Soviet political elite of either Japan's growing economic dynamism or that of the newly industrializing countries (NICs). East Asia's growing economic strength was transforming the regional order, but it would take a new generation of leaders in the Kremlin to appreciate and acknowledge these changes.

East Asia in the decade or so prior to beginning of the Soviet reform process was, from Moscow's perspective, a promising arena for expanding its presence and influence. The Soviet Union's chief adversary had retreated in defeat from Vietnam, with public and Congressional sentiment strongly against further international commitments. America's departure left Moscow's close ally Vietnam as the dominant military power in Southeast Asia. The Soviet Union supported Vietnam with substantial military and economic assistance and in exchange Vietnam granted the Soviet Union use of the port facilities at Cam Ranh Bay, formerly utilized by the United States.

Moscow's other major competitor in the region, China, had by the mid-1970s abandoned the radicalism of the Cultural Revolution and, following the death of Mao Zedong in 1976, embarked on a reform program that focused on domestic economic modernization. Hostile rhetoric by both sides continued well into the 1980s, but discussions on normalizing relations began in 1979 and, with a brief hiatus, survived the Soviet invasion of Afghanistan late that year. However, relations remained tense and the aging Brezhnev regime resisted making any significant concessions to Beijing. Soviet leaders were suspicious of the Carter administration's efforts to normalize relations with China, led by hardline anti-communist National Security advisor Zbigniew Brzezinski. Moscow supported Vietnam during its clash with China, in early 1979, through material assistance and by conducting military exercises as a form of intimidation along China's northern border. Moscow also protested the China–Japan friendship treaty of 1978, which included a clause opposing attempts by outside powers to establish hegemony in the region.

Soviet preoccupation with exercising military power in the Asia-Pacific region was illustrated by the nature of the Soviet build-up in the 1960s and 1970s. The first stage, starting in 1965, was primarily in response to a perceived threat from a hostile China. This was a quantitative expansion, as Soviet forces roughly doubled between 1965 and 1970. The second phase of the Soviet build-up, which began in the later 1970s, seems to have been less a response to any genuine threat than simply Moscow's asserting its perceived "rightful" position as a major player in regional politics. The bureaucratic momentum that characterized overall Soviet military growth during the latter Brezhnev period also played a role. Soviet forces during this period expanded both quantitatively and qualitatively, with SS-20 intermediate-range missiles, long-range Backfire bombers, and modern conventional weaponry replacing the second-line equipment previously stationed the Soviet Far East. Four divisions were deployed in Mongolia, one in the Kurils, and treaties of friendship and cooperation were signed with Mongolia and Vietnam in 1978.

In East Asia, the Soviet Union had no collective security mechanism comparable to the Warsaw Treaty Organization. Soviet proposals for an Asian collective security pact, which were obviously designed to isolate China, were ignored or rejected by most states in the region. Moscow did maintain bilateral treaties with North Korea, India, Vietnam, and Mongolia, and Soviet military presence in the latter two countries was important in Moscow's strategy toward the People's Republic of China. However, these allies were at best a mixed blessing. Vietnam was extraordinarily costly, absorbing some $1–2 billion per year in Soviet assistance, second only to Cuba. North Korea was internationally unpredictable, also expensive (though less so than Vietnam), and tended to side with Beijing more often than Moscow. Lastly, Mongolia provided a convenient staging ground for Soviet troops deployed against China, but little beyond that.

Trade during the Brezhnev period was conducted more as a subset of Soviet political and military goals than for purely economic considerations. The

USSR's major communist trading partners were Vietnam and North Korea. Vietnam was admitted to membership in the Council for Mutual Economic Assistance in 1978, and benefited from exports of cheap Soviet oil. North Korea was likewise a net drain on the Soviet economy—Pyongyang seldom repaid its debts to the USSR, or even acknowledged Soviet largesse publicly. Sino-Soviet hostility limited economic cooperation between the two communist giants in the 1970s. Trade with the PRC was very low during the 1970s, usually under $100 million per annum, and did not expand significantly until progress was made on normalization of relations in the Gorbachev period.

Soviet trade with non-communist Asian nations was concentrated in two countries—Japan and India. Japan assisted the Soviet Union in several development projects in Siberia and the Far East from 1965 on, despite a legacy of mistrust and hostility between the two countries. Relations with India were much better. The Soviet Union regarded India as a close friend and key actor in the nonaligned movement, and a critical ally against China. Soviet-Indian trade accounted for approximately 90 percent of all Soviet trade with South Asia—some 3.2 billion rubles in 1990—and Moscow provided India with 79 percent of weaponry purchased in the period from 1987–1991.[3]

Compared to Soviet trade with its Comecon partners and with Western Europe, trade with all Asian-Pacific nations was extremely low, constituting only about eight percent of total turnover. Moscow's trade with the newly industrialized economies (NIEs) was minimal to nonexistent, as was trade with the ASEAN nations, Australia and New Zealand, and the remaining Asian-Pacific nations. Ideology conditioned the Kremlin leadership to view economic relations almost exclusively as a tool of foreign policy, rather than an end in itself. Moscow was willing to bear the cost of subsidizing its friends provided the political payoffs were adequate. Conversely, Soviet leaders saw little to be gained from trading with capitalist Asian nations linked to the United States, aside from the exceptional case of Japan.

Soviet leaders were suspicions of multilateral organizations in the Asia-Pacific region—ASEAN, for example—that Moscow could not dominate. ASEAN's opposition to Vietnamese expansionism in Southeast Asia was responsible for much of Soviet hostility towards that organization. In general, the absence of strong multilateral institutions in Asia comparable to those in Europe was to Moscow's advantage. Rather than formulate a distinctive Asia policy, Soviet leaders frequently tried to apply in Asia methods that had worked in Europe. Thus, Brezhnev's 1972 proposal for an Asian collective security arrangement was inspired by Soviet goals as reflected in the CSCE process. Chief among these goals was isolating and containing a hostile China, and securing international recognition of the post-war boundaries, thereby legitimizing Soviet control of the Kuril Islands and disputed territories along the Sino-Soviet border.

To summarize, Soviet policy toward East Asia during the Brezhnev period was guided by traditional power considerations, focusing almost exclusively on expanding military might and neglecting the economic and diplomatic levers of international relations. This approach, which was frequently ineffective or even counterproductive, was heavily influenced by ideological and structural factors within the Soviet system. The Brezhnev elite, however, did not realize that its overbearing military presence alienated many states, and was clearly out of tune with the dynamic economic processes taking place in the Asia. Moscow's pretensions to superpower status not only resulted in heavy direct and opportunity costs, but also contributed to the growing political and economic crisis facing the USSR in the early 1980s. These domestic factors would fundamentally alter ties with the East Asian states.

Sources of Change in Soviet-East Asian Relations

In the early 1980s the Soviet system was confronted with a wide array of domestic problems—economic stagnation, growing cynicism and apathy, corruption, severe environmental pollution, and a increasing gap between elites and masses—that could not be effectively addressed within the existing political and economic framework. These internal difficulties were compounded by a dramatic reversal of the favorable international climate that existed in the 1970s, in East Asia and elsewhere. Finally, these problems coincided with a major generational change in the Soviet leadership, as the Communist Party officials who had advanced so rapidly under Stalin began to die off or retire.

The key factor undermining the status quo was the declining growth rates in the Soviet centrally planned economy, which had proved incapable of adjusting to the computer and information revolutions sweeping the developed world. Not only was the Soviet economy mired in primitive industrialism, but economic priorities had consistently slighted the consumer in favor of the heavy industry-military complex. By the later stages of the Brezhnev era Soviet consumers had, like their East European counterparts, come to expect a gradually improving standard of living. When these expectations were frustrated, as in Poland, the results could prove explosive.

Economic stagnation subverted the Communist Party's claim to organizational superiority over capitalism, striking at the very legitimacy of the Soviet-type systems. It also undermined Moscow's empire and its aspirations to superpower status in East Asia. The longstanding confrontation with China had proved especially costly. At the time of Brezhnev's death in November 1982 the Soviet Union had approximately 500,000 troops deployed on the border with China, with an additional 110,000 in Afghanistan and a division stationed in the Kuril Islands. Some 25–35 naval vessels were deployed at Cam Ranh Bay, along with a squadron each of Badger bombers and MiG–23 fighters. Vietnam was being subsidized at $1–2 billion per year, largely through low-cost oil deliveries. North Korea was granted favorable credit terms, and the Soviet Union provided assistance for Pyongyang's energy, oil refining metallurgy and chemical fertilizer industries, much of which was never openly acknowledged by Kim Il Song's regime.[4] Yet for all this "investment" the Soviet Union was not secure in East Asia, nor was it influential, nor was it genuinely respected. The Soviet military presence in the region did, however, generate a certain amount of trepidation, which led to support for the American naval build-up in the Pacific under President Reagan and strengthened U.S. alliances in the region.[5]

Of course, Soviet failures in East Asia were not solely responsible for the reassessments that led Gorbachev to implement "new thinking." Many other costly and unproductive foreign policies could be identified, such as the breakdown of detente, which were equally if not more critical to the Soviet leadership. But in East Asia, perhaps more clearly than elsewhere, the Soviet Union stood out as a clumsy, unidimensional superpower whose imperial ambitions could not be sustained.

A comprehensive reevaluation of Soviet foreign and domestic policies was undertaken during the transition period, with Central Committee Secretary Gorbachev directing a task force of the Party's leading social scientists. The recommendations of this group would form the basis for perestroika and new thinking, the fundamentals of which were announced at the April 1985 Plenum, just one month after Gorbachev became General Secretary.

In East Asia, the priorities were fairly clear. The first task was to accelerate existing efforts to normalize relations with the PRC, thereby reversing one of the greatest failures of Soviet foreign policy in the postwar era. In his autobiography, former Foreign Minister Eduard Shevardnadze estimated the conflict with China had cost the Soviet Union at least 200 billion rubles.[6] The Sino-Soviet split had also fractured the international communist movement, challenging Soviet aspirations to ideological primacy, and had provided Washington effective leverage against Moscow in East Asia. Reconciling with China would enable Moscow to effect savings through troop reductions along the border, and would put the Soviet Union in a more advantageous position vis-à-vis the United States.

Gorbachev had another reason for focusing on China in developing a new East Asia policy. China provided an example of what economic reforms could accomplish within the overall framework of socialist ownership and Communist Party control. Granted, Gorbachev did not start perestroika with agricultural reform, as had the Chinese (a major mistake, as it turned out). But central to new thinking was swallowing Soviet pride by admitting fallibility in ideological affairs, and a consequent readiness to learn from the example of more successful communist (and capitalist) states. More directly, improved relations could lead to highly beneficial trade between the complementary Soviet and Chinese economies. In fact, the first major agreement between the two countries was a $14 billion, five year trade pact was signed in July 1985, a full year before Gorbachev's Vladivostok speech.[7]

The 1986 Vladivostok initiative dramatized the importance of East Asia, in particular China, for Soviet foreign policy. Gorbachev's speech included new

concessions on the border question, applauded the expansion of economic cooperation between the two nations, and in general demonstrated a willingness to
compromise with Beijing that had been absent during the Brezhnev era. Political
relations improved noticeably following Gorbachev's speech, and trade experienced significant growth.[8] However, progress on the three major conditions for
normalization advanced by Chinese was stymied until late in the decade.

The turning point in Sino-Soviet relations, as in many other areas of domestic
and foreign policy, came in 1988–1989 as glasnost and democratization began
fundamentally to transform Soviet society. Consonant with liberalism's emphasis
on the centrality of domestic politics, genuine change in Soviet foreign policy
emerged as the authoritarian political structures and dogmatic ideology of the
system began to crumble. Gorbachev's announced withdrawal of all troops from
Afghanistan, his pledge to significantly reduce troops along the Sino-Soviet
border, and Soviet pressure on the Vietnamese to pull out of Cambodia signalled
a turning point in Sino-Soviet relations. Complete normalization of state and
party ties soon followed.

Normalization of Sino-Soviet relations altered the regional power balance.
China became less useful as an element in U.S. foreign policy, but this was offset
by the fact that the Soviet Union was reducing its threatening posture in Asia.
Tensions between India and China, and between India and Pakistan eased somewhat. Vietnam and North Korea lost much of their salience as alliance partners
as Sino-Soviet relations improved. With the Soviet economy continuing to deteriorate, it became increasingly difficult to justify providing generous subsidies to
these two nations. Conservatives were reluctant to abandon their communist
friends, but the costs—both economic and political—of preserving the old alliance structures were simply too high.

These calculations were most evident in changing Soviet policy toward the
two Koreas. Pyongyang was an expensive and often unreliable ally for Moscow,
but preserving a foothold on the Korean peninsula had been highly advantageous
in the Sino-Soviet–U.S. strategic competition. By 1988–1989, however, much of
North Korea's utility had disappeared, and a reformist Moscow was drawn toward the dynamic, capital-rich South. Olympic diplomacy opened the door for
business exchanges, joint ventures and formalized trade relations in 1988 and
1989. South Korea had the investment capital needed to help develop Russia's
Far East, and Soviet economic needs meshed with Korean President Roh Tae
Woo's goal of extracting concessions toward reunification from the North. Moscow approached Seoul gingerly in an attempt to avoid antagonizing North Korea,
but by summer 1990 Gorbachev had decided to establish formal diplomatic ties,
which were concluded at the end of September.[9]

During the Gorbachev period Moscow made concerted efforts to convince the
United States to reduce its military presence in the Pacific, including sending
then–Deputy Director of the USA and Canada Institute Andrei Kokoshin to
testify before Congress. However, actual Soviet reductions in the Far East and

the Pacific were modest compared to those along the Sino-Soviet border. Washington's specialists, and the Japanese government, cautioned against any naval arms limitations that would restrict U.S. maneuverability in the Pacific. For its part, Moscow refused to undertake more substantial reductions in forces arrayed against Japanese and U.S. forces barring greater Japanese flexibility on the Kuril Islands.

The long legacy of hostility between Japan and the USSR, compounded by the festering Kuril dispute, hindered any significant improvement in Soviet–Japanese relations under Gorbachev. Initial expectations that Japan would be eager to take advantage of new opportunities in a reforming Soviet Union were not realized. The Japanese, having restructured their economy, diversified their sources of raw materials imports, and implemented effective energy conservation measures since the first oil shock of 1973, were far less interested in Soviet natural resources than they had been in the 1960s and 1970s. Commanding the world's second largest economy, Tokyo found itself in a much stronger bargaining position vis-à-vis Moscow than at any time in the past. These factors, combined with the growing role of public opinion in Soviet foreign policy, constrained Gorbachev's options and ensured the April 1991 summit would not yield any major breakthroughs.

The countries of Southeast Asia and the Pacific were relatively less important to Moscow's new Asia policy than those of Northeast Asia, with the possible exceptions of Vietnam and India. India had generally been viewed as one of the major success stories of Soviet–Third World relations. Gorbachev sought to preserve this friendship, and to extend the pattern of Soviet–Indian relations to other states in the region. His speeches at Vladivostok and Krasnoiarsk asserted a new policy of seeking amicable ties with all Asia-Pacific nations regardless of ideological orientation. Greater economic cooperation was advocated with the ASEAN member nations, Australia and New Zealand, and the smaller Pacific island countries. In the year before the August coup, trade with Taiwan expanded rapidly.

For most nations in Asia, the Soviet Union's importance diminished as Gorbachev moved to cut back the country's military might. On the eve of the coup, Moscow had largely overcome its reputation as an aggressive, threatening power in Asia. This was due in part to Gorbachev's policies, and in part to perestroika's abysmal failures. The economic crisis had so weakened the Soviet Union that Moscow no longer posed a significant threat to the region, except through the possibility of internal disintegration in the Far East. Soviet economic difficulties and the chaotic political situation after 1989 discouraged many potential investors, frustrating a major Soviet goal underlying Gorbachev's reforms— the aspiration towards securing a larger role in the Asian-Pacific economic order.

Russia's Identity Crisis in Foreign Policy

With the collapse of the Soviet Union in late 1991, the Russian successor state faced a unprecedented set of circumstances. Internally, Russia's economy continued to decline, accompanied by further political decentralization. Internationally, Moscow's leaders now operated in a world where they had lost both their external empire in Eastern Europe, and the internal, contiguous empire of the former USSR. The new Commonwealth of Independent States, hurriedly assembled as a means of facilitating the USSR's breakup, was a poorly conceptualized, temporary expedient rather than a functioning mechanism for implementing foreign policy.

Russia's leadership confronted the demanding task of formulating foreign policies toward the traditional regions, with the added complication of having to design a strategy to deal with the "near abroad"—the fourteen new states that had emerged on Russia's western and southern borders. These new states remained linked economically to Russia through the legacy of highly specialized central planning. Moreover, three of them possessed nuclear weapons, and some 25 million ethnic Russians lived within their borders. Moscow was preoccupied with violent conflicts in the Caucasus and Central Asia, and the fighting in Yugoslavia, which involved kindred Serbs. Also worrisome was the potential for a nationalist backlash against Russians in the Baltic states, Ukraine and especially the Caucasus and Central Asia, where many Russians feared the rise of Islamic fundamentalism. For trade, investment and economic assistance the reformist leadership looked primarily toward Europe and the United States.

Russia's position in the Asia-Pacific region is not dramatically different from that of its communist predecessor, aside from the considerable weakening of its military posture. The loss of the Baltic states, Ukraine, Belarus and Moldova have physically brought Russia closer to East Asia, but it should be remembered that only 24 million of Russia's 145 million citizens live east of the Urals mountains. Most of Russia's industry and agricultural land is located west of the Urals. Siberia and the Far East remain for most Russians a backward frontier area, far from its political and economic centers. From Moscow's perspective, Siberia, the Russian Far East and East Asia are relatively remote and peaceful compared with Europe, Central Asia and the Caucasus. Since the opportunities and the potential challenges to Russian interests in East Asia are long-term, it is not surprising that more immediate tasks would take precedence, with Russia's East Asian policy shunted into a position of tertiary importance.

In many respects, Russia's national interests in East Asia are similar to those of the reforming Soviet Union under Gorbachev. Northeast Asia, defined here to include the Russian Far East, China, Japan, the Korean peninsula and Mongolia, ranks well above South or Southeast Asia and the Pacific islands. Moscow wants to attract foreign investment into the Russian Far East to facilitate the extraction of natural resources, assist in defense conversion, develop high value-added exporting industries, and in general raise the standard of living in this remote and inhospitable area. Expanding on policies established during the late 1980s, Russia has continued to pursue major reductions in armed forces along the Sino–Russian border, has withdrawn forces deployed against Japan, and has repudiated attempts at power projection in the Pacific. Russia's interests dictate that it must remain active in regional affairs, although the Yeltsin government has yet to establish a prominent new role for Russia in this vital region.

Northeast Asia: The First Tier

China, which is rapidly emerging as East Asia's dominant power, clearly occupies the central position in Russia's East Asia policy. As long as the country does not disintegrate from the contradictions of economic reform and continued political repression, China's high growth rates and military modernization will position it to assume a greater role in regional affairs over the next decade. Do China's aspirations toward a larger role in the region pose a military threat or in some way fundamentally challenge Russia's interests? Or will Moscow reconcile itself to a powerful China in order to realize the benefits of trade and economic cooperation?

In the years following Gorbachev's visit to Beijing, relations with China have followed a pattern of expanding economic cooperation and relatively good political relations. China's leadership is less concerned with a direct threat from former Soviet forces than with the impact of Russia's democratization on Chinese students and minorities in the border areas. Beijing had augmented its security forces in Xinjiang, Tibet and Inner Mongolia following the Tiananmen massacre in an attempt to contain discontent in these regions.[10] Economic cooperation is highly valued by both sides and trade, especially that across the borders in the Far East, has flourished. Renewed Russian-Chinese cooperation in the military sphere, in the form of advanced weapons sales, military exchanges, and confidence building measures, has characterized the new "constructive partnership."[11]

A new Russian policy toward China took several months to emerge from the debris of the disintegrating Soviet Union. A trade pact, the first official agreement since the end of the USSR, was signed in early March of 1992. China relaxed controls along its northern border in an effort to encourage economic cooperation with Russia and the newly independent Central Asian states. In February 1992 the Russian and Chinese parliaments ratified border agreements which, in the words of Russian Ambassador Igor Rogachev, resolved about 98 percent of the entire border.[12] However, additional negotiations failed to settle disputes over several islands near Khabarovsk and one in the Argun river.

Yeltsin's December 1992 visit to Beijing was heralded as the start of a new era in Russo-Chinese ties, characterized by close economic, technical and military cooperation, and amicable political relations. Some two dozen agreements were signed, including plans for Chinese participation in developing Siberian and Far Eastern resources, the projected construction of a two gigawatt nuclear reactor in China, and other scientific and technical forms of cooperation. Military cooperation figured prominently in the discussions. Ambassador Rogachev disclosed plans for Russia to help modernize 256 arms plants built by the Soviet

Union in the 1950s. President Yeltsin welcomed the opportunities for arms sales to China, noting that China had purchased a total of $1.8 billion in weapons and parts from Russia in 1992 (a total of 26 Su-27 jet fighters plus S-300 air defense missile systems). The two sides also agreed to accelerate joint negotiations on border issues, together with Kazakhstan, Kyrgyzstan, and Tajikistan, in an attempt to reach a settlement on the disputed Western borders.[13]

For the most part, political relations between Beijing and Moscow were friendly and stable during 1993–94. The nations' defense ministries signed confidence building measures to prevent incidents along the 4000 kilometer border, and Moscow offered Beijing technical assistance for their newly purchased Su-27 fighters and S-300 air defense systems. Foreign Minister Kozyrev visited Beijing early in 1994, and President Jiang Zemin met with Yeltsin in Moscow in September. The two leaders signed one agreement on de-targeting nuclear weapons, and another delimiting the western sector of the Russo-Chinese border. Additional agreements were reached on constructing a Russian nuclear power station in northeastern China, on further military cooperation, and on Russian assistance in constructing several major industrial facilities in China.[14]

Tensions occasionally surface, however. Moscow (together with Kazakhstan) protested China's October 1994 underground nuclear test at Lop Nor, asserting it dampened prospects for nuclear disarmament. Russian politicians and observers have voiced warnings about the uncontrolled influx of Chinese into Siberia and the Russian Far East, and suggested that the geostrategic rivalry between China and Russia would likely continue.[15] And although the two nations had agreed on the eventual transfer of 72 Su-27s, less than half had been delivered to Beijing by the beginning of 1995.

Enhanced trade has linked the Russian and Chinese economies more closely, especially in the remote border regions. The number of access points along the border has expanded rapidly between China's Heilongjiang province and Russia's Primorskii, Khabarovsk and Amur regions. Total turnover between the former Soviet Union and the PRC reached a high of nearly $7.7 billion in 1993, nearly double the 1991 level.

Sino-Russian trade has been constrained by questions of quality control, currency inconvertibility, and the degree of freedom granted to Chinese entrepreneurs operating in Russia. These factors combined to lower total trade turnover in 1994 to an estimated $3.8 billion, relegating China to fifth place among Russia's trade partners. Russian consumers resent the high prices charged for Chinese food products, clothes and other consumer goods, and view Chinese merchandise as second-rate. Chinese nationals are accused of engaging in shady business practices and organized crime rackets, leading regional governments to enact laws against Chinese owning property. Beijing, concerned about its reputation, has promised to implement strict controls backed by harsh punishments.[16]

While economic cooperation is a factor for stable, amicable Sino-Soviet relations, the changed geopolitical situation in Asia complicates relations between

Moscow and Beijing. There are three possible areas of contention: Mongolia, Central Asia, and Taiwan. Of these, Central Asia could be the most problematic over the long term.

The emergence of a nascent democracy and marketizing economy in outer Mongolia, long a satellite of the Soviet Union, has presented China with new economic opportunities together with the potential for political problems. With the normalization of Sino-Soviet relations, Mongolia lost much of its significance as a buffer state between the two communist giants. Russia pulled the last of its military forces out of Mongolia in late 1992, and reduced its subsidies to Ulan Bator. Chinese trade with Mongolia is expanding, a welcome development for China's resource-poor and relatively isolated inner regions. At the same time, Beijing is determined to prevent a Mongolian cultural and religious renaissance from influencing the 3.4 million Mongols living in Inner Mongolia.[17]

Russia's current preoccupation with domestic problems has pushed Mongolia into the distant background. Russia has maintained its ties with Mongolia and, at least as long as the reformers are in control in Moscow, favors continued democratic development there. Beijing's aged and cautious leadership is worried about the potential for "spiritual pollution" in the form of democratic ideas and Buddhist revivalism contaminating inner Mongolia. Neither country's interests would be served by pan-Mongolism. There are over half a million Mongols living in Russia, primarily in the border territories of Buriatia and Tuva, who might wish to integrate with a reunited Mongolia. Since China would only accept Mongol unity under its sphere of influence, such a development would heighten Sino-Russian tensions.[18] At present, however, the Mongolian question is overshadowed by the potential for political turmoil in Central Asia.

The four new Central Asian states strategically located between China and Russia have historically been subject to great-power struggles for influence. Turkey, Iran, Pakistan, India, and Saudi Arabia all have a stake in Central Asian developments. The ethnic groups of these regions share religious and cultural identities across borders and, with the breakdown of the Soviet Union, new lines of conflict, commerce and communication have emerged. Conventional arms have proliferated in the region, and one state—Kazakhstan—is a nuclear power.[19]

A central tenet of Moscow's foreign policy toward Central Asia involves extending protection to some ten million Russians residing in the region, and preserving stability along its vital southern borders. Russia has dispatched troops to resolve the conflict in Tajikistan, makes threatening noises in support of Kazakhstan's seven million ethnic Russians, and is on generally friendly terms with the region's authoritarian governments. Russia continues to regard Central Asia's external borders as its defensible borders, and is under domestic pressure to secure these frontier areas. This is in part a function of economics. Russia simply does not have the resources to construct an entirely new set of fortifications along the Russian–Central Asian borders.[20] More important, however, is the inability of the weak Central Asian states to maintain order without Russian help.

For its part, Beijing is alarmed about possible ethnic unrest in Central Asia spilling over into the border areas of northwestern China, with its large Uygur, Kazakh and Kirghiz populations. Xinjiang province has experienced several incidents of violent resistance since 1990, and there are reportedly two Uygur underground nationalist movements operating there.[21] Russia and China are also troubled the growth of Islamicized nationalism, and the consequent potential for influence by radical Muslim movements. Both Moscow and Beijing favor economic development in order to enhance political stability in the region. Central Asia's economic difficulties provide fertile ground for conventional and nuclear weapons proliferation linked to the Middle East and South Asia, areas of notorious instability.[22]

In its relations with the Republic of China, Russia has tried a delicate balancing act of expanding economic and cultural ties without antagonizing Beijing. Taiwan's External Trade Development Council opened an office in Moscow shortly after the August coup, and the first Russian–Taiwanese joint venture was set up in Taiwan. Trade grew significantly from 1992 to 1993, reaching $709 million; Russian exports comprised $638 million of this. Taiwan is importing metals (gold, aluminum, steel and scrap metal) from Russia, in exchange for electronics goods, computers, and clothing.[23] Moscow and Taipei also at one point explored the possibility of military sales, although nothing materialized from these discussions.

In any case, mainland China is far more important for Russian foreign policy, both politically and economically. The Yeltsin government has explicitly recognized Beijing's sovereignty over Taiwan by rejecting the concept of two Chinas. Moscow established coordination councils, arrangements similar to those existing with the United States and Japan, to handle economic and cultural matters with Taipei and avoid offending Beijing.[24]

On balance, common interests appear to outweigh competing interests in Sino-Russian relations. The two countries have virtually finalized agreements on their disputed border, and have achieved significant progress in bilateral arms control and confidence building measures. Russia and China are no longer targeting nuclear weapons against each other. Disputes about ideological primacy have been displaced by pragmatic cooperation in trade and economic development. Both countries favor a stable regional environment in the Asia-Pacific, and both seek to reduce tensions on the Korean peninsula.

However, enough significant differences remain to suggest that Sino-Russian relations will not become as close as they were during the 1950s. Political interests will diverge assuming continued democratization in Russia and the absence of political reform in China. China's military build-up may not directly threaten Russia in the near future, since Beijing's attention seems to be drawn more toward the territorial disputes in the South China Sea (China has emphasized developing sea and naval air power in preference to ground forces). However, Moscow cannot continue to supply advanced weaponry to Beijing without acknowledging that these weapons could fuel an arms race in the Asia-Pacific, and could be turned against Russia at some point in the future.

Russian–Japanese relations have been plagued by a long record of hostility, centered around the continuing impasse over the Kuril Islands. Political tensions between the two nations, and a basic lack of economic complementarity, ensure that frosty relations will probably endure through the remainder of the decade.

The exaggerated expectations for Soviet–Japanese reconciliation of the Gorbachev period have been replaced by a more sanguine recognition of long-term disagreements between Moscow and Tokyo in the post–Cold War era. Trade between the two countries declined by a third from 1991 to 1992, and tensions over the disputed Kuril Islands continued to frustrate efforts toward greater Russo-Japanese economic cooperation. A major battle between Russian conservatives and liberals developed over Yeltsin's plans to visit to Tokyo and the prospect, however remote, of a territorial solution.

In the months leading up to September 1992, the first date scheduled for a summit, the Russian press was filled with articles and letters debating the issue, while public opinion polls reported varying levels of opposition to concluding an agreement with the Japanese.[25] Nationalists in the Russian parliament and local officials from the Far East were adamant that the islands were sovereign Russian territory, and rejected as insulting any proposals to exchange these territories for Japanese investment.[26] A beleaguered Yeltsin avoided a politically fatal confrontation with conservatives by postponing his trip. Rescheduled for May 1993, the visit was once again canceled at the last minute, leading to considerable Japanese anger.[27] Yeltsin did finally visit Tokyo in October 1993, just after the attempted parliamentary coup, and a few minor economic and technical agreements were signed. The Russian president formally apologized for the mistreatment of Japanese POWs after WWII, but there was no progress on the Kuril issue.[28]

Russia's interests vis-à-vis Japan are frequently misunderstood in the West as well as by the Japanese. Public opinion on both sides has become more positive in recent years, but there still exists a legacy of mistrust from having engaged in several major conflicts over the past century. Many Russians are passionately convinced that the Kurils are rightfully theirs and should not be returned under any circumstances. Trading Russian territory for economic aid is anathema to many nationalists, who remain suspicious of foreign capitalism. The Russian military continues to argue that control of the Kurils is vital to protect Russian strategic submarines in the Sea of Okhotsk, and the military's political influence has been on the rise following Yeltsin's confrontation with parliament.

Most Japanese are likewise intransigent about any compromise on the islands. A few Japanese companies anticipate profits from doing business with the Russians, but the associated risks can be expected to outweigh the benefits in the foreseeable future, even with a resolution of the territorial issue. With the downturn in Japan's economy in the early 1990s, Japanese foreign investment has declined dramatically, and in any case Russia is considered one of the least attractive investment opportunities in the region. Those few Japanese firms doing business in the Russian Far East appear to be more interested in obtaining quick profits than undertaking long-term capital investments.[29]

Washington has sought to convince Japan that aiding Russia's fledgling democracy is crucial to regional and world stability. Barring any progress on the territorial issue, though, Tokyo has been reluctant to commit significant economic assistance. A package of $1.82 billion, primarily in the form of loans and loan guarantees, was announced in April 1993, prior to the Tokyo G–7 summit. In November 1994 Tokyo granted Russia a $530 million credit and agreed to defer repayment of some $280 million in debt incurred by the former USSR. Prime Minister Tomiichi Murayama informed First Vice-Chairman Oleg Soskovets Japan would support Russia's admission to GATT and the World Trade Organization, but reiterated Japan's longstanding position that genuine progress in resolving the territorial issues would have to preceed major improvements in economic cooperation.[30]

Considering the overwhelming nature of its internal economic and political problems, the military dimension of Russian-Japanese relations is a low priority for Moscow. With the impending cutbacks of U.S. forces in the Pacific, the threat from the Japanese-American alliance has receded. Over the long term, Russia cannot ignore the potential challenge posed by Japan. Russia's top military officers are concerned about the rapid deterioration of the Pacific Fleet, and some elements claim a strong defensive force, and continued Russian sovereignty over the southern Kurils, is necessary to protect the Sea of Okhotsk and the Far East coastline.[31] However, these voices seem to be in the minority. Overall, neither the central authorities in Moscow nor local officials in the Russian Far East are discernibly alarmed about a potential Japanese resurgence.

Other countries, however, are wary of the possibility of a militarily stronger Japan moving to fill the vacuum left by American disengagement. Two factors that could lead to the rapid growth of Japan's military power are Chinese military expansion and Beijing's attempts at power projection in the Pacific, and the emergence of a nuclear threat on the Korean peninsula. Either of these developments would undermine regional security, as would the sudden withdrawal of American military presence from the region. Some analysts are concerned about the growing arms race in the Asia-Pacific, in which the PRC and North Korea play a major role.[32]

The Korean peninsula remains important to Russian economic and security interests in Northeast Asia. Russia and North Korea share a border, and the former Soviet Union had extensive military and economic ties to Pyongyang. Russia intends to expand the relationships with South Korean government and business circles established under Gorbachev; preserve links to North Korea to encourage adherence to the Non-Proliferation Treaty, discourage terrorism or the use of military force, and secure repayment of the substantial debt owed to Moscow; and, more broadly, to maintain stability during the transition from Kim

Il Song's rule. Moscow appreciates that America's presence in South Korea helps maintain equilibrium on the peninsula, but would prefer the U.S. acquiesce in a greater role for Russia as a power broker on the peninsula.

Yeltsin's visit to South Korea in November 1992 was an attempt to formalize and strengthen ties that had developed in the later Gorbachev years, and to sort out debt and repayment problems that had constrained further economic cooperation. The two sides signed a pact pledging friendly relations based on democratic principles, human rights and the market economy. Yeltsin returned the "black box" and tapes—doctored, as it turned out to Seoul's embarrassment—from KAL flight 007. In an address to the Korean parliament, the Russian President called for the formation of a multilateral forum in the Asia-Pacific to work out a system of crisis management for the region. Several huge projects totalling $20–30 billion were discussed, including construction a natural gas pipeline from the Sakha Republic (Yakutia) through North Korea.

Russian and South Korean security interests are now closer than at any time in the past, and some modest forms of military cooperation have even developed. Defense Minister Pavel Grachev and Deputy Prime Minister Aleksandr Shokhin (the latter responsible for arms sales abroad) accompanied Yeltsin as part of the Russian delegation to Seoul in 1992. During the visit the two sides signed a memorandum on military-technical cooperation providing for military exchanges and naval visits between the ports of Vladivostok and Pusan. Yeltsin assured President Kim Young Sam, who visited Moscow in June 1994, that amendments to the 1962 Soviet-DPRK treaty no longer obligated Russia to side with North Korea the the event of a conflict. Late in 1994 Russia agreed to repay part of its Korean debt through the delivery of $187.5 million in weaponry, which Seoul intends to use for military research.[33]

To enhance its claim to great power status in East Asia, Russia has sought a larger role on the Korean peninsula. Moscow has advanced a number of proposals, including a "two plus four" peace conference bringing in Japan and Russia, an idea opposed by the Chinese who favor "two plus two" talks. Washington's decision to exclude Russia from the nuclear reactor accord with Pyongyang offended Moscow, which apparently hoped to sell $4 billion worth of light-water reactors to the North.[34] In brief, the South Koreans, Chinese and Americans have resisted accommodating Russia's pretensions, while Moscow has lost the limited influence it once had with North Korea.

There is significant potential for South Korean–Russian economic cooperation. Although ranking well behind Japan and China in terms of total trade turnover, South Korea's business giants are seeking investment opportunities in Russia and other CIS countries, and are aiding Russian factories in the difficult process of defense conversion. South Korea has more sophisticated technology and a larger supply of investment capital than does China, and appears to be more committed to long-term, cooperative ventures with Russia than do the Japanese. South Korean corporate groups, most notably Daewoo, together with the energy-poor North Korean government, are eagerly promoting the Sakha pipeline project. During Kim Young Sam's June 1994 visit to Moscow disputes over terms of the pipeline plan were ironed out, and each side committed $10 million for a joint feasibility study.[35]

Russian exports to Korea consist overwhelmingly of raw materials; in turn, it imports primarily consumer electronics and clothing. However, Russia's failure to repay $1.47 billion debt incurred by the former Soviet Union led South Korea to cancel all economic aid to Russia late in August 1993. Continuing negotiations have dealt with the issue of Russian credit problems, which have dampened trade possibilities. Total South Korean–Russian trade turnover in 1993 was $1.57 billion, a substantial increase from $859 million in 1992. Trade in 1994 was running at roughly the same level.[36]

Moscow's focus in the Asia-Pacific is primarily on the extent to which the adjacent states of Northeast Asia can assist in Russia's economic transformation. Russian leaders continue to assert that their country is a major regional player, but Russia is clearly perceived as a power in decline. The Soviet-era obsession with strengthening the Far East as a frontier military outpost against a potential security threat from Asia and the United States has been abandoned by all but the more militant nationalists. Efforts to expand presence and influence in Southeast Asia and the Pacific are similarly a thing of the past. Russian interests in this region, as noted in the following section, are almost exclusively economic and essentially marginal.

South and Southeast Asia: The Second Tier

Russia in its first year devoted very little attention in its foreign policy to the "second tier" states of South and Southeast Asia and the Pacific. Relations between Russia and its formerly close friend India were transformed by the end of the Cold War in Asia. India's role as a counterweight against China diminished as Moscow and Beijing ended three decades of hostility, and its importance as a friendly nonaligned country disappeared as international transformations made the concept of nonalignment irrelevant. However, the two countries' longstanding and extensive economic and military ties ensure that the relationship will not readily be abandoned by either party.

After a rocky start in which New Delhi was slow to accept the collapse of the Soviet Union, Prime Minister Narasimha Rao's government moved to grant Russia credits and humanitarian assistance, and established diplomatic relations with the successor states. India's Foreign Secretary J.N. Dixit concluded a political treaty in Moscow in January, and State Secretary Gennadi Burbulis visited India in May 1992, signing a five-year economic cooperation pact. A major source of irritation in economic relations, however, concerned the terms for repayment value of India's 10.5 billion ruble debt to Russia. After the ruble was allowed to float against the dollar, India preferred repayment of its outstanding debts according to current ruble value, rather than based on the old artificial rate of exchange. Moscow, as might be expected, has resisted this arrangement.

Russia and India also have a mutual interest in continuing defense cooperation. About 70 percent of India's military equipment is of Soviet origin and, like Beijing, Delhi needs spare parts and is interested in upgrading its air force. Moscow needs the income generated through arms sales. This coincidence of interests led to a testy dispute with the United States when Washington objected to a $350 million deal involving the sale of rocket engines and cryogenic technology to Delhi. The Bush administration claimed the agreement violated the Missile Technology Control Regime (MTCR). Russia, which is not a formal signatory to the MTCR but has agreed to abide by its principles, claimed the disputed technology did not have military applications.

American pressure over the sale continued during the Clinton administration. The United States formally imposed sanctions on the Russian agency Glavkosmos, and President Clinton strongly expressed U.S. opposition to the sale at the Tokyo G–7 summit in July.[37] Under pressure from Washington, and despite vociferous objections from the Indian government and conservatives in the Russian legislature, the Yeltsin government agreed to transfer only the engines, canceling the delivery of related technology. In exchange for Russia's adherence to the MTCR, Washington promised Glavkosmos access to the commercial satellite market and the right to participate in the U.S. space station program. While the liberal media praised the compromise as ultimately more beneficial to Russia than the original deal, former parliament speaker Ruslan Khasbulatov called it "a national disgrace," and Civic Union denounced the move as an infringement on Russia's independence in foreign policy.[38]

Moscow sought to preserve ties with its former ally Vietnam, but oil and weapons exports dropped off sharply after the coup, and formal military cooperation between the two nations ended in 1992. Russia has provided support for several power projects, and has assisted Vietnam in oil extraction, gold mining, biotechnology and agriculture. Trade was approximately $300 million in 1993, with Russia importing primarily food products from its former ally.[39]

Vietnamese-Russian relations have been complicated by an outstanding 10 million ruble debt, disagreements over Russian arms sales to Beijing, and continued Russian access to Cam Ranh Bay. In June 1994 Prime Minister Vo Van Kiet visited Moscow to discuss military cooperation and economic issues. The signing of a new, watered-down friendship treaty, which stipulated no more than bilateral consultations in the event of a crisis, was delayed by controversy over Russia's Cam Ranh Bay lease.[40]

Russia's relations with the remaining Southeast Asia countries have been friendly, but are developing slowly. The most notable recent development in Russia's relations with the ASEAN member-states has been Moscow's foray into the lucrative Southeast Asian arms market. Russia and Malaysia concluded a $775 million deal involving the sale of 18 MiG-29M jet fighters, the first instance of Russian arms sales to an ASEAN member state.[41] Russia is also competing with Australia to sell three diesel submarines to Malaysia. Moscow offered to trade Mi-17V helicopters in exchange for Thai rice and other consumer goods, and has negotiated with the Philippines on possible arms sales.

Funneling additional weapons into a region that is already in the middle of an arms race may not be the wisest policy. However, conservatives and representatives of the Russian defense industry are pressing Moscow to expand sales of weaponry, to reverse a dramatic decline in arms exports during 1992 and 1993. Southeast Asian nations have the currency reserves to buy weapons off the shelf and the level of development needed to produce advanced armaments through licensing and technology transfer.[42] Other countries, most notably the United States, have not refrained from capitalizing on regional demand for weapons. By expanding its arms exports Russia expects to stabilize the rapid decline in the defense industrial sector, minimize unemployment, finance defense conversion, earn much-needed hard currency, and in general promote greater social and economic order. Foreign Minister Kozyrev has even defended Russian arms sales to Southeast Asia as a factor for stability.[43]

Relations with multilateral institutions in the Asian-Pacific region, once a priority of Gorbachev's Soviet regime, stagnated under Yeltsin. Russia has had only modest success convincing Asian-Pacific countries that Russia deserves to participate on a fully equal basis in such institutions as the Asia-Pacific Economic Cooperation forum (APEC), Pacific Economic Cooperation Council (PECC), and Pacific Basin Economic Council (PBEC). Moscow participated informally in ASEAN's 1992 and 1993 post-ministerial conferences (PMC), and was admitted as a member of the ASEAN Regional Forum (ARF) in 1994. Russia is a full member of PECC, but does not hold membership in PBEC or APEC. Nor are any Russian organizations participating in the recently formed Council for Security and Cooperation in the Asia Pacific, a consortium of ASEAN, Japanese, American and Korean strategic studies institutes.[44]

Active Russian participation in Asia Pacific multilateral economic institutions has been constrained by Russia's general economic crisis, structural problems hindering development of the Russian Far East, and internal political conflict. In addition, many of the cooperation networks in the Asia Pacific are unofficial and informal in nature, drawing on leading business connections and independent research organizations. This particularly Asian form of cooperation is alien to Soviet and Russian practice.[45]

Russia's internal political battles have been extremely important in shaping the debate on policy toward East Asia and on Russia's foreign policy identity more broadly. Conservative and nationalist critics have exerted increasing influence over President Yeltsin's decisions in the region, and this pressure should not be expected to diminish in the wake of the September 1993 coup attempt. These forces deserve closer scrutiny.

Internal Politics, National Interests, and East Asia

Positioned between Europe and Asia, Russia has historically been ambivalent in defining its cultural identity.[46] During the first years of the new state the Yeltsin-Kozyrev foreign policy line was subject to strident criticism from conservatives within the Parliament and even within the executive organs of government, for adhering to an excessively Eurocentric orientation. By early summer 1992 opinion on foreign policy had divided between the "Atlanticist" Yeltsin reformers, who looked toward Europe and the United States for support and advice, and the "Eurasian" nationalists and conservatives, who were suspicious of Western capitalism and democratic processes.

Members of the Eurasian group were highly critical of the Yeltsin government's "excessive" reliance on the West, reflected in the choice of Sweden's Anders Aslund, Harvard's Jeffrey Sachs, and other Western "shock therapists" as advisers. Russia's economic future, critics claimed, was being placed almost exclusively in the hands of such Western institutions as the International Monetary Fund, World Bank, and European Bank for Reconstruction and Development. Even the formerly liberal presidential adviser Sergei Stankevich warned against continuing a purely opportunistic, pragmatic foreign policy that assigned Russia the role of a "junior partner" to the G–7 countries. Stankevich advocated greater attention to the "near abroad" CIS states, home to over 25 million Russian ethnics, and the "second-echelon" countries of Asia, Latin America, and Africa—countries historically and economically more comparable to the new Russian state.[47]

For more moderate and conservative Russians preoccupied with their country's disintegration Asia, particularly Japan, China and South Korea, provided examples of how satisfactory economic growth could be achieved under the guidance of an activist state. The strong state or corporatist model is more appealing to Russian nationalists than laissez faire economics propounded by Western economists because it coincides more closely with the traditional values of authoritarian Russian political culture.[48]

Divisions within the Russian leadership are reflected in a 1993 survey of foreign policy elites conducted by Germany's Friedrich Ebert foundation. This poll found Russia's foreign policy makers almost equally divided, with 52 percent characterizing themselves as "Westernizers," favoring a developmental strategy followed by the Western industrialized nations. By contrast, 45 percent claimed they were "Slavophiles," who believed Russia should follow a uniquely Russian path in world affairs.[49] Ambivalent attitudes can also be found among the general population. A survey conducted by the All-Russian Center for the Study of Public Opinion in late 1994 found 54 percent who agreed Russia could learn from the West, while 35 percent believed nothing good could be learned from Western nations. Older, less educated respondents tended to be more critical and suspicious of the West.[50]

Both nationalists and moderates criticized Yeltsin's government for shirking its responsibilities in maintaining stability in the Central Asia, virtually abandoning Vietnam and North Korea, and for yielding excessive concessions to the United States and NATO. Bowing to these pressures, Yeltsin and Kozyrev shifted Russian foreign policy away from its Eurocentric orientation toward a more independent stance. Policy toward the "near abroad" moved to first place on Russia's foreign policy agenda, at least rhetorically. Russian military forces were redeployed to ensure stability in the Caucasus and Central Asia, in keeping with Russia's new security doctrine. Russian troops were used to support conservative forces against a coalition of democrats and Islamic nationalists in Tajikistan, and to overthrow Dzhokar Dudaev's rebellious government in Chechnya. Yeltsin's recent visits to East Asian capitals, Moscow claimed, demonstrated a new Asian thrust in Russia's foreign policy.

Russia is still seeking to define a role for itself in the post–Cold War international order, and is reassessing its national interests both globally and regionally.[51] Moscow has not clearly spelled out its goals and interests in Asia and the Pacific, but it is possible to identify at least four factors that will shape Russia's East Asia policy in the near future. All four are closely related to and will be influenced by domestic political and economic circumstances.

First, there are no immediate security threats to Russia from its neighbors in East Asia. China and Japan may challenge Russia over time, and Korean instability may indirectly affect Russian security, but there is no threatening belligerent to command Moscow's attention and resources. The chaotic political situation in Russia's Far East is probably the single greatest security concern for Moscow, although the capital is generally neglecting its citizens in this part of Russia. The armed forces of the former Soviet Union are subject to a wide range of internal problems, including low morale, housing and food shortages, poor discipline, hazing, desertions, and illegal diversion of weapons. The Pacific Fleet has had difficulties paying for repairs on its ships. Withdrawal and demobilization of large numbers of troops from Afghanistan, Mongolia, and along the Sino-Russian border, together with desertions, has created new pressures on housing, jobs, and social services, making the Russian Far East one of the least hospitable places to serve. In addition, public antipathy to military secrecy, dramatic accidents such as the massive ammunition explosions near Vladivostok in 1992 and 1994, fear of radiation leaks from nuclear reactors, and dismay over environmental pollution have led to strong feelings of resentment against the military.

Compounding these problems, the major employers in many Far Eastern cities are defense-related industries, now severely affected by cutbacks in military spending. Given the large numbers of unemployed or underemployed and the high cost of living in the Far East, incentives to pilfer and resell military weapons and ammunition, both conventional and nuclear, are great indeed.[52] Attempts to gain control of conventional weapons are a frequent occurrence in the area.

The shortage of trained personnel and complete lack of discipline in the armed forces make theft of nuclear weapons or nuclear fuel a very real possibility, and there have been disquieting rumors about "misplaced" nuclear warheads. These events reinforce the perception that Moscow does not exercise full control over its Far Eastern military forces, a development that could easily jeopardize regional stability. Reestablishing full authority over these forces must be a priority of Moscow's in the immediate future.

Second, and related to the security question of problematic control over the armed forces, is formalizing a new legal relationship between Moscow and republic authorities. To a certain extent, the growing independence of Primorskii krai, Sakhalin oblast, the Sakha republic and other territories is a natural reaction to years of exploitation and neglect by Moscow. Some regional officials used their new-found autonomy to push reform beyond the bounds endorsed by Moscow.

There are more disturbing aspects to regional autonomy, however. Separatist movements have emerged calling for the formation of independent Siberian and Far Eastern republics. Cossack formations throughout the former Soviet Union, for example, have promised to defend Russian national interests, and several Cossack formations are located in eastern Russia. Former Sakhalin Governor Valentin Fedorov invited Cossacks to establish communities on the Kuril Islands, complicating the chances of reaching an agreement with Japan.[53] Constitutional order is needed to overcome the "war of laws" between center and locales that has resulted in a welter of contradictory regulations and has discouraged outside investment. Stabilizing the legal environment will facilitate economic growth, which is necessary to restore order in the Far East.

Much depends on whether the new Russian federal constitution and laws enumerating the economic powers of sub-national units will create a climate of political and economic stability in Russia's regional communities.[54] Russia's constitutional structure depends in turn on the outcome of the power struggle between liberal and conservative/nationalist politicians. Nationalist forces have pressured the leadership to strengthen central control over what remains of the empire, to prevent further fragmentation of the Russian state. Federalism is anathema to Russia's nationalists, especially the imperialist factions. Genuine autonomy for the Far East, however, is critically important if Russia is to continue to expand its economic links to the Asian-Pacific economies.

Third, Russia's domestic economic reform process cannot continue to rely exclusively on Europe and the United States, both for economic and political reasons. Even with the current downturn in Japanese and South Korean growth, these nations' economies remain robust. Japan, South Korea and Taiwan have considerable surplus capital, although uncertainty in the Russian economy, political complications and structural incompatibilities have precluded higher levels of cooperation. Trade and economic cooperation with China, which has the world's fastest growing economy, has had a positive impact on the isolated Russian Far East, as it has on China's northern border regions. Moscow is seeking to preserve economic ties with both India and Vietnam, and hopes to recoup much of the 20 billion rubles owed it by these countries. Finally, there is significant unrecognized potential for expanding trade and economic cooperation with the ASEAN nations, Australia and New Zealand.

Russia is formally involved in the UN Development Programme's proposed Tumen River Area Development Program, although its potential for stimulating growth in the Russian Far East is questionable. This project envisions investment of some $30 billion over 20 years to build up to eleven specialized harbors, air, rail and road terminals, power plants and telecommunications facilities, and the modern infrastructure to support an urban community of half a million. The concept is to utilize existing regional complementarities—South Korean and Japanese capital and technology, Russian natural resources, and Chinese and North Korean surplus labor—to create world-class port facilities rivaling Rotterdam's. Development within the zone is expected to have a spillover effect on surrounding areas, and promote growth in neighboring economic zones. Local Russian authorities have been fairly skeptical about the project given its planned location in what is now a wilderness area, and are concerned about potential environmental problems. In any case, little progress has been made to date on this ambitious project.[55]

Finally, those Russian officials who are members of the reformist camp accept the aspects of Gorbachev's new thinking that reject aggressive military posturing and imperialist ambitions. However, there remains considerable sentiment across the political spectrum favoring the reassertion of Russian power, if not to reestablish the old Soviet empire, then at least to vigorously defend Russian national interests in Central Asia, the Far East, and East Asia. In the aftermath of the September 1993 confrontation with parliament Yeltsin found himself more reliant on his supporters in the Russian military. This has resulted a more activist policy to restore order in the border regions of the Caucasus and Central Asia, in contrast to the more cautious approach of the Russian foreign ministry, and helped lead Yeltsin into the Chechnya quagmire.

Few other than followers of the rabid nationalist Vladimir Zhirinovskii, who seems determined to reestablish the old Russian empire at its most expansive boundaries, envision the forcible restoration of direct political control in the former republics, or a renewed attempt at power projection outside Russian Federation borders, in the Asia Pacific or elsewhere. Virtually all sides of the political spectrum are in agreement on maintaining good ties with China, and would avoid any actions that might jeopardize this vital relationship. Russia's major unfinished business in East Asia is the emotional issue of the Kuril Islands. Since there is no easy solution, this imbroglio may be expected to dominate Russo-Japanese relations and influence Russian domestic politics for some time to come.

With the end of the Cold War, Moscow and Washington find themselves in agreement on many issues in the Asian-Pacific region. Both are opposed to military confrontation or other forms of instability on the Korean peninsula, and are openly opposed to North Korea's efforts to develop a nuclear bomb. Russia is no longer interested in supporting communist states or movements in the region, and Sino-Russian reconciliation has eliminated a major source of leverage for would-be radical states. As a consequence, Vietnam and North Korea have been forced to moderate their policies or risk becoming increasingly isolated. The United States has encouraged its friends and allies in East Asia to provide financial support for Russia's incipient market economy. Russia accepts the continued presence of U.S. forces in the Pacific in order to guarantee regional stability, although being accorded equal status as a great power in the region is one of Moscow's foremost goals.

In a worst-case scenario, these common interests could quickly dissolve were a conservative/ nationalist regime to gain control in Moscow. Many of the conservatives have a visceral dislike for the United States, and regard continued Russian-American cooperation as subservient and insulting to Russian national dignity. Even the more obstinate stance adopted by the Yeltsin government has not thoroughly satisfied them. These political forces have little interest in attracting foreign investment into Russia, or participating in multilateral institutions. The world view of a conservative Russian government would be closer to those of the authoritarian states in East Asia than to the East Asian democracies.

Conclusion

Asia is contemplating a new regional order largely because of the dramatic transformations that have occurred within the former Soviet Union, changes which brought about the end of the Cold War. Russia's struggle to define a consistent East Asia policy is closely related to the bitter internal debate over Russia's political identity as a country straddling Europe and Asia. President Yeltsin and his fellow reformers, who have advocated liberal democratic values, may still wish to secure a place for Russia in the Anglo-European world. However, political pressure from nationalist groups and the military has forced Yeltsin's government to be more assertive than before in protecting Russia's interests in the former Soviet republics and along the periphery. The consequences of this more assertive approach, demonstrated most vividly in Chechnya, have been disastrous.

Russia can be expected to refrain from reverting to great-power imperialism, at least as long as the reformers stay in power in Moscow. Even a more nationalistic government would be hard pressed to justify adventures outside Russian borders. The strong domestic opposition to using military force against Chechnya suggests the general population, and much of the military, would not tolerate another Afghanistan. In any case, it would be years before Russia's military could again develop the capabilities of the late Brezhnev era.

Greater stability can be anticipated with the development of democratic constitutional mechanisms and some semblance of political normalcy. East Asia will not occupy center stage in Russian foreign policy priorities. Nor should East Asia fear an aggressive, expansionist Russia in the Asia-Pacific region, even if Russia would by some miracle manage to restore vitality to its damaged economy.

The situation could be different in the event of a conservative/nationalist victory in Moscow. Assuming a shift toward greater authoritarianism, nationalism, and possibly a messianic foreign policy inspired by a pan-slavic, Orthodox view of the world, such a regime would be more assertive in defending the Russian diaspora in Central Asia. An escalation of the bloodshed in Central Asia, an infusion of more weapons, and possible clashes with Russia's neighbors to the south and east should not be ruled out. A more hardline position on the Kuril dispute would rule out accommodation with Japan. A conservative government in Moscow would likely be more willing to use force to keep the union intact; for example, to prevent the Tuvinians and Buriat Mongols from aligning with a reunified Mongolia. The imperialist wing might take advantage of turmoil in the former republics to forcibly reincorporate territory under Russia's sovereign authority. A tougher position toward China on the territorial issue might surface. A conservative regime would almost certainly restrict foreign economic activity in Siberia and the Russian Far East, delaying economic development and exacerbating local hostility toward Moscow. Finally, the present level of Russian-American cooperation in the Asia-Pacific would decline if not disappear altogether.

No longer feared as a potential aggressor, a reformist Russia is now accepted in the region. This is encouraging, since a continued Russian presence can be a factor for moderation and stability, assuming the reformers or moderates stay in control in Moscow. The collapse of a Soviet threat undermines much of the rationale for a Chinese or Japanese military build-up, forcing these two nations and their neighbors to reassess their respective positions in East Asia's new regional order. Russia's potential role as moderator on the Korean peninsula, and its support for initiatives on building multilateral security institutions are to be welcomed after years of regional troublemaking.

Russia, like its East Asian neighbors, is a country in transition. Russia's size, history, talented population, and its enormous potential, ensure that Russia will continue to play a role in East Asian politics. But Russia's continuing economic crisis and political uncertainties, and its tenuous cultural ties to the Asia-Pacific, suggest that in the near future Russian and East Asian transformations will proceed along separate paths.

Notes

Research for this paper was supported by a grant from the International Research and Exchanges Board, with funds provided by the Andrew W. Mellon Foundation, the National Endowment for the Humanities, and the U.S. Department of State. Additional support was provided by a grant from the University of Louisville College of Arts and Sciences. None of these organizations is responsible for the views expressed.

1. Russia's relations with East Asia have focused primarily on the principal neighboring states of Northeast Asia—China, Japan and the Korean peninsula. Mongolia, strategically positioned between China and Russia, merits some attention. Central Asia's Turkic Muslim states are vitally important to Moscow—this region is very unstable politically, the Central Asian states are Russia's strongest supporters in the CIS, and there are large numbers of ethnic Russians living in Central Asia. However, the Central Asian region is beyond the scope of this paper and will be discussed only in the context of Russia's East Asian security concerns. On Central Asia, see Michael Mandelbaum, ed., *Central Asia and the World* (New York: Council on Foreign Relations Press, 1994); Amin Saikal, "Russia and Central Asia," in Amin Saikal and William Maley, Eds., *Russia in Search of Its Future* (Cambridge: Cambridge University Press, 1995); Alvin Z. Rubinstein, "The Geopolitical Pull on Russia," *Orbis*, Vol. 38, no. 4 (Fall 1994), pp. 567–583; and Martha Brill Olcott, "The Myth of 'Tsentral'naia Azii'," *Orbis*, Vol. 38, no. 4 (Fall 1994), pp. 549–565.

2. For a more complete discussion of change in Soviet policy toward Asia, see Charles E. Ziegler, *Foreign Policy and East Asia: Learning and Adaptation in the Gorbachev Era* (Cambridge: Cambridge University Press, 1993).

3. Ramesh Thakur, "South Asia," in Ramesh Thakur and Carlyle A. Thayer, eds., *Reshaping Regional Relations* (Boulder: Westview Press, 1993), pp. 155, 157.

4. V.I. Andreev and V.I. Osipov, "SSSR-KNDR: kursom vzaimovygodnogo sotrudnichestvo," *Problemy dal'nego vostoka*, no. 3 (March 1983), pp. 8–22.

5. Of course, the one exception to this was New Zealand's departure from ANZUS following the disagreement with the United States over port visits by nuclear weapons-bearing ships.

6. Eduard Shevardnadze, *The Future Belongs to Freedom* (New York: The Free Press, 1991), p. 58.

7. *Pravda*, July 11, 1985, p. 4.

8. Bilateral trade expanded from a low of $110 million in 1981 to $3.964 billion in 1991. Charles E. Ziegler, "Russia and the Emerging Asian-Pacific Economic Order," in Ramesh Thakur and Carlyle A. Thayer, eds., *Reshaping Regional Relations* (Boulder: Westview Press, 1993).

9. The formal date was move up several months after the truculent North Koreans insulted Foreign Minister Shevardnadze during a courtesy visit to explain the Soviet decision. See Peggy Falkenheim Meyer, "Gorbachev and Post-Gorbachev Policy Toward the Korean Peninsula: The Impact of Changing Russian Perceptions," *Asian Survey*, Vol. 32, no. 8 (August 1992), pp. 757–772.

10. Guocang Huan, "The New Relationship with the Former Soviet Union," *Current History*, Vol. 91, no. 566 (September 1992), p. 254.

11. "Constructive partnership" is the term used by the Russian Ministry of Foreign Affairs.

12. *Izvestiia*, April 22, 1992, p. 6.

13. See Radio Free Europe/Radio Liberty, *Daily Report* (December 18 and 21, 1992); *The New York Times*, December 18, 1992; and *China Daily* November 27, 1992.

14. Aleksandr Chudodeyev, "Russia and China: Partners But Not Allies," *Segodnya* (2 September 1994), in *Current Digest of the Post-Soviet Press* (hereafter *CDPSP*), Vol. 46, no. 36 (1994), p. 13.

15. *Izvestiia*, April 27, 1994; Aleksei Voskresenskii, "Vyyzov KNR i rossiiskie interesy," *Nezavisimaia gazeta*, September 16, 1994; and Vladimir Lukin, "Neither Fraternal Love Nor Fraternal Hatred," *Moskovskie novosti*, September 4–11, 1994, in *CDPSP*, Vol.

46, no. 36 (1994), p. 14. It is unclear how many Chinese illegals are currently in Russia. The estimates range from 50,000 to 2 million.

16. *Izvestiia*, July 17, 1993, p. 1. The trade estimate for 1994 is from the Russian ministry of foreign trade.

17. See *Far Eastern Economic Review*, April 9, 1992, pp. 16–20. Due to communist migration policies, Han Chinese now outnumber Mongols in Inner Mongolia by about five to one. This of course undermines the viability of any pan-Mongol movement.

18. For a more extended discussion of great power interests in Mongolia, see Marko Milovojevic, *The Mongolian Revolution of 1990: Stability or Conflict in Inner Asia?* (London: Conflict Studies #242, June 1991).

19. J. Richard Walsh, "China and the New Geopolitics of Central Asia," *Asian Survey*, Vol. 33, no. 3 (March 1993), pp. 272–284. It should be noted that Kazakhstan signed the NPT in February 1994 and has begun the process of transferring its 92 SS-18s to Russia for destruction.

20. See, for example, the interview with Deputy Foreign Affairs Minister Georgii Kunadze in *Nezavisimaia gazeta*, July 29, 1993, pp. 1,3.

21. Igor Rotar, "Etnicheskaia bomba na severno-zapade Kitaia," *Nezavisimaia gazeta*, August 3, 1994).

22. See Rajan Menon and Henri J. Barkey, "The Transformation of Central Asia: Implications for Regional and International Security," *Survival*, Vol. 34, no. 4 (Winter 1992–93, pp. 68–89; and Keith Martin, "China and Central Asia: Between Seduction and Suspicion," *RFE/RL Research Report*, Vol. 3, no. 25, June 24, 1994, pp. 26–36.

23. *Izvestiia*, April 2, 1994; *Nezavisimaia gazeta*, October 1, 1992, in *CDPSP*, Vol. 44, no. 39 (1992), p. 21.

24. It is not unlikely that Taiwan's overtures towards Russia were an attempt to prod the Bush administration into concluding a deal that would stimulate the ailing American arms industry, and improve the President's chances for reelection at the same time.

25. One poll commissioned by the conservative Russian National Party and conducted in Moscow in August found 72.3 percent of Muscovites and 91 percent of residents of other regions (who were visiting Moscow) opposed to returning the Kuriles under any circumstances. *Sovetskaia rossiia*, September 3, 1992, in *CDPSP*, Vol. 44, no. 35 (1992), p. 20. A poll published in the more liberal *Nezavisimaia gazeta*, August 26 and September 2, 1992, found 49.6 percent willing to return the islands. Two years later, in a poll conducted immediately following the October 1994 earthquake, 89 percent of Primorskii krai residents and 60 percent of Muscovites favored promptly returning the Kurils to Japan, citing Russia's inability to provide a normal standard of living for the island's residents as their primary reason. *Izvestiia*, October 13, 1994.

26. Fuel shortages in early spring of 1993 led local government officials to plead with the governor of Hokkaido for assistance, much to the annoyance of the Russian Ministry of Foreign Affairs. Japan earned additional goodwill br providing $1 million in assistance to the Kuril communities stricken by the earthquake. *Izvestiia*, October 14, 1994.

27. The complicated political maneuvering over Yeltsin's proposed visit is analyzed in Harry Gelman's excellent monograph, *Russo-Japanese Relations and the Future of the U.S.-Japanese Alliance* (Santa Monica, CA: RAND, 1993).

28. Radio Free Europe/Radio Liberty, *Daily Report*, October 12–14, 1993.

29. Interviews conducted during June-July 1993 in the Russian Far East.

30. *Segodnya*, November 29, 1994, in *CDPSP*, Vol. 46, no. 48, (1994), p. 19. Russia's debt at the beginning of 1995 was approximately $5 billion.

31. See Stephen J. Blank, *The New Russia in the New Asia* (Carlisle Barracks, PA: U.S. Army War College, July 22, 1994), pp. 18–27.

32. See Michael T. Klare, "The Next Great Arms Race," *Foreign Affairs*, Vol. 72, no. 3 (Summer 1993), pp. 136–152.

33. See *Izvestiia*, November 19 and December 20, 1992; Radio Free Europe/Radio Liberty *Daily Report*, June 3, 1994; Shim Jae Hong, "Silent Partner," *Far Eastern Economic Review*, December 29, 1994/ January 5, 1995, pp. 14–15.

34. Hong, "Silent Partner."

35. Data from Korean Trade Asociation and *Direction of Trade Statistics* (Washington, D.C.: IMF, December 1994), p. 166.

36. *RA Report*, no. 17 (July 1994), p. 112.

37. Radio Free Europe/Radio Liberty *Daily Report*, July 7, 1993.

38. The income from launching American satellites on Russian rockets was estimated at $700 million over 7–8 years. Vladimir Nadein, "Pervyi ser'eznyi spor mezhdu Rossei i SShA zavershen vygodnym kompromissov," *Izvestiia*, July 20, 1993; Daniel Sneider, "Russians Up in Arms About Cancellation of Rocket Deal," *Christian Science Monitor*, July 27, 1993.

39. *RA Report*, no. 17 (July 1994), p. 81.

40. Carlyle A. Thayer, "Russian Policy Toward Vietnam," in Peter Shearman, Ed., *Russian Foreign Policy* (Boulder, CO: Westview Press, 1995); and Thayer, *Vietnam's Developing Ties with the Region: The Case for Defence Cooperation*. ADSC Working Paper No. 24. Canberra: Australian Defence Studies Centre, Australian Defence Force Academy, June 1994.

41. Boris Rybak, "Russia Completes MiG–29 Export Deal," *Aviation Week and Space Technology*, Vol. 141, no. 6 (1994), pp. 28–29.

42. Klare, "The Next Great Arms Race;" *The Economist*, February 20, 1993, pp. 19–21.

43. Radio Free Europe/Radio Liberty, *Daily Report*, July 27, 1993.

44. See Paul M. Evans, "Building Security: The Council for Security and Cooperation in the Asia Pacific (CSCAP)," *The Pacific Review*, Vol. 7, no. 2 (1994), pp. 125–139.

45. For a review of Asian-Pacific economic cooperation organizations, see Stuart Harris, "Policy Networks and Economic Cooperation: Policy Coordination in the Asia-Pacific Region," *The Pacific Review*, Vol 7, no. 4 (1994), pp. 381–395.

46. Samuel P. Huntington has argued that the major fault lines along which future conflicts will emerge are civilizational. He suggests that "torn countries" incorporating different civilizations, such as Russia and Yugoslavia, are prime candidates for dismemberment. Russia is also torn in its civilizational identity, as are the examples Huntington cites of Turkey and Mexico. "The Clash of Civilizations?," *Foreign Affairs*, Vol. 72, no. 3 (Summer 1993), pp. 22–49. For a discussion of Russia's position in Asia, see Milan Hauner, *What is Asia to Us?* (Boston: Unwin Hyman, 1990).

47. Sergei Stankevich, "A Power in Search of Itself," *Nezavisimaia gazeta*, March 28, 1992, in *CDPSP*, Vol. 44, no. 13 (1992), pp. 1–4.

48. In July 1992 a symposium of prominent Russians and Japanese was held in Moscow to assess the relevance of the Japanese model for Russia in metallurgy and machine building, energy, chemical industry, transport, and the distribution of goods. The proceedings were published as a monograph. *Iaponskaia ekonomicheskaia model': vozmozhnosti primeneniia v vozrozhdaiushcheisia Rossii* (Moscow: Kompas interneshil, 1992).

49. N. Popov, "Vneshniaia politika Rossii," *Mirovaia ekonomika i mezhdunarodnye otnosheniia*, no. 3 (1994), p. 58.

50. Vadim Sazonov, "The West: Friend or Foe?" *Segodnya*, December 6, 1994, in *CDPSP*, Vol. 46, no. 49 (1994), pp. 14–15.

51. The closest Moscow has come to elaborating a coherent foreign policy is Yeltsin's

decree on "Basic Provisions of the Russian Federation's Foreign Policy Concept" of April 1993. See *Nezavisimaia gazeta*, April 29, 1993, pp. 1, 3.

52. In one case, over 200 people were arrested for looting and theft in a single day during the fire at Vladivostok's huge ammunition dump. Moscow Mayak Radio, in *Foreign Broadcast Information Service/Soviet Union*, May 18, 1992. This author was present at a meeting in Vladivostok (June 1993) where several Russians, clearly without official authorization, offered to sell Mig-29 and Mig-31 fighters to an American businessman.

53. *Far Eastern Economic Review*, August 27, 1992, pp. 46–47.

54. A 1993 draft law outlining the economic powers of subnational units is unclear in many respects. "Zakon Rossiiskoi Federatsii: O razgranichenii polnomochii mezhdu Rossiiskoi Federatsei i sub'ektami Federatsii v voprosakh mezhdunarodnykh i vneshneekonomicheskikh sviazei" (Draft: June 1993).

55. Much was written about the TRADP in 1992–93, but the unsettled situation in North Korea appears to have put the project on hold. See Euikon Kim, "Political Economy of the Tumen River Basin Development: Problems and Prospects," *Journal of Northeast Asian Studies*, Vol. 11, no. 2 (Summer 1992), pp. 35–48; *Far Eastern Economic Review*, January 16, 1992, pp. 16–17; Li Haibo, "Tumen River Delta: Far East's Future Rotterdam," *Beijing Review*, April 20–26, 1992, pp. 5–6.

4

China and the Stability
of East Asia

Robert S. Ross

The transformation of China's role in East Asia since the end of the Cold War has been both fundamental and far-reaching. Whereas during the Cold War China had been a strategically important actor in the global balance and a critical participant in the anti-Soviet/anti-Vietnam coalition throughout East Asia, it quickly lost much of its global and immediate regional strategic significance with the demise of the Soviet Union. Simultaneously, the collapse of the Soviet Union encouraged Chinese leaders to shift their strategic focus from concentration on immediate threats to vital Chinese security interests to a consideration of the long-term sources of regional instability and the prospects for renewed great-power rivalry in the twenty-first century.

But what the end of the Cold War could not change was China's importance to the stability of East Asia. China's geographic and demographic size, its location in relation to other regional great powers, and its growing economic and military potential guarantee that it will be a major force affecting regional stability. Constructive Chinese foreign policy will be required to establish an enduring post–Cold War East Asian order characterized by stability and cooperation. Nevertheless, there remains considerable uncertainty regarding China's emerging role in post–Cold War East Asia. Since the early 1980s, its economy has been growing at a remarkably rapid rate, and in recent years it has begun to emphasize military modernization through increased defense spending.

China's regional capabilities are clearly expanding. But the impact of these changes remains unclear. Chinese economic and military development can become a source of either stability or instability. Similarly, its relations with its neighbors in the region have the potential to contribute to their security and economic development or to become a source of significant insecurity. Development and consolidation of a stable East Asian order requires an understanding of the sources and instruments of contemporary Chinese security policy. It also requires an understanding of the options available for promoting a Chinese contribution to regional stability. The challenge is to use the current uncertainty both within China and throughout East Asia as an opportunity to encourage the development of trends conducive to regional stability.

China and the Cold War Balance of Power

During the final two decades of the Cold War, China was a major actor in regional polarization insofar as it played a key strategic role in the development of the anti-Soviet coalition. Whereas America and its allies throughout East Asia had been concerned that the U.S. defeat in Indochina would allow the Soviet Union to fill the resulting vacuum, China's regional presence compensated for Washington's reduced strategic role, thus minimizing the repercussions of the U.S. retrenchment on the regional balance. The local powers adjusted their foreign policies not by tilting toward the Soviet Union, but by improving relations with China. The "dominoes" did not fall; rather, they tilted toward China.

This trend was most clear in Southeast Asia. In 1974, after the United States had withdrawn from Vietnam, Malaysia normalized relations with Beijing. In 1975, in the aftermath of the fall of Saigon to North Vietnamese forces, Thailand and the Philippines normalized relations with China. China's anti-Soviet foreign policy and its significant regional presence allowed all three states to offset Vietnam's enhanced regional weight and the potential for an expanded Soviet regional presence by improving relations with Beijing. Although Singapore refrained from normalizing relations with China out of deference to Indonesia, President Lee Kuan Yew's frequent visits to Beijing beginning in early 1976 reflected a similar response to the U.S. defeat in Vietnam.

These formal diplomatic developments were matched throughout the 1970s and 1980s by active diplomacy between China and the countries in the Association of Southeast Asian Nations (ASEAN): Thailand, Malaysia, Indonesia, Singapore, Brunei, and the Philippines. This was particularly the case after 1978, when China became the strategic foundation for the regional coalition against the Soviet-Vietnamese alliance and the Vietnamese occupation of Cambodia. China's military contribution to the anti-Vietnamese resistance in Cambodia and its significant military presence on the Vietnamese border assured the region that China would resist any Soviet-Vietnamese efforts to further expand their military influence. Thailand was especially grateful for China's strategic presence, for it allowed it to resist the Vietnamese occupation of Cambodia, despite the presence of the Vietnamese military on the Thai border. On a larger scale, China provided the strategic backing for all of the ASEAN countries as they led the diplomatic drive at the United Nations and in other international forums to isolate Vietnam diplomatically and economically. Even Jakarta, which had failed to develop formal diplomatic relations with China, improved relations with Beijing in the context of ASEAN–China cooperation against Vietnam and the Soviet Union.

China's contribution to the anti-Soviet coalition was also evident in Sino-

Japanese relations. Japan had long sought to improve relations with China but had been constrained by U.S. opposition. Soon after Richard Nixon's visit to China in 1972, Japan established diplomatic relations with China. Just as China contributed to the security of the ASEAN states, so too did it contribute to Japanese security. In the context of the Nixon doctrine and U.S. unwillingness to bear the full burden of stability in Asia, China's regional weight and its anti-Soviet policy afforded Japan additional insurance against the Soviet Union. Despite Tokyo's reluctance to offend Moscow, it derived significant security from its relationship with China. As was the case for the ASEAN countries, the 1978 Soviet-Vietnamese alliance and the Vietnamese invasion of Cambodia, as well as the 1979 Soviet invasion of Afghanistan, enhanced China's value to Japanese security. Frequent diplomatic consultations and the initial development of Sino-Japanese trade, which required encouragement of Japanese business by the Japanese government, reflected the common interest in resisting Soviet power in Asia.

Moreover, Sino-Japanese cooperation and Sino-American cooperation contributed to stability on the Korean peninsula. Since China needed stable relations with Tokyo and Washington, Beijing helped restrain North Korea's more dangerous foreign policy tendencies. Although the Sino-Soviet conflict restrained Beijing from isolating Pyongyang and developing relations with Seoul, China's North Korea policy reflected considerable caution and Beijing's interest in stability. Thus, Japanese and American leaders had some confidence that Beijing would restrain Pyongyang from launching a war against South Korea.

Finally, China's bilateral Soviet policy played an important role in regional affairs. Its willingness to resist Soviet pressure and an escalating Soviet military presence on the Sino-Soviet border created a significant burden on Soviet defense expenditures. By the early 1980s, Moscow was deploying its most advanced weaponry in the Soviet Far East, including the Backfire bomber and the SS-20 ballistic missile, as well as large numbers of troops. The largest proportion of Soviet soldiers and weaponry in the Soviet Far East was deployed against China. According to former Soviet foreign minister Eduard Shevardnadze, the Soviet Union spent 200 billion rubles to develop the military infrastructure along the Sino-Soviet border.[1] Overall, China's adversarial Soviet policy inhibited Soviet flexibility in Asia and thus contributed to the security of all the states in the region that feared the power of the Soviet Union and its allies.

Thus, from the Sino-Soviet border, through the Korean peninsula, and down to the Malacca Strait, China was a conservative force. China's foreign policy enabled the 1950s and 1960s Cold War U.S.-led anti-Soviet coalition to be maintained despite America's reduced security role in the region. In Northeast Asia, China supported the status quo on the Korean peninsula, and in Southeast Asia, it cooperated with the ASEAN countries to compel Moscow and Hanoi to end their cooperation in Cambodia. Chinese policy also contributed to Japanese security by easing Japanese worries as the U.S. contribution to the Sino-Japanese defense relationship declined.

Ultimately, China's contribution to the anti-Soviet coalition played a decisive role in the evolution of the regional balance. In Southeast Asia, China's support for the anti-Vietnamese resistance and its military deployments on the Sino-Vietnamese border compelled Vietnam to engage in a long and costly defense effort. In conjunction with its economic isolation, which the ASEAN states enforced in international organizations, and reduced support from the Soviet Union, Chinese military pressure compelled Hanoi to withdraw from Cambodia. China's Soviet policy was also crucial to this development. When Soviet internal developments persuaded Gorbachev of the necessity of reducing the costs of Soviet foreign policy, he was faced with China's demand that he change Soviet Indochina policy as the price of improved Sino-Soviet relations. Chinese pressure helped persuade Moscow to end its support for Vietnam. Generally, the protracted Sino-Soviet conflict, in combination with the U.S.-Soviet conflict and Soviet economic policy, contributed to Soviet desire to transform its policies toward South Korea, Japan, and the ASEAN states. Along with the United States, Japan, and the NATO allies, China can take some satisfaction from having "defeated" the Soviet Union and "won the Cold War."

The Transformation of China's Security Environment

The Soviet Union was China's primary and almost sole security concern throughout the 1970s and most of the 1980s. It was the source of Chinese border concerns and of Vietnamese "regional hegemony" in Indochina. The collapse of the Soviet economy and the resultant retrenchment of Soviet military power in East Asia and the disintegration of the Soviet empire in Central Asia transformed China's security environment. The decline and disappearance of the Soviet threat not only allowed China to focus its attention on economic concerns, it also transformed the East Asian political environment in that economic diplomacy assumed increased importance vis-à-vis military competition in the ongoing rivalry for influence among the Asian states.

The first signs of Soviet problems appeared in the early 1980s, when the superpower confrontation hardened and the Soviet Army was unable to extricate itself from the war in Afghanistan. For the first time since the early 1970s, Moscow was on the defensive. As the 1980s developed, Soviet difficulties became increasingly intractable. The succession crisis continued to plague Soviet decision making, and the Soviet economy continued to worsen. The superpower agreement on intermediate-range nuclear missiles on essentially Washington's terms reflected the significant decline in Soviet capabilities. Moreover, Washington had negotiated in China's interest. Its demand for a "double-zero" agreement had compelled Moscow to remove its SS-20 missiles from the Soviet Far East, thus reducing the Soviet strategic threat to China.

The decline of Soviet strategic power was matched by the reduction of the Soviet presence in East Asia. As the Soviet economy collapsed and the superpower confrontation intensified, Soviet leaders concluded that the Sino-Soviet conflict was too costly. Moscow sought Sino-Soviet rapprochement to reduce the economic and strategic burden of Soviet foreign policy. In so doing, it was prepared to meet Chinese terms for rapprochement. By the time of the Sino-Soviet summit in May 1989, the Soviet Union had mostly resolved the three obstacles that China had insisted blocked rapprochement. In 1988 it signaled its reduced strategic and economic support for the Vietnamese occupation of Cambodia and encouraged Vietnam to withdraw its troops, it had withdrawn its own troops from Afghanistan, and it had significantly reduced its military presence on the Sino-Soviet border. Moreover, the Soviet Navy had begun to withdraw from Cam Ranh Bay, signaling the Soviet Union's declining power and its reduced regional presence. By 1989 the Soviet Union no longer posed a significant threat to Chinese security. Subsequent developments in 1990 and 1991 merely consolidated this trend, so that a Soviet policy reversal became inconceivable.

In this improving strategic context, China's policy priorities changed. Now that security concerns were declining, China's post-Mao leadership, having already discarded the ideological priorities of the Maoist era, reduced China's preoccupation with security and focused on the "four modernizations." Indeed, it was no accident that defense modernization was ranked fourth. A strong defense required a modern economy and in the new international context, policymakers were able to compel the military leadership to wait for a stronger economy to receive additional resources. Thus, the military budget remained fairly steady throughout the 1980s, while the economy and the annual budget expanded significantly. Moreover, the size of the military contracted, as over one-quarter of the troops were demobilized. Similarly, now that trade had become a source of growth and power, economic relations with the relatively benign Soviet Union became not only possible but desirable. First border trade and then state-level trade developed and expanded.

Complementing the international sources of Chinese policy change was the emergence of China's reform-minded leadership. Together they led Beijing to adopt policies designed to maximize economic growth. The introduction of market reforms in the domestic economy was matched by measures designed to facilitate economic relations with the advanced capitalist states. Thus, Chinese foreign trade and foreign investment in China quickly expanded. Similarly, China's diplomacy in Asia shifted from emphasis on opposition to Soviet hegemonism to efforts to develop bilateral economic relationships conducive to the acquisition of foreign capital and advanced technology. In the post–Cold War era, economic diplomacy replaced strategic diplomacy.

But the transformation of Chinese diplomacy has not only been driven by the economic opportunities provided by the new international environment and by new domestic priorities. It has also been driven by the prospect that renewed great power tension in East Asia could pose a significant strategic challenge to Chinese security. Chinese leaders believe that the current period of relaxation is not likely to endure beyond the turn of the century. On the contrary, they believe that the contemporary period is likely to be a mere breathing spell, during which time countries throughout East Asia will be both addressing issues they had neglected during the period of Cold War insecurity and preparing themselves for the inevitable resumption of great-power rivalry in Asia. As the report of the Communist Party's Fourteenth Party Congress maintained:

> The world today is undergoing a historic period of tremendous change . . . various forces are redividing and recombining. . . . The formation of a new political pattern will be protracted and complex.[2]

China's regional diplomacy thus reflects both the end of one era and the preparation for the emerging era.

The Post–Cold War Balance of Power and Chinese Security

Central to the direction of contemporary Chinese policy are the assumptions held by the elite about the transition and the primary determinant of its evolution. Beijing understands that economic sources of power are of increasing importance as the central element of comprehensive national power in an increasingly multipolar world. As one senior Chinese analyst explained, the "race for overall national strength and high technology" will "ultimately determine the balance of power in the world."[3] Another Chinese analyst observed that the 1990s are a "crucial period," during which the "results of . . . competition in national strength will decide the places of various countries in the world in the next century, and their roles in the new world order."[4] Similarly, "the major countries of the world are engaged in a competition to raise their overall national strength" as the world moves toward "multipolarization." In this context, "the balance of forces among the big powers is undergoing rapid change."[5]

China's primary concern regarding this emerging world order and the future balance of power focuses on the combination of Japan's preeminence in regional economic diplomacy and its corresponding regional authority. Chinese leaders fear that Tokyo's current economic foundation and the likely development of greater Japanese military power mean that Japan is the East Asian state best positioned to succeed in this post–Cold War climate and to emerge from the transition with the strategic advantage in the new balance of power. One commentator argued that as an "economic superpower," Japan is "vigorously pursuing 'superpower diplomacy,'" increasing its political influence in the Asia-Pacific region." Another analyst reflected that whereas the U.S. military and economic position in the region is "on the decline," Japan's "economic strength is gaining dramatically," resulting in "enormous political and economic influence on the ASEAN countries." At a minimum, Chinese leaders are asking whether in the 1990s, Japan, as an "economic superpower," will pursue "economic hegemonism."[6]

But concern about Japanese military power is also prevalent. When Japan sent minesweepers to the Persian Gulf, it signaled an initial step toward Tokyo's objective of becoming a "political giant" and "seek[ing] military backing for its bid to become a political power." Its decision to end its ban on sending troops abroad by agreeing to participate in UN peacekeeping activities revealed that having achieved economic power, Tokyo was "demanding a 'major political actor's' position." This ambitious objective also allegedly explains why Tokyo seeks a permanent seat on the UN Security Council and why China remains publicly ambivalent on this issue.[7] Thus, China was skeptical that former Japanese prime minister Kiichi Miyazawa's effort to develop a security role for Japan in Asia could overcome the region's "lingering memory of Asia's bitter past" and its "vigilance" against the revival of Japanese military power.[8]

Chinese fear of Japan's post–Cold War role in Asia is compounded by the uncertainty surrounding America's role in the region. Chinese leaders share with leaders throughout East Asia an appreciation of the role of the U.S.–Japan security treaty in minimizing Tokyo's security concerns and its incentive to expand its military capability. Thus, Beijing, like all the other East Asian leaderships, fears that a decline in America's regional presence would lead Japan to seek to protect its security through unilateral measures, including a defense buildup. Although such a development might well reflect Japanese insecurity in the context of U.S. retrenchment, there is sufficient suspicion of Japan in Beijing and elsewhere in East Asia to arouse concern that once Japan develops military power, it cannot be counted on to eschew an expansionist policy detrimental to its neighbors' security.

Further exacerbating Chinese concern is the state of U.S.–China relations. On the one hand, the Chinese hope that Washington will eventually come to its senses and recognize China's value to the United States in maintaining a regional balance of power as Japanese strength grows. On the other hand, Beijing must also be concerned that Washington's apparent inability to leave ideological considerations out of its China policy will undermine the potential for U.S.–China cooperation in an unstable Asia. Despite the recent improvement in relations and the unconditional extension of China's MFN trade status in 1994, it would not be alarmist on the part of Chinese leaders if they feared that American domestic politics would once again lead to tension in U.S.–China relations, with significant implications for Chinese security. Not only could differences over human rights once again affect U.S. policy toward China, but the Taiwan issue might also reemerge as a U.S.–China conflict of interest.

Thus, Beijing made a considerable effort to conciliate the United States during the latter half of the Bush administration in such areas as economic relations, missile and nuclear proliferation, and regional conflicts.[9] Beijing's efforts reflected not only the importance of the U.S. market to Chinese economic development, but also China's significant interest in maintaining the basis for future U.S.–China political cooperation, should that prove necessary. But despite their efforts and recent successes, Chinese leaders remain concerned that America's "ideological" human rights policy, its Taiwan policy, and its complacent view of Japan make the United States an unreliable participant in the politics of East Asia.

The combination of Japan's significant great-power potential in an era emphasizing technological advantage and the uncertainty surrounding both America's regional presence and U.S.–China relations demands that China prepare for the possibility of enhanced regional instability. At a minimum, Chinese leaders must promote a peaceful international environment in Asia in which to consolidate the basis for future cooperative relationships and maximize Chinese access to the sophisticated technologies of its more advanced Asian neighbors. Thus, China has been engaged in active "smiling diplomacy" with all of its neighbors from Northeast to Southeast Asia. The recent establishment of China–South Korea diplomatic relations, Beijing's welcome of the Japanese emperor, and the frequent visits to regional capitals by Chinese leaders all reflect this dynamic.

But just as important as Chinese summit diplomacy is China's effort to develop and consolidate both the military and economic instruments of diplomacy necessary to compete for influence in Asia. Thus, in addition to various bilateral sources of Chinese defense spending (discussed below), a major impetus for Chinese defense modernization is Beijing's concern about China's role in the overall regional balance of power into the twenty-first century. Indeed, the lesson of the 1991 Gulf War for China was that the most advanced technologies are critical elements in military power and, most important, that Chinese technology was woefully behind the levels of the advanced industrial countries.[10] Thus, prudence requires that China study today the technology that it may need in ten years, rather than wait until the need arises to develop first the technology and then the hardware. Moreover, the technologies that China would like to acquire are technologies that the United States, Russia, and Japan, for the most part, already possess, including aircraft carrier and missile-guidance technology. China is the weakest of the great powers in East Asia, and even a stable defense budget will not prevent it from falling further behind the others.

Chinese leaders' foremost security concern is the direction of the Sino-Japanese balance. Japan increased its defense budget throughout the 1980s, during which time in China there was a steady decline in the military's share of the state budget and, between 1983 and 1989, no growth in actual Chinese defense spending.[11] The pace of Japanese technology development and weapons acquisition has also far exceeded that of China. Japan has more major surface vessels than any other country in the world apart from the United States; it already deploys in East Asia more submarines, escort ships, and mine warfare units than the United States; and after the U.S. Seventh Fleet completes its scheduled downsizing, it will have more major vessels in East Asia than the United States. Moreover, this is a new and modern navy, having been built in the last fifteen years. Japan is also constructing an advanced jet fighter based on the technology of the U.S. F-16C/D that will be technologically superior to any aircraft that China can manufacture or import from Russia or from anywhere else, but with the important advantage of domestic production.[12] Finally, Tokyo's continued interest in plutonium-based nuclear reactors and its advanced civilian space program indicate Japanese possession of advanced strategic nuclear capabilities.[13] Thus, Japan is currently developing advanced military capabilities based on equipment and weaponry far superior to those that China possesses or can look forward to developing during the next decade.

But in addition to its concern about Japanese power, China also has a separate but complementary ambition to become a great power throughout the region. This objective reflects Chinese leaders' ambition to restore China to its historical place in East Asia as well as Beijing's long-term objective of minimizing Chinese dependence on other powers for security. China reluctantly depended on the Soviet Union for its security in the 1950s and on the United States in the 1970s and 1980s. Given its natural power endowments, it can realistically seek to establish sufficient power to independently protect its interests throughout Asia. But to do so, it must have an influential voice—a place at the table—in every regional negotiation. Thus far, however, Chinese military power is insufficient to reach this objective, and Chinese leaders cannot be sure that China's military capability in the foreseeable future will afford it either an independent security policy or a major role in regionwide issues.

Thus, China has increased its acknowledged defense budget by over 60 percent since 1990 while focusing its resources on the air force and navy in order to enhance its power projection capability. It has purchased advanced weaponry from Russia, including Su-27 fighter jets and surface-to-air missiles, and expressed interest in purchasing an advanced Soviet-built aircraft carrier from Ukraine. Given the controversy created by the Sino-Ukrainian negotiations and/or the cost of purchasing an aircraft carrier, however, Beijing decided to defer purchase or perhaps to develop its own aircraft carrier production facilities. It almost certainly has not given up the quest for power projection technology. China is determined to at least maintain its current position and to try to improve its position in the East Asian balance of power, and it cannot be expected to curtail its defense program.[14]

China's military buildup, while perhaps explicable as prudent policy, nonetheless creates a policy dilemma for Chinese leaders, for its defense policy is out of synch with its diplomacy. Contemporary post–Cold War trends call for a benign diplomacy emphasizing cooperation and economic development. Although Japan's significant technological head start may render any Chinese attempt to catch up, no matter how premature, fruitless, Chinese leaders are not prepared to cede the strategic initiative to Japan. Thus, Beijing seems to see no alternative to incurring the criticism of China's neighbors for its apparently unnecessary, counterproductive, and provocative defense policy.

While developing its military capabilities, Beijing has also been trying to develop the economic basis for great-power influence in East Asia. Japan already has such a regional economic role. Japanese trade with the region and Japanese direct investment in the Asian economies have yielded Tokyo an important role in the economic development of all the East Asian economies. Thus, China has been developing economic relations with its East Asian neighbors not only to attract the resources for economic development but also to develop regional influence, insofar as developed economic relations between China and its neighbors will compel them to consider their economic interests when making China policy across a wide spectrum of issues.

Beijing's regional economic objectives have been boosted by the phenomenal rate of Chinese economic growth since 1979. China is developing the domestic economy necessary to develop international economic power through trade and investment. Nevertheless, as with military power, it remains unclear whether Chinese economic growth will enable China to accrue economic power and thus political power. This will require that China develop an important role in the economic development of its neighbors. Only then will it have political influence.

The challenge for Chinese policymakers is clear. In order to be competitive in the emerging post–Cold War multipolar balance of power in East Asia, not only must China become a regionwide strategic power, it must also develop both the domestic economy and the corresponding economic diplomacy necessary to become a regional economic power. What is less clear, however, is Beijing's ability to meet this dual challenge.

China and the Emerging Strategic Order in East Asia

China's ability to respond to this challenge in East Asia varies according to the subregion. There are three subregions in East Asia: Northeast Asia, Indochina, and the area of Southeast Asia comprising Thailand and the countries in the South China Sea—the ASEAN countries. In each of these sectors, China has different capabilities and a different role in the local balance of power.

China and Northeast Asia

An affinity of strategic interests and economic complementarity between China and its Northeast Asian neighbors have already established the foundation for future political cooperation. The recent trend in Sino-Russian relations reflects the role of both strategic and economic factors in promoting cooperative relations. As the Soviet Union began to withdraw its forces from the Sino-Soviet border area and dismantle its nuclear missiles targeted on China, China began to reevaluate its Soviet policy and its posture on the Soviet role in Northeast Asia. As the Soviet challenge to China continued to recede, leading to the May 1989 Beijing summit, and China's concern about growing Japanese power increased, Beijing subtly but significantly adjusted its policy toward the Soviet-Japanese territorial dispute over the Kuril Islands. Whereas it had previously supported the Japanese position, by early 1991 it had adopted a neutral position on the dispute.[15] Since that time, the disappearance of Sino-Soviet strategic competition has enabled the resolution of the border conflict and the development of active border trade between Russia and China. Beijing thus turned its attention away from the Soviet Union and toward Japan as the Northeast Asian power most likely to challenge Chinese security interests in the twenty-first century.

Moreover, in this context of reduced security suspicions, Sino-Russian trade expanded. During the post-Soviet period, economic relations developed at a rapid but ultimately unsustainable rate. By 1993, China had become Russia's second-largest trade partner and the second-largest investor in the Russian Far East. But in 1994, due to a host of policy and economic changes in both countries, including the imposition of tariffs and border-control measures by Russia that curtailed the uncontrolled movement of Chinese traders deep into eastern Russia, economic relations settled into a more appropriate pattern. In 1994, two-way trade declined by approximately 50 percent over 1993 as China became Russia's ninth-largest trading partner. Nonetheless, in important respects China and the Soviet Union will remain significant complimentary economic partners. Inexpensive Chinese consumer goods, including textiles and foodstuffs, will remain appropriate to Russian market conditions, and Russian oil, steel, construction equipment and, as noted, military goods will continue to find a place in the Chinese market. Moreover, inexpensive Chinese consumer goods will continue to play an important role in alleviating the impoverished living conditions in the eastern sections of Russia and thus help to ease regional political dissatisfaction with Moscow's ineffectual economic policies.[16]

Moreover, border trade provides the context for heightened mutual confidence concerning border security and for reduced political tension. Not only has each side significantly reduced troop deployments along the border, but they have made progress toward an agreement for additional withdrawals. They have also agreed to various confidence-building measures, including an agreement on measures to prevent accidental war and a mutual no targeting of nuclear weapons agreement.[17] Political relations have also flourished. Russian president Boris Yeltsin's visit to China in December 1992 erased any suspicion that the two countries' contrary domestic political trajectories would disrupt the bilateral relationship. On the contrary, the visit bolstered confidence in both capitals that cooperation could be expanded, as reflected in the panoply of economic agreements that were signed. Since then, reciprocal visits by various leaders from both countries, including the September 1994 visit to Moscow by China's Communist Party secretary Jiang Zemin, have reinforced this trend.

Finally, the two sides have developed an important arms sales relationship, reflected in the military aircraft and surface-to-air missile agreements. Now that China no longer has access to Western military technology, Russian technology has become a very valuable base for its military modernization program. Meanwhile, Russia's most valuable export commodity is weaponry, and it is more than willing to sell military hardware to China in exchange for hard currency. As

Deputy Prime Minister Aleksandr Shokhin recently observed, "It is hardly sensible" for Russia "to turn away from this source of income which helps solve numerous problems facing the country."[18] Clearly, despite the rapid increase in the Chinese defense budget in recent years, Russia does not consider China a security threat. Indeed, given Russia's inability to resolve its differences with Japan and its continued economic and political predicament, Moscow may even welcome China's strategic presence in Northeast Asia.

China's success in developing relations with Russia contrasts with the ongoing difficulties in Russian–Japanese relations. As of early 1995, Tokyo and Moscow showed no signs of being able to resolve their territorial dispute over the Kuril Islands. Thus, in contrast to Beijing's success at arranging Sino-Russian summits, two scheduled visits to Tokyo by Yeltsin were abruptly canceled before he finally officially visited Tokyo in October 1993 because the territorial dispute remained at the top of the Japanese agenda. Moreover, for both economic and political reasons, Russian–Japanese economic relations have not expanded much beyond the low levels of the Cold War. Indeed, among the group of seven (G–7) countries, Japan has been the most reluctant to consider granting Russia significant economic aid. Even in the aftermath of the Tokyo summit, Chinese leaders remain confident that the level of Russian–Japanese cooperation will remain below that of Sino-Russian cooperation.[19]

Complementary levels of economic development also provide the basis for expanded economic relations between China and Korea and Taiwan. In these cases, however, as the less developed state, China has been the recipient of investment capital, and it has imported advanced technology. Since 1989, the annual average increase in two-way trade has been approximately 50 percent. Moreover, the amount of trade dramatically increased in the aftermath of normalization of relations in 1992. Total trade in 1993 was over $9 billion. In 1992 China was South Korea's fourth largest trade partner; in 1993 it had become South Korea's third largest trade partner. Moreover, the opening of direct air travel between the two countries in 1994 and the 1994 Seoul summit should encourage further expansion of trade.[20] Trade between China and Taiwan has also been rapidly expanding. In 1992 the mainland became Taiwan's second largest trading partner, and in 1993 total trade between Taiwan and the mainland reached nearly $14 billion, with Taiwan enjoying a substantial trade surplus.[21]

Investment in China by South Korea and Taiwan has also grown. South Korean investment in China has doubled each year since 1990. What began as a mere $170 million invested by small South Korean firms reached more than $1 billion in 1993. Moreover, this trend should continue, as relations have continued to consolidate since the 1992 normalization of diplomatic relations and the signing of the China–South Korea investment agreement. In 1993 China was the largest recipient of South Korean external investment, accounting for approximately 60 percent of total South Korean foreign investment. In 1994, the two sides signed a host of new agreements for cooperation involving large South

Korean corporations, including the joint production of commercial airplanes.[22] Investment in China by Taiwan has followed a similar pattern. In 1993, Taiwan investment in China increased approximately 600 percent over 1992 and total investment in China came to approximately $15 billion. By 1992 the mainland had become Taiwan's largest target of outbound investments, attracting over one-fifth of Taiwan's overseas investments.[23] The extent of Taiwan's growing dependence on the mainland economy is also reflected in the fact that its investments in the mainland are more than twice its combined investments in Indonesia, Thailand, Vietnam, the Philippines, and Malaysia. Taiwan's own assessment of these trends is that its dependence on the mainland will continue to grow and that this will have a detrimental effect on Taiwan's security. Of particular concern to Taipei is the possibility that growing Taiwan investment on the mainland will create a powerful interest on the part of Taiwan's financial community in ongoing economic cooperation with China. Thus, Taipei has adopted a "southern strategy," trying to encourage banks and industries to expand their investments in Southeast Asia.[24] Clearly, developments in Chinese economic relations with both South Korea and Taiwan have given Beijing influence on the direction of their foreign policies.

Complementing these economic developments is progress in China–South Korean political relations and reduced mainland–Taiwan tension. Normalization of relations between Seoul and Beijing in August 1992 and the ensuing China–South Korean summit in Beijing not only were diplomatic breakthroughs, they also were political breakthroughs for China insofar as they suggested South Korean interest in cooperating with China to offset Japan's regional presence.[25] Beijing and Seoul maintain vivid memories of Japanese occupation and are sensitive to Japan's military potential. And despite their inability to formally end the civil war and their ongoing competition for international legitimacy, Taiwan and the mainland have gone a long way toward depoliticizing their relationship and establishing the basis for resolving less high-profile issues through informal negotiations, which may ultimately provide the basis for negotiations over ending the civil war. The 1993 meeting in Singapore between China's Wang Daohan and Taiwan's Koo Chen-fu was an important breakthrough toward reduction of tension, and the 1994 agreements and further progress in 1995 toward additional agreements regarding such issues as hijackings and patrolling of the Strait of Taiwan and Taiwan's easing of trade restrictions in early 1995 suggest that additional opportunities for cross-strait cooperation exist.[26]

In contrast, in a situation analogous to China's position between Japan and Russia, South Korea and Taiwan have yet to develop a stable foundation for significant political ties with Japan. South Koreans in particular continue to harbor deep resentment toward Japan, and South Korean and Japanese leaders have yet to develop a stable, working, consultative relationship. Although South Korea and Japan have developed significant economic contacts, trade and societal relations are laden with tension. And both countries have incurred significant trade deficits with Japan. Finally, with the sole important exception of China,

North Korea's nuclear program and its economic and political policies have isolated it from the entire world.

Thus, in many respects, China has more advantageous than Japan with the other Northeast Asian states and shows early signs of developing the potential for participation in a loose anti-Japanese coalition in Northeast Asia based upon both strategic apprehension among all the parties (with the exception of Taiwan) toward Japan and China's strategic importance, as well as upon the economic complementarity and corresponding development of economic relations.

In this context, China is, as it has been since 1949, a great power in the Northeast Asian balance of power; it is playing a significant role in determining alignment patterns in Northeast Asia. Its intensive efforts to enhance its military power may augment its political stature in this region, but there will be no fundamental transformation of its capabilities. Its influence will continue to reflect its size on the mainland of Asia, so that naval and even air force modernization will only incrementally affect China's weight in the Northeast Asian regional balance. China has been and will remain a significant force in Northeast Asia.[27]

Thus, for both economic and political reasons, China is diplomatically well positioned to respond to the significant strategic challenge posed by great-power relations in Northeast Asia. At the same time, however, China continues to try to maximize its cooperation with Japan. Beijing recognizes that excessive Japanese isolation is conducive neither to Chinese economic and strategic interests nor to regional stability. Thus, Beijing has developed diplomatic and economic relations with Tokyo both to help China develop the economic foundation to contend with Japanese power and to give Japan a stake in bilateral and regional stability. In this respect, the Japanese emperor's 1992 visit to China was crucial to China's effort to establish the diplomatic basis for political and economic cooperation. Equally important, however, Sino-Japanese diplomacy and economic cooperation help to promote Japanese and Chinese interest in stable bilateral relations and provide the basis for reducing the possibility that future security problems will be interpreted in the worst light, thus precluding political solutions.

Contemporary Sino-Japanese economic and political relations are a source of satisfaction to China. Japan is China's second largest trade partner, and trade in 1992 increased by more than 25 percent over 1991; Chinese imports from Japan increased by over 36 percent and accounted for 20 percent of all Chinese imports. Moreover, in 1992 China was Japan's fourth largest export market. Although the Chinese market for Japan was considerably smaller than the U.S. market, it was relatively equal to the importance of Taiwan and South Korea for Japanese exports. And in 1993 Japanese exports grew by nearly 70 percent to over 17 billion U.S. dollars, assuming equal importance in overall Japanese exports as South Korea, Hong Kong and Germany.[28] Economic relations between the two countries are becoming increasingly dense and significant. Equally significant have been Japan's yen loans and development aid to Beijing, which by 1992 had totaled nearly 3.5 trillion yen since 1979.[29]

But what is most encouraging is the recent trend in Japanese direct investment in China. Through 1989, Japan had provided only 8 percent of the direct foreign investment in China, and this represented only 1 percent of Japan's total direct foreign investment and 6 percent of its direct foreign investment in Asia.[30] The dearth of investment aroused suspicions in China over Japanese attitudes toward China, particularly since as the minimal investment led to little technology transfer. This trend began a fundamental turnaround in 1992. Between March 1992 and 1993, new Japanese investment in China increased by 87 percent over the previous year and three times that of 1989–90, although total Japanese overseas investment dropped by 18 percent. By 1993 Japan had become the fourth largest investor in China, surpassing Germany.[31] These investment trends will further engage the two economies and may lead to greater technology transfer from Japan to China.

Thus, while China is concerned about Japanese power and has adopted various cautionary measures, including increased defense spending, it is also managing this relationship well. The Sino-Japanese economic relationship, the Japanese emperor's visit to Beijing in 1992, and ongoing high-level diplomacy, as well as Beijing's interest in downplaying the dispute over the Senkaku Islands, all suggest China's interest in maximizing the potential for mutual Sino-Japanese benefit, despite its apprehension. Rather than promoting a self-fulfilling prophesy, China is trying to manage a fragile and potentially destabilizing relationship by maximizing contemporary cooperation.

China and Indochina

China's position in Indochina is more complex than its position in Northeast Asia. On the one hand, China has emerged as the preeminent strategic power in Indochina, which assures it border security along its southern periphery. In this respect, China's position is more secure in Indochina than anywhere else in East Asia. Nevertheless, Beijing's authority is not based on either complementary strategic or economic interests between China and its Indochinese neighbors. Rather, its influence is based on coercive use of military power, and its economic importance in the region is declining.

Since the Soviet Union began to reduce its military presence in Indochina in 1988, China's regional military influence has experienced a corresponding increase. Having first expelled the French and then the Americans from Indochina, China finally expelled the Russians. Now that Beijing had no competitor for regional influence, it changed its Vietnam policy, content to normalize relations with Vietnam on Chinese terms. One of the first signs of Chinese satisfaction with the strategic trend in Indochina was the curtailment of Chinese military incursions into Vietnamese territory, which had required Hanoi to maintain a high state of military preparedness. China also agreed to open the border to trade between local residents. Then, shortly after Vietnam's January 1989 announcement that it would withdraw its troops from Cambodia by September 1989, the Chinese Foreign Ministry received a Vietnamese Foreign Ministry official for the first time since 1978.[32] By early 1991 Hanoi had sent six delegations to Beijing, while China had sent only one delegation to Hanoi. Then, after Vietnamese Communist Party general secretary Do Muoi and Premier Vo Van Kiet visited Beijing in November 1991 and the formal normalization of relations was concluded, in February 1992 Beijing sent Foreign Minister Qian Qichen to Hanoi. This was the highest-level Chinese delegation to visit Vietnam since the early 1970s. This trend culminated in December 1992, when Premier Li Peng visited Hanoi. Li was the first Chinese premier to visit Vietnam since Zhou Enlai. The two sides also reopened air and train service between the two countries and opened numerous ports to trade. In 1991, the value of two-way border trade between Vietnam and Guangxi Province alone was over $150 million. Overall trade has also been increasing significantly. Total trade more than doubled from 1992 to 1993, reaching $400 million.[33]

China's relationship with Laos has also improved in recent years. Vietnam's preoccupation with domestic economic problems, its troop withdrawal from Laos in 1988, and its lack of Soviet strategic support meant that Vientiane had both the occasion and the need to improve relations with China. Likewise, Beijing, for the first time since the 1970s, saw the opportunity to establish a presence in Laos. In these circumstances, China and Laos began economic exchanges along the border and then improved political relations. In October 1989 Chinese leaders welcomed Lao Party Secretary Kaysone Phomivane to Beijing for the first Sino-Lao summit since the 1970s, and in December 1990 Li Peng paid a reciprocal visit to Vientiane. In 1990 the two sides also signed an interim border agreement calling for a joint aerial survey of the boundary. Furthermore, in an apparent contemporary strategic equivalent to Chinese road building in northern Laos in the 1970s, during the 1990s the two sides will cooperate in the development of an airfield in northern Laos.[34]

Sino-Cambodian relations show a similar trend. In the light of retrenched Vietnamese power and Hanoi's diminished ability to contribute to Phnom Penh's economic or strategic security, Phnom Penh has the need and the opportunity to pursue Cambodia's traditional postindependence diplomatic practice of developing cooperative relations with both Beijing and Hanoi. In current strategic circumstances, only good relations with Beijing can bring peace to Cambodia and permit political stability, regardless of the composition of the Cambodian leadership. Hun Sen's willingness to hold SNC meetings in Beijing in 1992 under defacto Chinese auspices indicates that this trend had already begun in the early stages of the peace process. And, as Prince Sihanouk observed, that the SNC chose China as its first country to visit after the signing of the Comprehensive Political Settlement expressed Cambodian "respect for the Chinese government and people."[35] Similarly, recent Chinese diplomacy reflects Beijing's confidence in its regional authority and a corresponding willingness to work even with the

Vietnamese-installed "puppets" within a coalition leadership. China not only welcomed the SNC, including Hun Sen, to Beijing in July 1991, before the conclusion of the peace negotiations, but has consistently treated the Hun Sen leadership with greater respect than it has the other factional leaders, with the exception of Prince Sihanouk. In July 1992 Chinese premier Li Peng and Foreign Minister Qian Qichen welcomed Chea Sim to Beijing in his capacity as a senior member of the Phnom Penh faction, thereby according the Phnom Penh leadership equal and independent status among the contending factions.[36] China has sought peace in Cambodia regardless of the composition of the Cambodian leadership, confident that any Phnom Penh leadership will accommodate Cambodian foreign policy to Chinese power, both to offset Vietnamese power and to promote Chinese support for domestic stability in Cambodia. Thus, Beijing quickly signaled all the Cambodian parties of its support for the outcome of the 1993 UN-administered elections, despite the poor performance of the Khmer Rouge. Beijing was clearly pleased by the victory of the royalist party and the participation of Prince Sihanouk in the postelection government.[37]

Thus, by exercising its power, China has compelled its neighbors in Indochina to seek friendly relations with Beijing. Nevertheless, however advantageous this may be to Chinese interests, the contrast with China's diplomacy in Northeast Asia is both striking and important. Whereas China's Northeast Asian neighbors have willingly sought consolidated relations with China to achieve their foreign political and economic objectives, Vietnam, the most important state in Indochina, has been a reluctant suitor driven by weakness; it is unhappy with its strategic isolation and is determined to extricate itself from China's shadow. The Sino-Vietnamese dispute over the Paracel Islands will also continue to arouse Vietnamese opposition, particularly as China tries to block Vietnamese efforts to attract Western oil drilling in the disputed waters.[38] Moreover, given Vietnam's economic backwardness and its thirst for foreign capital and advanced technology, Hanoi will have only limited interest in developing close economic relations with China. On the contrary, it will develop economic relations with the advanced industrial economies, especially Japan, both for the economic benefits and in order to maximize its foreign policy independence from China's regional preeminence. This trend will certainly accelerate now that Hanoi has access to World Bank funds and the United States has normalized economic relations with Vietnam.

China's concern about Vietnamese interest in attracting outside participation in its economic development is reflected in the Chinese defense modernization program. The development of naval capabilities and landing facilities for military aircraft on Woody Island in the Paracel Islands in the northern South China Sea and the aircraft modernization program seek to ensure China a dominant strategic position in Vietnamese coastal waters and a dominant position vis-à-vis Vietnam into the twenty-first century.[39] Its cooperative policies toward Laos and Cambodia reflect similar objectives. Despite China's satisfaction with current developments in Indochina, it is also hedging against future uncertainty.

Thus, China's position in Indochina is better than at any time since the nineteenth century. Nonetheless, despite the improbability that a challenge to Chinese strategic authority will develop in the region, Beijing's advantageous relationship with Vietnam is based on coercion rather than Vietnamese choice, and Chinese leaders must consider the likelihood and implications of greater Vietnamese policy independence.

China and the ASEAN States

China's role among the ASEAN states is the most limited of its East Asian roles. In Northeast Asia, China is welcomed as a strategic asset by Moscow and Seoul, and it has good economic relations with all of the Northeast Asian countries; in Indochina, it is respected for its strategic power. But among the ASEAN states, China is neither sought out for strategic benefit by smaller powers seeking security within the great-power balance of power nor respected for its strategic presence. Moreover, China has yet to become a significant economic power among the ASEAN states. Thus, the region can give secondary consideration to China's interests with little concern either for the strategic or economic opportunity costs or for potential retribution.

In the strategic realm, the end of China's struggle for secure southern borders has undermined its ability to maintain cooperative relationships with the ASEAN states. In the post–Cold War era, not only is China less important to the global balance, it is also less important to the security of the ASEAN states. When the Soviet Union withdrew its military power to its Northeast Asian coastal waters and Vietnam, economically destitute, withdrew its forces from Cambodia, China lost its vital strategic role in the eyes of the ASEAN states. Moreover, China's minimal ability to project power beyond its coastal waters means that maritime Southeast Asia has little to fear from China's military power. Indeed, China's contribution to the Cold War strategic order in Southeast Asia was a function of its military power in Indochina. It never was and still is not a strategic power in maritime Southeast Asia. Thus, China cannot count on either the necessity for cooperation or coercive power to ensure cooperative relations with the ASEAN countries.

Moreover, China is not an important economic partner of any of the ASEAN states. On the contrary, China remains primarily a competitor of Thailand, Malaysia, Singapore, and Indonesia for international markets, and, with the partial exception of Singapore, there is little bilateral trade between China and the ASEAN countries.[40] Moreover, China's combined trade with all six of the ASEAN countries was only approximately 10.5 billion in 1993, approximately equal to total Sino-South Korean trade and considerably less than total trade between China and Taiwan. Singapore is China's most significant trade partner among the ASEAN states, yet in 1993 it ranked only seventh in total trade among Chinese trade partners, and had only 60 percent of the combined trade between Russian and China and less than half of combined Sino-South Korean trade. Most revealing, China was only Singapore's tenth largest export market, absorbing a mere 2.6 percent of total Singapore exports.[41] Similarly, the ASEAN countries have not participated in significant direct foreign investment anywhere, much less in China. Of the ASEAN countries, Singapore is the largest ASEAN investor in China but its actual investment in China during 1993 was less than $500 million.[42] Thus, despite China's rapidly developing and modernizing economy, there continues to be little economic exchange between China and the most developed countries of Southeast Asia.[43] There does not seem to be much likelihood that this will change in the foreseeable future. Ultimately, it is not GNP but economic relations that provide economic power. Thus, China is likely to remain handicapped by its inability to develop significant economic relations with the ASEAN states.

Further complicating China's role in Southeast Asia are its claim to the disputed Spratly Islands and its defense policy. Portions of the Spratly Islands are also claimed by Malaysia, Brunei, the Philippines, Vietnam, and Taiwan. But unlike the claims of the other states, China's territorial claim encompasses all the islands and extends to the southern reaches of the South China Sea—that is, to the waters just off the coast of Malaysia and Brunei, creating legitimate security concerns in both these countries.

China has numerous interests in the islands. The most commonly cited interest is the minerals, including oil, in the surrounding ocean floor. This, however, is not the most significant interest. China lacks the technology to mine the southern waters and the military capability to protect such efforts. And, given the uncertainty over ownership, international corporations will not contract with China to mine these waters. Moreover, the most promising sites for oil exploration are in the East China Sea and the northern areas of the South China Sea.[44]

Nevertheless, China does have a number of important interests in the islands. First, its claim to the southern Spratly Islands creates sufficient uncertainty to inhibit other states from mining the surrounding waters. Second, its claim to the islands creates the legal fiction of Chinese territorial waters, enabling Chinese vessels to navigate the region under this useful cover. Third, possession of a limited number of islands astride the shipping lanes of Southeast Asia may one day provide China with aircraft carrier equivalents, potentially enabling China to prevent Japanese naval domination of the South China Sea, should Tokyo decide to resurrect its aircraft carrier production industry in the context of heightened regional tension. Finally, for domestic political reasons, Chinese leaders are loath to compromise China's position. China has claimed these territories since at least the nineteenth century, and any leader who compromised the Chinese position would encounter extreme opposition, similar to that which any Russian leader would encounter should he return the Kuril Islands to Japan. Having once made the claim, Chinese leaders are now unable easily to withdraw it.[45] Moreover, the political obstacles to compromise are particularly salient now that Chinese leaders are in the midst of the succession to Deng Xiaoping's leadership.

But whatever China's motives, its expansive territorial claim undermines its diplomacy toward the ASEAN states. Further compounding apprehensions of China in East Asia, particularly in Japan and Southeast Asia, is the trend in China's defense spending and military acquisitions. The most ambitious goal of China's power projection development program is the development of strategic power in the coastal waters of the ASEAN states. Just as in other aspects of its East Asia policy, China is motivated by its aspiration to become a regionwide power and by its concern for the combination of Japanese capabilities and the prospect of continued U.S. strategic retrenchment in Asia. Indeed, the Asian region in which U.S. retrenchment will be most apparent is Southeast Asia, where American security interests are relatively minor and its relative economic presence is dwindling.

Nevertheless, however serious and ambitious China's defense program, its power projection capabilities remain primitive. Even with air refueling technology, China will require aircraft carrier capabilities to establish a credible military presence and to support offensive naval and land operations in the southern South China Sea. The U.S. navy, which possesses the world's most reliable military technology and unsurpassed maintenance efficiency, requires three aircraft carriers in order to maintain one aircraft carrier on location at all times. Given China's ongoing inability to keep its far-less sophisticated vessels at sea for even short durations, actual Chinese power projection would seem to require more than three aircraft carriers. And China will not be able to buy such power projection capabilities. Not only will it not find suppliers for the requisite number of vessels (what country would want to facilitate Chinese acquisition of power projection capabilities?), but Beijing would also not be able to afford the combined cost of the carriers, the larger number of required support vessels for the carriers, and the associated technology to protect the vessels and manage the logistics of such a complex operation as deploying a carrier task force. Thus, Chinese power projection capabilities will require indigenous production capabilities. But should China start development of aircraft carrier production in the near future, it would not have the minimum number of three carriers required for rudimentary power projection until after the year 2010. Moreover, it is not even clear whether China could succeed in developing reliable aircraft carrier capability. The technology, management, and training required for aircraft carrier operation is more sophisticated than any other military operation.[46]

China's limited strategic presence and offensive capabilities in maritime Southeast Asia are reflected in the division among the ASEAN states regarding recent developments in Chinese defense policy. Indonesia has expressed the most alarm over Chinese defense and territorial policies, despite the fact that Jakarta does not claim any of the Spratly Islands, whereas Singapore, Thailand, and the Philippines have expressed relatively more sanguine attitudes, despite their greater vulnerability to Chinese power. For the most part, China's emerging post–Cold War relationships with the ASEAN countries reflect traditional regional attitudes toward China rather than the direct implications of Chinese policy for each state's security or its reputed strategic presence in the region.

Whereas during the Cold War Indonesia and Malaysia had raised the alarm over China's reputed ability to manipulate overseas Chinese and subversive communist parties, in the post–Cold War era they have expressed alarm over the security implications of Chinese military and territorial policies. These countries have always opposed China's regional presence and continue to do so by focusing on new issues. Indeed, it is no accident that Malaysia has been able to work out a joint exploration project with Vietnam involving disputed territory in the South China Sea but has been unwilling to do so with China. Kuala Lumpur has traditionally viewed Vietnam as a local counterweight to Chinese power. Similarly, it is revealing that Indonesia, the country farthest from the Chinese mainland and the most powerful of the ASEAN states, has been particularly outspoken about the Chinese threat. Jakarta has always considered China a rival for regional leadership. In contrast, Singapore, Thailand, and the Philippines, despite the latter's territorial conflict with China, tended throughout the 1970s and 1980s to see China in a less threatening light and have expressed only moderate concern over recent developments in Chinese foreign policy. Indeed, Thailand has developed close military ties with China and is the largest purchaser of Chinese weaponry in East Asia, acquiring Chinese missile escort ships, tanks, artillery, and armored personnel carriers.[47] Singapore welcomes China's regional presence as a counterweight to Malaysian and Indonesian power. At times, the Philippines has been far more concerned with Japan's potential military power, albeit less so than the Northeast Asian countries. Finally, all of these countries have a far greater economic stake in relations with Japan than in relations with China, which makes it politically easier for them to express their suspicions of China than of Japan.

Thus, in contrast to Northeast Asia, in maritime Southeast Asia there is much less fear of Japanese power and minimal Chinese economic presence, and, in contrast to both Northeast Asia and Indochina, China has minimal strategic presence. As a result, the ASEAN countries, even those inclined to downplay China's military capabilities, have relatively less interest in developing relations with China, and policy toward China has been derived from local strategic dynamics. Moreover, insofar as the gap between the Chinese and Japanese economic presence in Southeast Asia continues to grow and there is little likelihood that the United States will be able to offset the growth of Japanese economic power and corresponding Japanese political presence, China's limited regional influence must be viewed with concern by the Chinese leadership.[48]

Nonetheless, of all the subregions of East Asia, maritime Southeast Asia is the least important to Chinese security. Geographic distance and separation by water reduce the significance of developments among the ASEAN countries for Chinese interests. Thus, the overall pattern of the relationship between Chinese influence and Chinese interests in East Asia is relatively favorable to regional stability. China faces the most serious strategic challenge in Northeast Asia, where the presence and vital interests of all the great powers are the greatest, but it also has developed the most successful diplomacy in this region. In Indochina, Chinese diplomacy is perhaps the weakest, given traditional Vietnamese animosity for China and China's weak economic role in this area. But its relationships with Cambodia and Laos and its dominant military position on its southern border, which is its most secure border in Asia, go a long way toward satisfying Chinese security objectives. Chinese foreign policy faces the greatest obstacles in maritime Southeast Asia, where it lacks strong economic and military instruments of diplomacy, but this is the region of least importance to Chinese security, so that China may well be able to accommodate itself to a relatively secondary strategic role in the region. Overall, Beijing's diplomacy has created a very favorable environment for the pursuit of Chinese objectives.

The Uncertainties of the Transition

Thus, China's position in East Asia varies with the particular subregional environment. China is best positioned in Northeast Asia and faces the greatest challenge in maritime Southeast Asia. Indeed, current diplomatic and economic trends in the regions that matter most to Chinese security favor Chinese interests, so that Beijing has little incentive to adopt destabilizing policies aimed at revising the regional order. Nonetheless, throughout the region there remains considerable uncertainty over the potential for change in Chinese policy.

In Northeast Asia, the challenge to China is the management of Korean unification and its aftermath. As the state with the most influence in Pyongyang, however limited its influence may be, China has the most responsibility for trying to contain the repercussions for stability on the Korean peninsula of the North Korean succession and the inevitable increased exposure of North Korean society to the situation in neighboring countries. Thus, in the interest of stability in Northeast Asia, China must try to persuade the post–Kim Il Song leadership to begin the process of reform during the current period of stability and thus ease the difficulties of the postsuccession North Korean leadership. Equally important, Beijing has an interest in curtailing Pyongyang's nuclear program, as a nuclear-armed North Korea could further undermine stability on the peninsula and encourage Japan to develop its own nuclear weapon program.

Therefore, Beijing has exposed the numerous North Korean leaders who have visited China to China's modern, open-door cities, thus underscoring both the benefits of reform and the disadvantages of North Korea's ideological isolation and economic backwardness. China's South Korea policy has had a similar impact. Improved relations between Beijing and Seoul have encouraged Pyongyang to accommodate international demands regarding its nuclear program and to start down the path of peaceful unification, thereby easing contemporary peninsular tension. Finally, Beijing has used what little influence it has on North

Korea to try to persuade Pyongyang to comply with the demands of the International Atomic Energy Agency and the United Nations Security Council and to reach agreement with the United States, while simultaneously trying to minimize the prospects for war on its border.[49]

Nonetheless, acknowledgment of China's limited influence on Pyongyang underscores the possibility that the ongoing North Korean succession could lead to a domestic convulsion with international consequences. There is no predicting what an embattled and besieged communist leadership might do to maintain its control over North Korea, including using force against South Korea. Thus, it behooves China to underscore its opposition to such a development and to consider the appropriate response. In particular, the consolidation of Chinese–South Korean ties affords Beijing the opportunity to assure Seoul of its intentions during such a crisis so as to reduce the possibility that China and South Korea would find themselves competing for influence among contending North Korean factions, leading to misperceptions in North Korea and South Korea over the benefits of and/or the necessity for using force.

Uncertainty also surrounds the impact of a unified Korea, regardless of the process of unification, on regional stability and China's policy in Northeast Asia. A united and stronger Korea with a common border with China would transform the strategic environment in Northeast Asia. Indeed, it is hard to imagine a Chinese interest in unification, given the current combination of dominant Chinese influence in Pyongyang and complementary Chinese–South Korean strategic interests. But regardless of Chinese interests, unification may well be inevitable in the aftermath of the succession. Ultimately, a more powerful and independent Seoul, possessing a common border with China, will likely strike a more independent posture in Northeast Asia. This, too, will require Chinese adjustment, in that Beijing will no longer be able to depend as much on South Korean self-interest to promote Korean suspicions of Japan and a corresponding consolidation of Chinese–South Korean relations. Once again, the best means of ensuring a peaceful evolution in Northeast Asia is communication and the development of a stake in stability. Current Chinese policy toward both Koreas and toward Japan is an appropriate mechanism for coping with this uncertainty.

Mainland–Taiwan relations, despite the current positive trend, could also be a source of instability. On the one hand, China certainly has every interest in maintaining the current situation. Its modernization program benefits from Taiwan's economic activities on the mainland, and the trend in both economic relations and intersocietal ties lessens Taiwan's ability to risk conflict with Beijing. Moreover, tension across the Taiwan Strait could well impede China's ability to develop relations with other Asian countries, as an aggressive Taiwan policy would be likely to elicit suspicions of Chinese ambitions throughout Asia. Nonetheless, Beijing has made it clear that it would not tolerate Taiwan's declaring independence from the mainland and that it is prepared to use force against Taiwan under such circumstances. Although the current Taiwan leadership understands the danger of declaring independence and insists that Taiwan is part of China, as Taiwan continues to democratize, the independence issue may become hostage to partisan politics. Under such circumstances, electoral politics may eventually lead Taipei to declare Taiwan independent from the mainland.

Beijing's influence over Taiwan domestic politics is marginal at best. Its current policy combines offering Taiwan the benefits of trade, openness to inter-societal contacts, and reduced cross-strait tension with the threat of force should Taiwan declare itself independent. Although the threat of force may be provocative, its deterrent value should not be ignored. Chinese renunciation of the use of force would considerably reduce the risk to Taiwan of declaring independence and would possibly elicit a declaration of independence and a violent Chinese response. For this reason and because of Chinese domestic politics, Beijing will not change its position until the civil war is formally ended.

Indeed, in addition to its regional aspirations and its concern for the East Asian balance of power and its security position in Indochina, China's defense policy is also influenced by Beijing's concern for the balance of power across the Taiwan Strait. China seeks sufficient military power to dissuade the Taiwan leadership from risking a declaration of independence and to coerce Taiwan to retract such a declaration should deterrence fail. One motivation for the acquisition of Russian Su-27s was concern that given Taiwan's indigenous technology and its access to U.S. weaponry through the 1980s and into the 1990s and the mainland's continued reliance on 1950s Soviet military technology, Beijing's deterrent would progressively erode in the 1990s and encourage the Taiwan independence movement. The development of the Chinese navy has a similar objective. Although aircraft carriers would be superfluous in dealing with Taiwan, as Chinese land-based aircraft would be well within range of all targets in Taiwan, modernization of other vessels, including a new generation of destroyers and submarines, would enhance China's ability to impose a blockade on Taiwan's shipping should Taipei declare independence and, thus, also enhance Chinese deterrence.[50]

But Taiwan's acquisition of 60 French Mirage jets and 150 American F–16s and its production of its Indigenous Defense Fighter (IDF) have rendered China's air and naval deterrent capabilities even less effective than they were before Beijing purchased the Su-27s.[51] Indeed, after the acquisition of the Mirages and the F-16s, Taiwan will have the largest force of fighter planes in Asia. Thus, China is far from satisfied with the current situation in mainland–Taiwan relations and views with alarm the growing authority in Taiwan politics of the Democratic Progressive Party and its frequent advocacy of an independent Taiwan.

The best means of furthering the current trend in mainland–Taiwan relations is for the two sides to negotiate reduced tension. This process is politically sensitive both in Beijing and on Taiwan. Nonetheless, continued trade and societal relations and unofficial negotiations, such as the 1993 Wang–Koo talks, may well provide the confidence necessary for the two sides to discuss political issues and to develop enhanced mutual interest in stable relations. This is inherently an intra-Chinese process that can be solved only by Beijing and Taipei. Nonetheless, the United States has a certain ability to influence the course of negotiations. But whatever the pros and cons of various policy initiatives, including U.S. arms sales to Taiwan, and the level at which diplomacy is conducted, Washington should resolutely refrain from suggesting any preference whatsoever for one solution or another to the Chinese civil war, particularly concerning the merits of an independent Taiwan. Nothing would be more disruptive of mainland–Taiwan relations and of regional stability.

Developments in Southeast Asia will also require Chinese adjustment and tolerance. In Indochina, although China now possesses strategic preeminence, its economic position will quickly and significantly decline. Chinese leaders are sensitive to Hanoi's continued hostility to and distrust of China and its eagerness to extricate itself from Chinese power. Indeed, Vietnam's historical and contemporary resentment of Chinese authority in Indochina and its extreme economic backwardness have encouraged Hanoi to use economic diplomacy to free itself from the constraints of Chinese power and to modernize its own economy. Given China's own severe demand for hard currency and high technology, there is simply little it can offer Vietnam to alter Hanoi's economic and strategic calculus.

Thus, before long Vietnam will have extensive economic relations both with the local powers in Southeast Asia and with Japan. In 1992 and 1993 Japan was Vietnam's largest trading partner whereas China was Vietnam's eighth-largest trade partner in 1993. Continuation of this will inevitably lead to a diminution of Chinese economic influence in Vietnam and, to a lesser extent, throughout Indochina. There is little that Beijing can or should do to obstruct this trend. Vietnamese modernization is a legitimate objective, and China simply lacks the capabilities to play a central role in the modernization process. It must, therefore, reconcile itself to a reduced economic presence in Indochina.

Beijing appears willing to accommodate itself to Vietnamese economic independence. Nonetheless, it is concerned about the prospect of Japan's becoming the dominant economic power in Indochina. It perceives the Japanese eagerness to develop relations with Hanoi and has expressed concern over the implications of a developing Japanese political presence in Indochina. One Chinese analyst warned of Japan's "pronounced interest" in Indochina.[52] The optimum regional response to Chinese fear is to neither deny it nor resist it. Concern for Japanese aspirations is regionwide. Rather, the appropriate response is to promote diversity in Vietnamese economic relations, thus minimizing the prospect of Vietnamese dependence on Japan for economic well-being. The recent trend is encouraging. Singapore is a major trading partner of Vietnam, and Taiwan is the largest investor in Vietnam. The U.S. role in the Vietnamese economy will also begin to develop. Nonetheless, the Japanese role will probably increase. Thus, Washington should do what it can to promote American investment in and trade with Vietnam, thereby helping both the U.S. economy and regional stability.

Given their concern over Japanese intentions, Chinese leaders would welcome such an American policy toward Vietnam. After many years of immobility in Vietnam policy, the Clinton administration has moved in this direction. This trend can only be beneficial for regional stability.

Finally, there remains much uncertainty surrounding China's policy toward maritime Southeast Asia. But whereas in Northeast Asia and Indochina the uncertainty centers on China's response to a potentially changing environment, in Southeast Asia China may well be the agent of change. Unless China's economic role in the region expands beyond its limited relationship with Singapore, the combination of economic weakness and military potential could lead Beijing to emphasize the role of its military to compensate for its inability to compete for regional influence through economic diplomacy. Regardless of China's limited relative military potential, this would create heightened insecurity and tensions throughout the region. Should regional alarm over Chinese military modernization coincide with tension over the Spratly Islands, the potential for conflict would be considerably increased.

Thus far, however, China's policy regarding the Spratly Islands reflects its understanding of the dangers of arousing the hostility of the ASEAN countries. It has not occupied any of the islands claimed by Malaysia or Brunei, thus avoiding increased tension with the most influential ASEAN states. To the extent that China's primary interest in the Spratlys reflects strategic concerns, it may be satisfied with the islands it now occupies. Moreover, in an effort to defuse the issue in Chinese relations with ASEAN, since 1991 Beijing has proposed that all the claimants defer the sovereignty dispute and cooperate on joint exploration of the disputed waters. China's approach seems to be gaining support throughout the region. Thus, the status quo over the Spratlys may well endure, reducing the likelihood of escalated conflict.[53]

Thus, scenarios in which China is a source of instability or exacerbates preexisting regional tendencies toward instability are not difficult to imagine. It is Beijing's unenviable position to be surrounded by potential hot spots involving Chinese interests. In this context, Chinese diplomacy has approached regional conflicts with a multifaceted policy designed to maximize Beijing's ability to manage peacefully the transition to the post–Cold War order while simultaneously preparing for the emergence of counterproductive developments, particularly by developing its military power. Given these cross-cutting trends in Chinese policy and Beijing's view of the potential dangers in the post–Cold War era, tension over any of the myriad sources of potential instability could easily be exacerbated should it coincide with Chinese domestic instability associated with the succession to the leadership of Deng Xiaoping. Chinese policy toward the succession politics in North Korea and Seoul–Pyongyang relations, toward a Taiwan declaration of independence, and even toward territorial disputes in the South China Sea could well be influenced by the temptation of Chinese politicians deeply embroiled in a succession struggle to adopt extreme nationalistic or ideological positions in the pursuit of parochial political interests. Alternatively, possible Chinese domestic policies during the succession, including measures to suppress dissent and democracy demonstrations, might well elicit retaliatory measures from the United States and other Western powers, which would further lessen the interest of succession-minded Chinese leaders in pursuing policies conducive to stability and encourage Chinese efforts to develop unilateral security measures, including even greater efforts to expand its military capability. Furthermore, any of these developments could elicit countervailing policies from other regional powers, contributing to spiraling tension. The Hong Kong issue could also play such a role. In the midst of a succession crisis, should Beijing adopt military measures to suppress a Hong Kong democracy movement, regional suspicions of Chinese ambitions might be exacerbated.

Despite China's current diplomatic successes, and precisely because of the potential for both regional instability and political instability in China, the diplomatic challenge is, for the short term, to reduce the Chinese tendency to assume the worst strategic implications in local conflicts, particularly in Northeast Asia, and, over the long run, to encourage China to reconcile itself to the combination of dominant strategic power in Indochina and secondary influence in maritime Southeast Asia. For these trends to develop, not only must China maintain its diplomatic confidence regarding Northeast Asia and Indochina, but it must also be convinced that Japan will not use its economic presence in Southeast Asia to undermine China's strategic security or significantly expand its offensive military capabilities.

Conclusion: China and Multilateral Diplomacy in East Asia

The key bilateral relationship most likely to affect stability throughout East Asia is the Sino-Japanese relationship. China's pre–World War II experience with Japan predisposes Chinese leaders to see the worst in Japanese policy. Similarly, China's size and rapid economic growth and its periodic Japan bashing predispose Japanese leaders to assume the worst about China. In East Asia, this is the potentially most disruptive relationship. Thus, in addition to ongoing expanded economic and cultural relations, focused communication across the East China Sea about strategic issues is required to mitigate counterproductive influences. A first and encouraging step in this direction was the May 1993 Sino-Japanese agreement to establish a bilateral security dialogue. In January 1995, the two sides held their second discussion at of security issues. These talks provide an opportunity for both sides to raise issues of concern, including Japan's growing political role in Asia and China's growing defense budget, as well as common concerns, such as the North Korean nuclear program. Similarly, in June 1993, Chinese and Japanese officials held the first round of consultations on maritime security in the East China Sea.[54] These dialogues may ultimately encourage greater transparency in both the Chinese and Japanese militaries, helping to reduce mutual suspicions and minimizing the risk of inadvertent conflict. Given the current secrecy and resulting suspicion involving so many aspects of the Chinese military, including the defense budget, this would be a welcome development.[55]

Contemporary Chinese foreign policy permits cautious optimism regarding Beijing's future contribution to regional stability. But if China were to engage in multilateral diplomacy, providing a relatively less rigid and forced agenda than bilateral discussions and encouraging regional communication, additional optimism would be warranted. An appropriate venue for this dialogue would be a four-plus-two meeting concerning the Koreas. The agenda would simultaneously focus on a significant regional issue—stability on the Korean peninsula—and allow for a bilateral Sino-Japanese dialogue without drawing excessive attention to the prospect for Sino-Japanese conflict. Given America's interest in the Korean peninsula and its continued leadership role in Northeast Asia, it is up to Washington to promote such a multilateral dialogue.

In Southeast Asia, a similar dialogue among China and the ASEAN countries already exists. Leaders of China and the Southeast Asian countries pay frequent visits to one another's countries, and China participates in the annual ASEAN Post-Ministerial Conference. Moreover, China participates in the security dialogue in the ASEAN Regional Forum (ARF) with the six ASEAN countries and their seven dialogue partners, including Japan and the United States.[56] All of these forums provide Beijing with an opportunity to discuss its Southeast Asia policy with its ASEAN neighbors in a multilateral setting. What is lacking is an official-level dialogue among the claimants to the Spratly Islands. Nonetheless, it is encouraging that a unofficial dialogue among the claimants has been developing since 1990 under Indonesian auspices and that this dialogue has evolved into a series of meetings of working groups. The first such working group, composed of scientists from all of the claimants, met in May 1993.[57] Given the firm opposition to Chinese claims in the region and China's rigid posture, the current level of dialogue among the claimants to the Spratlys may reflect the maximum possible institutionalization of a dialogue over the disputed islands for the foreseeable future. Nonetheless, a regularly convened official-level dialogue, while not resolving the territorial dispute, would provide a setting for discussions that might alleviate concerns over Chinese ambitions and help to defuse any military tension that might develop.

What remains to be considered is Chinese participation in formal and region-wide institutions and arms control discussions. China is a member of the Asia Pacific Economic Cooperation (APEC) forum. This provides a setting in which China can hold discussions with its neighbors on bilateral or regional economic issues. But APEC is simply too large and its membership too diverse to permit it to serve as an institution for resolving conflicts over economic issues.

Formal multilateral security institutions also have limited ability to persuade the Chinese to participate in arms control. As this is a state's most sensitive security issue, such negotiations can be held only among the parties immediately concerned. Yet China's interest in even bilateral arms control negotiations with the other East Asian powers, with the exception of negotiations with Russia over land forces, is difficult to imagine. Given the technological distance China must cover to catch up with its regional rivals, it lacks both the negotiating leverage necessary to extract significant compromises from its rivals and the motivation to constrain its own program. Moreover, the structural dissimilarities between Chinese forces and those of its neighbors, with the exception of Russia, would make trade-offs exceedingly difficult.

Thus, the remaining promising option is confidence-building measures. Although of limited immediate value, confidence-building measures can weaken proclivities to reach worst-case conclusions about a potential adversary. Thus, they might help reduce China's predilection to believe the worst about Japan's defense program, for example. Furthermore, over time such multilateral efforts may also contribute to greater transparency in the Chinese military and ease suspicions of Chinese intentions throughout East Asia. It is thus in the interest of East Asian countries to encourage the dialogue between the Chinese and Japanese military establishments and the formation of a Northeast Asian security dialogue.

Over time, Chinese participation in such regional dialogues may persuade Chinese policymakers of the regionwide value of multilateral institutions. Although Beijing currently tends to see membership in such institutions merely as necessary to prevent regional isolation and as an opportunity for information collection, prolonged involvement may lead Chinese policymakers to appreciate the role that Beijing can play in simultaneously promoting regional stability through multilateral diplomacy and Chinese national interests throughout Asia. There is little harm in such efforts, while the benefit to the region could be considerable.

China's participation in regional institutions is growing. China also appears to be doing well at managing well its bilateral relationships with its most difficult counterparts, including Japan, North Korea, Taiwan, and the other claimants to the Spratly Islands, given the existing conflicts of interest and China's determination to modernize its defense industry. Thus far, Chinese diplomacy has responded well to the post–Cold War transition in East Asia, and China, per se, does not yet appear to be a destabilizing force. It is welcomed by its neighbors on mainland Northeast Asia, it is a status-quo power in Indochina, and it remains a secondary strategic and economic power in maritime Southeast Asia.

Thus, the most likely source of instability involving China will be Sino-Japanese mistrust and the impact of Chinese intervention in unpredictable and unplanned events, such as developments in North Korea or Taiwan. The regional objective should be to promote China's confidence in its security so that Chinese leaders, even in the middle of a succession crisis, will not be inclined to perceive the worst in Japan's growing authority in Southeast Asia or to consider it necessary to intervene in regional conflicts, thus undermining the security of its neighbors.

The development of U.S. policy toward Asia will be a vital element affecting China's perceptions of its security and its response to changes in its neighbors' policies and to regional instability. The Sino-Japanese relationship may be the most important bilateral relationship for maintaining peace in East Asia, but America's role in the region will be a crucial determinant of the ability of China and Japan to manage the relationship. As two Chinese analysts explained, "Change in U.S. strategy and policy will be a dominant factor influencing great power relations" in Asia.[58] Thus, what Singapore prime minister Goh Chok Tong said for the entire region is especially true for China's relations with its neighbors: "A U.S. that remains engaged in the region will make it easier for China, Japan, Korea, ASEAN and the Indochinese countries to have comfortable relationships with each other."[59] In particular, an engaged United States will help both to minimize Chinese fears of resurgent Japanese militarism and to dissuade China from overreacting to local conflicts and to incremental change in Japanese policy.

Maintaining regional stability will also require continued efforts on the part of all of the great powers to develop cooperative working relationships with one another. China must be part of this process. As Russia and China have gone a long way toward establishing such a relationship and Japan has avoided the pitfalls of extended post–Beijing massacre recriminations and has opened a bilateral security dialogue with Beijing, Washington remains conspicuous in its inability to establish a regular security dialogue with China. Given its central role in shaping Chinese security concerns, the United States should waste no time in, at a minimum, establishing a regular, high-level security dialogue with the Chinese leadership, including the military leadership. In conjunction with the Sino-Japanese dialogue and Chinese participation in multilateral institutions, a U.S.–China dialogue would further engage China in regional affairs and expand the region's understanding of Chinese decision making and defense planning. It is in the interest of all the East Asian countries that such a dialogue develop, and they have all encouraged the United States to avoid harming U.S.–China relations. Reflecting the view of his ASEAN colleagues and most of East Asia, the Malaysian prime minister explained that "As a potential economic and political power [China] has to be reckoned with. It would be in the interest of the Asia-Pacific countries to ensure that China becomes constructively engaged in regional affairs."[60] All of East Asia would benefit if Washington were to heed his advice in making China policy.

Notes

1. *Xinhua,* July 4, 1990, in *Foreign Broadcast Information Service, Daily Report: China* (hereafter cited as *FBIS/China*), July 6, 1992, pp. 5–6.

2. *Xinhua,* October 20, 1992, in *FBIS/China,* October 21, 1992, p. 16.

3. Wang Shu, "Study Thoroughly the Global Competition for Economic Power—Grasp the Foundation of Changes in the International Situation," *Liaowang,* March 16, 1992, in *FBIS/China,* April 9, 1992, pp. 3–4.

4. Ren Zhengde, "Turbulent International Situation—Multipolar, Changeable, Eventful," *Liaowang,* August 3, 1992, in *FBIS/China,* August 25, 1992, pp. 1–5.

5. Tang Tianri, "The Post-Bipolarization Year of Tremendous Change," *Ban Yue Tan*, no. 24 (December 25, 1992), in *FBIS/China*, February 10, 1993, p. 7.

6. Wan Guang, "Evolution of the Postwar Asia-Pacific Pattern and Its Prospects in the 1990s," *Liaowang* (overseas edition), no. 33 (August 13, 1990), in *FBIS/China*, 5 August 24, 1990, pp. 2–3; Lin Xiao, "Shake Off the Influence of the Cold War—ASEAN Members Adjust Their Foreign Policies," *Shijie Zhishi*, no. 21 (November 1, 1989), in *Joint Publications Research Service, China Report* (hereafter cited as *JPRS/China*), February 15, 1989, pp. 4–5; Tao Bingwei, "On the Asia-Pacific Situation in the 1990s," *Guoji Wenti Yanjiu*, no. 1 (January 1990), in *FBIS/China*, May 14, 1990, p. 16. Also see, for example, Tian Zhongqing, "The Pattern of International Relationships in the Asia Pacific Region in the 1990s," *Guoji Zhanwang*, no. 3 (February 8, 1990), in *JPRS/CAR*, May 29, 1990, pp. 6–9. For an in-depth analysis of this problem, see Allen S. Whiting, *China Eyes Japan* (Berkeley, CA: University of California Press, 1989).

7. Sun Zhenhai and Gao Hong, "1993 nian Riben Xingshi Wenti yu Jinhou Zhanwang (Problems in Japan's Situation in 1993 and Prospects for the Future), *Riben Wenti Ciliao* (Materials on Japanese Studies), no. 1, 1994; *Xinhua*, January 3, 1992, in *FBIS/China*, January 3, 1992, pp. 18–19; Tang Tianri, "Why Did Japan Pass 'Bill on Dispatching Troops Abroad'?" *Fazhi Ribao*, June 11, 1992, in *FBIS/China*, July 1, 1992, pp. 7–8; *Kyodo*, May 29, 1993, in *FBIS/China*, June 1, 1993, pp. 3–4. It is important to note that China's reaction to recent Japanese developments is, to a greater or lesser degree, shared by various countries throughout the region. See *Far Eastern Economic Review* (hereafter cited as *FEER*), June 25, 1992. For a recent statement on the UN, see *Xinhua*, July 2, 1993, in *FBIS/China*, July 2, 1993, p. 1.

8. *Xinhua*, January 18 1993, in *FBIS/China*, January 19, 1993, pp. 13–14; *Xinhua*, January 19, 1993, in *FBIS/China*, January 22, 1993, pp. 11–12.

9. For an extended discussion of these issues in U.S.–China relations, see Robert S. Ross, "The United States and China in the 1990s: Facing the Issues," in Gerrit Gong and Lin Bi-Jaw, eds., *Sino-American Relations in a Time of Change* (Washington, D.C.: Center for Strategic and International Studies, 1994).

10. For Chinese analysis of the importance of technology during the Gulf War, see, for example, *Haiwan Zhanzheng* [Gulf War] (Beijing: Military Science Press, 1991); *Haiwan Zhanzheng Xinzhan Moulue* [New military strategy of the Gulf War] (Beijing: National Defense University Press, 1992); *Gao Jishu Zhanzheng* [High-technology war] (Beijing: National Defense University Press, 1993). Also see the reports of the Chinese military intelligence investigation in *Cheng Ming*, March 1, 1991, in *FBIS/China*, March 5, 1991, p. 5, and the report of the National Defense University study in *Tangdai*, March 9, 1991, *FBIS/China*, March 14, 1991, p. 31. The military newspaper, *Jiefang Junbao*, also made an extensive analysis of the importance of high technology in the war. *Jiefang Junbao*, April 19, April 26, May 3, and May 10, 1991, in *FBIS/China*, May 29, 1991, pp. 47–54. In the year following the Gulf War, Beijing initiated a nationwide campaign stressing the importance of using advanced technology in both military and civilian production. See, for example, *Xinhua*, May 23, 1991, in *FBIS/China*, May 24, 1991, pp. 22–23; *FBIS, Trends*, May 30, 1991, pp. 42–46; Commentator, "Enterprises Should Heighten Their Sense of Urgency in Applying High and New Technology," *Xinhua*, May 18, 1991, in *FBIS/China*, May 23, 1991, pp. 47–48; Beijing International Service, April 16, 1991, in *FBIS/China*, April 19, 1991, pp. 26–27. On the development of the campaign, see, for example, *Renmin Ribao*, June 14, 1991, in *FBIS/China*, June 28, 1991, p. 39; *Xinhua*, June 10, 1991, in *FBIS/China*, June 13, 1991, pp. 26–27.

11. For the CIA analysis, see James Harris et al., "Interpreting Trends in Chinese Defense Spending," in Joint Economic Committee, Congress of the United States, *China's Economic Dilemmas in the 1990s: The Problems of Reforms, Modernization, and*

Interdependence (Armonk, NY: M. E. Sharpe, 1992), pp. 676–77.

12. For a comprehensive discussion of Japan's military capability, see Norman D. Levin, Mark Lorel, and Arthur Alexander, *The Wary Warriors: Future Directions in Japanese Security Policies* (Santa Monica, CA: Rand, 1993); Michael W. Chinworth, *Inside Japan's Defense: Technology, Economics, and Strategy* (Washington, DC: Brassey's, 1992).

13. For a discussion of ongoing Japanese plans to stockpile plutonium, see *FEER*, March 3, 1994, p. 13. Also see the acknowledgement of Japanese nuclear capability by Japan's Prime Minister Tsutomu Hata in *New York Times*, June 22, 1994.

14. For a careful analysis of current Chinese defense spending, see Paul H.B. Godwin, "'PLA Incorporated': Estimated Chinese Military Expeditures," paper prepared for the IISS/CAPS conference on "China's Economic Reform: The Impact on Security Policy," July 8–10, 1994, Hong Kong.

15. See *Kyodo*, March 21, 1991, in *FBIS/China*, March 21, 1991, p. 1.

16. For a full discussion of the Chinese and Russian sources of the economic problems in 1994, see, for example, Hou Baoquan, "Zhong E Bianjing Maoyi de Xin Wenti he Xin Quxiang" (The New Problems and the New Trend in Sino-Russian Border Trade), *Dongou Zhongya Yaniju* (East European and Central Asian Studies), no. 3, 1994; Xiong Xiaoqui, "Zhong E Maoyi Jiangwen Touxi" (A Full analysis of the Cooling Down of Sino-Russian Trade), *Dongou Zhongya Yaniju*, no. 5, 1994. For 1993 trade statistics, see International Monetary Fund, *Direction of Trade Statistics Yearbook, 1994* (Washington, D.C.: International Monetary Fund, 1994).

17. *Xinhua*, July 13, 1994, in *FBIS/China*, July 13, 1994, p. 7.

18. *Xinhua*, December 1, 1993, in *FBIS/China*, December 6, 1993, p. 6.

19. For Chinese analyses of the ongoing difficulties in Russo-Japanese relations, see Xiao Bin, "Yeliqin Fang Ri yu Ri E Guanxi" (Yeltsin Visits Japan and Japanese-Russian Relations), *Riben Wenti Ciliao*, no. 2, 1994; Gao Ke, "Ri E Guanxi de 'Lingtuhua' de Wenti (The Issue of "Territorialization" in Japanese-Russian Relations), *Dongou Zhongya Wenti*, no. 5, 1994.

20. *Xinhua*, February 22, 1993, in *FBIS/China*, February 24, 1993, pp. 11–12; *Zhongguo Tongxun She*, March 25, 1994, in *FBIS/China*, March 30, 1994, p. 14; *Renmin Ribao*, March 26, 1994, in *FBIS/China*, March 29, 1994, pp. 13–14; *Xinhua*, July 27, 1994, in *FBIS/China*, July 28, 1994, p. 7; *FEER*, July 28, 1994; International Monetary Fund, *Direction of Trade Statistics Yearbook, 1994*.

21. *China News Analysis*, March 5, 1994, in *FBIS/China*, March 8, 1994, p. 67; Beijing Central People's Radio, August 9, 1992, in *FBIS/China*, August 12, 1992, p. 64; *Xinhua*, July 15, 1992, in *FBIS/China*, July 21, 1992, pp. 62–63; *China News Analysis*, March 19, 1993, in *FBIS/China*, March 19, 1993, p. 76; *China Daily*, April 3, 1993, in *FBIS/China*, April 5, 1993, p. 54.

22. *Liaowang*, June 1, 1992, in *FBIS/China*, June 12, 1992, pp. 9–10; *FEER*, July 23, 1992, p. 53; *FEER*, September 17, 1992, p. 79; *Xinhua*, February 22, 1993, in *FBIS/China*, February 24, 1993, pp. 11–12; *Renmin Ribao*, March 26, 1994, in *FBIS/China*, March 29, 1994, pp. 13–14; *China Daily*, March 28, 1994, in *FBIS/China*, March 28, 1994, p. 15; *Xinhua*, June 6, 1994, in *FBIS/China*, June 7, 1994, pp. 7–8; *FEER*, April 21, 1994.

23. *China New Analysis* (Taipei), February 9, 1994, in *FBIS/China*, February 9, 1994, p. 68; *Xinhua*, July 15, 1992, in *FBIS/China*, July 21, 1992, pp. 62–63; *China News Analysis*, April 1, 1993, in *FBIS/China*, April 1, 1993, p. 64; *China Daily*, April 3, 1991, in *FBIS/China*, April 5, 1993, p. 54; *FEER*, July 28, 1994. Some estimates place the amount of investment as high as 30 billion dollars. *Zhongguo Tongxun She*, January 31, 1994, in *FBIS/China*, February 1, 1994, p. 69.

24. *China News Analysis* (Taipei), July 14, 1994, in *FBIS/China,* July 15, 1994, pp. 41–42; *China News Analysis* (Taipei), January 15, 1994, in *FBIS/China,* January 18, 1994, pp. 37–38; *China News Analysis* (Taipei), March 9, 1994, in *FBIS/China,* March 9, 1994, pp. 69–70. For the Taiwan authorities' own extended assessment of Taiwan's growing dependence on the mainland, see Kao Koong-Lian, *Trade and Investment across the Taiwan Straits: Maintaining Competitive Advantage, Pursuing Complimentarity* (Taipei: Mainland Affairs Council, Executive Yuan, 1993).

25. See the discussion in *New York Times,* August 25, 1992; *FEER,* October 8, 1992, pp. 10–11.

26. *FEER,* August 18, 1994; *New York Times,* August 9, 1994; *International Herald Tribune,* January 14–15, 1995.

27. The exception to this pattern is the impact of Chinese military modernization on the mainland–Taiwan balance of power. This is discussed below.

28. *Xinhua,* March 9, 1993, in *FBIS/China,* March 10, 1993, p. 6; *FEER,* September 9, 1993, pp. 46–49; International Monetary Fund, *Direction of Trade Statistics Yearbook, 1994 .*

29. *Renmin Ribao,* September 9, 1992, in *FBIS/China,* September 24, 1992, p. 12.

30. Shuichi Ono, *Sino-Japanese Economic Relationships: Trade, Direct Investment, and Future Strategy,* World Bank Discussion Papers, no. 146 (Washington, DC: The World Bank, 1992), p. 17.

31. Editorial Committee of the Chinese Foreign Economic and Trade Yearbook, *Zhongguo Duiwai Jingji Maoyi Nianjian* (Chinese Foreign Economic and Trade Yearbook) (Beijing: Zhongguo Shehui Chubanshe, 1994), pp. 707–709; *FEER,* September 9, 1993, pp. 46–47; *China Daily (Business Weekly),* July 11–17, 1993, in *FBIS/China,* July 12, 1993, pp. 19–20.

32. Also see the critical commentary, "A Step Forward," in *Renmin Ribao,* January 12, 1989, in *FBIS/China,* January 12, 1989, p. 9.

33. *Zhongguo Xinwenshe,* August 4, 1992, in *FBIS/China,* August 10, 1992, p. 11; *Xinhua,* August 6, 1992, in *FBIS/China,* August 7, 1992, p. 4; International Monetary Fund, *Direction of Trade Statistics Yearbook, 1994.*

34. *Xinhua,* August 25, 1990, in *FBIS/China,* August 27, 1990, p. 8; *Xinhua,* August 1, 1990, in *FBIS/China,* August 2, 1990, pp. 4–5.

35. *Xinhua,* April 8, 1992, in *FBIS/China,* April 9, 1992, p. 15.

36. See the coverage in *Xinhua,* July 12, 1992, in *FBIS/China,* July 13, 1992, pp. 13–14.

37. See, for example, China Radio International in Cambodian, June 5, 1993, in *FBIS/China,* June 7, 1993, p. 14; China Radio International in Cambodian, June 11, 1993, in *FBIS/China,* June 14, 1993, p. 20; China Radio International in Cambodian, June 10, 1993, in *FBIS/China,* June 11, 1993, pp. 5–6.

38. For recent Chinese criticism of Vietnamese efforts to exploit these waters, see *Xinhua,* June 16, 1994, in *FBIS/China,* June 16, 1994, p. 2; *Agence France Presse,* July 19, 1994, in *FBIS/China,* July 19, 1994, p. 8. Thus far, Vietnam has not been able to persuade foreign firms to drill in this area.

39. On China's development of the islands, see, for example, *Renmin Ribao* (overseas edition), January 9, 1991, in *FBIS/China,* January 16, 1991, p. 46; *Zhongguo Tongxun She,* January 10, 1991, in *FBIS/China,* January 10, 1991, pp. 36–37. On Chinese economic activities in the disputed waters, see *FEER,* July 9, 1992; *FEER,* September 24, 1992.

40. For a recent discussion of this issue, see Fred Herschede, "Trade between China and ASEAN: The Impact of the Pacific Rim Era," in *Pacific Affairs,* vol. 64, no. 2 (Summer 1991).

41. International Monetary Fund, *Direction of Trade Statistics Yearbook, 1994.*

42. Editorial Committee of the Chinese Foreign Economic and Trade Yearbook,

Zhongguo Duiwai Jingji Maoyi Nianjian, pp. 707–709. Official figures for Singapore investment in China fails to capture the significant Singapore investment that goes to China through Hong Kong firms. Nevertheless, these figures provide a rough indicator of the overall Singapore involvement in the Chinese economy.

43. For an alternative view of China's economic role in Southeast Asia, see Nicholas Lardy, "China's Growing Economic Role in Asia," in *The Future of China, NBR Analysis*, vol. 3, no. 3 (1992).

44. For a discussion of Chinese drilling priorities, see *FEER*, February 11, 1993.

45. For documentation of nineteenth- and early twentieth-century Chinese claims and European recognition of those claims, see *Woguo Nanhai Zhudao Shiliao Huibian* [Compilation of Historical Documents on China's South Sea Islands] (*neibu faxing*), (Beijing: Dongfang Chubanshe, 1988).

46. For the CIA analysis of Chinese naval capabilities, see Robert Skebo, Gregory K.S. Man, and George Stevens, "Chinese Military Capabilities: Problems and Prospects," in Joint Economic Committee, *China's Economic Dilemmas in the 1990s*, pp. 671–73. Cf. John Garver, "China's Push through the South China Sea: The Interaction of Bureaucratic and National Interests," *The China Quarterly*, no. 132 (December 1992).

47. *Xinhua*, July 24, 1994, in *FBIS/China*, July 27, 1994, p. 10; *Wen Hui Bao* (Hong Kong), in *FBIS/China*, July 6, 1990, p. 14; *Zhong Hua Ribao* (Bangkok), in *FBIS/China*, December 13, 1990, p. 19; *FEER*, December 8, 1988.

48. On the trends in Japanese trade and investment within East Asia, see *FEER*, June 9, 1994.

49. Prior to the death of Kim Il Song, Beijing signaled Pyongyang that should North Korea fail to accommodate IAEA demands, it was prepared to allow United Nations Security Council sanctions against North Korea and might comply with the sanctions. See *Ta Kung Pao* (Hong Kong), June 3, 1994, in *FBIS/China*, June 6, 1994, pp. 9–10; *AFP*, June 2, 1994, in *FBIS/China*, June 3, 1994, p. 1.

50. For a report on the destroyer, see *Xinhua*, January 30, 1993, in *FBIS/China*, February 1, 1993, p. 29.

51. On Taiwan's plans for the IDF, see China Broadcasting Corporation News Network (Taiwan), February 10, 1993, in *FBIS/China*, February 12, 1993, p. 62; China News Agency (Taiwan), March 19, 1993, in *FBIS/China*, March 19, 1993, p. 77.

52. Tian, "The Pattern of International Relationships in the Asia Pacific Region in the 1990s"; *Xinhua*, July 31, 1991, in *FBIS/China*, August 1, 1992, pp. 18–19. For Vietnam's reaction to China's policies toward the disputed offshore islands, see *FEER*, July 16, 1992.

53. For a discussion of the various claims, see Robert Sutter, *East Asia: Disputed Islands and Offshore Claims—Issues for U.S. Policy*, CRS Report to Congress (Washington DC: Congressional Research Service, Library of Congress, July 28, 1992). On the tentative emergence of a consensus in 1994, see *FEER*, August 11, 1994; *FEER*, June 30, 1994. For an extended Chinese analysis of the dispute and the potential for joint exploration of resources, see Ji Guoxing, *The Spratlys Disputes and Prospects for Settlement* (Kuala Lumpur: Institute of Strategic and International Studies, 1992).

54. *Renmin Ribao*, January 15, 1955; *Xinhua*, July 3, 1993, in *FBIS/China*, July 6, 1993, p. 9.

55. *Kyodo*, May 29, 1993, in *FBIS/East Asia*, June 1, 1993, p. 3; *New York Times*, May 30, 1993.

56. See the report of the visit to Beijing by Malaysian prime minister Mahathir in *Voice of Malaysia*, June 16, 1993, in *FBIS/China*, June 16, 1993, p. 10. Also see *FEER*, April 29, 1993, p. 26; *FEER*, June 3, 1993, p. 18. The regular ASEAN dialogue partners are the United States, Japan, Canada, the European Community, Australia, New Zealand, and South Korea.

57. *Xinhua,* May 31, 1993, in *FBIS/China,* June 2, 1993, pp. 2–3. Also see Frank Ching, "Scientific Meetings Being Held to Reduce Spratlys Tension," *FEER,* May 27, 1993, p. 30.

58. Yan Yang and Chu Dao, "Ya Tai Diqu Anquan Wenti ji Gefang de Jiben Taidu" [Strategic issues in the Asia-Pacific region and the basic attitudes of various sides], *Xiandai Guoji Guanxi,* no. 7 (1994), p. 3.

59. *International Herald Tribune,* July 6, 1993.

60. *FEER,* June 24, 1993, p. 13. The one obvious exception to this belief would be Vietnam.

5

Japan as an Asia-Pacific Power

Mike M. Mochizuki

In recent years, the most striking shift in Japanese foreign policy has been the growing emphasis on the Asia-Pacific region. In December 1992, an advisory council appointed by then Prime Minister Miyazawa Kiichi outlined a framework for Japan's regional policy regarding security dialogues, economic cooperation, and the promotion of mutual understanding.[1] A month later, Miyazawa toured Southeast Asia to strengthen relations with the states in the Association of Southeast Asian Nations (ASEAN). He called for a long-term vision for peace and security in the region and proposed a "Forum for the Comprehensive Development of Indochina."[2] On another front, Ozawa Ichiro, who played a critical role in provoking Miyazawa's fall from power in summer 1993 by leading a faction out of the ruling Liberal Democratic Party, has argued that "Japan must clarify its diplomatic stance of emphasizing the Asia-Pacific region." In his best-selling book, *Nihon Kaizo Keikaku*, he called for a special policy coordination relationship with countries in the Asia-Pacific region by establishing a permanent "Asia-Pacific Cabinet-Level Council."[3] Soon after becoming prime minister, Hosokawa Morihiro explicitly engaged the issue of Japan's responsibility for the Pacific war and apologized for his country's malicious behavior during thirty-five years of colonial rule over Korea. Prime Minister Murayama Tomiichi, the first Social Democratic prime minister since 1947, followed up on this theme during his state visits to South Korea and Southeast Asia in the summer of 1994 by expressing remorse about Japan's imperialist past as well as bearing economic benefits. Both diplomatic initiatives represent an effort to liberate Japanese policy towards East Asia from the shackles of its historic past and establish the political foundations for a more prominent regional role.

These developments are indicative of the growing Japanese interest in the Asia-Pacific dimension of its foreign policy. After the end of World War II, advocates of Asianism usually belonged to either the political right or the political left. Rightists invoked Asianism as an expression of nostalgia for Japan as a great power. Leftists promoted Asianism as an expression of guilt about military expansionism and of resentment toward the United States for its betrayal of postwar democratization. The political and intellectual mainstream, however, tended to downplay or even reject Japan's Asian identity in favor of an affinity with the West—especially the United States.[4] Therefore, what is striking about both Miyazawa's Asia-Pacific study group and Ozawa's call for an Asia-Pacific policy is that they both come out of Japan's mainstream and not from the extremes.

Reasons for this rise of what some have called a "new Asianism" are not difficult to identify.[5] One is the problematic future of U.S.–Japan relations. With the end of the Cold War and the collapse of the Soviet Union, the basic geopolitical foundation of this bilateral alliance has disappeared. Japan's chronically huge trade surplus with the United States and the intense competition between the two countries in high-technology fields are likely to provoke increasingly tough responses from the United States. Although East Asia still cannot substitute for the United States in terms of economic and strategic importance, it does serve as a hedge against a worsening of U.S.–Japan relations. A strategy to embed the bilateral relationship in the context of an Asia-Pacific community might increase Japan's degrees of freedom with respect to the United States and give Japan some leverage in reducing America's degrees of freedom—that is, reducing America's capacity to act unilaterally against Japanese interests.

Second, the end of the Cold War has also begun to shift some of the long-standing fault lines in East Asian international relations. Seoul has adroitly normalized relations with both Moscow and Beijing. Relations between Russia and China, which many analysts had believed to be permanently antagonistic for geopolitical, cultural, and historical reasons, have improved remarkably—even to the point of security cooperation. And Hanoi is now actively reaching out to other Asian capitals as well as Tokyo and Washington in its quest for greater economic integration with the region. This diplomatic fluidity is finally pushing Japan to emerge from its foreign policy conservatism and consider greater activism in East Asian affairs.

Third, economic trends are steering Japan to look more carefully at Asia. The creation of a unified European market and the signing of the North American Free Trade Agreement (NAFTA) have prompted Japanese officials to promote economic cooperation in the Asia-Pacific region more vigorously in order to discourage European and American exclusionary policies. Although Japan invested vigorously in the United States during the 1980s to overcome U.S. protectionism, such investments have become less attractive to Japanese businesses. Lower labor costs make the East Asian economies more profitable for Japanese direct investments than the United States, Canada, and Western Europe. Moreover, with their rapid growth rates, the nations of East Asia are now the most promising partners for further Japanese economic expansion.

Fourth, with the end of the Cold War, the regional security environment has become more uncertain and possibly more threatening. The possible nuclearization of North Korea poses an acute military threat to Japan, and the prospect of a chaotic and even violent Korean reunification process provokes anxiety among

Japanese policymakers. In the longer term, the growth of Chinese power and the emergence of a reunited Korea will present Japan with formidable diplomatic and even security challenges, especially if the United States reduces its military presence in the region. Moreover, given the distrust that still exists among countries in the region, economic success is likely to result in the expansion of military budgets and the technological modernization of military forces. All of these trends are compelling Japan to search for new regional security architectures.

Finally, a focus on East Asia fits nicely with Japan's own international orientation and the predilections of its bureaucratic institutions and political elites. Since their perspectives on foreign affairs tend to be less ideological and more limited in geographic scope than those of their American counterparts, Japanese leaders will naturally give greater weight to developments in East Asia than to those in distant regions. After the disastrous failure of its first attempt to create an East Asian co-prosperity sphere, Japan tended to soft-pedal the East Asian dimension of its foreign policy and to stress its ties with the United States. But with the passage of nearly five decades since the end of the Pacific War, Japanese are now less reluctant to talk openly about their cultural affinity with other East Asians. Although suspicions about Japanese power remain, Japan's economic miracle is inspiring the other East Asian countries to model their own success stories on Japan's example. Emulation by its neighbors on the economic front is giving Japan a greater sense of self-confidence about its ability to provide regional leadership.

In pursuing a more activist regional policy, Japan is not downgrading its relations with the United States. The bilateral alliance with the United States remains central in Tokyo's post–cold war calculations. But Japan is gradually recalibrating the various dimensions of its foreign policy within a framework of comprehensive security. A greater focus on East Asia should make its diplomacy more balanced and less hamstrung by the United States. Not surprisingly, Japan's growing influence in the region is most prominent in the economic realm. But even in the political-military arena, Japan is readjusting its previous policies in order to cultivate a more benign strategic environment.

The Economic Dimension

Japanese economists have tended to project an optimistic view of East Asia's economic development. They often invoke the metaphor of flying geese in V formation, with each nation developing in harmony with others. National economies would be enlisted into a regional system according to their ability to produce high-value-added products in a multilayered chase process. Each tier of nations would engage in trade patterns appropriate to its position in the international division of labor. The advanced countries would aid the industrialization of the developing countries by providing capital and technology. The appealing feature of this vision is that all of the nations in the region would be economically dynamic, advancing technologically in an orderly fashion.

This flying-geese model of regional development has its origins in the pre–World War II ideas of Akamatsu Kaname, who anticipated many of the notions of contemporary product-cycle theory.[6] In the postwar period, former Foreign Minister Okita Saburo has been one of the most vocal advocates of this vision in Japanese government circles. More recently, Watanabe Toshio, an economist at the Tokyo Institute of Technology and a member of Prime Minister Miyazawa's discussion group on the Asia-Pacific region, has written numerous works refining Akamatsu's original conceptualization and analyzing contemporary economic developments in the region. He has argued that over time, the relationship among national economies will become less hierarchical as the late developers take advantage of technology transfers from the more advanced countries to narrow the gap in their ability to produce higher-value-added products. The regionwide division of labor will thus become less vertical as a result of what Watanabe calls "a chain-like succession of structural change" (*kōzō tenkan no rensa-teki keiki*).[7] This dynamic will minimize economic exploitation of the less-developed countries by the more advanced ones. Eventually, economic integration in the Asia-Pacific region will come to resemble the more horizontal pattern of the European Community. Such an evolution of the regional economic system would not only serve Japan's economic interests, but also help to mitigate the geopolitical competition among countries in the region. Greater economic interdependence would reduce the incentives for states to threaten to use force to resolve international disputes. And interstate relations would be viewed in more positive-sum, rather than zero-sum, terms.

In concrete terms, the above conception of harmonious regional development distinguishes three sets of economies that can be ordered according to their levels of economic modernization: (1) the East Asian newly industrializing economies or NIEs (South Korea, Taiwan, Hong Kong, and Singapore); (2) the ASEAN (Association of Southeast Asian Nations) Four (Indonesia, Malaysia, the Philippines and Thailand); and (3) the reformist communist states of China and Vietnam. As the most advanced economy in the region, Japan must perform at least three critical functions for this vision to work. First, it must make its capital available to the less-developed economies so that they can improve their industrial capabilities. Second, it must transfer its technology so that the follower economies can manufacture higher value-added products. Third, while providing intermediate goods, Japan must absorb a sufficient amount of output from the developing economies while they are still engaged in export-led growth and their domestic demand is limited. To what extent is Japan fulfilling these functions?

Promoting Regional Economic Development

Regarding the first role, that of capital supplier, Japan is the largest source of foreign capital for the Asian economies. In 1992, Japanese capital flow to developing countries in Asia was over $10.2 billion, or about 38.6 percent of the total amount going to this region. The United States was second with about $5.28 billion or 19.9 percent of the total.[8] In terms of Official Development Assistance (ODA), Asia continues to be the largest recipient of Japanese aid. In 1993, the amount of ODA disbursements to Asia was $4.86 billion, or 59.5 percent of the total aid program. Japan's aid to Asian countries is now more than two-and-a-half times that of the United States. Of the ASEAN countries, Indonesia, the Philippines and Thailand have consistently been among the top eight recipients of Japanese economic assistance, and Malaysia has also frequently ranked in the top ten. In recent years, Japan's aid programs have focused increasingly on supporting the development efforts of reformist communist states in East Asia: China and Vietnam. One year after the June 1989 Tiananmen crackdown, Japan was the first advanced industrial country to resume its aid to China. In 1991, China became Japan's largest ODA recipient after Indonesia. In December 1994, Tokyo announced a three-year (1996–98) aid package that will give China an average of ¥190 billion in assistance per year.[9] This initiative will make China the top ranking country for Japanese aid. After the conclusion of the Cambodian peace agreement in October 1991, Japan urged Vietnam to cooperate with the United States regarding information relevant to American serviceman missing-in-action.[10] When U.S.-Vietnamese relations subsequently improved (albeit still short of full normalization) in November 1992, Tokyo quickly ended its freeze on official assistance to Vietnam and extended a commodity loan of about ¥45.5 billion ($365 million) to help pay for imports.

There has also been a change in the nature of Japan's assistance programs to East Asia. Whereas before the primary objective was to promote access to raw materials, Japanese aid programs are now emphasizing the cultivation of export-oriented manufacturing industries through the promotion of joint ventures and technical training as well as infrastructure development. As part of this shift in thinking, Japan announced in August 1986 the New Asian Industries Development Plan (or New AID Plan) for the ASEAN countries which mandated the coordination of private investment, trade, and ODA so that they would become "three sides of one body" (*sanmi-ittai*). In December 1987, the government announced a $2 billion loan package as part of this initiative.[11]

The Asian Development Bank (ADB) also serves as a conduit for supplying Japanese capital to East Asia. In 1991, ADB's loans totaled $4.89 billion. Japan and the United States are the largest shareholders in this regional development bank with 16.3 percent each. Japan, however, provides 37 percent of the ADB's soft loans, compared to only 17 percent for the United States. To pay for its operations, the bank has tapped heavily into Japanese yen bond markets. The yen is the ADB's principal borrowing currency and accounts for nearly 40 percent of its gross and outstanding borrowings. Having succeeded in economic development, the East Asian NIEs are no longer borrowers from the bank. Even Thailand has repaid its ADB loans without borrowing more. Consequently, the major borrowers from the ADB among the ASEAN Four are now Indonesia, the Philippines, and Malaysia.[12]

Commercial lending is another way in which Japan provides capital. Currently, Japan's commercial banks lend about $6 billion per year to the rest of Asia, which amounts to roughly 20 percent of their total foreign loans. The total outstanding loans in the region come to about $51 billion, or 10 percent of Japanese banks' global exposure. Bank of Japan officials have stated that a larger portion of new commercial lending is likely to go to Asia to the United States and Europe. A major reason for this is the fact that given the region's higher growth rates, return on assets tend to be higher and loan defaults lower.[13]

The most dramatic change in Japanese capital flows to East Asia has taken place in foreign direct investments (FDI). The steep appreciation of the yen after the 1985 Plaza Accord compelled Japanese corporations to move a large part of their lower-value-added, labor-intensive production overseas, especially to the East Asian economies. Japan's annual FDI in the East Asian NIEs soared from $718 million in 1985 to a peak of $4.9 billion in 1989. Despite some decline since then, Japanese FDI in these economies totaled $2.4 billion in 1993. These investments increasingly reflect an interest in developing parts supplier networks rather than merely building assembly plants. Direct investments to the other ASEAN states have also increased comparably. Japan's annual FDI in the ASEAN Four expanded from $596 million in 1985 to a peak of $3.24 billion in 1990. The increase was sharpest for Thailand (from $48 million in 1985 to $1.28 billion in 1989) and for Malaysia (from $408 million in 1985 to $880 million in 1991). According to the U.S.-ASEAN Council, while U.S. investments were dominant in Southeast Asia in 1970, Japan's investment position in the region had become approximately twice that of the United States by 1990. In 1990, new Japanese direct investments in the ASEAN states exceeded those of the United States by a four-to-one margin.[14] In recent years, Japanese investments indicate a booming interest in China. With the traditional reluctance of Japanese firms to invest in China having all but disappeared, FDI in China shot up from about $579 million in 1991 to over $1.69 billion in 1993. Japanese investment activity in Vietnam is also beginning to pick up.

In terms of the regional distribution of FDI, the Japanese emphasis in East Asia does not seem to be so striking at first. As Figure 5.1 shows, despite the relative increase of direct investments in East Asia, the United States and Europe are still the largest investment targets. But the trend for outward investments in manufacturing is more dramatic. In 1985, 52.0 percent of Japan's foreign manufacturing investments went to North America and 13.7 percent to Europe. Only 19.6 percent of such investments went to Asia. But in 1993, while the proportion of Japan's manufacturing FDI to North America dropped to 37.2 percent and the percentage to Europe was 18.3, the proportion of manufacturing investments to East Asia rose to 32.2 percent. In the near future, East Asia is likely to surpass North America as the foremost geographic target for FDI in manufacturing.[15] Japanese firms have found investments in Asia to be much more profitable than those in the United States. Whereas only 20 percent of the direct investments in

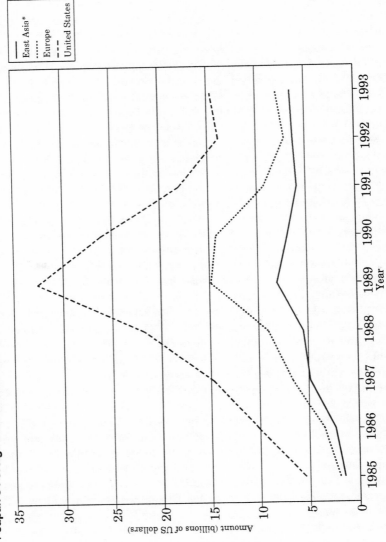

Figure 5.1 **Japan's Foreign Direct Investment**

Source: Japanese Ministry of Finance.
*East Asia includes China, Hong Kong, Indonesia, Malaysia, Philippines, Singapore, South Korea, Taiwan, and Thailand.

America showed a profit within two years, 80 percent of those in East Asia did so. Moreover, the higher projected growth rates for the region compared to North America, Latin America and Europe will make East Asia the most attractive investment target of Japanese firms in the coming decade.[16]

Russia and North Korea remain low priority countries from the perspective of Japanese capital. Whereas Japan articulated the notion of separating politics and economics to promote economic ties with China, it has clung to the principle of the inseparability of politics and economics (*seikei fukabun*) to constrain its economic ties with Russia. The territorial dispute continues to be the major impediment to a large-scale Japanese aid package to Russia. In an attempt to engineer a breakthrough in Soviet-Japanese relations just prior to Soviet President Mikhail Gorbachev's visit to Tokyo, Ozawa Ichirō (then secretary-general of the ruling Liberal Democratic Party) reportedly worked with the Ministry of International Trade and Industry (MITI) and business leaders to put together a major aid package of $26 billion in spring 1991 as a *quid pro quo* for meaningful Soviet concessions on the territorial question.[17] Gorbachev, however, was in no position to make such concessions given the intense domestic pressures that he faced, and the summit between him and Prime Minister Kaifu Toshiki yielded little progress. Although hopes for another breakthrough were raised after the failed Soviet coup and the collapse of the Soviet Union, they were again dashed when Russian President Boris Yeltsin abruptly canceled his scheduled visit to Tokyo in September 1992. Yeltsin finally visited Tokyo to meet with Prime Minister Morihiro Hosokawa in October 1993. Although the summit improved the atmosphere of bilateral relations, it did not lead to much progress on the territorial issue.

To keep from falling behind the Western nations, however, Japan has made moderate compromises in its policy of not separating politics and economics. Japan has provided modest amounts of humanitarian aid to Russia and is participating in economic assistance efforts channeled through international organizations. Moreover, the inseparability doctrine does not preclude private-sector trade and investments and large-scale projects for resource development. But without strong government backing such as loan and investment guarantees, Japanese corporations will continue to be reluctant to invest in Russia. In fact, many business executives believe that given the present situation in Russia, making huge investments or providing large amounts of aid would be like pouring money into a black hole. Rather than wasting capital on Russia, they would rather focus on Southeast Asia and China. Consequently, they probably welcome their government's hard-line stance on the territorial question because it gets them off the hook.

Despite this impasse in Russo-Japanese relations, joint ventures such as the oil and natural gas project off Sakhalin Island have continued to move forward. Moreover, MITI officials have shown enough interest in Russian economic reform to present a report in May 1992 outlining their policy suggestions to the

Russian government. In contrast to the free-market orthodoxy contained in the International Monetary Fund's (IMF) blueprint for economic restructuring, they have called for policies similar to those pursued by Japan after World War II, including centrally guided "priority production programs" to ensure an adequate supply of critical industrial goods, strategic allocation of capital through government and private financial institutions, and preferential tax policies to encourage capital accumulation.[18] The Japanese are also watching with interest the efforts to create free economic zones in the maritime regions of the Russian Far East.[19]

Although North Korea remains the main country in Northeast Asia outside the reach of Japanese business, Korean residents in Japan who are aligned with the Pyongyang regime have provided North Korea with large amounts of foreign capital through remittances. Having been largely abandoned in economic terms by its two patrons (China and the Soviet Union), North Korea now faces a severe economic crisis and is under acute pressure to open itself up to foreign investments. The surprise visit to Pyongyang of LDP leader Kanemaru Shin in October 1990 at first suggested that Japan might relieve some of this pressure by paying reparations and normalizing relations. But Japan's Foreign Ministry successfully reined in this bold move, using the reservations expressed by Seoul and Washington as well as indications that Pyongyang has been trying to develop nuclear weapons. At this point, Japan has little economic incentive to move ahead of either South Korea or the United States with North Korea. The 1994 nuclear agreement between Pyongyang and Washington, however, could open the way for limited Japanese business involvement in North Korea. Japan is expected to fund a major portion of the light-water nuclear reactors that are to be provided to North Korea as part of this accord.

Concerning Japan's second role, that of technology provider, the Japanese government tends to define this task in terms of education and training. For example, it emphasizes that the ASEAN Four countries suffer from an acute shortage of technicians and that this shortage is impeding foreign direct investments. Consequently, official agencies such as the Ministry of International Trade and Industry have recommended the establishment of Industrial Technology Training Centers in the various ASEAN countries.[20] Although such efforts are welcome, the East Asian economies are much more interested in the technologies belonging to the Japanese private sector. Japanese firms, however, have been generally cautious about transferring technology for fear of aiding potential rivals—especially in the East Asian NIEs.

For example, South Koreans have frequently complained that Japanese firms are willing to license only older-generation technology. In the period 1985–90, Japan accounted for 1,829 instances of technology transfer to South Korea out of a total of 3,860 instances, or about 47.4 percent. The total licensing costs of these Japanese technology transfers, however, amounted to only about 31.9 percent of the costs of all the international technology transfers to South Korea. The average value of Japanese transfers in 1985–90 was $0.66 million, whereas the average value of U.S. transfers (of which there were 1,116) was $1.66 million. The relatively lower value of Japanese licensing fees seems to confirm Japan's reluctance to transfer the more advanced technologies. To explain this reluctance, Japanese firms point to South Korea's inadequate protection of intellectual property rights and the inability of Japanese companies to apply for South Korean patents on products as well as processes—a privilege accorded to American and European firms.[21]

Japanese companies seem to be less hesitant about transferring technology when it is done in the context of developing business partners overseas. For example, in Taiwan, Japanese firms are providing technical assistance to local producers so that they can become suppliers of high-quality parts to Japanese subsidiaries. In this context, Taiwanese firms signed 105 technical assistance contracts with Japanese counterparts in 1990. This figure surpassed the number of contracts concluded with U.S. (50) and European (30) firms.[22]

Finally, how is Japan doing as an absorber of the productive output of the East Asian economies? In large part because of yen appreciation, Japan's imports from the East Asian NIEs increased substantially from about $9.8 billion in 1985 to over $26.9 billion in 1993, a jump of 174 percent. Japan's import performance relative to that of the United States has also improved: whereas Japan imported only 25.2 percent of the amount that the U.S. imported from the East Asian NIEs in 1985, it imported nearly 41.8 percent of the amount of U.S. imports in 1993. Imports from the ASEAN Four have also increased. In 1985, Japan purchased about $16.7 billion of goods from these developing countries; but in 1993, it bought over $29 billion—a rise of almost 74 percent. Although the ASEAN Four countries primarily served as raw material suppliers in the past, even these developing states are beginning to export more manufactured goods to Japan.

Accompanying this increase in Japan's absorption of East Asian goods, however, has been a sharp expansion of its exports to the region. During the 1985–93 period, Japan's exports to the East Asian NIEs grew by nearly $58 billion, or almost 257 percent. Consequently, despite yen appreciation, Japan's trade surplus with the East Asian NIEs increased by about $40.9 billion, or over 323 percent. There has also been a surge in exports to the ASEAN Four, from about $7.3 billion in 1985 to over $32.7 billion in 1993 (a jump of over 348 percent). This trend reflects the growing demand for Japanese capital goods as these developing countries promote their manufacturing capabilities. Consequently, Japan's trade balance with the ASEAN Four has shifted from a deficit of $9.41 billion in 1985 to a surplus of over $3.74 billion in 1993. China is the one major country in East Asia that goes against this trend in Japanese trade patterns. Although Japan had a trade surplus with China of almost $6 billion in 1985, it posted a deficit of about $3.3 billion in 1993. But this statistic may be somewhat misleading in light of the dramatic increase of Japanese exports to Hong Kong—from $6.5 billion in 1985 to nearly $22.7 billion in 1993. A significant portion of these Hong Kong directed exports may be ultimately going to mainland China.

In the aggregate, the East Asian economies now represent a much larger export market for Japan than either the United States or the European Community (see Figure 5.2). Therefore, even while Japan's imports from the region have increased significantly, the steeper rise in exports to the region have caused Japan's trade surplus with East Asia as a whole to swell from about $9.2 billion in 1985 to nearly $54 billion in 1993 (see Figure 5.3). The U.S. trade pattern is generally a mirror image of Japan's. Although America's export performance to the East Asia region excluding Japan has improved substantially (from $24.9 billion in 1985 to over $74.9 billion in 1993), imports from the region have grown even more (from about $51.8 billion in 1985 to over $125.5 billion in 1993). Consequently, the U.S. trade deficit with East Asia (excluding Japan) has ballooned from about $26.9 billion in 1985 to nearly $50.6 billion in 1993 (see Figure 5.4). Although much of this deficit is with China ($22.8 billion in 1993), the United States also has net deficits with the East Asian NIEs ($14.5 billion) and the ASEAN Four ($13.3 billion). While the U.S. deficit with the East Asian NIEs has declined by 31.3 percent from 1985 to 1993, the deficit with the ASEAN Four has increased by 126.4 percent. Also during the 1985–93 period, the U.S. trade deficit with Japan rose from $43.5 billion to over $60.5 billion. In short, as Japan's trade surplus with East Asia has grown so has America's trade deficit with the region (see Figure 5.5). Put differently, Japan has a large and growing trade *surplus* with *both* the United States and East Asia, while the United States has a large and growing trade with *both* Japan and East Asia.

Despite the tendency for Japan to purchase more of the East Asian output, the United States remains the chief absorber of the region's production. Japan has not expanded its absorption of the output of East Asia's growing productive capacity at the rate necessary to restrain further increases in East Asian exports to the United States. Although it is not evident from the aggregate trade statistics, a significant portion of the expansion of Japan's two-way trade with the East Asian NIEs and the ASEAN states seems to be managed by Japanese multinational business networks, or *keiretsu*. To overcome high labor costs at home, Japanese corporations are establishing production and marketing subsidiaries in the East Asian countries. In addition to selling and sourcing in the local market, these subsidiaries then export some of their output back to Japan, as well as exporting intermediate goods and higher value-added parts from their affiliates in Japan. In short, Japanese business networks are cultivating a system of "captive" exports and imports between Japan and the rest of East Asia.[23] Such a system works to the advantage of Japanese corporations because they can modulate the trade flows so as to minimize the dislocative effects on affiliate firms back in Japan. But this practice also has two other consequences. It can restrain the expansion of East Asian manufactured exports to Japan, and it can cause a major part of the output of Japanese subsidiaries in East Asia to be exported to third markets like the United States.[24]

Figure 5.2 **Japan's Direction of Exports**

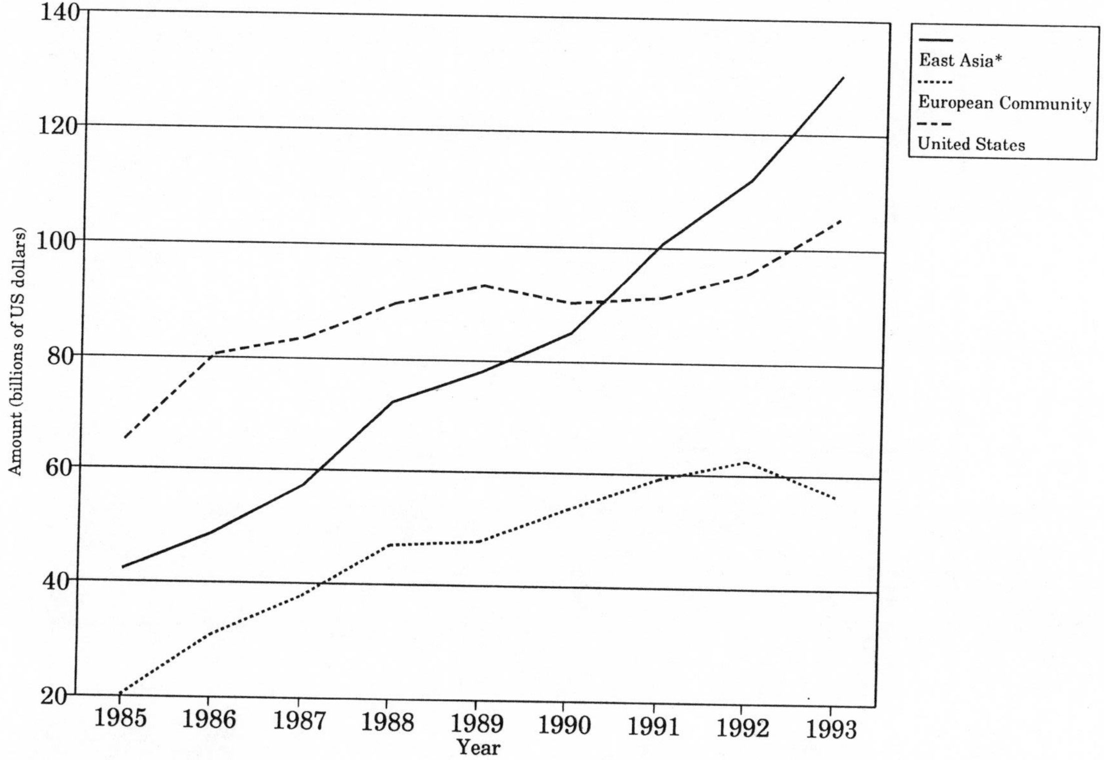

Legend:
— East Asia*
······ European Community
– – – United States

Y-axis: Amount (billions of US dollars) — 20, 40, 60, 80, 100, 120, 140

X-axis: Year — 1985, 1986, 1987, 1988, 1989, 1990, 1991, 1992, 1993

Source: Japanese Ministry of Finance.
*East Asia = NIEs, ASEAN 4, and China.

136

Figure 5.3 Japan's Trade with East Asia

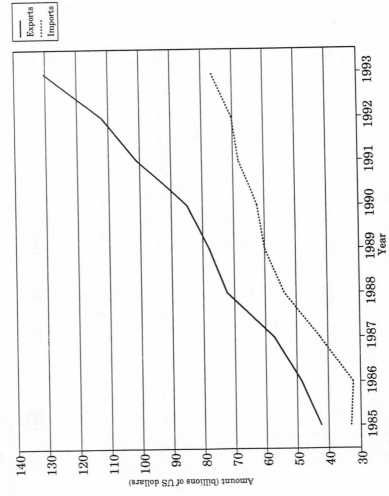

Source: Japanese Ministry of Finance.
*East Asia = NIEs, ASEAN 4, and China.

137

Figure 5.4 **U.S. Trade with East Asia**

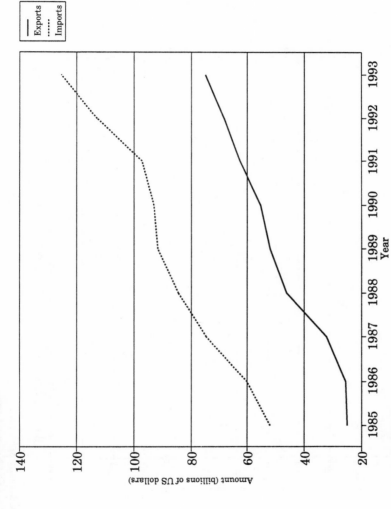

Source: U.S. Department of Commerce.
*East Asia = NIEs, ASEAN 4, and China.

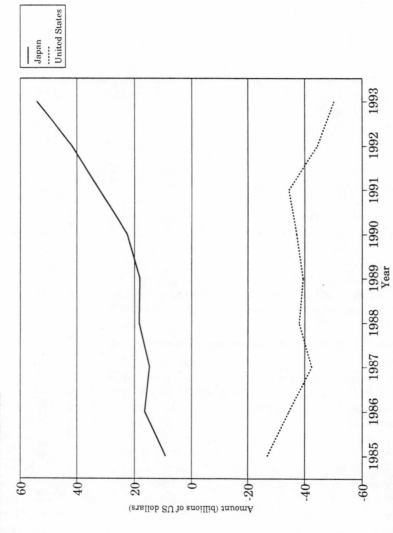

Figure 5.5 **Trade Balances with East Asia**

Sources: Japanese Ministry of Finance and U.S. Department of Commerce.
*East Asia = NIEs, ASEAN 4, and China.

The above analysis shows that Japan's primary role has been to provide the East Asian NIEs and the ASEAN Four with capital, technology, and intermediate goods. Using these inputs, the East Asian NIEs and the ASEAN Four have, in turn, developed their own manufacturing capabilities. As the flow of Japanese capital has increasingly taken the form of direct investments, Japanese corporations have managed to expand their business networks in East Asia through joint ventures with local governments and firms and through the establishment of subsidiaries. On the technology transfer front, Japanese firms seem extremely cautious about making technology transfers to actual and potential East Asian competitors. However, they appear more willing to transfer technology if this is done in the context of joint ventures with local entities or with the aim of cultivating local suppliers. As in the case of direct investments, Japanese firms are using technology transfers as an instrument to expand their business networks in the region. Although Japan has undeniably increased its imports from the East Asian economies, it is the United States—and not Japan—which still serves as the primary foreign absorber of East Asia's productive output.[25] By expanding its network capitalism into the East Asian NIEs and the ASEAN Four, Japan has both improved and organized the productive capabilities of these economies. But Japan has not adequately assumed the role of importer. Despite the increase in regional economic integration, a self-contained regional economic bloc involving Japan, the East Asian NIEs, and ASEAN is impossible because most of these economies are net exporters. Until the leading East Asian economies, including Japan, become larger demand absorbers, regional economic harmony will be contingent on access to the U.S. market.

Regional Economic Organizations and Groupings

Japan has been generally favorable to the development of regional economic organizations and sensitive to the concerns of the less powerful states in the region. In August 1977, during his visit to Southeast Asia, then prime minister Fukuda Takeo enunciated what has come to be known as the Fukuda Doctrine, which clearly articulated Japan's support for ASEAN solidarity.[26] Although his successor, Ohira Masayoshi, actively supported the concept of Pacific Basin cooperation, he hesitated to push for a regionwide, government-based organization after the misgivings expressed by the ASEAN countries. Therefore, in active partnership with Prime Minister Malcolm Fraser of Australia, Ohira initially backed the creation of a nongovernmental tripartite forum consisting of business, government, and academic representatives. The Pacific Economic Cooperation Conference (PECC) held its first meeting in Canberra in 1980.[27] PECC has been serving the purpose of facilitating the exchange of information, the discussion of trade, investment, and technology issues; and the development of a regional consensus on such subjects.

In 1989, regional institution building went a big step further with Australian

Prime Minister Robert Hawke's initiative to create a cabinet-level consultative mechanism: the Asia Pacific Economic Cooperation (APEC) forum. Although Australia took the lead in a public sense, the Japanese—especially former Prime Minister Nakasone Yasuhiro and MITI—vigorously backed such an institution. In fact, because the initiative came from Hawke and not from a Japanese leader, the move did not provoke strong opposition from other countries in the region on the grounds that Japan might seek to use APEC for the purpose of economic domination. Japan's own Ministry of Foreign Affairs (MOFA) initially expressed concern that APEC might be misconstrued as moving Japan in an Asiatic direction, away from the West, but when U.S. Secretary of State James Baker announced American support for the new organization, MOFA's reservations subsided. The first meeting of APEC was held in Canberra in November 1989 and attended by cabinet ministers from twelve countries: the six ASEAN states, Australia, Canada, Japan, New Zealand, South Korea, and the United States. Two years later, the People's Republic of China, Taiwan, and Hong Kong were formally admitted to the organization as "three Chinas" at APEC's third meeting held in Seoul. The formalization of APEC has proceeded incrementally. A permanent secretariat was established in Singapore in 1992. A year later, the heads of state of all the APEC member countries except Malaysia attended the meeting in Seattle, thus initiating the practice of annual region-wide summits. The November 1994 APEC summit in Indonesia yielded a declaration for achieving free trade in the region by the year 2020. In November 1995, Japan will be hosting in Osaka the next APEC meeting. This summit could prove to be critical for this fledgling organization since the regional leaders will have to consider more concrete plans for trade and investment liberalization beyond the general proclamations.

The most controversial proposal for a regional grouping thus far has been Malaysian Prime Minister Mahathir Mohamad's call for an East Asian Economic Group (EAEG) consisting of most of the Asian APEC members plus Vietnam, Myanmar, and the Pacific islands, but excluding the United States, Canada, and Australia. The other ASEAN states managed to dilute the Malaysian proposal from a formal grouping to a noninstitutional caucus that would "discuss issues of common concern to East Asian economies, and meet as and when the need arises."[28] Although supporters of Mahathir's initiative would like to see Japan play a leading role, the Japanese government has refused to endorse even the watered-down caucus version for fear that it would exacerbate tensions with the United States. In fact, prior to the third APEC meeting, U.S. secretary of state Baker wrote a letter to foreign minister Watanabe Michio asking Japan not to participate in the East Asian Economic Caucus (EAEC) because by excluding North America, the caucus would "divide the Pacific region in half."

The EAEC issue, however, has triggered some tense exchanges between Japan and the United States about economic regionalism. For example, former foreign minister Okita Saburo has argued that the EAEC would "counterbalance emerging organizations in Europe and North America and . . . improve the bargaining position of Asian countries."[29] Many Japanese business leaders have criticized Baker's sharp repudiation of the EAEC by pointing out that the United States was in fact drawing a line down the Pacific by signing the North American Free Trade Agreement. President Bush countered such criticisms of NAFTA by proposing "a strategic network of free-trade agreements across the Atlantic and Pacific." But in identifying partners for free-trade agreements across the Pacific, an official in the U.S. Commerce Department mentioned a number of countries, but noticeably excluded Japan.[30] The implication was that since Japanese business practices posed invisible trade barriers, the negotiation of a free-trade agreement with Japan would be counterproductive.

The controversy over the EAEC and NAFTA highlights the basic dilemma of Japan's regional economic policy. East Asian access to the U.S. market is critical if Japan's vision of regional development to work because Japan and many of the other East Asian economies are either unwilling or unable to expand imports fast enough to absorb the region's growing output. That is why Japan promotes organizations such as APEC as a way to discourage American protectionism. That is why all official Japanese documents and reports refer to the "Asia-Pacific," not "East Asia." By connecting "Asia" and "Pacific" with a hyphen, the Japanese are affirming the essential trading link between East Asia proper and North America. But here is the problem. Because the East Asian economies tend to be net exporters (and Japan is the worst of them all) and the United States is the main absorber of their exports, there are strong incentives for the United States not only to adopt protectionist measures, but also to negotiate a free-trade agreement in an area where it is still economically dominant (*viz.,* NAFTA). By encouraging other East Asian economies to adopt the Japanese strategy of export-led development, Japan is aggravating the problem.

Japan may seek to develop closer relations with its economic partners and emulators in East Asia so as to increase its leverage over the United States and to prevent America from being protectionist or pursuing managed trade. But such a strategy is likely to push Washington further in the direction of economic regionalism. Or it may even encourage Washington to outflank Japan by reaching out to other countries in East Asia that value liberal access to the U.S. market more than modulated access to the Japanese market. By excluding Japan as a possible partner in trans-Pacific free-trade agreements, Bush administration officials were hinting at the second possibility. This kind of U.S.–Japanese sparring about the regional economic order threatens to escalate into an open conflict over economic influence and to spill over into the security arena. The only way to establish a stable equilibrium would be to use forums like APEC not to keep the United States from defecting from free trade, but rather to promote greater imports by Japan and the East Asian NIEs.

The Political-Military Dimension

During the Cold War period, the security system in the Asia-Pacific region was generally stable and provided a firm anchor for Japanese security policy. The

United States, as part of its containment strategy, forged a network of alliances across the Pacific, of which the security treaty with Japan was a critical component. Since it was in America's strategic interest to protect Japan against possible threats from continental East Asia (mainly the Soviet Union), Japan could afford to have a relatively relaxed view of its security environment. Therefore, domestic debates about defense policy tended to focus on constitutional and ideological questions, with very little attention given to geopolitical factors.[31]

Within this overall bipolar Cold War system, there were nevertheless some geopolitical shifts in East Asia. The most important was the changing alignments of China. The Sino-Soviet alliance deteriorated into a split. During the Nixon administration, the United States sought to increase its international leverage by opening up to China as well as pursuing a détente policy with the Soviet Union. After the collapse of détente, in the later years of the Carter administration, the United States tried to draw China into an anti-Soviet coalition in East Asia. But these geopolitical shifts did not challenge Japan's basic policy of allying with the United States. In fact, the shift in America's China policy removed a long-standing source of irritation from U.S.–Japan relations and allowed Japan to normalize relations with China. Although Japanese leaders were skeptical about U.S. attempts to forge a security relationship with China against the Soviet Union, Japan did modernize its military forces and promote defense cooperation with the United States to counter the increase in Soviet military deployments in East Asia. Japan, thus, gradually evolved from a reluctant to a more active ally of the United States.

The Changing Regional Security Environment for Japan

Given that the Soviet threat and the Cold War provided the main geopolitical rationale for the U.S.–Japan alliance, the Soviet collapse and the Cold War's dènouement will inevitably have consequences for Japan's security policy. Of course, the end of the Soviet-American competition removes the danger (however unlikely) that Japan might become embroiled in a global military conflict. But this does not mean that all is well for Japanese security. Although the regional security environment may not be threatening in a direct sense, it is nevertheless worrisome. The following concerns affect Japanese security calculations.

One involves America's security commitment to Japan and the U.S. military presence in East Asia and the western Pacific. The United States now wants to collect a "peace dividend" by reducing its military forces in East Asia as well as Western Europe and to concentrate on domestic economic renewal. Japan has no problems with the modest military retrenchment plan for East Asia outlined by the Pentagon. Its real concern is whether this plan is politically sustainable in Washington at a time when America is seeking to cut the budget deficit. Japan's massive trade surplus with America and its modest security burden will certainly work against Tokyo's appeals for the United States to sustain a sizable force in

Northeast Asia. Further increases in Japanese host-nation support will help alleviate charges of free riding, but may not be politically sufficient at a time when the threat to U.S. security is unclear.

But why should Japanese defense policymakers be so concerned about a possible U.S. withdrawal? Why not embrace the pacifist view that the end of the Cold War provides an opportunity to terminate military alliances and to rid Japan of the last vestiges of the U.S. occupation? There are two reasons for the concern. First, given Asian suspicion about the reemergence of Japanese militarism, Japan's security linkage with the United States is essential to allay regional fears. As long as Japan has good relations with the United States, the various countries in the Asia-Pacific region will permit the expansion of Japanese economic power. But if Japan were to become uncoupled from the U.S. security linkage, they would be likely to become more fearful of Japanese domination and much less receptive to Japanese trade and investments.[32] Second, despite the collapse of the Soviet Union, there are still potential threats to Japanese security interests in the region. Therefore, for the United States to abandon the security linkage could very well cause the kind of Japanese remilitarization that its Asian neighbors fear. So what are these potential threats?

First, there is the Russian problem. With the Cold War over, the scenario that Russians might threaten the Japanese archipelago to gain a military advantage over the U.S. navy or to counter U.S. maritime strategy is now unthinkable. The Russian threat in terms of intentions has clearly disappeared. But Japanese defense analysts still worry about the Russian military deployments that remain in Northeast Asia (submarines, warships, bombers, and fighter aircraft). And there are indications that Russia is upgrading some weapons systems in the Far East and transferring some of its forces from the European theater east of the Urals.[33] What makes these capabilities especially worrisome is the current fluidity in Russian politics. The democratic revolution could very well fail and yield a xenophobic Russia. On the other hand, the outbreak of political chaos would raise the specter of "loose nukes." Moreover, the nationalistic fervor that prevents Yeltsin from making concessions on the territorial issue certainly does not reassure Japan about Russia's long-term intentions. Consequently, military analysts in Tokyo argue that Japan must remain vigilant and continue to modernize its forces while maintaining close security cooperation with the United States.

Second, China is beginning to emerge as a geopolitical problem. One factor is the danger of political instability or even civil war, which could cause a massive flow of refugees toward Japan. Consequently, although Japan condemned the Tiananmen massacre, it has been much less strident than the United States about condemning human rights abuses. For Japanese leaders, Chinese stability is probably more important than Chinese democratization. Another factor that makes China a security problem is military modernization. China is now engaged in expanding its naval and air power as well as modernizing its nuclear forces. One immediate motivation for this is China's interest in pressing its claims to the Spratly and Paracel Islands.[34] Although this buildup in the South China Sea does not threaten Japan directly, it raises concerns about the security of the sea lanes to Southeast Asia and beyond—especially now that the United States has withdrawn from the Philippines. The recent agreement by Russia to sell China advanced military equipment and technology will certainly fuel the growing anxiety in the Japan Defense Agency (JDA) about Chinese military power.[35] Finally, the questions of Hong Kong's reversion and Taiwan's security compound the China problem for the Japanese.

Third, the Korean peninsula poses a multifaceted security challenge for Japan. For one thing, there is the danger of a nuclear North Korea. The JDA's Defense White Paper of 1992 mentioned for the first time the possible threat to Japan from the new missiles being developed by Pyongyang. Another problem is the process of reunification. One possible scenario is the emergence of a reformist authoritarian regime in North Korea after the death of Kim Il Song. While maintaining tight political control, such a regime could follow the Chinese model by gradually opening its economy to the outside world and increasing its interaction with South Korea. Reunification would take place only after considerable progress in North Korean reform. But just as likely—if not more likely—is reunification triggered by a rapid collapse of the northern regime. Under these circumstances, the process could become chaotic and even violent, with repercussions for Japan. Finally, Japan has concerns about a postunification Korea. Given the animosity that Koreans still feel toward the Japanese for the period of colonial domination, Japan could confront a militarily powerful and hostile Korea.

Finally, many of the countries in the region face imminent political transition periods triggered by generational change or internal pressures for democratization. While holding the promise of stable democratic development, they also suggest the danger of internal political instability. This would have the most direct consequences for Japan in the geographically proximate countries of Northeast Asia. But given Japan's growing investments in Southeast Asia, the problem of instability goes beyond the issue of refugees. In sum, whereas formerly Japan could focus almost entirely on the Soviet threat, it must now deal with multiple and complicated uncertainties and potential threats.[36]

Possible Japanese Strategic Responses

How might Japan respond to this changing regional security environment? Theoretically, there are four general options.

First, Japan could pursue a strategy of security autonomy and become a great power in the traditional sense. Calculating that the U.S. security commitment is no longer reliable in the post–Cold War era and that the regional security environment is threatening, Japan might shift from its defensive military posture and acquire significant power projection capabilities—perhaps even nuclear weapons. Predictions that Japan will inevitably develop military power commensurate with its economic capabilities usually assume some conception of what a "normal" nation-state ought to be.[37] Nation-states seek to maximize their power. And since military force is the ultimate arbiter of power in the anarchic world of international politics, Japan will surely choose to acquire nuclear weapons or conventional power projection capabilities. By building up its military, Japan will at a minimum gain international prestige. Such a course would also give Japan the ability to resist foreign pressures and the leverage to compel other nations to act in accordance with Japanese interests, however defined.

The problem with this option is that it would aggravate the existing distrust in the region. Rather than making Japan more secure, it is likely to make it more insecure by provoking greater militarization by its neighbors, such as China, Russia, and even Korea. This option would also undermine Japanese efforts to expand its business networks throughout East Asia. Furthermore, if this option is not provoked by explicit U.S. abrogation of the security relationship, a policy of security autonomy is likely to antagonize the United States and even put Japan on a military collision course with its former ally. Understandably, there are few proponents of such a strategy in Japan today. Even prominent nationalistic voices like Ishihara Shintarō and Etō Jun favor neither developing a nuclear capability nor challenging the United States geopolitically in the Pacific.[38] Despite the noisy sound trucks of right-wing groups and Japanese confidence in their economic prowess, pacifism or antimilitarism born out of the tragic experience of World War II still runs deep in Japanese elite and mass culture.[39]

Nevertheless, one cannot completely rule out remilitarization. Two international developments could lead Japan to adopt a great military power strategy independent of or antagonistic to the United States. One possibility involves security abandonment by the United States in the context of a threatening geopolitical environment in Northeast Asia. Under this scenario, Washington would end its security guarantee for Japan (including the abrogation of the bilateral security treaty and the termination of extended nuclear deterrence) at a time when the environment in Northeast Asia was becoming more threatening to Japan. A threatening Northeast Asia could involve one or more of the following developments: the emergence of a xenophobic Russia, a China that is rapidly expanding its naval and nuclear capabilities or one that is undergoing an intense civil war, and a unified and highly armed Korea hostile to Japan. Without a security guarantee from the United States, Japanese leaders would probably see no realistic choice but to expand the military to protect Japan's territorial integrity. And in such a geopolitical environment, public opposition to both constitutional revision and rearmament would be likely to wane.

The other possibility involves military intimidation by the United States. This is the scenario sketched out by George Friedman and Meredith Lebard in their book *The Coming War with Japan*. They argue that even after military retrenchment, the United States will choose to remain a global naval power. If the economic power balance continues to shift in Japan's favor and Washington is unable to win meaningful trade concessions from Tokyo, then the United States could use its naval capabilities to manipulate Japan's oil supplies from the Middle East. Japan would then respond by building up its own naval forces to prevent the United States from engaging in such blackmail.[40] This scenario rests on the assumption that with the collapse of the Soviet Union, intense economic competition between Japan and the United States will spill over into the military arena. But this replay of the past is a bit far-fetched. It was not an economically competitive Japan that provoked the naval arms race in the 1930s and ultimately the U.S. naval blockade. Rather, it was Japan's military expansion on the Asian continent in the context of a domestic social and economic crisis.

Although the probability of either security abandonment or military intimidation by the United States is extremely low, Japan can hedge against these worst-case scenarios by maintaining a dynamic defense industrial base.[41] Its stockpile of plutonium, which was originally intended to reduce foreign energy dependence, could also be used to develop a nuclear arsenal. In other words, Japan could have the capability to transform itself rapidly into a great military power if such a need were to arise. In the meantime, even those who want Japan to play a more prominent role in world affairs tend to advocate such a role only in the context of the alliance with the United States and international cooperation.

A second strategic option would be for Japan to abrogate the security treaty with the United States and develop a cooperative security regime in East Asia. Advocates of this course see the collapse of the Soviet Union as removing the only credible threat to Japan. They are confident that increasing economic interdependence and prosperity will gradually reduce the historical distrust that exists among countries in the region. Therefore, the worst thing that Japan could do would be to continue to modernize its military forces.[42] Rather, Japan should drastically scale back its Self-Defense Forces and resist U.S. pressures to participate in multinational military operations such as the Desert Storm action against Iraq in 1991. Japan could, however, contribute to United Nations peacekeeping activities by organizing with other Asian countries an Asian Standby Force modeled after the Nordic Standby Forces that were established by Denmark, Finland, Norway, and Sweden as a corps for UN service. Such a mode of participation would allay Asian fears of resurgent Japanese militarism. Moreover, since such a corps would be under the command of the UN secretary general and not the Japanese government, it would not violate the constitution.[43]

To replace the old network of Cold War alliances, Japan should advocate the construction of a multilateral security system. It can do this by negotiating confidence-building measures with countries in the region and agreements to reduce military deployments. As the only target of a nuclear attack in history, Japan also has a moral obligation to promote the denuclearization of the Asia-Pacific region by first formalizing its three non-nuclear principles into law and then appealing to other nations in the region to follow its example. Such a course would be the most effective way to prevent the acquisition of nuclear weapons by North Korea.[44]

Proponents of this option tend to be the pacifists and socialists who advocated unarmed neutrality during the Cold War period. With the Cold War over, those who tend to see the world primarily through an economic lens may also find this position attractive. But the invasion of Kuwait by Iraq in August 1990 and the rise of ethnic conflicts throughout the world have had the net effect of making many Japanese who were traditionally pacifists more realistic about international politics. Consequently, there is not a strong movement in Japan for terminating its security linkage with the United States.

A third strategic course would be to try to reshape the alliance system with the United States into a broad maritime coalition to counter actual or potential threats emanating from continental East Asia. In addition to Japan and the United States, members of such a coalition might include South Korea, Taiwan, the ASEAN countries, and Australia. The key security concerns would be China and North Korea, and Russia if the democratic revolution should fail. This option would have several advantages. First, it would provide a new geopolitical rationale for the U.S.–Japan security alliance and the American military presence in the region. Second, it would be consistent with the harder line on China that seems to be emerging in the United States because of human rights and trade issues. Third, it would provide Japan with an opportunity to consolidate its political ties with South Korea, Taiwan, and the ASEAN states. Fourth, it would give Japan a chance to build on its participation in UN peacekeeping operations in Cambodia to assume a more active security role in the region beyond its borders without exacerbating regional anxieties. In fact, in the wake of Japan's positive contribution to the Cambodian peace process, Southeast Asian leaders are gradually warming up to a more prominent Japanese security role.

The major problem with this option is that it would work against Japan's current policy of trying to integrate China into the regional economic system. Despite concerns about China's military buildup, most Japanese leaders prefer to improve relations with Beijing in hopes of moderating Chinese behavior. Moreover, if U.S. relations with China do deteriorate, Japan could promote regional stability by serving as a link between the two. If Japan opted to join the U.S. in pursuing hard-line policies, China would be likely to respond with greater hostility and a more energetic military modernization program. Another flaw in the maritime coalition approach is the Russian factor. Despite the difficulties of Russian reform, the United States is far from ready to drop all hope of economic and democratic stabilization. Consequently, at this juncture, Washington is unlikely to welcome the notion of a maritime coalition even if it finds the recent moves toward Sino-Russian military cooperation problematic.

Whether or not Japan will pursue this balancing strategy will depend in large part on the future evolution of China and the response of other regional actors. Most strategic analysts in Japan see China's military modernization as an inevitable result of its economic growth and its quest for great-power status. They also believe that China is likely to be unyielding in its territorial claims and its opposition to foreign intervention in domestic politics. This vision of a "greater China" could steer other countries in the region to balance against China. For example, some of the key ASEAN states and the Indochina countries could cooperate to counter the rise of Chinese power and influence. And the Western democracies (especially the United States) could challenge China more vigorously regarding its handling of human rights and democratization, its neomercantilist trade policies, and its arms transfer policies.[45] In such circumstances, Japan would be under a great deal of pressure to join an effort to contain China. However, Japan, as well as other regional actors, would reject the construction of such a maritime coalition against China if China were to embrace a cooperative vision for Asia based on economic interdependence and move in a more democratic direction. At this point, most Japanese leaders still hope that China will take this latter course. The historic visit to China by the Japanese emperor in October 1992 can be interpreted as an effort to lay the diplomatic foundation for such regional cooperation. As one noted Japanese politician put it, "Japan and China should link hands and create a cooperative relationship like the one France and Germany have built up in the four decades since World War II. This is essential . . . if we hope to make the years after 2000 an 'Asian century.' "[46]

The fourth and final option would be to maintain the security relationship with the United States and a modern defensive military force, while encouraging regional and subregional dialogues on security as well as on economic issues. This course would allow Japan to guard against potential geopolitical rivals under the U.S. security umbrella, while hedging against U.S. military retrenchment by promoting regional security cooperation. Present trends suggest that this strategy is garnering the greatest support in Japan. Progressive intellectuals affiliated with the leftist parties have heretofore been the most active proponents of a cooperative security regime in the Asia-Pacific region based on confidence- and security-building measures (CSBMs). But now even government officials and intellectuals in the conservative mainstream are embracing the notion of regional security discussions as a complement to the alliance with the United States.[47] At the same time, the Japan Socialist Party and many pacifists have come around to acknowledging for the time being the positive role of the U.S.–Japan security treaty and the Self-Defense Force. In other words, this fourth option offers Japan a chance to bridge the long-term ideological divide that has often paralyzed domestic decision making on security policy issues. Since this strategy is the one that Japan is most likely to pursue in the foreseeable future, a more detailed discussion of this option is warranted.

Comprehensive National Security

Japan's strategy in the post–Cold War era is likely to be comprehensive in nature, linking political-military and economic instruments and combining bilateral, regional, global, and unilateral approaches. In concrete terms, it will have the following components.

At the bilateral level, the central relationship for Japan will continue to be that with the United States, and the greatest challenge to this relationship will be on the economic front. Up until now, Japan has responded to U.S. pressures on trade issues by a variety of means: the reduction of tariffs and nontariff trade barriers while minimizing the detrimental effects on domestic economic sectors; the negotiation of "voluntary" export restraints and other market-share arrangements in such sectors as steel, automobiles, and semiconductors; and an increase in direct investments in the United States and the forging of corporate alliances between Japanese and American firms. These efforts have certainly helped to prevent a stridently protectionist coalition from emerging in the United States. But with the end of the Cold War, the United States has become less restrained about pressing its economic interests and less concerned about the negative impact of tough policies on the bilateral security relationship. Even Pentagon officials have come to recognize that a continuation of the huge trade imbalance will have a corrosive effect on the alliance.

The Bush administration pursued a policy of aggressive liberalism through the Structural Impediments Initiative (SII). The 1989–90 SII process was one of the most intrusive efforts to harmonize the domestic economic structures of two industrial giants. Japanese negotiators insisted that both sides must undertake measures to mitigate the trade problem. In the end, SII yielded a two-way agreement in which Japan agreed to increase public works spending, relax regulations in the retail sector, reform land-use policies, and enforce antitrust laws more effectively. The United States agreed to reduce the federal budget deficit, encourage long-term planning horizons among corporate executives, increase spending on commercial and scientific research, develop more effective workforce training programs, and promote exports.[48]

President Clinton has taken this aggressive approach a step further. While it continues to press Japan to liberalize its economic policies, the Clinton administration believes that "leveling the economic playing field" by focusing on deregulation and transparency is insufficient given the preferential trading practices of Japanese firms. Washington is now insisting on objective measures or criteria to track progress on foreign access to the Japanese market at both the aggregate and sectoral levels. Japan, however, is adamantly resisting this Clinton strategy to correct the trade imbalance. Charging Washington with embracing managed trade, Tokyo officials have ironically assumed the role of champions of free trade. They argue that numerical targets for imports would run counter to domestic efforts at deregulation.

The best way to reestablish a stable equilibrium in U.S.–Japan relations would be for Japan to shift decisively away from its neomercantilist economic policies and business practices. The current process of political realignment could ultimately facilitate such a change by galvanizing social and political forces more supportive of consumer and worker interests than those of producers. The recent adoption of a hybrid electoral system combining single-seat constituencies and proportional representation will encourage further realignments and reaggregation of political forces. A two-party system, or something close to it, may emerge, and elections may come to be contested more on the basis of policy choices than of distributive politics and the mobilization of well-organized interests. Greater weight would be given to urban middle-class voters, who are more likely to support consumer over producer interests. Moreover, elections could produce clearer mandates, enhancing the power of political leaders over the bureaucracy and therefore their ability to effect major policy shifts. Such is the theory. But there isn't much ground for optimism in the near future. The short-lived Hosokawa government failed to meet expectations about initiating sweeping economic reforms. Although the formation of the surprising coalition between Liberal Democrats and Social Democrats has ended the wide ideological divide on security policy, it has also stalled the movement for deregulation and economic liberalization. Given the political uncertainties, politicians have tended to defer to the bureaucracy on major economic policy issues. Key proponents of reform like Ozawa Ichiro, Hata Tsutomu, and Takemura Masayoshi have failed thus far to articulate an effective strategy for resolving economic tensions with Washington. They still lack the power, if not the will, to overcome bureaucratic resistance and promote the necessary changes. Consequently, for the time being, Japan will continue its policy of making marginal adjustments in hopes of satisfying the United States.

Another component of Japan's policy toward the United States will be the maintaining of the security relationship even after the disappearance of the Soviet threat. To do so, Japan will increase its host-nation support for U.S. forces to about 73 percent of the costs of stationing U.S. forces in Japan exclusive of American salaries or 54 percent of the costs inclusive of salaries. By making it much cheaper to keep American forces in Japan than to station them in the United States, Tokyo hopes to defuse charges of free riding on America's security guarantee and to limit U.S. military retrenchment in East Asia. Although bilateral defense technology cooperation was originally seen as a way to strengthen the U.S.–Japan alliance, the controversy over the FSX codevelopment project has called into question the wisdom of this approach.[49] Japan will also support, within the constraints of domestic politics and economic interests, America's foreign policy agenda in East Asia.

The first post–Cold War test in East Asia of the resiliency of the trans-Pacific alliance has been the problem of North Korean nuclearization. While insisting that North Korea must cooperate fully with International Atomic Energy Agency (IAEA) inspectors to verify its adherence to the Nuclear Non-Proliferation Treaty, Tokyo has been more cautious than Washington about an open confrontation with Pyongyang. From Japan's viewpoint, the risk of war on the Korean peninsula is a greater concern than North Korean nuclearization—that is, as long as U.S.-extended nuclear deterrence remains effective in the face of a North Korean nuclear threat. The nuclear agreement between the United States and North Korea has defused the situation for the time being, but the question remains whether Pyongyang will abide by the accord. If the agreement were to fall apart, Washington could once again press for economic sanctions against a recalcitrant North Korea and would expect Tokyo to back this effort by cutting off financial flows from Japan to North Korea. If the standoff with North Korea were to reach a crisis point, Washington would expect Tokyo to cooperate with U.S. and South Korean forces to counter possible aggression from North Korea. Any hesitancy on the part of Japan to support the United States in such a crisis would severely weaken, if not rupture, the bilateral alliance.

Human rights and democratization policy will also test the relationship with the United States. Rather than being as assertive as Washington about promoting human rights, Tokyo officials stress the tension between economic modernization and political liberalization. Modernization may ultimately lead to democratization, but the process is unlikely to be smooth and may require periods of repression to preserve stability. Although senior Japanese diplomats recognize that human rights are indeed universal—not just Western—values, they believe that confrontational approaches to promoting them are not always effective.[50] Differences in Japanese and American approaches will be most evident in the case of the Asian countries, especially China. Japan will also diverge with the United States on Russia policy. Despite the setbacks in the reform process in Russia, one of the priorities of U.S. foreign policy is to support democratic stabilization and economic liberalization in Russia by expanding aid programs to Russia and by providing security reassurance. The territorial dispute with Russia has restrained Japan from offering major economic assistance beyond what is necessary to stay in step with the United States and other Western powers. The Japanese are also skeptical that any external aid effort—no matter how massive—will have a decisive impact on Russian internal developments.

Next to that with the United States, the bilateral relationship of central importance to Japan in the Asia-Pacific context will be that with China. Japan's policy will exhibit a tension between two calculations. On the one hand, Japan will seek to expand its economic links with China and to integrate it into the regional economic system. In addition to the attraction of a huge market for Japanese products, the promotion of economic interdependence with China would be a way of moderating China's external behavior. Given its proximity, a China in domestic turmoil would be threatening to Japan because of the flow of refugees. Many Japanese analysts believe that the best way to help stabilize China in the long run is to support its quest for economic prosperity. Tokyo will therefore work to keep relations with Beijing on a positive diplomatic footing. If relations between Washington and Beijing sour further, then Tokyo may try to play a mediating role. On the other hand, Japan will be wary of China's inevitable rise as a political-military giant. Consequently, it will have every incentive to strengthen its ties with other East Asian countries that share a similar concern about China. This also means that even if Sino-American relations deteriorate, Japan will want to avoid straying too far from the American position.

The other great power in the region—Russia—will be less important in Japan's strategic calculations. This reflects Russia's current preoccupation with domestic problems and its economic weakness. Nevertheless, Japan will try to prevent this bilateral relationship from becoming openly hostile. Some Japanese strategists are beginning to look beyond the territorial issue in order to engage Russia on security issues. They support involving Russia in multilateral security dialogues such as the recently established ASEAN Regional Forum. They are deeply interested in getting Moscow to transfer its SSBNs from the Sea of Okhotsk to the Arctic Ocean to facilitate Russian military retrenchment in Northeast Asia. Japan would also like to promote the dismantling of Russian nuclear weapons and prevent Russia from disposing of nuclear waste from submarines in the Sea of Japan. Although Japan's raw material needs are not as acute as before, it remains interested in cultivating access to the rich resources in the Siberian Far East. In the longer term, a revitalized Russia is likely to reemerge as a formidable actor in Northeast Asia. Therefore, as in the case of China, Japan will continue to be vigilant about Russia.

At the regional level, Japan will seek to develop a regional community that will be hospitable to its interests. This effort will have economic, security, and cultural dimensions. In terms of economics, Japan will use its foreign aid programs and extend its business networks to keep East Asian countries receptive to Japanese economic expansion. It will promote incipient regional economic institutions like APEC as ways of managing regional economic interdependence. At this point, Japan appears to be serving as a bridge between the Anglo-American member states of APEC, which favor the negotiation of formal agreements on trade and investment, and the East Asian countries, which prefer to keep APEC as primarily a discussion forum. Japan's regional economic policy faces two major challenges. First, Japan must become a larger absorber of excess East Asian production. Otherwise, Japan's huge trade surpluses with both North America and the rest of East Asia will exacerbate, rather than mitigate, the historical distrust of Japan that remains in the region. Second, Japan must demonstrate through its trade, investment, and technology transfer policies that it is not seeking to preserve a hierarchical economic relationship with the other East Asian countries.

In terms of regional security policy, Japan will promote security dialogues in the region to complement—not to replace—the network of security alliances between the United States and its Asia-Pacific partners. The aim will be to hedge against a substantial drawdown of U.S. forces in the Pacific. Through these dialogues, Japan will push the consideration of CSBMs to discourage arms races and lower the possibility of military conflict. During a July 1991 meeting with foreign ministers from the ASEAN countries, then foreign minister Nakayama

Tarō proposed the convocation of annual high-level consultations among the nations represented in the ASEAN Post-Ministerial Conference (ASEAN-PMC) as "a process of political discussions designed to improve the sense of security among us." The Nakayama proposal was especially noteworthy because it was made despite American reservations about creating new security organizations.[51] A year later, Prime Minister Miyazawa echoed this initiative when he talked openly about forming an Asian version of the Conference on Security and Cooperation in Europe (CSCE).[52]

Soon after the election of Bill Clinton to the U.S. presidency, a high-level Japanese diplomat explicitly articulated Japan's policy as a "two-track approach." One track involves "efforts to solve on-going conflicts and disputes in such subregions as the Korean peninsula, Cambodia and the South China Sea" and to create "subregional frameworks of international cooperation for political stability and security." The other track entails the promotion of "a region-wide security dialogue at the ASEAN-PMC and eventually also in the context of APEC." The purpose of this process would be "to enhance the level of mutual reassurance among the countries in the region."[53] It would build upon the ongoing trend toward greater regional economic interdependence and cooperation to discourage geopolitical competition. Although representatives from ASEAN originally resisted these Japanese ideas for regional and subregional security discussions, they have become much more receptive. Moreover, the Clinton administration, in contrast to its predecessor, has also come out in support of this initiative. As a consequence, the ASEAN Regional Forum (ARF) was formed to discuss regional security issues and held its inaugural meeting in 1994.

Finally, there is a cultural dimension to Japan's regional policy. Efforts to internationalize the educational system have dramatically increased the number of Asian students in Japan. The study of the Japanese language is becoming more prevalent among Asians. The export of Japanese popular culture (from karaoke to video games) has also made Asians more open to Japanese influence. But at the same time, the legacy of Japan's imperialist past continues to make regional relations uneasy. In this context, Prime Minister Hosokawa Morihiro's statement during his first press conference after assuming office in August 1993 was a breath of fresh air. In response to a journalist's question, Hosokawa stated without ambiguity that Japan had engaged in a "war of aggression" and that he felt that it was wrong. But the positive impact of this candor quickly dissipated when several nationalistic politicians sharply criticized the prime minister in the Diet for giving such a one-sided interpretation of the Pacific War and for making Japan vulnerable to demands for compensation and increased aid packages from the East Asian countries.

At the global level, Japan's strategy has two dimensions. One concerns Japan's identification with the advanced industrial democracies of the West, as symbolized by the G–7 summit. Although it may be reluctant to take a lead in this community of nations, it will avoid falling too far out of step on issues of importance to the West. Consequently, Japan in the end accepted partial liberalization of its rice market so as not to become the spoiler of the Uruguay Round GATT negotiations. It became more flexible on the question of aid to Russia when French president Francois Mitterrand suggested that the 1993 G–7 summit scheduled for the summer in Tokyo be moved to an earlier date at another place in order to support Yeltsin's reform efforts. But at the same time, Japan recognizes that it is the only non-Western country represented in the G–7 summit and therefore sees an obligation to articulate common Asian perspectives in such circles.

The other dimension of Japan's global strategy is international cooperation in the context of the United Nations. In June 1992, after a long and difficult deliberative process, the Japanese Diet enacted a United Nations Peacekeeping Operations law. The legislation permitted the government to dispatch Self-Defense Forces abroad as part of UN peacekeeping efforts on condition that they not engage in combat operations.[54] Soon after the bill's passage, Japanese forces were sent to Cambodia to join the UN peacekeeping operation there. Despite initial concerns about Japanese remilitarization, the reaction in Southeast Asia to the Japanese peacekeepers has been surprisingly positive. In addition to this contribution to UN security activities, Japan has also become the second largest donor to the United Nations, after the United States. It provides 12.5 percent of the financial contributions for UN peacekeeping operations, while the United States contributes 30.4 percent.

Two factors motivate Japan's growing activism in the United Nations. First, by becoming more involved in the UN, Japan hopes to strengthen its security ties with the United States and the West generally in the post–Cold War era. Second, by participating directly in UN security activities, Japan seeks to gain a permanent seat on the UN Security Council. Although the passage of the UN peacekeeping bill is a welcome development, the Japanese public is still far from embracing the concept of collective security, which would ultimately involve the use of military force against aggressive states. Participation in collective security operations might be politically and constitutionally possible if Japan's Self-Defense Forces (JSDF) came under direct UN command, rather than just being part of a multinational coalition as in Desert Storm. But as long as the United Nations is unable to guarantee Japan's own security, conservative leaders will resist the incorporation of the JSDF into a UN force. One way to overcome this political impasse would be to create a separate unit for UN collective security actions, but such a bifurcation of the Japanese military faces strong opposition from conservative political circles as well as from the JSDF itself. The other alternative would be to tackle the constitutional constraint directly by moving to revise the postwar document. Although the Japanese are now more willing to talk openly about constitutional revision, opposition to such a move within Japan as well as from other Asian countries remain strong.

Finally, even while trying to avoid isolation by pursuing a comprehensive security strategy based upon bilateral, regional, and global approaches, Japan will also maintain a modern and effective defensive military force. With the collapse of the Soviet Union and the end of bipolarity, Japan has scaled back the defense spending schedule originally laid out in the five-year Medium-Term Defense Plan for 1991–95.[55] Although this move may slow the pace of Japan's defense modernization, it will not stop the modernization program itself. Japan will still be acquiring airborne warning and control systems (AWACS), Aegis-equipped destroyers, multiple-launch rocket systems, Patriot surface-to-air missile systems, surface-to-ship missile launchers, and other advanced weapons.[56] Given the uncertainties in Northeast Asia, especially on the Korean peninsula, the Self-Defense Forces very much want to have a robust defensive conventional capability. Barring a dramatic change in the international environment, such as the end of America's security commitment, however, Japan is unlikely to develop an offensive capability, such as aircraft carriers, long-range bombers, or medium- or long-range ballistic missiles.

Force for Regional Harmony or for Regional Tensions?

Japan has been a positive force in the region in two basic ways. First, by restraining itself on rearmament, Japan has not aggravated the geopolitical distrust that still exists among regional actors. Second, Japan has promoted regional economic development through capital and technology transfers. It has also contributed by providing an effective model of development that other economies in the region can emulate, with appropriate variations. But the flip side of this positive contribution is this. Japan is reaping a large portion of the economic benefits of East Asia's economic dynamism, while the United States continues to provide the critical collective goods of regional security and a large and open market as an absorber of East Asian productive output. Moreover, by encouraging other East Asian economies to pursue export-led growth, Japan is exacerbating the regional gap between export production and import absorption. Japan has been relatively successful in insulating itself from the deleterious effects of this gap. By aggressively expanding its business networks throughout East Asia, Japan has been able to modulate trade and capital flows so as to minimize the economic and social dislocations at home as regional interdependence deepens. By contrast, the United States, following more liberal economic policies and business practices has been less successful in cushioning the dislocative effects of East Asian competition on its own businesses and workers.

Consequently, by making the United States less willing to provide the collective goods (a market of last resort and regional security) that are critical to regional harmony, Japan is unwittingly causing the regional order to become less stable. For all the obvious reasons, Japan cannot take the place of the United States as the ultimate guarantor of regional security. Domestically, the Japanese public is still unwilling to have the nation play such a role, and any effort to do so would certainly destabilize the region by provoking strong countermeasures from neighboring states.

There are also few indications that Japan will dramatically shift away from its neomercantilist economic policies and business practices to absorb more of the East Asian output and to reduce its trade surplus with the United States. Morita Akio of the Sony Corporation called upon Japan to turn away from its relentless pursuit of economic expansion, but his views did not receive much support from the business community—especially since the Japanese economy went into a deep recession.[57] The split in the ruling Liberal Democratic Party and the unprecedented formation of a seven-party coalition government led by Hosokawa raised expectations about structural change. For example, the coalition partners declared their support of deregulation and a reduction of working hours to an average of 1,800 hours per year. But the Hosokawa government collapsed soon after winning passage of its electoral reform legislation. Given the fluidity of the party system, politicians are now more focused on adapting to the new electoral system than on changing Japan's foreign economic policy or business practices significantly . And ironically, despite the selection of the first Social Democratic prime minister since 1947, the Social Democratic Party is now so weak and confused that it is unable to develop a social democratic alternative to neomercantilism by forging a worker-consumer coalition.

On the security front, recent Japanese initiatives for regional security dialogues with an eye toward confidence- and security-building measures are positive developments for regional security. So is Japan's contribution to the peace process and peacekeeping operation in Cambodia. Such efforts will make it more possible for the United States to reduce some of its military burdens in the region without provoking a destabilizing arms race. But on the economic front, recent Japanese hints about using Asia-Pacific organizations as leverage to keep U.S. markets open to East Asian goods could backfire by pushing Washington in a more hemispheric direction. It could even cause the United States to outflank Japan by negotiating trade agreements with other East Asian economies. In the final analysis, therefore, the most important contribution to regional stability and harmony that Japan can make is to expand its absorptive capacity. This may be a tall order given the nature of Japanese domestic politics and business practices; but if Japan does not move forthrightly in this direction, it may undermine the regional economic system from which it has benefited so immensely.

Notes

1. Known as the "Discussion Group to Think about the Asia-Pacific and Japan in the 21st Century," this advisory council was chaired by Ishikawa Tadao, president of Keio University, and encompassed academics, business leaders, and former government officials—many of whom have specialized in Asian affairs. The full text of this report can be found in Watanabe Toshio (ed.), *Ajia wa kó kawaru* (Tokyo: Tokuma Shoten, 1993), pp. 345–62.

2. Paul Handley, "Japan's Clarion Call," *Far Eastern Economic Review*, vol. 156, no. 4 (January 28, 1993), pp. 10–11.

3. Ozawa Ichiro, *Nihon kaizo keikaku* (Tokyo: Kodansha, 1993), pp. 150–57.

4. Saitō Seiichirō, "The Pitfalls of the New Asianism," *Japan Echo*, vol. 19 (Special Issue, 1992), pp. 14–15 [originally published as "Shin Ajia shugi no kansei," *Voice*, November 1991, pp. 206–19].

5. Saitō, "The Pitfalls of the New Asianism," pp. 15–16.

6. Akamatsu Kaname, *Keizai Shin-chitsujo no Keisei Genri* (Tokyo: Risosha, 1944). For an excellent discussion of the flying-geese model of development, see Susumu Awanohara, "Japan and East: toward a New Division of Labor," *Occasional Paper 1* (Honolulu: East-West Center, August 1989).

7. Watanabe Toshio, *Ajia shin chōryō* [Asia's New Tide] (Tokyo: Chūō Kōronsha, 1990), pp. 34–68.

8. *Geographic Distribution of Financial Flows to Developing Countries: Disbursements, Commitments, Economic Indicators 1989/1992* (Paris: Organisation for Economic Co-operation and Development, 1994).

9. Charles Smith, "Eager to Please: Tokyo Sets Aside Own Rules in China Aid Package," *Far Eastern Economic Review*, January 26, 1995, pp. 25–26.

10. Susumu Awanohara, "Decent Interval: Japan May Pre-Empt U.S. on Vietnam Aid," *Far Eastern Economic Review*, April 30, 1992, pp. 12–13.

11. David Arase, "U.S. and ASEAN Perceptions of Japan's Role in the Asian-Pacific Region," in Harry H. Kendall and Clara Joewono (eds.), *Japan, ASEAN, and the United States* (Berkeley: Institute of East Asian Studies, 1991).

12. Anthony Rowley, "Nice to Be Needed: ADB Treads a Careful Path Through a Jungle of Ideologies," *Far Eastern Economic Review*, May 7, 1992, pp. 41–42, 46–49.

13. Anthony Rowley, "In Their Own Backyard: Japanese Foreign Ventures to Tap Asian Capital Markets," *Far Eastern Economic Review*, March 19, 1991, p. 40.

14. Margo Grimm, "Japan and ASEAN: Aspects of a New Interdependence," *Japan Economic Institute Report No. 12A* (March 27, 1992), pp. 2, 4.

15. Nomura Sogo Kenkyujo and Tokyo Kokusai Kenkyu Kurabu (eds.), *Chokusetsu toshi de Ajia wa nobiru* (Tokyo: Nomura Sogo Kenkyujo, 1994), p. 14.

16. "The Second Wave: Japanese Investment in Asia," *The Economist*, November 7, 1992, pp. 87–88.

17. *Yomiuri Shimbun*, March 21, 1991; and "Japan, Gorbachev and the Price of Peace," *The Economist*, March 30, 1991, p. 33.

18. Anthony Rowley, "To Russia with Pride: Japan Offers Economic Model," *Far Eastern Economic Review*, August 13, 1992, pp. 59–60. See also Yukitsugu Nakagawa, "Reflections on Restoring the Former Soviet Union: Can the Japanese Experience Help?" *IIGP Policy Paper #92E* (Tokyo: International Institute of Global Peace, June 1992).

19. Mark Clifford, "On the Brink: Soviet Far East Poised for Big Economic Transformation," *Far Eastern Economic Review*, August 15, 1991, p. 40.

20. Tsūshō sangyō shō (ed.), *90 nendai no tsusan seisaku bijon* (Tokyo, 1990), p. 99; and Report of the Council for the Promotion of Asia-Pacific Cooperation, "Toward an Era of Development through Outward-looking Cooperation" (June 1989), pp. 69–72.

21. Tadashi Saito, "New Strains in Japan–South Korea Economic Relations," *Japan Economic Institute Report No. 27A* (July 17, 1992), pp. 8–9.

22. Tadashi Saito, "Japan's Economic Relations with Taiwan," *Japan Economic Institute Report No. 27A* (July 19, 1991), pp. 10–11.

23. Grimm, "Japan and ASEAN: Aspects of a New Interdependence," pp. 4–7; and Okazaki Hisahiko, "Ajia cho-daiken' e no shin senryaku" [A New Strategy for an Asian Super Sphere], *This Is Yomiuri*, August 1992, pp. 69–70.

24. Dennis J. Encarnation, *Rivals Beyond Trade: America Versus Japan in Global Competition* (Ithaca: Cornell University Press, 1992), pp. 180–81.

25. Heizo Takenaka, "The Macroeconomic Management of the Asia-Pacific Region: The Growing Significance of Japan's Role," in FAIR Conference (the Second Asia-Pacific Conference), *The Asia-Pacific Region in the 1990s—Cooperation for Sustainable Development and the New World Order*, vol. 1 (Tokyo: Foundation for Advanced Information and Research, 1991), pp. 117–24.

26. Charles E. Morrison, "Japan and the ASEAN Countries: The Evolution of Japan's Regional Role," in Takashi Inoguchi and Daniel I. Okimoto, eds., *The Political Economy of Japan*, vol. 2: *The Changing International Context* (Stanford, CA: Stanford University Press, 1988), pp. 421–22.

27. Peter Drysdale, *International Economic Pluralism: Economic Policy in East Asia and the Pacific* (New York: Columbia University Press, 1988), pp. 215–20.

28. Michael Vatikiotis, "The Morning AFTA: Asean Takes Tentative Step toward Free-Trade Area," *Far Eastern Economic Review*, October 24, 1991, p. 65.

29. Shim Jae Hoon and Robert Delfs, "Block Politics: APEC Meeting Clouded by Fears of Regionalism," *Far Eastern Economic Review*, November 28, 1991, pp. 26–27.

30. Margo Grimm, "Impact of North American Trade Pact Scrutinized, *Japan Economic Institute Report*, no. 35B (September 18, 1992), p. 5; and Margo Grimm, "Japan Raises Concerns about North American Trade Pact," *Japan Economic Institute Report*, no. 41B (October 30, 1992), p. 5.

31. Hideo Otake, "Defense Controversies and One-Party Dominance: The Opposition in Japan and West Germany," in T.J. Pempel, ed., *Uncommon Democracies: The One-Party Dominant Regimes* (Ithaca, NY: Cornell University Press, 1990), pp. 128–61; and Donald C. Hellmann, "Japanese Politics and Foreign Policy: Elitist Democracy within an American Greenhouse," in Inoguchi and Okimoto, eds., *The Political Economy of Japan*, vol. 2, pp. 345–78.

32. Okazaki, " 'Ajia cho-daiken' e no shin senryaku," pp. 69–70.

33. Tai Ming Cheung, "The Eastern Front: Russian Military Deployment in Asia Sparks Concern," *Far Eastern Economic Review*, November 26, 1992, pp. 26–28.

34. Nayan Chanda, "Treacherous Shoals: South China Sea," *Far Eastern Economic Review*, August 13, 1992, pp. 14–17.

35. Carey Goldberg, "Yeltsin Sees Chance to Help Modernize China's Weapons," *Los Angeles Times*, December 18, 1992.

36. Morimoto Satoshi, "Nihon no bō'ei keikaku o minaose" [Reassess Japan's Defense Planning], *Voice*, August 1992, pp. 192–201.

37. Chalmers Johnson, "Japan in Search of a 'Normal' Role," *Daedalus*, vol. 121, no. 4 (Fall 1992), pp. 1–33.

38. Ishihara Shintaro, *The Japan That Can Say No* (New York: Simon and Schuster, 1991), pp. 55–56; and Ishihara Shintarō and Etō Jun, *Dankō "No" to ieru Nihon* (The Japan That Can Say a Firm No) (Tōkyō: Kōbunsha, 1991), pp. 170–83.

39. Peter J. Katzenstein and Nobuo Okawara, "Japan's National Security: Structures, Norms, and Policies"; Thomas U. Berger, "From Sword to Chrysanthemum: Japan's Culture of Anti-militarism," *International Security*, vol. 17, no. 4 (Spring 1993), pp. 84–150.

40. George Friedman and Meredith Lebard, *The Coming War with Japan* (New York: St. Martin's Press, 1991), p. 211.

41. Steven Vogel, "The Power behind 'Spin-Ons': The Military Implications of Japan's Commercial Technology," in Wayne Sandholtz et al., *The Highest Stakes: The Economic Foundations of the Next Security System* (New York: Oxford University Press, 1992), pp. 55–80.

42. Asai Motofumi, *Nihon gaikō: hansei to tenkan* (Tokyo: Iwanami Shoten, 1989), pp. 158–99.

43. Tatsurō Kunigi, "Toward a Renaissance of the United Nations," *Japan Quarterly,* vol. 38, no. 1 (January–March 1991), p. 25.

44. Asai Motofumi, *Amerika ga Nihon o tataku honto no riyu* (Tokyo: Goma Shobo, 1990), pp. 198–207.

45. Okazaki Hisahiko, "China Must Shed 'Middle Kingdom' Mentality," *The Daily Yomiuri,* February 8, 1993. See also Okazaki Hisahiko, "Chūgoku mondai saihō," *Chūō Kōron,* vol. 108, no. 3 (February 1993), pp. 30–51.

46. Kakizawa Kōji, "A New Stage in Sino-Japanese Ties," *Japan Echo,* vol. 20 (Special Issue 1993), pp. 49–50.

47. Nakasone Yasuhiro, Murakami Yasusuke, Satō Seizaburō, and Nishibe Susumu, *Kyōdō kenkyū: Reisen igo* (Tokyo: Bungei Shunjū, 1992), pp. 217–19.

48. NHK Shuzaihan, *Nichi-Bei no shototsu* (Tokyo: Nihon Hoso Shuppankai, 1990); and Leonard J. Schoppa, "Gaiatsu and Economic Bargaining Outcomes," *International Organization,* vol. 47, no. 3 (Summer 1993), pp. 353–86.

49. Gregory W. Noble, *Flying Apart? Japanese-American Negotiations over the FSX Fighter Plane* (Berkeley: University of California Institute of International Studies, 1992).

50. Ikeda Tadashi, " 'Ajia-shugi' de nai Ajia gaiko o," *Gaiko Forum,* no. 65 (February 1994), pp. 58–59.

51. Michael Vatikiotis, "The New Player: Japan Takes More Assertive Regional Role," *Far Eastern Economic Review,* August 1, 1991, p. 11.

52. "CSCE Ajia-ban mo" [A CSCE for Asia as Well], *Yomiuri Shimbun,* July 15, 1992.

53. Yukio Satoh, "Structuring a New Partnership with the Clinton Administration," *Washington-Japan Journal,* Winter 1993, pp. 14–15.

54. Naoki Saito, "The Passing of the PKO Cooperation Law: Japan's Struggle to Define Its International Contribution," *International Institute for Global Peace Policy Paper,* no. 102E (November 1992).

55. Robert Delfs, "The Vanishing Threat: Opposition Parties Combine to Demand Defence Cuts," *Far Eastern Economic Review,* February 20, 1992, pp. 10–11.

56. Norman D. Levin, Mark Lorell, and Arthur Alexander, *The Wary Warriors: Future Directions in Japanese Security Policies* (Santa Monica, CA: Rand, 1993), pp. 37–77.

57. Morita Akio, "A Critical Moment for Japanese Management," *Japan Echo,* vol. 19, no. 2 (Summer 1992), pp. 8–14.

6

The United States and the Asia-Pacific Region in the Post–Cold War Era

Donald S. Zagoria

Accused by critics of having failed to develop a coherent foreign policy vision for the post–Cold War era, President Clinton and his foreign policy team have begun to respond to the challenge. By the middle of 1994, the Clinton team was voicing several major themes. First, economics is assuming a new centrality in international relations and to be strong abroad, the United States must have a strong economic base at home. In an increasingly global economy, Washington must seek to harness that economy for the benefit of its own people. To do this, the United States must get its own economic house in order, make trade a priority element of American security policy, improve economic coordination among the major industrial powers, and promote steady expansion in the developing world, especially in East Asia, which now constitutes a rapidly expanding market for U.S. exports.

Second, the successor to a doctrine of containment should be a strategy of enlargement of the world's free community of market democracies. The highest priority in such a strategy is to strengthen the bonds and the sense of common interest among the major market democracies in Europe, Japan, and North America. Another important priority must be to help ensure the success of democracy in Russia and in the world's other new democracies.

Finally, in promoting global peace and security, the United States must try to stop the spread of weapons of mass destruction, be prudent in cutting its military budget, and be prepared to use multilateral mechanisms such as the United Nations more than previously, but only under certain conditions and when multilateralism serves to protect American interests.

With specific regard to East Asia, the Clinton administration's policy was spelled out in greater detail than before during the president's trip to Japan and South Korea in July 1993 and at the summit meeting of the Asia Pacific Economic Cooperation (APEC) forum hosted by the United States in Seattle in November 1993.[1] The basic U.S. goal in the Pacific, said the president, would be to join with Japan and others in the region to create a "new Pacific community." This community needs the support of both economic and security pillars. The economic pillars include a revived partnership between the United States and Japan and progress throughout the region toward more open economies and greater trade. The security pillars include a continued U.S. military commitment to the region; stronger efforts to combat the proliferation of weapons of mass destruction; new regional dialogues on common security challenges; and support for democracy and more open societies throughout the region.

Clinton's speeches in Asia and in Seattle went some way toward calming the fears of many Asians that the United States, preoccupied with domestic challenges, was preparing to retreat from that important region of the world. Still, there are a number of difficult challenges to be faced, and the region is waiting to see how well U.S. deeds match U.S. rhetoric.

In this essay, I want first to discuss the post–Cold War economic and strategic environment in East Asia. Then I want to emphasize the growing geopolitical and economic importance of East Asia and to assess the extent of U.S. leverage in the region. I will go on to discuss the Clinton administration's East Asia policies under three headings: security issues, economic issues, and the promotion of human rights and democracy. Finally, I want to discuss some of the principal challenges and opportunities that the administration is likely to face in East Asia in the coming years.

The New Strategic Environment

Both optimists and pessimists can make strong arguments for their different assessments of the security situation in East Asia now that the Cold War is over. Let me begin with the case for optimism.

First, the region is at peace. This contrasts sharply with the situation in the former Soviet Union, the Balkans, and the Middle East. The current situation is also in contrast to the region's past. During the past half century, there has been a civil war in China, a war in Korea, several Indochina wars, the Sino-Soviet border conflict, the Sino-Vietnamese war, and the Cambodian civil war, to name only the most prominent conflicts in post–World War II East Asia.

A second cause for optimism is that the market-friendly, export-oriented economies of the region are booming, with the highest rates of growth in the world. Economic growth in the Asia-Pacific region is expected to continue despite recession in Europe and slow growth in the United States. And this economic dynamism will have a number of positive political results. Because peace and stability are preconditions for trade and investment, the states of the region have acquired a big stake in a more relaxed international environment and in the continuation of an open, liberal trading system. Even China and Vietnam, two states still led by communist parties, have adopted an outward-oriented, market-friendly growth strategy. Such a strategy will inevitably lead to a greater degree of transparency and pluralism.

A third factor contributing to optimism is the spread of democracy. South Korea and Taiwan have recently joined the ranks of the democracies, and, after a brief period of military rule, Thailand has once again established a civilian government. In Cambodia, a huge turnout for elections sponsored by the United Nations has led to the formation of a new, legitimate government for the first time in several decades. The spread of democracy in East Asia, moreover, is not simply a fortuitous development. Rather, it is the product of powerful forces now at work throughout the region, especially economic growth, which has produced a liberal middle class, and the telecommunications revolution, which makes it impossible for governments to isolate their own people from global developments.

A fourth factor leading to optimism is the recent beginning of multilateral economic and security institutions in a region that has never had them. An economic group of seventeen states—the Asia Pacific Economic Cooperation Forum—was formed in 1989 and is mapping out a strategy for trade and investment liberalization. The United States hosted the first APEC summit meeting in Seattle in November 1993, and the meeting was attended by most of the top leaders in Asia. At the same time, a new Regional Forum of the Association of Southeast Asian Nations (ASEAN) has also come into existence. This group, which now includes all of the major powers, met for the first time in 1994. It is likely to concentrate on increasing military transparency and resolving or pre-empting regional conflicts.

A final cause for optimism is that the risk of a conflict between any two of the four major powers in the region—the United States, Russia, Japan, and China—is lower than at any time in this century. This may have a great deal to do with the existence of nuclear weapons and the enormously increased cost of military conflict between major powers. It may also have something to do with a factor stressed by liberal theorists of international relations—the opportunities, through trade, investment, and the development of technology, to increase power without resorting to force of arms.[2]

The pessimistic case for East Asia stresses the many potential sources of instability in the region and the likelihood that the relative decline of U.S. power, accompanied by the rise of Japan and China, will give birth to great-power rivalries of the sort common throughout history.[3] Trade tensions between the United States and Japan are growing as the Cold War glue that bound the two allies together is melting. Japan and China, while cooperating economically, still eye each other warily. Russia and Japan are still divided by a territorial dispute over the Kuril Islands. The United States and China are at odds over trade, missile sales, and human rights, and, until recently, the United States threatened to withdraw China's Most Favored Nation (MFN) trade privileges unless China improved its human rights performance.

Meanwhile, prior to a recent nuclear freeze agreement it signed with the United States, North Korea was threatening to leave the nuclear nonproliferation regime, a development that could encourage proponents of nuclear weapons development in both South Korea and Japan. Also, many countries in the region are modernizing their armed forces, and there is the danger of an arms race.

Finally, the rise of China is viewed by many realist theorists of international relations as an inevitably destabilizing phenomenon in the years and decades ahead. In this view, the rise of new great powers has always disturbed the existing equilibrium and frequently led to "hegemonic wars."[4] Because China's power potential is so enormous, accommodating it will be difficult.

It is important to understand that both the optimists and the pessimists are pointing to significant trends in the region. Either view could prove to be right. Much depends on what happens in the years ahead, on the future of the global economy, on the domestic politics of key countries, on the nature of political leadership, and on many other factors. The challenge for policymakers in the United States and Asia will be to find ways to accelerate the positive trends while coping with, and reducing, the potential sources of tension.

Let me now turn to examining Asia's rising economic and strategic importance and the implications of all this for the United States.

East Asia's Growing Strategic Importance

Any assessment of U.S. interests in East Asia must begin with the fact that the global balance of power is increasingly shifting toward the Pacific. Consider the following:

- East Asia, with almost half of the world's population, is the most rapidly growing region of the world. By the end of the century or in the early part of the next century, according to the International Monetary Fund (IMF), it will account for 30 percent of world GNP, while the United States will represent only 18 or 19 percent.
- East Asian central banks today control approximately 42 percent of total world central bank reserves. Because of very high savings rates in the region, which exceed 30 percent of national GNPs, East Asia has the world's largest pool of capital.
- East Asia is at the center of world trade. Its trade with Europe and North America is greater than the trade between the two other major industrial regions.
- Japan is already the second largest industrial economy in the world and could well catch up to the United States in total GNP in the early part of the next century.
- China is the fastest-growing country in the world and, according to conservative estimates by American specialists, already has a GNP of about $1.2 trillion.

- The newly industrial economies in East Asia, such as Taiwan, South Korea, Singapore, and other ASEAN countries, are among the fastest growing countries in the world. According to one projection, Asia, excluding Japan, will have a GNP of more than $5 trillion by 2020.
- Several East Asian countries are quite advanced in high-technology industries, and a number of them are beginning to develop modern defense industries.

In sum, East Asia is destined to be a center of world power in the next century. A stable and increasingly democratic East Asia allied with, or friendly to, the United States and integrated into a trans-Pacific community could be a potent force for U.S. security and for global prosperity and stability. But an East Asia that is increasingly alienated from the United States, that develops a rival economic bloc, and that pursues policies inimical to U.S. interests could be a very serious threat to U.S. security and to global stability.

United States Leverage in the Pacific

For at least the remainder of this decade, the United States will continue to have considerable strategic and economic leverage in East Asia. On the strategic side, all these countries want the United States to remain engaged as the principal outside balancer because they regard the United States as a relatively benign power needed to check more troubling neighbors with whom they have had a long history of conflict.

In Northeast Asia, a continued United States presence is wanted to keep a cap on Japan's defense capability, to balance a rising China, to ensure against a revival of an authoritarian, expansionist Russia, and to deter a Stalinist dictatorship in North Korea, which now threatens to develop nuclear weapons. In Southeast Asia, the United States is wanted to balance China, which has territorial disputes with several governments in the region over the Paracel and Spratly Islands, and which is steadily increasing its power projection capabilities. Since many of the countries in the region are dependent upon imports of oil from the Middle East and Persian Gulf, the United States is also wanted to guarantee the security of the sea lanes.

No other country in East Asia could replace the United States as the security guarantor. If the United States Seventh Fleet were to be withdrawn from the Pacific, the most likely development would be a naval arms race between Japan, China, and other East Asian powers. The resulting instability would almost certainly harm the region's prosperity and security.

The United States also has considerable economic leverage in the region. Virtually every country wants to increase trade and investment relations with the United States. For most countries in East Asia, the United States is the first or second largest trading partner, the largest market, and an important source of investment. Although intraregional trade within East Asia is growing rapidly, more than half of East Asia's trade still goes outside East Asia, and a substantial part of this is with the United States.

Furthermore, it is not in the interests of the East Asian countries to be dominated economically by Japan. Yet Japan is by far the largest of the economies in the region, the principal provider of development assistance, and the largest source of new investment. Most countries in the region therefore have an interest in encouraging more U.S. trade and investment in East Asia in order to balance the economic role of Japan. And the Japanese themselves have a strong stake in a continuing U.S. economic presence in East Asia because they know that without a growing economic stake, the U.S. interest in maintaining its military commitments may dwindle. If this were to happen, Japan would have to contemplate filling the vacuum, a step that would almost certainly arouse considerable domestic opposition as well as security concerns throughout the region.

There is yet another reason why East Asia wants the United States to remain engaged in the region. That is because the United States continues to be the most crucial player in a number of global and regional issues that are bound to be of continuing concern. These issues include maintaining a liberal international and regional trading system, strengthening the United Nations and regional peacekeeping systems, resolving a number of outstanding regional security conflicts, and halting the spread of nuclear weapons and missiles.

The Clinton Administration's Agenda in the Pacific

Let me turn now to summarizing what seem to be some of the major themes of the Clinton administration as it seeks to develop a post–Cold War agenda for East Asia. In a number of recent speeches, the president has outlined an ambitious agenda for U.S. policy. This agenda includes the promotion of U.S. interests in regional security, economic cooperation, and the development of human rights and democracy throughout the region. It reflects the expansion of U.S. interests beyond the post–Cold War policy of containment.

Clinton's Security Agenda in the Pacific

In his speech to the South Korean National Assembly in July 1993, President Clinton went a long way toward allaying widespread fears in the region that a Democratic president preoccupied with America's economy would opt for a policy of retreat and disengagement from the Pacific. Clinton went out of his way to distance himself from the last Democratic president, Jimmy Carter, who announced his intention to withdraw U.S. ground troops from South Korea soon after he took office. Clinton affirmed in Seoul that the bedrock of America's security role in the Pacific must be a continuing military presence and that U.S. troops would remain in South Korea "as long as the Korean people want and need us here." Moreover, he announced that any further reductions in American forces in South Korea would be frozen pending clarification of the North Korean nuclear threat. And he warned Pyongyang that its use of nuclear weapons would lead to the total destruction of North Korea.

The president also reaffirmed the five U.S. security agreements with Japan, Korea, Australia, the Philippines, and Thailand and the intention of the United States to maintain "a substantial forward presence" in East Asia, so that the region could focus less energy on an arms race and more energy on the peaceful race toward economic development.

The second security theme developed by Clinton in Seoul was the determination of his administration to combat the spread of weapons of mass destruction and their means of delivery. The president urged North Korea to reaffirm its commitment to the Nuclear Non-Proliferation Treaty (NPT), to fulfill its full-scope safeguards obligations to the International Atomic Energy Agency (IAEA), and to implement bilateral inspections under the South–North Nuclear Accord. And he expressed concern over what he called North Korea's commitment to "indiscriminate sales" of its Scud missiles and its efforts to develop and export an even more powerful missile with a range of 600 miles or more—enough for North Korea to threaten Japan.

A third security theme developed by President Clinton in Seoul was the commitment of his administration to developing new regional dialogues on common security challenges. The president said there was no need for the Pacific to develop a single security institution such as NATO to meet the new security challenges in the region because there was no single threat. Rather, the challenge was to develop a variety of new arrangements to meet multiple threats and opportunities. Significantly, the president said that the United States was prepared to involve and engage China in this enterprise, but he warned that China cannot be a full partner in the world community until it respects human rights and international agreements on trade and weapons sales.

In sum, Clinton used his South Korea trip to signal a number of U.S. security concerns in the region while seeking to reassure the Asians that the United States intended to maintain its security commitments and its forward presence. Perhaps the most important signal was the symbolism of a newly elected Democratic president choosing to go to South Korea so early in his administration—it was only his second overseas trip—and to emphasize security rather than economic issues while there. The contrast between the Clinton and Carter administrations could not have been greater.

The Economic Agenda in the Pacific

It was while he was in Japan that the president unveiled his economic approach to the Pacific. Clinton said that his first foreign policy priority would be to create a new and stronger partnership between the United States and Japan. He thus took a substantial step away from the strident and confrontational rhetoric about Japan that had marked the first few months of his presidency. The president noted that the two countries together account for nearly 40 percent of the world's economic output, that neither nation could thrive without the other, and that the economic relationship benefited both nations. Yet, he warned, in contrast to the U.S. relationship with all other wealthy nations, the United States had a huge and chronic trade deficit with Japan. This imbalance could not, he went on, be attributed solely to unfair Japanese barriers and, indeed, was in part simply a tribute to Japanese abilities to produce high-quality, competitively priced goods. But it was also clear that U.S. markets were more open to Japanese products and investments than Japanese markets were open to U.S. goods and capital. This imbalance hurt not only American workers and businesses but also Japanese consumers. And this was why the United States sought a new framework for trade on macroeconomic, sectoral, and structural issues.

The second economic building block of the Pacific community, Clinton argued, must be a more open regional and global economy. An essential starting point would be the successful completion of the Uruguay Round of the General Agreement on Tariffs and Trade (GATT). But the United States would also work to reduce regional trade barriers. And the most promising forum for debating these issues was the newly formed organization for Asia-Pacific Economic Co-operation. The seventeen members of APEC account for nearly half of the world's total output, and they include most of the fastest-growing economies in the world.

In sum, Clinton went some distance in Tokyo toward calming Japanese fears that the new U.S. administration was going to be protectionist and confrontational. His rhetoric on the trade issues was more measured than it had been earlier in his administration, suggesting that he would develop a more balanced approach to reducing the chronic trade deficit, an approach that was in fact not too different from that of his predecessor.

The Democracy Agenda in the Pacific

While in East Asia, President Clinton also forcefully argued that in addition to its security and economic goals, the third U.S. priority in building a new Pacific community must be to support the wave of democratic reform sweeping the region. This was not, the president suggested, a moral crusade. Rather, there were concrete U.S. interests in the spread of democracy. Open societies were better able than closed societies to address and resolve the frictions that economic growth creates. A free press roots out corruption. The rule of law encourages and protects investment. Democracy also guarantees regional peace and stability because democracies do not wage war on one another, engage in terrorism, or generate refugees. Democracy is also the best guarantor of human rights.

Responding to those in East Asia who argue that democracy is unsuited for

Asia or that Asian culture places a higher emphasis on harmony than on individual rights, Clinton declared that the growing number of democracies and democratic movements in the region demonstrates that democracy is the aspiration of the East Asian peoples themselves.

Challenges and Opportunities in the Pacific

The crucial test of the Clinton administration's policies in East Asia will, however, not be its rhetoric and declarations. Rather, the true test of the administration will be how well it responds to a number of challenges and opportunities that are already on the horizon.

Developing Durable and Comprehensive Ties with Japan

The most important challenge for the United States will be to develop a new post–Cold War policy toward Japan that integrates security, political, and economic concerns and that accords Japan the highest priority in U.S. global strategy. One of the major foreign policy failures of the Bush administration was its inattention to Japan. Former secretary of state James Baker spent less than a week in Japan during the entire four years of the Bush administration, and Baker's successor, Lawrence Eagleburger, twice conceded in speeches after he left office that the failure to build comprehensive and durable political ties with Japan was one of his biggest regrets. The single most important test of the Clinton administration's foreign policy in Asia will be whether it makes a serious effort to build such ties and whether it succeeds.

From an American point of view, there are three ways to look at Japan: largely as an economic rival, largely as a potential partner, or as a country with which the United States will continue to have many important common interests while being an economic rival. It is the last of these views that is held by this writer.

The United States and Japan share a strong common interest in maintaining global peace and stability and an open international trading system. Both have an interest in strengthening the United Nations peacekeeping regime. Both want to halt the spread of nuclear weapons and missiles. Both want a prosperous and unified East Asia. They also share common interests in virtually every key region of the world. Both want China to continue its progress toward market reform; both want Russia to maintain progress toward market reform and democracy; both want to see the peace process in the Middle East bear fruit.

Without a solid and harmonious U.S.–Japan relationship, none of these goals can be achieved. Indeed, if relations sour, the worst fears of the realists will be realized. Japan will eventually conclude that the United States is an unreliable ally, and that it must thus develop its own military power, including nuclear weapons, and assume the leadership of an East Asian security bloc. But none of these developments are inevitable, as some realists seem to think.[5] Much depends on United States policy in the years and decades ahead.

Fortunately, the most noteworthy feature about current Japanese thinking on foreign policy is the lack of support for a foreign policy approach that weakens Japanese links with the United States. A go-it-alone Gaullist policy draws little support in Japan. The Socialist Party has abandoned its traditional policy of unarmed neutrality. An Asianist approach advocating Japanese leadership of an East Asian bloc excluding the United States has failed to attract broad support. And few serious Japanese strategic thinkers believe that the U.S.–Japan alliance can be replaced by a collective security arrangement focused on the United Nations.

The dominant position in Japan's foreign policy debate is the internationalist position. This approach advocates that, while maintaining its alliance with the United States, Japan should play a larger economic and political, but not military, role in the international community.[6]

There are a number of reasons why alternative foreign policy options are not attractive to most Japanese strategic thinkers. First, the postwar period, in which the United States and Japan have been allied, has been a period of enormous success for Japan. Japan has enjoyed unprecedented peace and prosperity since the end of World War II, and most Japanese are hesitant to change a course that has been so successful.

Second, there is acute recognition within Japan of Japan's substantial vulnerabilities. Japan imports all its food and energy; has little offensive power-projection capability to protect its sea lanes of communication; is culturally isolated from most of the rest of the world; continues to rely heavily on the U.S. market for its exports; is the object of widespread suspicion in the rest of Asia; and is surrounded by two nuclear powers, Russia and China, with each of whom it has had troubled relations in the twentieth century.

Third, the alliance with the United States solves Japan's key geopolitical dilemma: It is a maritime power separated from the Asian mainland; it confronts huge land powers on the mainland—Russia and China—and its security would be threatened if the nearby Korean peninsula fell into the hands of a hostile power. To cope with this geopolitical dilemma, Japan, since emerging as a modern nation, has sought alliances with the Anglo-Saxon naval powers. Japan's alliance with Great Britain (1901–22) helped Japan counter tsarist Russia's aims in Korea and Manchuria. And during the Cold War, the alliance with the United States ensured that no hostile power would control the southern part of the Korean peninsula opposite Japan. Thus, the Anglo-Saxon powers have been essential partners in resolving Japan's security dilemma.[7]

But although the United States and Japan share a large number of common interests, they are also economic rivals. They will compete for markets and for primacy in the high-technology industries of the twenty-first century. Although Japan may open its markets to a greater extent than in the past, it is unlikely to abandon completely the neomercantalist economic strategy that has served it so well in the past.

The United States must therefore continue to try to pry open Japanese markets. During the past year or two, agreements have been reached to liberalize Japan's financial markets and its construction industry. The Bush administration also negotiated a number of sectoral agreements to open particular Japanese markets. These market-opening efforts should continue. But the main priority for the United States should be getting its own economic house in order, not bashing Japan. Innumerable studies have indicated that even if Japan were to open all of its markets completely to American goods, the chronic bilateral trade deficit would still be huge. The main problem for the United States is to reverse its internal consumption/savings ratio. Since 1980, the United States has consumed almost $1.5 trillion more than it has produced, while Germany and Japan have accumulated more than $1 trillion in future demands on American assets. The United States must reverse this pattern of dependence on foreigners by increasing its domestic savings and investment rates. As many economists have pointed out, "as long as a country consumes more than it produces, it will experience a trade deficit and a corresponding reliance on foreigners to finance it." Vigorous efforts to open external markets cannot alter this.[8]

In addition, the United States must strengthen its own industrial base by increasing domestic investment in industrial plant and equipment, in human capital, and in new technology. In recent years, the United States has had a very small investment rate, less than half that of its rivals in Europe and East Asia.

In sum, the United States needs an East Asia policy that recognizes that Japan is its most important partner in the region, that it shares many fundamental common interests with that country, and that continued security and political cooperation are essential to the maintenance of regional peace and stability, while at the same time understanding that the United States and Japan are economic rivals. To develop a more effective East Asia policy and to compete more effectively with Japan, the United States needs both to pry open closed markets and, perhaps more importantly, to resolve many of its own domestic economic problems.

Maintaining a Favorable Balance of Power

A second foreign policy priority for the United States is closely related to the first priority. The United States should seek to maintain the military forces necessary to preserve the favorable balance of power in the Pacific. The current military balance minimizes Japan's temptation to become a major military power, deters potential regional troublemakers, reduces the likelihood that a new arms race will develop, and, over the longer run, ensures that the Pacific will not be dominated by a single hegemonic power. All these developments will promote regional stability and the prospects for peaceful competition among the great powers.

To accomplish this goal, the United States needs to maintain a substantial military presence in the region. This means that the United States must maintain substantial ground forces in South Korea to reassure Seoul of its intent to deter and resist a North Korean attack. It must also continue to maintain a home port for an aircraft carrier battle group in Japan, thus providing a visible symbol of the ongoing value of the U.S.–Japan mutual defense treaty. Finally, it must continue to deploy a strong and visible naval presence throughout the region, making use of the port facilities of various regional partners in Northeast and Southeast Asia. Should the United States maintain such force levels, it will also possess substantial air force capability throughout the Pacific.

Maintaining an adequate U.S. military presence in the Pacific should not be an overly onerous assignment. American forward-deployed forces in East Asia now constitute only about 6.3 percent of U.S. total military forces and account for only about 15 to 20 percent of the total U.S. defense budget. The U.S. military presence in East Asia is a highly cost-effective investment.

Developing Stable Relations with China

A third priority for the United States in East Asia should be to stabilize relations with China. Some analysts say that China has lost its strategic importance to the United States because of the end of the Cold War and the collapse of the Soviet Union. In this view, the United States no longer needs to cultivate good relations with China because it no longer needs to balance Soviet power. This is an extremely shortsighted view.

China remains of considerable strategic importance to the United States for a number of reasons. It is an influential member of the international order. More than one of every five human beings live there. China possesses nuclear weapons, and it exports nuclear technology. China launches satellites and sells missiles. It represents a huge and growing market. It is one of the world's richest civilizations. It holds a permanent seat on the UN Security Council. China's cooperation is needed to resolve key Asian security issues, including the North Korean nuclear problem.

Thus, a return to Sino-American confrontation would be extremely destabilizing for the region. China has the capacity to harm U.S. interests in many areas of the world, particularly in Asia, and the United States needs to prevent or limit possible Chinese expansionism by encouraging present trends toward a market economy and by integrating China into a regional economic and security structure. The Clinton administration should try to work with Beijing on issues where the two countries' interests converge and to bargain hard on issues where the United States has significant differences with China. But blanket trade sanctions, such as removing China's MFN status, are counterproductive, because they work against the economic forces promoting Chinese openness and reform. Nor would they be supported by U.S. allies and friends in the region. The sanctions would thus be ineffective and would undermine U.S. economic and political interests throughout the region.

Finally, as China's economic and military capabilities grow in the late twentieth and early twenty-first centuries, as they inevitably will, much will depend on how the other regional powers cope with China's rising power. Whether China uses its growing authority to promote regional stability or to undermine the interests of its neighbors may be significantly determined by the policies of others toward China, particularly the policies of the United States.

The basic choice is between containing and accommodating China. And there are several reasons why containment is not now a sensible policy. First, China is no longer, as it was in the 1950s and 1960s, a revisionist or revolutionary power intent on overthrowing the established international order. On the contrary, China requires a long period of peace and cooperation with other powers in the Pacific while it carries out its ambitious policies of reform and modernization at home.

Second, although U.S. and Chinese interests and values conflict in several areas, such as China's abuse of human rights and missile sales, there are other areas in which the two nations have common interests, including preventing North Korea from developing nuclear weapons, bringing peace to Cambodia, increasing trade, ensuring that East Asia continues to be peaceful and prosperous, and developing Asian regional institutions. Thus, the United States must develop the capacity to develop a more normal relationship with China, in which it confronts disagreements in one corner of the relationship while developing cooperation in other areas.

Third, few, if any, Asian countries would join the United States in pursuing a policy of containment of China. Virtually every country in the region is steadily improving its economic and political relations with China, including those that are apprehensive over increasing Chinese military power. They all believe that a stable and secure East Asia can best be achieved by trying to integrate rather than to contain China. And they all would like to see the United States improve its relations with China.

Fourth, China presents significant economic opportunities for American companies. Many U.S. manufacturing and high-technology companies are beginning to increase their investment in China. China already provides a lucrative market for American companies specializing in power generation, telecommunications, energy exploration, aircraft, farm machinery, and many other areas. The loss of these markets would be highly detrimental to employment in these industries. On the other hand, the potential market expansion in these industries is considerable and would significantly benefit both domestic employment and economic growth.

Finally, none of the central U.S. goals in East Asia can be achieved without some degree of cooperation with China. It will be impossible to develop viable regional institutions such as APEC and the Asean Regional Forum or to resolve a number of regional conflicts without China's constructive participation. And it will be impossible to liberalize the trade and investment regime in East Asia without including China.

Differences between the United States and China over human rights will continue because the Chinese leadership is determined to maintain control and to suppress dissidence in the interest of preserving stability. And China is unlikely to become a democracy in the foreseeable future. Still, the East Asian experience suggests that there are two powerful forces working for democratization all over the region—economic development and the telecommunications revolution. Already there is more political change in China than is generally understood in the West. The old tools of indoctrination are no longer effective. The old communist ideology is largely discredited. There has been some attempt to codify the legal system. As a result of small businesses springing up across the country, much of the society is now outside the control of the Chinese Communist Party. The prosperous coastal provinces, in particular, are able to defy the conservative Beijing leadership on many issues.

The challenge for the United States will be to develop a policy toward China that balances its strategic, economic, and human rights concerns. Denying China MFN status would have been counterproductive. It would have deprived China's reformers of their economic base, devastated the economy of Hong Kong, the principal outpost of free trade in Asia, and done significant damage to Taiwan's economy as well. It would also have endangered those remaining areas of potential U.S.-Chinese cooperation on issues such as Korea, nuclear testing, and missile control.

The Clinton administration acted wisely in abandoning linkage between China's MFN status and its human rights policies. Moreover, the administration has recently begun to resume high-level diplomatic and military contacts with China, most of which were suspended after Tiananmen. This, too, is a sensible policy. Suspending such dialogues was irrational. Even during the height of the Cold War, the United States did not suspend high-level meetings with the Soviet leadership. The most urgent need is for the United States to resume a variety of Cabinet and high-level dialogues with China that would be designed to clarify areas of difference and potential areas for cooperation between the two countries. The work of all three joint Sino-American commissions (on science and technology, commerce and trade, and economics) should be resumed. High-level contacts between senior U.S. and Chinese military leaders should be expanded to clarify differences between the countries on China's nuclear testing and sales of missiles. China's recent agreement to adhere to the guidelines of the Missile Technology Control Regime and to discuss a comprehensive nuclear test ban are positive signs.

The North Korean Nuclear Issue

Another high priority for the United States in Asia should be the halting of nuclear and missile proliferation. This means drawing both China and North Korea into the nuclear and missile arms control regimes.

North Korea denies that it is building nuclear weapons, but suspicions were raised in March 1993 when it stopped allowing full inspections of its nuclear facilities and subsequently announced its intention of withdrawing from the Nuclear Non-Proliferation Treaty. After the United States held two rounds of high-level talks with Pyongyang in June and July 1993, North Korea announced that it would resume negotiations with the IAEA over the issue of nuclear inspections. And after eighteen months of difficult negotiations, the United States and North Korea finally reached an accord in which Pyongyang agreed to freeze its nuclear program in exchange for oil shipments from the United States, help in constructing new light-water reactors, and an exchange of liaison offices. Although this agreement has come under fire both in Seoul and in Washington, it appears to have been the only realistic alternative short of military action. And the Clinton administration deserves praise for obtaining this agreement. The challenge in the future will be to ensure that Pyongyang abides by the agreement and halts its nuclear weapons program.

Dealing with Regional Conflicts

Another high priority for the United States in the Pacific should be to work with other countries to prevent or reduce regional conflicts. The principal sources of conflict in East Asia are (1) the remaining cases of divided states, namely the two Koreas and China–Taiwan; (2) the unresolved territorial disputes, and (3) the continuing uncertainty that surrounds the future of Cambodia.

One of the most promising ways to defuse these conflicts, as Robert Scalapino has suggested, is through a situation-specific set of concentric arcs. In the case of Korea, the first arc is composed of the two Koreas. The prime ministers of the two states have been meeting regularly and have signed two important agreements on nonaggression and nonproliferation. The second arc is composed of the four major powers that have long been involved in Korea—the United States, China, Russia, and Japan. All four powers have an interest in stability in the Korean peninsula, and all have been working to achieve that goal. Beyond the four powers, there lies yet another arc—international bodies such as the IAEA.

In the China–Taiwan case, the first arc is again composed of the two parties most directly involved—China and Taiwan. Economic and cultural ties are growing and a liaison body for handling disputes is in place. At the same time, a second arc exists—namely the United States and Japan, who together have considerable military and economic influence on both parties. The policies of these two powers pose obstacles to any declaration of formal independence by Taiwan, an action that might trigger a militant Chinese response. Both countries recognize only one China. At the same time, the United States and Japan also pose obstacles to any Chinese aggression against Taiwan, since China cannot be sure whether the United States would forcibly resist any attempt China might make to use military force against Taiwan. Moreover, Japan's response to a Chinese use of force would undermine China's economic and political diplomacy throughout the region.

In the case of the Spratly Islands territorial dispute, the first arc is composed of China, Vietnam, Taiwan, and the ASEAN countries directly involved. The annual meeting of the ASEAN Post-Ministerial Conference (PMC) would be the logical second arc. The Spratlys dispute has been discussed at this forum in recent years. And Indonesia has sponsored a number of informal discussions on the Spratlys. Any development leading to improved relations should be encouraged.

In the case of the Russo-Japanese territorial dispute, only the two powers directly concerned—the first arc—are now involved, and there has been little progress toward settlement so far. But the United States and China can play some role in influencing developments.

In sum, for resolving regional conflicts in Asia, the United States should encourage a variety of bilateral and multilateral negotiations among interested parties. Nevertheless, this situation-specific, concentric-arc approach should be supplemented by broader regional and subregional security dialogues that would include all the powers in the region. A Southeast Asian regional security dialogue is now in place in the form of the ASEAN-PMC and the newly established ASEAN Regional Forum. These should be supplemented by a North Pacific security dialogue which might include the four major powers—the United States, China, Japan, and Russia—along with the two Koreas, Canada, and Mongolia.

Dealing with the Remaining Leninist States

Yet another broad challenge that the United States faces in East Asia is that of dealing with the remaining Leninist states—China, North Korea, and Vietnam. The future policies of these three states will be one of the critical factors determining whether Asia remains stable in the years ahead. The East Asian neighbors of these three states all hope for a gradual economic and political liberalization. They want neither a plunge into chaos nor rigid authoritarianism.

The United States needs to consult closely with its East Asian allies and friends about how to develop policies toward the three Leninist regimes that will encourage such gradual liberalization. Already there is considerable movement toward a market economy in China and Vietnam. And even in North Korea, there are signs that some groups want to open up economic relations with the outside world.

The major task for the United States should be to support constructive change in the Leninist states through various forms of economic, political, and cultural interaction. It should try to draw these countries into a wide-ranging dialogue on the principal issues relating to security and development. Isolating them will only feed the cause of extremism.

It is for this reason that the United States should expand and regularize high-level dialogues with Chinese leaders, continue the process of normalizing relations with Vietnam—which all of its friends and allies would support, and which would benefit American businesses—and maintain the high-level dialogue with North Korea.

A More Coherent U.S. Economic Policy

A final challenge for the Clinton administration will be to develop a coherent trade promotion strategy in East Asia. Such a strategy requires several prongs. It should include continuing pressure to open East Asia's markets while at the same time promoting the opportunities of American companies to compete more effectively in the region.

Over the last fifteen years, East Asia has surpassed Europe as America's most important overseas trading partner. Some estimates indicate that Pacific trade will be double the volume of Atlantic trade by the year 2000. In 1992, East Asia absorbed almost one-third of the total $422 billion in U.S. exports. The ASEAN countries in Southeast Asia are among the United States' fastest-growing export markets. They constitute a potential market of some 330 million people. Between 1986 and 1991, U.S. exports to Thailand quadrupled; to Singapore they tripled; and to all the ASEAN countries they increased by about 2½ times. Many of these countries, along with Korea and Taiwan, welcome American business as a counterweight to economic domination by Japan.

Unfortunately, however, in most of the region, U.S. investment is not keeping up with that of Japan, or even of Taiwan and South Korea. Since trade follows investment, the U.S. share of trade in the region is not increasing as rapidly as it should. In the 1980s, for example, the United States barely maintained its modest share of 16 percent of the exports to the ASEAN countries, while Japan raised its share to 24 percent.

Nor are several crucial sectors of American industry positioning themselves in East Asian markets.[9] One example from the automotive industry will suffice. Two-thirds of the unit volume growth in the international automotive industry in the 1990s will come from the blistering expansion of the East Asian car market. Firms participating in that growth will see tremendous volume increases as key new East Asian markets surge by 20 to 30 percent a year. In the ASEAN countries alone, consumers purchased 275,000 cars and light trucks in 1975; this increased to 864,000 units in 1990, and is expected to explode to 2,000,000 units by the year 2000. However, not a single American automobile producer is yet positioned to be more than a token player in any of East Asia's booming automobile markets.

There are many reasons why some sectors of American industry and some American companies are not as competitive in East Asian markets as they should be. One important factor, however, is that in Japan, financial arrangements, information on regulations, markets, and customs, and marketing support are provided by huge Japanese trading firms. In the United States, no similar public or private service trade promotion programs exist, despite the established programs in the U.S. Department of Commerce. The result is that many American firms, particularly small and medium-size firms, may be missing the boat in East Asia.

The potential for a growing U.S. corporate presence in East Asia is considerable. Indeed, American investment in East Asia is growing, albeit from a relatively small base. And some American companies have improved their competitive position in Asia over the last five years, while many expect to improve their position over the next five years. But it is time for the United States to develop a more coherent strategy for expanding the U.S. economic presence in East Asia. Revitalizing America and expanding exports to East Asia are inextricably connected. East Asia is America's fastest growing export market, and exports account for a growing portion of our economic growth.

The challenge for the Clinton administration, and for American business, is to work cooperatively toward developing a strategy that will enhance the competitiveness of American firms in the fastest-growing sector of the world economy. Bilateral trade toughness and negotiating market access agreements is one prong of such a strategy. A firm approach has sometimes borne real fruit. In 1992, the United States negotiated sixteen market access agreements with Japan, and, according to U.S. trade negotiators, trade in negotiated sectors increased faster than trade in other sectors. And in 1992, U.S. pressure prompted China to accept important agreements on market access and intellectual property rights.

A second and complementary approach would be to develop a more coherent policy to promote exports. This will require streamlining machinery for export promotion and using aid programs to help American business. Many trade analysts consider the United States to be the world's biggest export underachiever. Less than 10 percent of the U.S. economy, compared with an average of 19 percent among major trading partners, derives from exports. One big reason for this is that the United States has no coherent strategy for promoting exports. Consider the following:

- Support in Washington for export programs is haphazard, underfunded, and focused on farm sales, which represent only 10 percent of U.S. exports.
- The United States ranks last among its major trading partners in per capita government expenditure on export promotion.
- The U.S. Export-Import Bank covers less than 2 percent of export-finance transactions, versus an average of 15 percent in the developed world.
- Eighteen government agencies share export promotion responsibilities, while ten have export financing programs.
- Small and medium-sized industries are underrepresented among U.S. exports. Just sixty-six companies account for 54 percent of all U.S. exports.

United States aid programs in particular need to be reexamined. The United States needs to take a leaf out of the Japanese book and begin to tie aid to the needs of American business. This is especially the case in obtaining access to East Asia's huge infrastructure business. Building East Asia's dams, highways, ports, and telecommunications networks is potentially the most lucrative part of the region's economic development, and many U.S. companies have the capacity to compete effectively with any foreign companies in this area. Yet America lacks a strategy for exploiting infrastructure development in East Asia. Japan has obtained a large portion of this infrastructure development business in Asia by providing development assistance to East Asian countries that is either directly or indirectly tied to Japanese firms. The United States, on the other hand, now provides little development aid to Asia, and its aid projects are tied not to infrastructure but to "basic human needs."

Conclusion

For most of the twentieth century, and certainly during the Cold War, United States foreign policy was focused largely on Europe, and the formulation of that policy was dominated by a Eurocentric group within the American foreign policy establishment. During the remaining decade of the twentieth century and into the next century, no region of the world will be more important for U.S. interests than the Pacific. This new reality will require a number of adjustments, both within the American government and within the U.S. business community.

Individuals with background in Asia and with knowledge of East Asian languages and culture should be promoted to higher positions within the foreign policy bureaucracy. Either the secretary of state or his deputy, and at least some of the key players in the National Security Council, should be Asia hands. For their part, U.S. companies should train more of their executives in East Asian languages and culture. Expertise in East Asia will be a vital factor in all aspects of U.S. dealings with East Asia.

The Clinton administration has begun, in its first year and a half in office, to make the transformation required to elevate East Asia in its foreign policy priorities. But there are still serious doubts in East Asia about the depth of the U.S. commitment to the region and about U.S. priorities. The challenge for the administration in the year or two ahead will be to address these doubts.

Notes

1. For President Clinton's major speeches in Asia, see "Fundamentals of Security for a New Pacific Community," delivered to the South Korean National Assembly, printed in U.S. Department of State, *Dispatch,* July 19, 1993, vol. 4, no. 29; and "Building a New Pacific Community," speech delivered at Waseda University in Japan, *Dispatch,* July 12, 1993, vol. 4, no. 28.

2. See in particular Richard Rosecrance, *The Rise of the Trading State* (New York: Basic Books, 1987).

3. For the classic "realist" argument that the fundamental nature of international rela-

tions has not changed over the millennia and that the differential growth in power of the various states in the system undermines the stability of the status quo, see Robert Gilpin, *War and Change in World Politics* (New York: Cambridge University Press, 1981).

4. Ibid.

5. For an argument that Japan and Germany will sooner or later seek to become great powers with nuclear weapons, see Kenneth N. Waltz, "The Emerging Structure of International Politics," *International Security,* Fall 1993.

6. For this typology of Japanese foreign policy positions, I am indebted to Professor Seizaburo Sato of Tokyo University.

7. The need for Japan to ally with the Anglo-Saxon rival powers in order to ensure its security has been a constant theme in the writings of Hisashi Okazaki, a retired Japanese diplomat and Japan's preeminent writer on strategic issues.

8. For the paragraphs above and below, see the important argument advanced by Theodore H. Moran, "An Economics Agenda for Neorealists," *International Security,* Fall 1993.

9. See the statement by Kenneth Courtis to the House of Representatives, Committee on Foreign Affairs, United States Congress, February 17, 1993.

Part III:
The Local Powers

7

Korea in the Cold War and Its Aftermath

Robert A. Scalapino

In a world of extraordinary change, the challenges confronting Korea in its relations with others have shown elements of remarkable continuity. For centuries, Korea—united or divided—has attracted the attention of its big Pacific-Asian neighbors, and frequently their involvement in its internal affairs. Despite periodic efforts to isolate itself from the external world, Korea has inevitably been drawn into the geopolitics of the immediate region of which it constitutes the physical center. A shrimp among whales, a midget among giants, Korea has nevertheless been deemed important, whether to a regional balance of power or as a buffer state. History thus provides an appropriate background for the events that followed World War II.

The Emergence of Two Koreas

Korea's fate in the immediate postwar era, to be sure, was in considerable part unplanned and unintended. The war's finale came so quickly that the Russians had to hasten to claim the concessions granted them at the Yalta Conference. For Moscow, the Asian portion of the conflict was a six-day war. Yet the historic Russian interest in the Korean peninsula was easily rekindled. Korea's northern borders are only a few scant miles from important Siberian ports, including the vital naval base, Vladivostok. Moreover, at a point along the Tumen River, Chinese, Russian, and Korean borders are briefly joined.

The Soviets moved swiftly across Manchuria into Korea against a disintegrating Japanese army. Korea could easily have been unified in August 1945, but it would have been unified under Soviet control, and with an evolution similar to that which subsequently took place in the North. Under those conditions, the Russians would have finally won the Russo-Japanese War of 1904–1905—a war fought principally over Korea. The problem for Moscow was the Americans. Already, deep suspicions existed in Washington that both in Europe and in Asia, the USSR intended to expand its influence, making Eurasia a vast reservoir of communist power. Since the Pacific War had been largely an American–Japanese war, it was natural that the United States would assert its right to participate in the occupation of the Korean peninsula. However, its nearest troops were in Okinawa, and its presence did not come until the landing of U.S. forces under General J.R. Hodge on September 9.[1]

Under the circumstances, the Russians were initially accommodating. Based on an American-Russian agreement, the thirty-eighth parallel became the dividing line between Soviet and American occupations. At first, there was hope that Korean unification would be only briefly delayed. A few months later, a tentative agreement was reached among the wartime allies to establish a four-power trusteeship of Korea for five years. The Moscow Declaration of December 1945, however, was bitterly opposed by most Koreans, and was quickly abandoned. In any case, it could never have worked effectively.

In the unfolding Cold War context, the U.S.–USSR negotiations over Korean reunification that followed came to nought. Even as these negotiations were taking place, each side was attempting to create a political system in its own image. By the fall of 1948, two Koreas had been formally established, testimony to the ideological-strategic division that now marked the Eurasian world. The Republic of Korea was proclaimed in Seoul on August 15, 1948, the third anniversary of the end of Japanese rule. The Democratic People's Republic of Korea was set up in Pyongyang on September 10, less than one month later.

The two Korean leaders who had risen to the top in Pyongyang and Seoul symbolized both the differences and the similarities of the two Koreas. Kim Il Song was thirty-six years of age, a child of Chinese and Russian nurturing, supposedly a committed Marxist-Leninist, and yet soon to wage an internal power struggle against other Russian and Chinese proteges and to find in nationalism his best weapon. It was the monolithism—political and economic—of Leninism, not its internationalism, that attracted Kim.[2] Syngman Rhee was a full three decades older, influenced by Western-style democracy after decades of exile in America, including a Ph.D. at Princeton. He was prepared to see a market economy created and a civil society apart from the state exist (provided it was not too intrusive). In the final analysis, however, Rhee, like Kim, was a fiery Korea-centered nationalist who wanted a minimum of interference from either Americans or domestic opponents. Communism and democracy—with Korean characteristics—had been precariously launched, testifying to the influence of the world's current superpowers.

Within less than two years after the emergence of two Korean states, a hot war erupted on the Korean peninsula, one directly or indirectly involving each of the four large states that had a stake in Northeast Asia.[3] The Korean War was to cast its shadow over regional and, indeed, global relations for decades. In its unfolding, moreover, it revealed much about the nature of security and politics in the new era that has had relevance down to the present.

First, Kim Il Song's attack upon the South was to the United States an egregious example of communist expansionism, and it was widely assumed that both the USSR and the newly born PRC were intimately involved. Thus, despite reservations, President Truman came to the decision that the North's action could not go unanswered. Significantly, this event represented the first time in an important setting that the United States played the role of catalyst in seeking to rally international support via the United Nations to halt aggression. A strong drive was undertaken to make the defense of the ROK a multilateral effort. To be sure, it was always recognized that the United States was the only non-communist nation with the capacity and will to make a major military commitment. But while burden sharing in this era was more symbolic than real, the effort of the United States to move from unilateralism to multilateralism has its antecedents in the Korean War.

The events of this period were also significant in an entirely different sense. The war stands as a classic example of misread signals—and for this the United States bears heavy responsibility. In Europe, the peace was maintained, however precariously, because the United States was credible, at least as far as West Europe was concerned. But with respect to Asia, Washington misled the Communists, allowing them to believe that the United States would not intervene on behalf of the South. The withdrawal of American forces from South Korea in 1949 had been followed by statements by Secretary of State Dean Acheson, the Joint Chiefs of Staff, and others indicating that the ROK was not within the perimeter of American defense commitments. Thus, Kim Il Song could tell Stalin in the spring of 1950 that the likelihood of American involvement was very slight, and that aided by hundreds of thousands of dissident South Koreans (a figure grossly exaggerated), his forces could "liberate" the South in a few weeks. Unfortunately, it was not the last time that the U.S. government made the grave error of misleading opponents; Vietnam and Iraq followed.

A third aspect of the picture warrants attention. The behavior of the key states was based less on ideological considerations than on perceptions of national interest, a fact with continuing, even growing relevance to later events. While not posing objections to Kim's plan, Stalin was exceedingly cautious, not wanting to provoke a frontal Russian-American confrontation. Thus, the Russians avoided open participation, although Soviet pilots covertly took part, Soviet air protection was pledged to China, and ample Soviet military supplies were provided (most of them sold, not given). The USSR did not consider its stake in Korea great enough to risk a global war. Indeed, Russian behavior was sufficiently minimal to lay the seeds for the subsequent Sino-Soviet cleavage.

At the outset, although Mao had been informed of the plans, he and his associates did not believe that China would be involved. When Kim faced the prospect of a crushing defeat, however, a decision had to be reached. Divided counsels existed, but Mao carried the day with the argument that if the United States were not stopped here, it would pose a greater threat to China later. This decision exacted a heavy price in lives, economic plans, and global image, but it rested on a leader's perception of national interests.

The U.S. decision to prevent the conquest of the ROK was based upon ideological as well as strategic grounds, but that decision raised certain issues that remain of critical importance, as the agonies from Vietnam to Bosnia have revealed. The Korean War was the first protracted limited war fought by the United States. There was no desire to escalate the conflict into an all-regional or global war. But can a democratic society successfully fight such a war, or will not an attrition of public support occur, undermining the will of the nation? And should soldiers be asked to fight "with one hand tied behind their backs"? Further, if the tactic of limited war is to be employed, what constitutes victory? What are the goals, and can they be attained by this means? No consensus on the answers was forthcoming then, nor is it now.

Meanwhile, the Korean War induced a new U.S. security structure for Asia, different from, but nearly as comprehensive as, that for Europe. The emphasis was on Northeast Asia—South Korea, Taiwan, and Japan via bilateral treaties— but Southeast Asia was not overlooked. The Southeast Asia Treaty Organization (SEATO), established in 1954, included Thailand and the Philippines, and via a separate protocol, support was extended to South Vietnam, Laos, and Cambodia. Thus, events on the Korean peninsula had caused the United States to create a broad balance of power in Asia, as it had previously done in Europe.

Japan was one nation that benefited directly from the Korean War. Its long-term security was strengthened not only by the defeat of the North's effort to extend its control to the whole of the peninsula, but also by the stronger commitment of the United States to Japan's defense, symbolized by the Mutual Security Treaty. Japan was now free to place its priority on economic growth, and indeed, the U.S. procurement of supplies from Japan during the war provided a powerful stimulus to that process.

The Korean conflict not only produced a new balance of power in East Asia; it also resulted in an altered configuration of power on the peninsula itself. Henceforth, China was an influence with which to reckon; in some degree, Beijing had returned to its historic position of primacy, at least in the North. Yet Russia remained a massive military power in Northeast Asia and, along with Eastern Europe, of great importance to Pyongyang in terms of economic and military supplies.

The Challenges of Shifting Major Power Relations
Upon the Two Koreas

As the quarrel between China and Russia unfolded after 1956, Pyongyang swung into the Chinese orbit ideologically, with estrangement from Moscow sharply rising toward the end of Khrushchev's regime. Yet during the Cultural Revolution, Chinese radicals attacked Kim vigorously, causing the DPRK to look once again to Moscow.

The dilemma for the DPRK was clear. The split between the two Communist giants offered certain opportunities—but also certain risks.[4] From the end of the Korean War, Kim Il Song had determined to end Pyongyang's satellite status. His new weapon, *chuch'e* (self-reliance), was useful both in eliminating his domestic opponents and in fortifying his regime against any external threat. Nationalism could also be used in an appeal to southern compatriots. The Sino-Soviet cleavage offered the chance to play off one of his big neighbors against the other. A position of equidistance, with the ability to tilt first one way, then the other, in answer to policies by the giants presumed to be detrimental to the North's interests or representing troublesome pressure, seemed logical. Kim and his colleagues knew that neither the Soviet Union nor China wanted the other to obtain a strong priority in North Korea, given its strategic importance.

On the other hand, as the Sino-Soviet rift deepened, the pressures upon Pyongyang from both sides intensified. Moreover, neither Moscow nor Beijing had North Korea as the center of its concerns; thus at various times both followed policies that were strongly antithetical to DPRK interests as perceived in Pyongyang. Consequently, equidistance for any protracted period was impossible, and at certain points, North Korea was even inclined to take a "plague on both your houses" position. Until it had other strings in its bow, however, the latter policy was far too dangerous to be sustained for long, although by drawing into itself even more tightly than in the past, the North sought to fend off certain efforts by Russia and China to extend their influence over DPRK policies.

The Republic of Korea faced no such dilemma in the international realm in the years following the Korean War. Whatever the inner qualms in Seoul about American naïveté regarding the suitability of its political system for Korea, and despite periodic anger at certain American policies, the U.S. security commitment was strongly desired and, at this point, fully credible. Further, Washington was the source of extensive economic assistance. Nor was there any alternative on the horizon. The antipathy to Japan remained intense, even after diplomatic relations were established in 1965. Western Europe was remote and largely indifferent.

For the United States, the problem was the failure of South Korean democracy, symbolized by the military coup that brought Park Chung Hee to power in 1961. How deeply did one intervene in a client state to ensure that one's own political values were maintained, or alternatively, did one withdraw support even if this proved costly to one's larger interests? For several decades, South Korea epitomized the conflict between ideology and national interests for the United States, with the United States periodically putting pressure on Park for greater democratization to ease its conscience, and in this case having considerable leverage.[5]

Meanwhile, under the prevailing conditions, North–South relations remained minimal and wholly hostile during the 1960s, marked by various efforts of the North to disrupt the South. The major nations were of little help in inducing a reduction of tension during this period. The Brezhnev era in the Soviet Union was marked by a dull bureaucratism, underwritten by cronyism and corruption. During the Cultural Revolution, the Chinese were angry at virtually everyone, especially the USSR and the United States, until Mao realized that the tension with the USSR might result in open conflict and decided to smile at Washington. The United States was ever more deeply involved in Vietnam. Japan was wholly concentrating upon its meteoric economic climb, content to confine foreign policy to economics.

At the beginning of the next decade, however, several regional developments occurred that were to affect both Koreas, illustrating how intimately connected were trends in North–South relations and external stimuli. As the 1970s opened, Beijing's leaders, setting ideology aside, showed a greater determination than at any time in the recent past to develop an American card in dealing with the Russians. The new American president, Richard Nixon, and his key foreign policy adviser, Henry Kissinger, also had reasons for desiring a change in U.S.–PRC relations. The decision had been made to withdraw from Vietnam "with honor," and it was hoped that China could help. More important, that nation provided a potent counterforce to the Soviet Union.

These developments were not lost on the North and South Koreans. To the North, Chinese actions sent a powerful signal that, like all nations, the PRC would follow its perceived national interests, not those of Pyongyang. To the South, American abandonment of South Vietnam signaled the possibility of a more general withdrawal from Asia.[6]

It was in this setting that a new chapter in North–South relations unfolded. On August 12, 1971, the South Korean Red Cross, acting on the initiative of the Park government, proposed a meeting with the North Korean Red Cross to discuss the problem of Korea's divided families. The reunification issue had become increasingly important in South Korean politics, and this too promoted the ROK initiative. Two days later, the North responded, accepting the proposal, and suggesting a September meeting in Panmunjom. It took ten months before agreement on an agenda was reached on June 16, 1972, but at least communications had been established.

Whether the Chinese played any direct role in persuading the North to enter such negotiations is still unclear. In any case, a more dramatic step took place on July 4, 1972, when after secret high-level meetings, a joint North–South communiqué was issued. The three principles outlined in that communiqué were to be oft quoted in the years ahead: unification through independent Korean effort without external interference; unification through peaceful means, without the use of force by either side; and national unity "transcending differences in policies, ideologies, and systems." Further, a South-North Coordinating Committee was created to implement the agreements as well as to "solve various existing problems."[7]

The events of early 1972 indicated that startling changes in North–South relations were conceivable when conditions—domestic and international—provided impetus. Yet the aftermath of the July declaration proved to be a major disappointment. After some sporadic improvements, the situation returned to the minimalism and animosity of previous times. Domestic and international factors each contributed to this end. Domestically, both North and South faced certain challenges. The DPRK was now confronted with growing economic problems, and it viewed the striking economic success of the Park government with increasing alarm. To risk a step-by-step approach to unification, as the South was urging, commencing with economic and cultural exchanges, could be threatening. Thus, the North took a stance in favor of far-reaching political and military measures at the outset, including a proposal for a meeting of representatives of both sides on an equal basis, involving all parties and social organizations in each society. It was the perfect formula for a monolithic state seeking to coopt elements within a pluralistic rival. This body was supposed to create a Confederation of Koryo, a federation under which powers would be allocated, some joint, some separate. The DPRK formula was "one nation, one state, two systems, two governments." At the same time, Pyongyang proposed a drastic reduction of military forces on both sides, to reach 100,000 for each government, accompanied by the removal of all American troops from the South.

Meanwhile, in the South, the political system tightened even as the economic advances continued. By means of the Yushin Constitution, Park could perpetuate himself in power, and political freedoms were progressively circumscribed. In August 1973, Kim Dae Jung, a leading liberal critic and former presidential candidate against Park, was kidnapped by Korean CIA agents in Tokyo. He would have been murdered had not the American government, discovering the plot, sternly intervened. This episode not only increased tension between the ROK and the United States, but also raised serious problems with Japan.

The North remained heavily dependent upon the Soviet Union for economic and military support, but the Soviet government, and especially Soviet intellectuals, privately regarded the DPRK system as a perversion of Leninism, and the cult of Kim as absurd. But not wanting China to gain a strong advantage, they continued to provide aid. The North's relations with China were once again cordial, but the Sino-American friendship that was blossoming prompted a question in Pyongyang: Could Beijing be a more effective spokesman for the North's interests in the West, or would this development limit the North's options?

As the 1970s progressed, the DPRK placed increased emphasis upon ties with the so-called Third World. Assistance to revolutionary movements was downgraded in favor of state-to-state relations. Efforts to become a part of the Non-Aligned Movement (NAM) were stepped up, culminating in the DPRK's admission to that body in 1975. The strategy was clear: By reaching out to the developing world, the North could not only enhance its competitive position with the South, but also have some ties other than those with the badly fractured—and unreliable—communist bloc.[8]

As the decade came to a close, the two Koreas were both forced to adjust to complex conditions at home and abroad. And insofar as international relations were concerned, both Koreas could only react in a largely defensive manner; neither had the capacity to take initiatives or shape events.

In the ROK, attention was focused almost exclusively on the domestic situation. By the fall of 1979, political unrest was widespread. The combination of economic dynamism and political authoritarianism was becoming increasingly nonviable. At a critical juncture, on October 26, Park was assassinated by the KCIA head, Kim Jae Kyu, a supposed close friend and intimate adviser. A period of instability and uncertainty ensued, with another military man, General Chun Doo Hwan, coming to power in the late summer of 1980. Previously, on May 18–26, an uprising in Kwangju, triggered by the arrest of Kim Dae Jung, had been bloodily suppressed by the military. A new authoritarianism was being imposed.

ROK relations with the United States remained troubled. Indeed, when President Carter came to office in 1976, he had been committed to a withdrawal of U.S. forces from South Korea by 1982, partly because of Park's repression of human rights. Yet many Americans, in Congress and elsewhere, and America's key ally, Japan, strongly opposed such action as risking another conflict on the Korean peninsula. The idea was abandoned. A proposal was advanced in 1979 for a trilateral meeting involving the United States, the ROK, and the DPRK to discuss a peace treaty and related matters. The DPRK, bitterly disappointed over the scrapping of the troop withdrawal program, rejected the Carter–Park proposal. The North's true objective—then and later—was to achieve bilateral negotiations with Washington. As the 1980s opened, however, the United States kept its military commitment to the South.

While relations with the United States and Japan remained delicate, the ROK began to reach out internationally, competing with the North. Chun undertook several trips in 1981–1983, starting with the five ASEAN states and later including four African nations. He was at the beginning of an even more extensive trip when he narrowly escaped death in Rangoon, with 17 of his key officials killed in a bombing undertaken by North Korean agents. Seoul hosted the Asian Games in 1986, and climaxed its achievement with the Summer Olympics in 1988, the latter event being attended by both China and the Soviet Union, despite Pyongyang's boycott.

The DPRK continued to struggle with its domestic economic problems while seeking to discern which way the rapidly shifting international winds might blow next. Politically, the drive was now intensified to make certain that Kim Jong Il, the Great Leader's son and heir apparent, was made acceptable and progressively furnished with the necessary authority or at least its imagery. Kim Il Song and his close associates wanted "iron-clad, monolithic unity," with no succession crisis.

On the international front, the trends were initially favorable to the North. At the beginning of the 1980s, the opportunity to maintain access to both China and

Russia by feinting and weaving, using a combination of supplication and veiled threat, seemed to have improved. Having failed in its effort to punish Vietnam, and witnessing the substantial increase in Soviet power in Asia, both to the north and the south of its borders, China did not want to alienate Pyongyang. Thus, even though China had normalized its relations with the United States and was now increasing its economic relations with the ROK, it took special pains to reassure a suspicious DPRK of its complete loyalty, and a succession of Chinese leaders visited the North Korean capital.

As for the Soviet Union, it was locked in an escalating arms race with the United States, yet its faint overtures to Beijing to discuss differences were seemingly belied by its actions. Hence, it too had no desire to alienate the North. And by 1984, the North was prepared to seek improved relations with Moscow without sacrificing its ties with Beijing. If China could adjust its policies toward the ROK, the DPRK could redress the imbalance in its China–USSR relations. Trade with Russia had been on the increase since 1980. Soviet attacks on China's "collaboration with imperialists" and its criticism of increasing PRC contacts with the South were privately welcomed in Pyongyang. In this period, Moscow saw a threat in a U.S.–PRC–Japan alignment, and such a warning found a ready audience in the DPRK ruling circle. Thus, in May 1984, Kim made his first trip to Moscow in twenty-three years. He had visited China several times, and even Eastern Europe, but the USSR had long been avoided. Important gains followed: a treaty on boundary issues and agreements on economic transactions; an April 1985 communiqué signed by foreign ministers Kim Yong Nam and Andrei Gromyko denouncing "the U.S.–Japan–South Korea alliance," and a Soviet agreement to support the DPRK reunification proposal as well as the withdrawal of American forces from the peninsula. Russia also announced its opposition to the simultaneous admission of the two Koreas to the United Nations, a position in line with the DPRK stand.

Kim Il Song was to visit the Soviet Union again in October 1986, after the advent of Mikhail Gorbachev to power.[9] At that time, he expressed support for the economic development program being initiated, and praised Gorbachev as "a staunch Marxist-Leninist and talented political activist." These were words not repeated.

The early 1980s, however, proved to be the lull before the storm. During the years after 1985, shifts on the international front were to profoundly affect the Korean peninsula. The relative strength of the two Koreas, their respective relations with the major states, and their role in the region were all to be dramatically altered.

On the domestic front, great strides continued to be made by South Korea, both economically and politically.[10] In the years 1987–1990, for example, growth averaged 10.9 percent, and in 1991, per capita GNP was U.S. $6,498, probably five times greater than that of the DPRK. By 1991, the total trade volume exceeded U.S. $150 billion. South Korea, like the other newly industrial economies (NIEs), was en route to becoming a medium-sized industrial power with an expanding reach to China and Southeast Asia as well as to the West. Economic problems, to be sure, were not absent. The very rapidity of the growth as well as changes in the international economic environment demanded important reforms, as the incoming Kim Young Sam government was to acknowledge in 1993. On balance, however, South Korea was a striking success story economically.

In the political realm also, the developments were of major significance. Chun Doo Hwan deserves credit for abiding by his pledge to step down after one term as president and permitting the 1987 elections to take place under liberalized conditions. His successor, Roh Tae Woo, will go down in Korean history as the individual who enabled democratization and economic development to be successfully combined for the first time in Korean history. In the 1990s, the self-styled Sixth Korean Republic had joined the ranks of the world's democracies. And as will be noted shortly, Roh's foreign policy was strikingly successful, especially his reaching out to the Leninist and ex-Leninist states, a policy defined as *Nordpolitik*.[11]

In contrast, as the 1990s opened, the DPRK was sustaining negative growth rates, fueled by both the collapse of the Soviet Union and the increasing internal weaknesses of an outmoded Stalinist economic strategy that featured autarky in an age of rapid technological advances and growing interdependence. The calls for improvement in food supplies, other consumer goods, and, above all, energy testified to the somber economic conditions.

On the political front, the drive to install Kim Jong Il as the top leader, presenting him with the key party and military positions, reached a climax in the 1992–1993 period, just prior to his father's death. In a regime so intensely personalized, the leadership qualities of the younger Kim matter greatly, and a sizable mystery surrounds that question since he has seldom met foreigners for a substantive conversation or even functioned publicly before his subjects except in ceremonial roles.

The End of the Cold War and Its Implications for the Koreas

In the midst of grave internal difficulties, the North was also buffeted by foreign currents. To understand the challenges and opportunities confronting the two Koreas internationally, one must first turn to their interaction with the four principal states of the region.

When Gorbachev assumed leadership, the Soviet Union's Asia policies were moribund. The Sino-Soviet relationship remained hostile, exacting a heavy price from both parties; no settlement with Japan had been achieved; the balance sheet on Korea was still favorable to China, notwithstanding certain gains; Indochina was a substantial cost without perceptible benefit; relations with ASEAN were minimal; and Afghanistan was a political and military disaster. The new Russian leader set out to change this, with his 1986 Vladivostok speech the opening salvo. In that address, Gorbachev made it clear that improving relations with China had top priority, and that the USSR was prepared to make certain policy changes to achieve that goal.

At Vladivostok, and later at Krasnoyarsk, Gorbachev sketched a new set of policies aimed at reducing Russian military burdens, creating a climate for confidence building, and concentrating upon cooperation. These policies, coupled with his efforts to achieve rapprochement with the United States, signaled the onset of a new era for Asia and for the world. But Gorbachev was a reformer, not a revolutionary—and too late, he discovered that he had let loose a revolution that he could not control. The initial signs came in Eastern Europe. Free from Soviet overlordship, throughout the region communist regimes began to fall throughout the region. And suddenly, the revolution came to Moscow, accelerated by the failure of the August 1991 coup.

North Koreans, like their Chinese and Vietnamese colleagues, watched these events with incredulity, followed by a mixture of anger and apprehension. The motherland had deserted socialism. Gorbachev—and, even more, his successor, Yeltsin—was a traitor and a renegade. When Hungary became the first ex-Leninist country to establish diplomatic relations with the ROK on February 1, 1989, the DPRK angrily downgraded relations and condemned Budapest as selling out for capitalist gold. Poland followed the same course eight months later, and Pyongyang organs asserted that the collapse of Polish socialism had been caused by imperialist ideological and cultural infiltration. But when all the Eastern European states moved in a similar fashion, it was no longer possible to do other than accept the inevitable. The overthrow of Nicolae Ceausescu was especially bitter because North Korea had considered Rumania its counterpart in foreign policy, Bucharest having maintained its independence from Moscow. Pyongyang had kept close relations with the Rumanian leader.

The heaviest blows were yet to come. In early September 1990, Foreign Minister Eduard Shevardnadze journeyed to Pyongyang to inform the North Koreans that the USSR would shortly recognize the ROK, and also that DPRK–USSR economic relations would have to be put on a hard currency basis, with international market prices prevailing. Kim and his colleagues were enraged, and the meetings were very bitter.[12] Despite some effort to contain the vituperation in public speeches and organs, North Korean–Russian relations remain very cool as of early 1995. More important, the precipitous decline of trade with Russia, including that in such critical commodities as oil, produced deepening economic problems, as noted. Meanwhile, the improvement in Russian–South Korean relations was symbolized by the fact that both Gorbachev and Yelstin made trips to South Korea during their respective terms in office. South Korean industrialists have shown considerable interest in economic activities in Siberia, restrained only by the miserable condition of the Russian economy. On the cultural front, there has been a tremendous expansion of relations.

The People's Republic of China was to undertake changes in its Korea policies nearly as dramatic as those of Moscow.[13] Beijing leaders told Pyongyang in the spring of 1991 that the PRC could not veto the ROK request for admission to the United Nations. Thus, the DPRK was forced to abandon another principle long held sacred and accept the dual admission of the two Koreas to the UN. Then, predominantly for economic reasons, China decided that the time had finally come to accord the ROK diplomatic recognition. For some time, while the DPRK had been its formal wife, the ROK had been its favorite concubine. Now, a second marriage was performed.

The PRC's recognition of South Korea did not provoke the same outcry in the North as the earlier action of the Soviet Union. In part, this was because the Chinese leaders handled the matter in a highly sophisticated manner, informing the key North Korean leaders in ample time, and continuously assuring them that in no way would this interfere with their commitments to the DPRK or a continuance of such assistance as could be afforded. In part, the resigned DPRK acceptance of the Chinese action was a product of the recognition that China represented the last, best hope for a meaningful security and political relationship, given the collapse of Leninism in the West.

Confronted with the necessity of having to adjust to cross-recognition by its erstwhile allies and dual admission to the United Nations, and facing the increasingly urgent necessity of economic reforms, the DPRK now gave more serious consideration to its relations with Japan and the United States. There had been certain efforts in the past. For example, the North had sought to use *Chongryon* (the pro-Pyongyang General Federation of Koreans in Japan) and also the Japanese Left plus a portion of the Liberal Democratic Party to foster improved relations. And from the early 1980s, the DPRK had sought contact with American–Koreans and also with others, especially American Congressmen. Yet these efforts were sporadic and of limited consequence. Only with the events of 1988 and thereafter did Pyongyang authorities undertake efforts to reach out to Japan and the United States more seriously.

When the Kanemaru mission to Pyongyang took place in October 1990, a new chapter seemed to open in Japan–DPRK relations. At first, it appeared that Japanese policy, under the impetus of a powerful faction of the LDP, would move rapidly to a two-Koreas policy. However, with both Seoul and Washington expressing concern, the Japanese foreign ministry took control, and conditions relating to normalization were set forth, of which the Japanese demand that the nuclear issue be resolved became the most crucial.

Japan could be a major source of economic support for the DPRK, as it has been for the ROK for some three decades. As yet, however, relations between the two countries remain minimal and cool. The negotiations looking toward normalization have been thorny and subject to frequent disruptions. Indeed, negotiations broke off in November 1992. Such issues as compensation for past Japanese policies, the freedom to travel of Japanese women married to Koreans living in the North, and the "comfort women" of World War II remain unresolved. DPRK propaganda against Japan continued to be vitriolic, and the under-lying ethnic prejudices on both sides have been scarcely concealed.

Pyongyang sees the United States as the paramount power in Northeast Asia, strongly influencing if not controlling the policies of the ROK and Japan with respect to it. While this view is based on an exaggeration of Washington's capaci-ties, there can be little question that certain American actions pertaining to Korea had a decisive impact on developments on the Korean peninsula after 1990.

First, the United States gradually loosened restrictions on North Korean insti-tute personnel seeking to visit the United States for conferences and granted DPRK officials somewhat greater rights of travel within the country. Vastly more important was the Bush administration's decision to remove ground-based tactical nuclear weapons globally, and to apply this policy specifically to the ROK. This action, unfolding in the fall of 1991, took the North by surprise. When coupled with the later decision to suspend the Team Spirit military exer-cises for one year and the agreement by the United States to participate in an official meeting with the DPRK in January 1992, three large carrots had been extended to Pyongyang. At the same time, Washington made it very clear that the security ties with the ROK were firm, and that U.S.–ROK consultations would be continuous, with progress in North–South relations along with a satis-factory resolution of the nuclear inspection issue critical to long-term im-provements in U.S.–DPRK relations.

Against this background, seemingly dramatic developments occurred both with respect to North–South relations and in connection with the North's policies relat-ing to the Nuclear Non-Proliferation Treaty to which it was a signatory. At the fifth meeting of the two sides' prime ministers, held December 11–13, 1991, the two parties accepted an Agreement on Reconciliation, Non-Aggression, and Ex-changes and Cooperation between South and North. The twenty-five-point agree-ment covered the full range of security, political, economic, and cultural issues, and pledged to set up a series of subcommittees to implement every provision.[14] While certain pledges seemed unlikely to be effectuated in the near term, the agreement held out the promise of a giant step forward in North–South relations if even a portion of its provisions could be carried out in the months ahead.

Further, eight days after President Roh's statement of December 18 that there were no longer any nuclear weapons in South Korea, the first inter-Korean nuclear talks took place, and on December 31, an agreement on a nonnuclear Korean peninsula was signed by the two parties. On January 7, 1992, a statement was issued by the DPRK Foreign Ministry asserting that the government had decided to sign the Nuclear Safeguards Accord, have it ratified at an early date, and accept inspection by the International Atomic Energy Agency (IAEA) at a time mutually agreed. It was on this precise day that the Team Spirit exercises were suspended. The Safeguards Accord was signed on January 30 and ratified by the DPRK Supreme People's Assembly on April 9, and in June, inspections of the Yongbyon nuclear facilities began.

The promises of early 1992, however, were destined not to be fulfilled. After a hopeful start, the inspections of DPRK sites became bogged down in controversies between the IAEA and North Korean authorities, particularly over the issue of two undeclared sites that the DPRK insisted were merely "military installations," but with external evidence indicating otherwise. By the autumn, the ROK and the United States announced that unless progress were forthcoming the Team Spirit exercises would be resumed, and in March 1993 such exercises took place. In response, the DPRK, in the name of Marshal Kim Jong-pil, supreme commander of the Korean People's Army, announced that the country was being placed on a "semi-war" status, and tension was built up in the North through a series of mass rallies. Further, on March 12, the DPRK announced that it was withdrawing from the Nuclear Nonproliferation Treaty because of the "nuclear threats" of the United States and the "unfair demands" of the IAEA.

Despite these actions, there were signs that the North did not want to go over the brink. In May, Pyongyang allowed an IAEA visit, notwithstanding its earlier announcement. There followed two rounds of high-level talks between the United States and the DPRK that resulted in the North's "suspension" of its NPT withdrawal and the outline of an altered DPRK nuclear energy program that was to become the basis for a later agreement. Nonetheless, progress was agonizingly slow, although in a variety of ways the DPRK signaled its desire to use the nuclear card to establish a new relationship with the United States.

The year 1994 opened on an uncertain note. Initially, contention and confrontation continued to be prominent features of the scene despite the permission granted for IAEA inspection of declared nuclear sites and the continuance of U.S.–DPRK talks. The undeclared sites remained off-limits, and when IAEA inspectors did not arrive at the time announced for the change of fuel bars in the Yongbyon reactor, the process was begun without their presence; they arrived a few days later, announcing that a satisfactory inspection was not possible.

Under these circumstances, moves toward UN sanctions got under way, with the United States playing a leading role. The sanctions route promised to be difficult. China made it clear that it opposed sanctions. Japan and South Korea, while publicly supportive, had private reservations. In the case of Japan, its politically divided Korean population of some 700,000, together with the increasingly fragile nature of Japanese politics, constituted troublesome problems. For their part, key South Korean authorities realized that high North–South tension would strengthen the extremities—Left and Right—on the ROK domestic political front; moreover, the possibility of a collapsed North, with the huge economic and political costs to the South that would be involved, was not a scenario to be desired. Nor did the South want a U.S.–PRC confrontation.

In this setting, and while progress toward a peaceful resolution seemed frozen, former President Jimmy Carter made his trip to Pyongyang in mid-June and proved to be a useful vehicle for the North, in the person of Kim Il Song himself, to set forth a conciliatory policy of being willing to curb its nuclear program along lines earlier outlined, to be done in the context of a comprehensive U.S.–DPRK agreement. Kim also announced that he was prepared to hold a summit meeting with Kim Young Sam in the near future so as to lay the foundation for a new era in North–South relations.

However, the sudden death of Kim Il Song on July 8 created new uncertainties. His son and designated heir, Kim Jong Il, announced that he would abide by his father's wishes, and the U.S.–DPRK Geneva talks proceeded. Yet prospects for a summit meeting in the near future vanished under the new conditions, and North Korean propaganda against the Kim Young Sam government continued at the highest decibel levels. It was clear that the North wished to focus exclusively on the United States.

On October 21, a Framework Agreement was signed between the United States and the DPRK whereby the North agreed to freeze its ongoing nuclear program and allow IAEA monitoring (but with the inspection of the two undeclared sites postponed up to five years). In exchange, it was to receive shipments of heavy oil, starting three months from the date of the agreement, and the international funding of a new nuclear power program based on light water reactors. A consortium, the Korean Energy Development Organization (KEDO), involving the United States, the Republic of Korea, and Japan, has been created for the latter purpose.

The events after 1990 reveal a new type of approach to a specific regional or subregional conflict or tension that has security implications for others. I have labeled that approach one of concentric arcs. The term *arcs* is used rather than *circles*, since arcs, being open-ended, enable contact and interaction between various levels. The end of the Cold War has enabled the major states to downgrade ideological differences and big power rivalries, and focus more clearly upon mutual interests. Nowhere has this trend had greater implications than with respect to the Korean peninsula.

The first and all-important arc is that involving North and South Korea. Their dialogue, official and unofficial, will be crucial to any fundamental resolution of the Korean issue, whatever temporary roadblocks ensue. The second arc, however, has been of equal importance, namely, that of the four major states so long and so importantly involved in the Korean problem—the United States, China, Russia, and Japan. Beyond this arc is a third that can be brought into play: international bodies, from the United Nations and its auxiliary bodies to the International Atomic Energy Agency and various economic bodies, including the Asia Pacific Economic Cooperation forum (APEC) and the World Trade Organization (WTO). The interaction of these arcs with the domestic and international climate enabled such advances as were made with respect to Korea in the recent past.

North–South Relations—Key Factors

Using these arcs as a basis for analysis, what are the key issues and trends as the decade of the 1990s advances? In the all-important North–South relationship, the gulf remains significant despite the promising events of 1991–1992.[15] At an earlier point, the fundamental problem appeared to be a deep difference of opinion by the two parties as to how to approach unification. The ROK had long insisted upon a step-by-step approach, commencing with economic and cultural interaction. After trust had been built, the two governments could proceed to resolve political and military issues. The DPRK had argued for major political and military moves at the outset, consisting of a confederation created by a joint council composed of all parties and social organizations, drastic mutual reductions in the military forces of the two sides, and the removal of American forces from the South. It had also favored contacts between various nongovernmental organizations, thereby playing upon the South's growing pluralism and taking advantage of its own monolithic structure.

These differences appeared to have been bridged by the December 1991 agreements since these stipulated simultaneous advances on all fronts—economic, cultural, political, and security. By the end of 1992, however, after some ninety rounds of contacts and dialogues among the various subcommittees earlier established, no tangible progress had been achieved. Moreover, two issues were now juxtaposed: the renewal of the Team Spirit military exercises and DPRK nuclear activities.

Nevertheless, the Kim Yong Sam administration, inaugurated on February 25, 1993, took a conciliatory posture, issuing various statements to indicate its strong interest in seeing the North–South dialogue go forward, signaling a willingness to consider various forms of economic assistance and interaction if the nuclear question was resolved, and undertaking such gestures as the release of Li In Mo, a guerrilla fighter on behalf of the North who had been imprisoned for some thirty-four years. His right to return to the North had long been demanded by Pyongyang.[16]

These statements and actions, however, did not produce any immediate results. For months, no talks were conducted. Intra-Korean trade, which had reached U.S. $209 million in 1992, dropped sharply.[17] Both sides issued new statements pertaining to their mutual relations and the issue of unification. The ROK, insisting that it wished to pursue a policy of engagement with, not containment of, the North, outlined a three-phase approach starting with acts of reconciliation and cooperation, advancing to the creation of a South-North Commonwealth, and ending with the creation of a single, democratic republic. The DPRK set forth a "Ten-Point Program of Great Unity," reiterating many of the themes that had been outlined in previous proposals.[18]

There was little that was new in the unification programs of the two parties, and a retreat from the promises of late 1991 seemed to have taken place. The South insisted that progress hinged upon a resolution of the nuclear issue, while the North argued that the nuclear problem was an issue between it and the United States, not a factor in North–South relations. It also insisted that a new round of talks between special envoys looking toward a summit meeting be initiated as the next step, but by the fall of 1993, it had demanded two preconditions for such talks: The South must abandon all military exercises and give up "international collaboration" with respect to the nuclear issue, meaning consultation and joint planning with the United States and Japan. Scheduled meetings were canceled, although as winter approached, talks about talks were taking place.

Then came the dramatic events of 1994. As the United States and North Korea bargained, and in the process engaged in threats and counterthreats, South Korea—although fully consulted by its American ally—appeared to be on the sidelines. At the point when UN-imposed sanctions seemed imminent, Seoul made it clear publicly that it would support this action, although privately, as we have noted, it had some concerns.

The visit of former President Jimmy Carter to Pyongyang on June 15 was initially viewed with considerable negativism in Seoul. Carter's record with respect to Korea was not highly regarded, nor was his knowledge about the current issues seen as sufficient. Yet when it was announced that Kim Il Song had agreed to a summit meeting with Kim Young Sam, it opened up the possibility of a new era in North–South relations. Thus, the sudden death of President Kim on July 8 represented a sharp setback, possibly exacerbated when the ROK government refused to express condolences, citing Kim's key role in starting the Korean War. The North was to use this issue repeatedly in the months ahead as a reason for continued denunciations of Kim Young Sam and his government. In reality, however, the advent of Kim's son and heir to power was sufficiently protracted and complex to rule out any possibility of a summit meeting in the near term at least.

On another front, however, the South appeared to take center stage, albeit in an appropriately face-saving manner. The core of the U.S.–DPRK October agreement, as noted earlier, was that the North would forgo its current nuclear program for one based on light water reactors, with initial shipments of oil to replace nuclear power, followed by external financial and technical assistance in the construction of the new program, to be spread over a number of years. From the beginning, the United States had made it clear that the ROK must play a central role in the latter program. KEDO, the vehicle established to enable the shift, involved the United States as chair, with the ROK and Japan being members, and with both the funding and the reactors heavily dependent on the South, perhaps up to 80 percent of the necessary costs. The DPRK was not happy about the prominent role of the ROK as it made clear in early 1995.

Nonetheless, major South Korean firms are being solicited by the North for investment in the Rajin-Sonbong special economic zone and in certain other select areas as well. The ROK government has responded by loosening restrictions on economic interaction with the North, and a number of *chaebol* are sending representatives to the North to explore opportunities. The South has also moved to permit remittances to be sent legally to family members in the North. These actions represent a potentially fruitful course to induce greater North–

South interaction of a positive nature. The DPRK government has provided increasing evidence that it recognizes the absolute necessity of improving its economy—concentrating on food production, light industry, and infrastructural needs, especially energy. The future of Kim Jong Il or any other leader now depends on performance, with charisma in short supply.

The evidence strongly suggests that there are two groups within the DPRK political elite that are destined to be critically important in the years ahead: the military and the technocrats. In both cases, moreover, a generational change is, or will shortly be, under way, with the old Kapsan guerrillas that clustered around Kim Il Song passing from the scene and somewhat younger elements emerging in the top ranks. Among these, many potential agents of economic change exist.

There are thousands of returned students who studied in Eastern Europe, Russia, and China in recent decades, many majoring in science and technology. They know something of the wider world and its potentials. In addition, there are approximately 100,000 Koreans now living in the North who once lived in Japan, and many get remittances from relatives still in Japan or are connected with some of the joint ventures sponsored by *Chongryon,* the pro-DPRK Federation of Koreans in Japan. They too know a different system. And there are many military and diplomatic personnel who have been stationed abroad, including the West. The nature of the global revolution cannot be hidden from them.

One should be cautious in predicting the future of North–South relations, especially since domestic as well as international factors will influence events. A certain political fragility exists in the ROK at present, evidenced by the readjustments that are taking place in both major political parties. This is a development on which the DPRK may be tempted to play. Conditions in the North—political as well as economic—are also fluid and difficult to predict, as has been emphasized. Trends there will be vital in determining how cautious or bold Pyongyang will be in seeking to broaden contacts with others, and especially with the South. The South, moreover, will insist that the nuclear issue be fully resolved, that it be a party to any peace treaty, and that its security relations with the United States continue during this uncertain period.

However, the signs now point to expanded North–South relations, first economic, then cultural, leading on to political-security issues of fundamental importance. Barring collapse of the North, reunification does not appear to be at hand. And clearly, there is a risk to the North in opening up to the South too rapidly or too extensively, given the huge gap between them in developmental terms. But hopefully, the North's needs and the South's flexibility will lead to less tension and more positive interaction over time, even if the path is rocky at points.

The Second Arc—Positions of the Major States

One of the principal reasons for the North's relative lack of interest in moving forward with North–South negotiations is that its present priority is to focus heavily upon cementing ties with its one-time bête noire. Thus, we must turn to the second arc.

The United States—A Leadership Role

As noted earlier, the sweeping actions of the United States in announcing the withdrawal of nuclear weapons from South Korean soil in the fall of 1991 and the decision reached with the ROK to suspend Team Spirit military exercises for 1992 contributed in a major way to the DPRK agreement to allow IAEA inspections at its Yongbyon facility. After six inspections, however, the North ordered all IAEA activities halted, charging that the IAEA was not being "impartial" and that certain IAEA officials were under the influence of "American imperialism." Behind this charge lay the fact that in examining its nuclear residue, the IAEA had used more sophisticated laboratories than those employed in Europe previously, namely, Lawrence Livermore and Los Alamos. Furthermore, it had been given photos taken by U.S. satellites purportedly indicating that nuclear waste was buried in the vicinity of two buildings that DPRK authorities labeled "purely military installations." This information was shown to Northern representatives in early 1993.

The DPRK promptly announced that it would never allow "special inspection" of those facilities, and charging the IAEA with bias, on March 12, filed a letter of resignation from the Non-Proliferation Treaty, of which it had been a member since 1985.[19] It was the first nation to take such an action. In the succeeding weeks, a series of events unfolded: on May 11, the UN Security Council, acting on the basis of earlier IAEA board decisions, passed a resolution urging the North to remain in the NPT and accept international inspections, calling for additional actions if the North failed to comply. China abstained in the vote, and made it clear that it did not favor the application of sanctions, but wanted the matter handled through diplomacy.

After extensive consultations with the ROK and Japan, and conversations also with China, the United States opened medium-level official talks with the DPRK in New York on June 2, with Robert Gallucci, assistant secretary of state for political and military affairs, and First Deputy Foreign Minister Kang Sok Ju the respective heads of the two delegations. The United States had insisted that the talks focus on the nuclear issue, looking forward to the return of the DPRK to the NPT and an acceptance of full IAEA safeguard inspections.

The joint statement issued on June 11 asserted that the two parties had agreed to principles of "assurance against the threat and the use of force," peace and security on a nuclear-free Korean peninsula, including "impartial application of full scope safeguards," mutual respect for each other's sovereignty, noninterference in each other's internal affairs, and support for peaceful reunification. In the context of a continuance of the dialogue, the DPRK "decided unilaterally to suspend as long as it considers necessary" its withdrawal from the NPT.[20]

The June 11 statement signaled both the positions and the tactics that were to be pursued in the months ahead. The provisions regarding the nonuse of force, respect for sovereignty, and support for peaceful unification did not represent new positions on the part of the United States, yet the willingness to continue the dialogue at a higher level than the talks that had been taking place in Beijing and to hold the dialogue in New York indicated a conciliatory position by Washington, with the hope that a structure of incentives, combined with the serious economic problems of the North and other factors, would elicit a constructive response.

For its part, the North took a face-saving means of retreating from its NPT withdrawal, "suspending" that decision rather than reversing it, and being able to insert the term "impartial" to indicate its objections to past IAEA connections with the United States. It had taken the minimal actions required to prevent the issue from being brought before the Security Council. By implication if not explicitly, it had agreed to accept IAEA inspections again, and the promise of support for the North-South Joint Declaration of December 31, 1991, suggested but did not stipulate a return to a North–South dialogue on the inspection issue. In exchange, the North got its most urgent desire: a continuation of the DPRK–U.S. dialogue, hopefully on a prolonged basis.

After intensive U.S. consultations with allies and China, a second round of talks with the DPRK took place at Geneva, July 14 to 19. The structure of U.S. incentives and deterrents was being refined, with the former given greater prominence. In the July statement, the United States indicated that "as a part of a final resolution of the nuclear issue" and with the assumption that issues specifically relating to it could be resolved, the United States would support the introduction of light water–moderated reactors in place of graphite reactors, exploring with the DPRK ways in which such reactors could be obtained. The former reactors were less susceptible to use in a weapons program. From the North's standpoint, U.S. support would mean the elimination of various broad legal and economic barriers that had been placed upon it, thus supporting a general developmental program.

In exchange, the North agreed that "full and impartial application of IAEA safeguards" was essential to achieving a meaningful nonproliferation regime, and pledged that it would begin consultations with the IAEA, looking toward inspections. It was also agreed that the two parties would meet again within the next two months to discuss matters involved in resolving the nuclear issue and "to lay the basis for improving overall relations between the DPRK and the U.S."[21]

Just prior to the Geneva meetings, President Clinton had paid a two-day visit to Seoul, on July 10 and 11. In his speech to the National Assembly, Clinton asserted, "our goal is . . . certifiable compliance [with IAEA inspection requests]" and providing "strong support for the South-North Nuclear Accord." He further stated that the future of the Korean peninsula was for the South and North to shape, thus signaling that the U.S. priority was to encourage North–South dialogues. The United States was seeking to reassure the ROK that its interests would be safeguarded, whatever advances were made in the U.S.–DPRK talks.

Repeated frustrations followed. After several weeks of negotiations, three IAEA inspectors were allowed to go to Yongbyon on September 1 to check the monitoring instruments installed there, but the discussions yielded no progress on the issue of inspecting the so-called military buildings. Moreover, much time was spent on the issue of impartiality despite the IAEA's insistence that there were no prohibitions against help from whatever source in obtaining thorough data relating to its tasks. Thus, at a five-day IAEA conference attended by 114 member states that opened on September 27, the North Korean issue was placed on the agenda despite the violent objections of the DPRK delegate, Li Sung Hyon, and a resolution critical of the North's attitude was passed overwhelmingly. In response, the DPRK atomic energy minister announced that the meetings scheduled for October 5 to 8 for discussion of future IAEA inspections were being canceled.

It was not surprising that Gallucci had earlier announced during a September visit to Seoul that progress with respect both to the IAEA inspections and the North–South dialogue was insufficient to permit a third U.S.–DPRK meeting at this point.

During this period, the DPRK had also refused to attend all unofficial and quasi-official American-sponsored conferences except for one united front operation involving obscure American and South Korean figures. In addition, it had requested the postponement of the scheduled visits of individual Americans— except that of Congressman Dan Ackerman, head of the Asian Subcommittee of the House of Representatives Foreign Affairs Committee. He was accorded a meeting with Kim Il Song, and allowed to cross the DMZ as he had requested. No substantive advances were made, but this act underlined the ardent desire of the North for official contacts.

Unpublicized meetings between a State Department representative and officials of the DPRK UN mission in New York continued, and by the end of October, it appeared that the United Stated had further refined its structure of incentives and made these known to North Korean officials. If regularized IAEA inspections were permitted and the North–South dialogue went forward, the U.S.–DPRK dialogue could be resumed, the Team Spirit military exercises would be suspended or canceled, and the prospects for a general improvement in bilateral relations would be greatly improved. If little or no progress were made on the key issues, the U.S.–DPRK dialogue would remain suspended, and given the fact that the film and batteries for IAEA inspection cameras were running out, the IAEA would certainly report its inability to conduct inspections to the UN.

A cautious optimism existed at this point that the DPRK would permit regular inspections, but the issue of the two installations seemed more thorny. Prospects for a North–South special envoys meeting also appeared to be improved. Yet the past record suggested that negotiations on all matters would be lengthy and frustrating. There was no evidence that the minimalists had lost control of policymaking in the North.

What were the underlying factors shaping the North's policies?[22] Observers speculated that three considerations were of importance. First, the DPRK had discovered in the nuclear issue a card of major importance in dealing with the United States. Thus, it would hold on to that card, using it sparingly and hoping to obtain maximum concessions.

Second, the discrepancies between the statements of DPRK leaders that they had neither the capacity nor the desire to produce nuclear weapons (as well as their official reports on activities at Yongbyon) on the one hand, and the test evidence plus the satellite photos on the other hand, suggested deception. If such a deception had taken place, would not that revelation cause a great loss of face? No leadership wants to be proven to be falsifiers before the world.

Third, domestic politics may have played a significant role.[23] The events of the spring of 1993 coincided with the effort to consummate the succession of Kim Jong Il, including his assumption of leadership of the DPRK armed forces. Given the dismal economic picture and the uncertainties regarding the younger Kim's leadership, it was useful to be able to use the renewal of Team Spirit exercises and the impasse over "special inspections" to have him proclaim a "life or death" crisis, calling for the mobilization of all citizens on behalf of the fatherland. Patriotism and loyalty are always potent weapons, especially in a society like the DPRK. Moreover, a tough policy might strengthen Kim Jong Il's ties with the military, a critical determinant of power in this state.

Whatever the mix of factors influencing DPRK policies, the months ahead saw a continuation of brinksmanship on the part of the North, and a U.S. response that varied in toughness or threat with the circumstances. In January 1994, the North once again agreed to negotiate with the IAEA on inspection issues, and at the same time working-level U.S.–DPRK contacts were resumed in New York. The next several months saw signs first of progress, then of the North's retreat on the inspection matter. United Nations sanctions, pushed by the United States, seemed imminent, despite the problems noted earlier.

With the IAEA having adopted a sanctions resolution on June 10 and the DPRK announcing on June 13, the eve of the Carter visit, that it would withdraw from the IAEA, the picture seemed bleak. Yet beneath the surface, discussions were taking place. Thus, the announcements coming out of the Carter–Kim discussions that IAEA inspectors would not be expelled from the country despite the announced DPRK withdrawal and the provisional agreement for a third set of high-level U.S.–DPRK talks were connected and not without a background. Only Kim's agreement for a North–South summit was a major surprise.

The new round of Geneva talks got under way on the very day that Kim Il Song died and were thus postponed. However, they resumed the following month, with an agreed statement on August 12 that signaled the major points ultimately contained in the October 21 Framework Agreement. In the latter accord, as noted, the DPRK agreed to shift its nuclear program to the use of light water reactors, to freeze its current program, to remain in the NPT, and to allow safeguard inspections. This is to include "all inspections deemed necessary by the IAEA" (the undeclared sites) "when a significant portion of the LWR project is completed, but before delivery of key nuclear components." Cooperation with respect to the 8,000 spent fuel rods was also pledged.

For its part, the United States agreed to serve as leader of a consortium that would finance and supply the LWR project, and also to assure the delivery of heavy oil supplies pending the project's completion. The two sides agreed to move toward reducing trade and investment barriers as well as those in the telecommunications field, to open liaison offices in the two capitals, and, after suitable progress, to establish diplomatic relations.

This agreement evoked controversy in the United States, as might have been expected, with some arguing that the United States had gotten too little, given too much. Its defenders insisted that the alternatives were far less attractive, that sufficient safeguards with respect to compliance were built into the agreement, and that it offered a route to long-term tension reduction and the opportunity to bring North Korea into the region and the world, thereby inducing evolutionary change in this troubled society rather than an explosion that might wreak widespread damage.

As 1995 opened, there were certain hopeful signs. Compliance with the October Agreement on the part of both parties had thus far been fully satisfactory. Difficult issues and complex bargaining, however, lay ahead. One issue that loomed up was the North's interest in moving from the armistice that has prevailed since the end of the Korean War to a peace treaty. The United States insists that the ROK be a party to such a move, with the DPRK thus far holding out for a bilateral accord.

There are other issues that are likely to affect the timing and extent of U.S.–DPRK diplomatic relations, among them human rights and various security issues and, above all, the status of North–South relations. Yet as the crisis over the U.S. helicopter intrusion into the North in December 1994 indicated, when the chips are down, the DPRK still values the American connection, and for a variety of reasons—economic, political, and strategic. Thus, it will not overturn the recent gains lightly. And from an American perspective, the present course—with all of its uncertainties and hazards—offers better prospects than earlier routes, especially in a period when the North's domestic future is dominated by uncertainty.

Japan—A Neighboring Power

Another key actor in the second arc is Japan. As noted, Tokyo continues to operate under the handicap of the long-standing ethnic animosities between Japanese and Koreans.[24] This is the one issue upon which there is considerable unity between North and South, although various ROK leaders are seeking to reduce the emotional antagonism toward Japan that affects so many citizens, especially the older generations. Recent Japanese leaders' apologies for Japanese behavior during World War II may have helped, although there have also been periodic efforts by others to justify past Japanese actions. Moreover, there are a wide range of issues, from those of colonial policies to the "comfort women" for Japanese soldiers, that remain.

At some point, Japan would like to establish a two-Koreas policy in the same manner as China, and earlier, as noted, it was negotiating with Pyongyang to this end. Those negotiations have been broken off, and Tokyo has indicated that it regards a resolution of the nuclear issue as of critical importance. It is also greatly concerned about the North's missile program. On May 29 and 30, 1993, the DPRK tested a Rodong–1 missile reportedly with a range of 600 miles or more—sufficient to reach major Japanese cities. For this and other reasons, the ROK and Japan have been engaged in closer consultation and sharing information on military as well as other matters, and discussions relating to a jointly sponsored antimissile program are ongoing between Japan and the United States.

There is no pressure from the Japanese business sector to establish diplomatic relations with the DPRK, since the North has very limited attractiveness as an investment or market site at present. Moreover, old debts owed Japanese firms remain unpaid in some cases. In contrast, the South has been a major market for Japan, especially in high-tech products and components. Like many other countries, the ROK runs a trade deficit with Japan, and that has become a contentious point. However, economic relations are too important to both countries to permit a major crisis.

As of early 1995, Japan–DPRK negotiations had not resumed, despite various Japanese overtures, and the North's propaganda against Japanese policies remained intense. Should the North's interaction with the United States continue to advance positively, however, an opening in DPRK–Japan relations is very likely to follow, possibly in swift fashion as was the case in Sino-Japanese relations after the U.S.–PRC opening in the early 1970s.

China, the Big Neighbor on the Doorstep

China represents yet another major actor within the second arc.[25] As indicated earlier, after a period of growing economic and cultural ties with the ROK, the PRC government took successive steps toward a two-Koreas policy despite the danger of arousing DPRK wrath and the uncomfortable parallels that might be drawn with the issue of China–Taiwan. At present, the economic ties between China and the ROK dwarf those with the DPRK. The Chinese–South Korean relationship, however, remains unbalanced, with political and strategic relations far more fragile than those on the economic front. Chinese leaders continue to proclaim their support for DPRK socialism and maintain economic relations of critical importance to the North.

The Chinese dilemma is acute. On the one hand, the PRC does not want to lose its position with respect to North Korea, being mindful of the strategic position of that country and the very sizable Korean population living in northeast China, and being anxious to work with DPRK leaders on such projects as the Tumen River development. Moreover, even if they have substantial private doubts regarding the North's *chuch'e* socialism, and especially its cult of personality, and private fears regarding its future, Chinese leaders do not want a chaotic North Korea on their border, nor would they be overjoyed to see a unified Korea that was a showplace of democracy. Yet ties with the South are steadily growing, and beyond this, China does not want any part of Korea to have nuclear weapons. To have had the issue brought to the United Nations would have been most painful. Hence, China's exhortations to all parties have been to continue on the diplomatic path, and it has promised to serve as facilitator to various negotiations, always insisting that its influence on the North is limited.

For the present, since the negotiatory path appears to be succeeding—at least in the case of U.S.–DPRK relations—China is greatly relieved. Should official North–South relations remain at an impasse or worsen, China can be expected to wrestle with the question of what policies would serve its interest best, probably seeking to stake out a position between those of the adversaries, however difficult such a move proves to be, while counseling both to take a peaceful route. In any case, one can be certain that China will always take the Korean issue seriously and insist upon being a participant in whatever developments ensue.

Russia—A Lesser Actor

Russia also has a strong interest in the Korean peninsula. Key ports of the south Siberian coastline lie within close range of the two Koreas, and Russian provincial leaders look toward growing economic interaction with the two Koreas, especially the South, in supporting programs like the Greater Vladivostok developmental project.

As noted earlier, however, Russian diplomacy in recent years has not been as skillful as that of China in consummating a two-Koreas policy that keeps all parties at least minimally happy. Deep bitterness and distrust of the Russians now permeates the DPRK leadership, although Pyongyang is gradually coming to terms with the new order, recognizing that it has both an economic and a military need for a better relationship with Moscow. Trade and certain joint ventures are advancing. Nevertheless, coolness between the two governments remains the dominant condition. Russian leaders have been sharply critical of the North's purported nuclear activities, and of its supposed biological and chemical weapons stockpiles as well. They have sought to prevent unemployed Russian scientists from going to the DPRK. For their part, DPRK leaders along with others, were quick to condemn Russia for dumping nuclear waste in the Sea of Japan, and for various "hostile statements" emanating from Russian sources, including the release of documentary materials relating to the founding of the DPRK and the Korean War that have little in common with the official North Korean versions. Indeed, they conclusively establish Kim's responsibility for launching that war.

For the near term at least, Russia will be a minor actor in the Korean drama, and resentful of that fact. In the longer run, however, as Siberia develops economically, it will increasingly look East even as Russia west of the Urals looks West. Then, Korea—divided or united—will loom increasingly large in Russian eyes, both economically and strategically.

The Role of International Institutions

Let us now turn briefly to the third arc, that of international bodies—the United Nations, the UNDP, and various other agencies. Here, the current contrast between North and South is particularly striking. The ROK has emerged as a significant regional force, its economic reach extending into the whole of East Asia. Correspondingly, it has been an active participant in the activities of the World Bank and the International Monetary Fund. Moreover, it is an enthusiastic supporter of APEC and a participant in the embryonic unofficial and quasi-official bodies seeking to probe security issues in the region, including the ASEAN Regional Forum (ARF). As is well known, the United Nations has been involved in the issues of the Korean peninsula since the early post-1945 era, and it will be officially involved in any final movement from a Korean War armistice to formal peace.

In contrast with the ROK, the DPRK is involved with international agencies in a very modest way, principally with the UNDP. The latter body has not only sponsored various conferences relating to a Tumen River project that would involve the two Koreas, China, and Russia, but also provided some economic assistance to the North. The DPRK joined that body in June 1979 and has received aid in three phases, totaling some U.S. $82 million. Most recently, on March 25, 1993, the UNDP agreed to help in raising coal production and promoting the development of a tourist industry. Having joined the United Nations in 1991, the DPRK is also in a position to broaden its international ties, and some Northern authorities have indicated an interest in becoming part of APEC as well as other regional and international agencies.

In sum, the trends are in the direction of strengthening the activities of the third arc as it pertains to the Korean peninsula. Here, economics and the broad policy decisions of the DPRK will be key determinants. Current signs, however, point to a North Korea that will seek to use a variety of international agencies in its quest for future development.

Looking Ahead

Looking ahead, what are the prospects, first with respect to the two Koreas? Given the fluidity of the situation, it would be unwise to posit a single scenario, either for domestic developments or for Korea's impact upon the regional order. However, several possibilities with some estimate of probability can be outlined.

One scenario would be the collapse of the DPRK as a result of internal economic and political crises, followed by its absorption into the Republic of Korea. This is the so-called German formula that has been frequently discussed in the South and elsewhere. Thus far, the efforts to inject a new vitality into the DPRK's economy by fostering special economic zones and joint ventures with foreign entrepreneurs have had very meager results. If the lengthy impasse over the nuclear issue has now ended, however, various foreign companies, and notably those of South Korea, will show a greater interest in investment—as current trends clearly indicate. The DPRK has one significant asset: a labor force that has basic education and is available at low cost. Further, both South Korea and the United States have lightened the restrictions on trade and investment with the DPRK. On the other hand, many factors are likely to inhibit most foreign investors, especially given the intense competition for such investment throughout Asia. To make the DPRK economically attractive to outsiders is likely to be a prodigious task.

North Korea currently earns foreign exchange principally by military sales, and it is alleged that agreements have been sought or consummated with Iran, among others, relating to the sale of sophisticated military hardware, including medium- and long-range missiles, in exchange for oil and other commodities. The North vigorously denies such assertions. In any case, unless a dramatic shift of policy takes place, and can be sustained, it is difficult to see how the North can avoid falling further behind its neighbors economically.

Coupled with economic problems is the thorny issue of succession, as noted earlier. The propaganda extolling Kim Jong Il is so extravagant that one wonders how it could be credible even to those drugged by decades of eulogies to Kim's father. Virtually all careful observers of the Korean scene, including Russians and Chinese who have had personal contact with the two Kims, express reservations—in varying degrees—about Kim Jong Il—his personality, his health, his lifestyle, his leadership qualities.

There are many potential variations of a collapse scenario. It seems most likely that it would have to involve splits among the elite. There is very little chance of a revolution from below, given the nature of North Korean society. If serious factionalism developed within the elite over such issues as economic reform, policies toward the ROK, or relations with the United States, one dangerous possibility would be the internationalization of the domestic struggle. What if one faction turned to China and asked for support, pledging comradeship in return? The dilemma for Beijing would be acute, and all its Asian neighbors would anxiously await the decision. Less likely but not impossible would be a move on the part of one element in the struggle to turn toward the South, or at least to make tempting ROK involvement, military or otherwise.

It is easy to see how developments such as these could quickly produce a regional crisis of major proportions. An armed struggle on the Korean peninsula, whatever its dimensions, would almost certainly exacerbate tensions among the major states of Northeast Asia. But even if the North were to collapse with relatively little trauma, that unlikely event would create enormous hardships for the ROK, as noted. To inherit a poverty-stricken people who have had absolutely no preparation for political participation in a democratic society would be a tremendous strain. The ROK would need major economic assistance from countries like the United States and Japan. And it would be wholly absorbed in its internal problems, with its near-term contributions to a regional order correspondingly limited.

A different alternative would be a DPRK that returned to the pursuit of rigid policies both at home and with respect to others, retreating from the current efforts to turn outward economically, fearful of their consequences. In that event, the threat of violence would hang over the Korean peninsula, with the ROK feeling that it had to maintain a strong military defense, including rapid modernization of all facets of conventional weaponry. And if the DPRK were proven to be developing nuclear weapons, a desire to match that action would grow in the South despite many counterarguments. Clearly, Japan would also feel deeply apprehensive, with the issue of its own military posture being periodically reexamined. Tension would build throughout Northeast Asia.

A third and possibly more likely alternative for the DPRK would be the strengthened role of a modernizing elite, a prospect suggested earlier. A combination of second- and third-generation military and technocratic figures would steer policies in the direction of accelerated economic reform, with the political order remaining authoritarian. The model, broadly speaking, would be that previously pursued by China. It now seems clear that voices urging this course are emerging in the North despite past failures and current obstacles.

Obviously, the implications of these alternative scenarios are very different, not only for the ROK, but for the region as a whole. As noted, the collapse scenario in any of its forms is likely to cause grave problems for the South, and place corresponding burdens on neighboring countries. Their actions, especially under conditions of protracted tension on the Korean peninsula, would be of critical importance.

The combination of continued rigid policies at home and brinkmanship abroad would likewise cause tensions to mount, both between the two Koreas and on the international stage. Almost certainly it would evoke sanctions in some form if long continued, and then the capacity of the major states to pursue cooperative or collective policies would be tested.

If the third alternative were to unfold, an authoritarian-pluralist system bearing some similarity not only to China but to South Korea of an earlier vintage would probably evolve at home, replete with various advances and retreats. Economic and cultural intercourse with the South would expand rapidly. Diplomatic relations would be eventually established with Japan, and at some point, with the United States. These developments, in turn, could lead to reductions in DPRK military expenditures, participation in certain regional economic bodies, and other benefits—and risks—of greater involvement with the region of which it is a part. Clearly, this is the alternative that all parties outside the DPRK would desire, and, if present trends continue, it is a reasonable—but not certain—prospect.

Turning to the ROK, the future seems easier to discern. Despite the economic problems of the present, the ROK economy remains basically strong. Growth in 1994 was over 8 percent. The steep wage increases that exceeded gains in productivity appear to have ended. In addition, the government has promised further internationalization of the economy, including the accelerated opening of Korean markets, extensive deregulation, tackling the problems of low capital investment and the trade deficit, structural adjustments favoring support for small and medium business, and the promotion of research and development, partly through cooperation with such foreign enterprises as the high-tech industries of the United States.

If promise is translated into performance, Korea should be able to strengthen its already impressive trade and investment abroad, most notably in Asia. Like others, it is enthusiastic about the China market, and ROK trade with and investments in the PRC will continue to advance rapidly. If economic conditions in Russia improve, Siberia is another likely site for extensive ROK economic activity.

In sum, the internationalization of the ROK economy, already well underway, will accelerate. The ROK will become an important part of several natural economic territories (NETs) involving a combination of labor, resources, capital, technology, and managerial skills. These economic entities are cutting across political lines, transforming the topography of East Asia, quite possibly representing a development with more far-reaching consequences—economic, political, and social—than any event of our times. Already, the Shandong province–ROK NET and that involving the East Sea (known by the Japanese as the Sea of Japan) are prominent examples. If political conditions permit, a NET like that envisaged in the Tumen River delta could bring the two Koreas into close economic interaction. Then the process of eventual fusion would be smoother.

Meanwhile, like others, South Korea profits from and worries about its close economic ties with Japan, as suggested earlier. From that nation, the ROK obtains many components as well as finished products in the high-technology field. Its trade deficit with Japan has reached uncomfortable levels, but with Korea's needs, given its march up the technological ladder, the deficit shows scant signs of diminishing.

Economic relations with the United States also involve certain problems, reflecting the broader issues confronting competitive capitalist societies that come from different cultural traditions, are at different stages of development, and have pursued different economic strategies. ROK trade with the United States is currently more or less in balance. The problems have been in other areas: limited market access for the United States despite past promises, intellectual property protection; and dumping. With the sweeping reforms promised by the Kim administration, will past American grievances be significantly altered?

In any event, South Korea is now a medium-sized industrial power. Consequently, it can be expected to have a stronger voice in such organizations as APEC and GATT, with greater responsibilities placed upon it as well.

The economic dimension is only one aspect of the ROK's relationships with other Pacific–Asian nations. Politically, the greater openness in the South in recent years makes it certain that both domestic and foreign policies will be subject to debate and disputation. In recent times, the Kim Young Sam government has dipped in popularity according to public opinion polls, and, as noted, there are internal cleavages in both of the South's two major parties. The broad trend, however, is away from the extremities: Both the radical student movement and the military right have diminished support. The chances for a successful experiment with democracy seem promising.

At the same time, nationalism is rising in the ROK, and with it, a stronger assertiveness. To a sizable majority of citizens, the ties with the United States remain crucial. But the nature of the relationship is shifting from clientism to a demand for partnership. Hence, on all matters—economic, political, and military—careful handling and full consultation between Washington and Seoul will be necessary if the relationship is to remain healthy.

As one looks ahead, the key variables remain those of domestic policies, North and South, and the course of relations between these two states. If a cooperative relationship can gradually be built and peaceful unification ultimately comes as the end product of a process, not as the result of a single dramatic act, this will be a major achievement. Then, with the two economic and political systems acquiring greater compatibility, the Koreas—and, finally, Korea—will be an actor of ever-greater importance. In the posthegemonic era, the role of medium powers has become increasingly important and the Republic of Korea is already foremost in that category. A unified, democratic Korea with an outward-looking economy would be a major force in Asia and beyond.

Notes

1. For an account of political developments in South Korea in the weeks immediately after August 15, 1945, and the early U.S. Occupation policies, see Robert A. Scalapino and Chong-Sik Lee, *Communism in Korea,* vol. I (Berkeley: University of California Press, 1972): 233–312; for developments during the same period in the North under Soviet tutelage, see ibid., 313–81.

2. For a recent, well researched biography of Kim, see Dae Sook Suh, *Kim Il Sung:*

The North Korean Leader (New York: Columbia University Press, 1988). Kim's own presentation of his early life has recently been published in various languages. In English, see Kim Il Sung, *Reminiscences—With the Century,* vols. 1 and 2 (Pyongyang: Foreign Languages Press, 1992).

3. There have been innumerable accounts of the Korean War, written from a great diversity of perspectives. Three revealing memoirs are Harry S. Truman, *Memoirs by Harry S. Truman,* vols. 1 and 2 (New York: Doubleday and Co., 1956); Dean Acheson, *Present at the Creation* (New York: W.W. Norton, 1969), and Nikita Khrushchev, *Khrushchev Remembers* (Boston: Little, Brown, 1974). Relatively objective accounts of recent vintage include John Merrill, *Korea: The Peninsular Origins of the War* (Newark, NJ: University of Delaware Press, 1989); Chae-Jin Lee, ed., *The Korean War—40-Year Perspectives* (Claremont, CA: The Keck Center for International and Strategic Studies, 1991). For a fascinating account of Kim Il Song and the war—but one impossible to check for accuracy on a number of points, see the work of a Russian-Korean who uses the pseudonym Lim Un, *The Founding of a Dynasty in North Korea—An Authentic Biography of Kim Il-song,* English edition (Tokyo: Jiyu-sha, 1982). Recently, materials from the Russian archives on the Korean War have been made available to scholars, and they are of major importance.

4. For various perspectives on DPRK foreign policy, see Robert A. Scalapino and Hongkoo Lee, eds., *North Korea in a Regional and Global Context* (Berkeley, CA: Institute of East Asian Studies, 1986); see also Byung Chul Koh, *The Foreign Policy Systems of North and South Korea* (Berkeley: University of California Press, 1984). For an earlier work, see William J. Barnds, ed., *The Two Koreas in East Asian Affairs* (New York: New York University Press, 1976).

5. An analysis of South Korean politics during this period can be found in John Kie-Chiang Oh, *Democracy on Trial* (Ithaca, NY: Cornell University Press, 1968); David C. Cole and Princeton N. Lyman, *Korean Development: The Interplay of Politics and Economics* (Cambridge, MA: Harvard University Press, 1971); and Sung-Joo Han, *The Failure of Democracy in South Korea* (Berkeley: University of California Press, 1974).

6. This author had a lengthy conversation with President Park Chung-Hee in 1969, during which Park expressed serious concerns about American plans. He asserted flatly that the United States was going to withdraw from South Vietnam, and that there would be heavy pressures upon the Nixon administration to conduct a more general strategic withdrawal. "You must give me time to prepare for these events," he asserted. His subsequent preparations were to include the Yushin Constitution and a general trend toward stronger authoritarian rule, in anticipation of having to go it alone.

7. For details, see Scalapino and Lee, op. cit., I: 677–83.

8. For an overview dealing with both domestic and foreign policies of the two Koreas, see Young Whan Kihl, *Politics and Policies in Divided Korea—Regimes in Contest* (Boulder, CO: Westview Press, 1984).

9. For a brief Russian view of the Pacific-Asian theater as of 1990 and current Soviet policies, see Gennady I. Chufrin, "A Soviet View," in Chong-Sik Lee, ed., *In Search of a New Order in Asia* (Berkeley, CA: Institute of Southeast Asian Studies, 1991), pp. 42–51.

10. Seven articles written between late 1988 and 1994 provide a comprehensive overview of ROK policies during this period: Han Sung-Joo, "South Korea in 1988, A Revolution in the Making," *Asian Survey,* January 1989, 29–38; Young Whan Kihl, "South Korea in 1989: Slow Progress toward Democracy," *Asian Survey,* January 1990, 67–73; Young Whan Kihl, "South Korea in 1990: Diplomatic Activism and a Partisan Quagmire, *Asian Survey,* January 1991, 64–70; Hong Yung Lee, "South Korea in 1991: Unprecedented Opportunity, Increasing Challenge," *Asian Survey,* January 1992, 64–73; Victor D. Cha, "Politics and Democracy under the Kim Young Sam Government: Something Old,

Something New," *Asian Survey,* September 1993, pp. 849–63; and John Merrill, "North Korea in 1993: In the Eye of the Storm," *Asian Survey,* January 1994, pp. 10–18; and Samuel S. Kim, "North Korea in 1994: Brinkmanship Breakdown and Breakthrough," *Asian Survey,* 35, 1 (January 1995), pp. 14–30.

11. See Johngseh Park, "Korea's *Nordpolitik:* Its Background and Future Prospects in the Post–Cold War Era," *Institute Reports* (New York: East Asian Institute, Columbia University, May 1991).

12. Private conversation between the author and a Soviet foreign ministry official who had accompanied Schevardnadze, Vladivostok, September 1990. Reportedly, North Korean authorities threatened that Soviet "desertion" would leave them no alternative but to develop their own "modern" weapons program, turn to others for support and cease to trust the USSR. Instead of reacting with concern, as the DPRK officials may have expected, Schevardnadze responded that the DPRK would of course have to determine what was in its interests.

13. Official Chinese views on general Pacific–Asian developments during this period include Ma Xusheng, "Thoughts on the Question of Establishing a New International Order," *Foreign Affairs Journal* (Beijing), December 1991, 12–18; Li Luye, "The International Situation and a New International Order," *Foreign Affairs Journal* (Beijing), December 1991, 19–23; and Wu Zhan, "A Chinese View," in Chong-Sik Lee, ed., op. cit., 52–68.

14. The full text of the agreement was published by both South and North. See "Agreement on Reconciliation, Nonaggression, and Cooperation and Exchange between the North and South," *Korea News-Views,* Korean Information Office, Embassy of Korea, Washington, DC, December 14, 1991; *Press Release,* No. 31, Democratic People's Republic of Korea Mission to the United Nations, December 1, 1991.

15. Excellent analyses of North-South relations in the 1991–1992 period are to be found in Chong-Sik Lee and Se-Hee Yoo, eds., *North Korea in Transition* (Berkeley, CA: Institute of East Asian Studies, 1991); Michael J. Mazarr, et al., eds., *Korea 1991—The Road to Peace* (Boulder, CO: Westview Press, 1991); and Donald J. Clark, ed., *Korea Briefing, 1992* (Boulder, CO: Westview Press, 1992).

16. The position of the Kim government is set forth in detail by Tae Hwan Ok in his essay, "The Unification Policy of the Kim Young Sam Government and Prospects for South-North Relations," paper presented at the CSIS-RINU Conference, Washington, DC, October 27–28, 1993.

17. On North–South economic relations, see Ha-cheong Yeon, "Inter-Korean Trade and Economic Cooperation: Status and Prospects," in Gerrit W. Gong, Seizaburo Sato, and Trae Hwan Ok, eds., *Korean Peninsula Issue and U.S.–Japan–South Korea Relations,* vol. 2 (Washington, DC: Center for Strategic and International Studies, 1993), pp. 1–57. See also Il-Dong Koh, "Complementarity of Industrial Structures between North and South Korea," paper for the IEAS-East-West Center-Korean Association for the Study of Socialist Societies, Berkeley, December 11–13, 1991; Sungwoo Kim, "Recent Economic Policies of North Korea: Analysis and Recommendations," *Asian Survey,* September 1993, 864–78.

18. An official translation of the Ten-Point Program is contained in the DPRK Permanent Mission to the UN Press Release, April 8, 1993, entitled "President Kim Il Sung's Work—10-Point Programme of Great Unity of the Whole Nation for Reunification of the Country."

19. The March 12 statement is carried in the DPRK Permanent Mission to the UN Press Release, March 12, 1993.

20. For the June 11 statement as reported in the North Korean press, see *The People's Korea,* June 19, 1993, p. 1.

21. The July 19 statement is carried in *The People's Korea,* July 24, 1993, pp. 1, 8.

22. A perceptive article is that by Andrew Mack, "The Nuclear Crisis on the Korean Peninsula," *Asian Survey,* April 1993, 339–59.

23. On political trends in North Korea, see Byoung Yong Lee, "Trends in Domestic Politics and the Economy of North Korea," *RINU Newsletter,* vol. 2, no. 2, June 1993, 1–4; Yinghay Ahn, "Elite Politics and Policy Making in North Korea: A Policy Tendency Analysis," *The Korean Journal of National Unification,* vol. 2, 1993, 85–104. A broad analysis is contained in this author's *The Last Leninists—The Uncertain Future of Asia's Communist States* (Washington, DC: The Center for Strategic and International Studies, 1992) and his "Communism in Asia," *Problems of Post-Communism,* Fall 1994, 3–10.

24. For one perspective, see O. Sonfa, "The Cultural Roots of Japanese-Korean Friction," *Japan Echo,* vol. 20, Special Issue, 1993, pp. 23–28.

25. For a recent account from a Chinese perspective, see Chai Zemin, "Development of Sino-Korean Relations and Northeast Asia," *Foreign Affairs Journal* (Beijing), September 1993, 10–18.

8

A Giant Treads Carefully: Indonesia's Foreign Policy in the 1990s

Michael R.J. Vatikiotis

As Indonesia moves confidently into the last decade of the twentieth century, with its economy growing more surely, helped by a track record of social and political stability, there are distinct signs that Jakarta is adopting a higher diplomatic profile in the region and beyond. A number of changes in the external and internal dynamics of foreign policy appear to have coincided and combined to set Indonesia on a more outward-looking course. Indonesia is the largest country in Southeast Asia. With a population fast approaching 200 million, Indonesia accounts for almost half the ASEAN region's total population and is the fourth most populous country in the world. As such, Indonesia's contribution to regional stability is probably far greater than that of any other Southeast Asian state. Also, with the end of the cold war, new strategic significance has been assigned to East Asia. The focus of world affairs has moved away from the lumbering military antics of northern hemisphere superpowers, toward the economic dynamism of mid-sized regional powers in Asia. Indonesia is potentially one of these powers. This being the case, it is pertinent to search for the source and inspiration of foreign policy and suggest its possible impact on the region as a whole.

Indonesia's foreign policy is conceptually governed by pioneering nationalist Mohamad Hatta's view that it should be "free and active" (*bebas dan aktif*). But like so many conceptual formulations decided upon by the country's founding fathers, the "free and active" formula is often hard to deduce from actual policy. Rather, it seems that foreign policy has been characterized by an inherent duality driven by circumstances and an innate sense of pragmatism not uncommon to the region. At times, there have been those who favored adopting a low profile in international affairs, preferring policies which helped the country concentrate on internal economic, social, and political goals. Others have argued, at times per-

suasively, that resilience and internal unity can be best be enhanced by projecting Indonesia more actively on the international stage. Linking these two extremes is a view that only when Indonesia is domestically secure and stable can
an active foreign policy be prosecuted safely and effectively.

Historically, Indonesian foreign policy has swung between these two poles,
resulting in phases of active and passive diplomacy. Roughly speaking, there
have been three phases. The early 1950s saw the more passive pragmatists
successfully articulate a "free and active" foreign policy. As Herbert Feith puts
it, this independence was only mildly expressed and involved no overtly anti-
Western postures.[1] But as it developed, Sukarno's fiery brand of nationalism
generated excessive political energies, especially after the suspension of constitutional democracy and the imposition of Guided Democracy in the late 1950s.
Ties with the communist bloc strengthened after the mid-1950s. The Soviet
Union and China supplied Indonesia with modern weaponry, including long-
range Tupolev bombers. Armed with these and a stridently anti-imperialistic
brand of rhetoric, Sukarno embarked on a more assertive, confrontational foreign
policy.[2]

Sukarno's virulently nationalistic and anti-Western policies led to unprofit-
able alliances with China, North Korea, and the Eastern bloc, confrontation with
Malaysia, and enhanced suspicion of Indonesia in the region. After coming to
power in 1966, President Suharto made peace with Malaysia and restored a sense
of pragmatism, seeking peaceful relations with regional neighbors and much-
needed aid from the more prosperous noncommunist West. In December 1967,
Suharto declared that henceforth Indonesia would give first priority to creating
regional stability and cooperation among Southeast Asian states, and to ensuring
that relations with the outside world yielded what he called "real and material
benefits for both parties and particularly for Indonesia."[3]

The New Order's reliance on foreign aid and friendly markets for its exports
bred an acutely pragmatic, and therefore bland, foreign policy focused on restoring better relations with Indonesia's neighbors and wooing donor countries in the
West. The inherent antipathy toward foreign capital and investment, which
stemmed from the nationalist struggle against the Dutch, was replaced by better
relations with Western countries, allowing foreign investment to begin pouring
in. Only Indonesia's membership in the Non-Aligned Movement (NAM) survived Sukarno. And even identification with the NAM was, until recently,
masked by Suharto's reluctance to parade himself at international gatherings.
Consciously spurning Sukarno's globe-trotting, bombastic style, until the end of
the 1980s Suharto opted for a low international profile.

Preoccupied for the most part with domestic development, Jakarta's genuine
views about its immediate neighbors in the Association of Southeast Asian Nations (ASEAN) and the larger Asian powers beyond became difficult to identify.
Although, with the benefit of hindsight, it could be said that this neglect of a
forward foreign policy deprived Indonesia of the chance to play the leading role

in Third World politics that Sukarno initiated, few dispute the advantages that ensued. By restraining the militant spirit kindled at the 1955 Asia-Africa conference in Bandung and focusing on internal development, President Suharto paved the way for the establishment of ASEAN and heralded the present era of harmonious intrastate relations in the region. Indeed, Indonesia's conscious containment of its aspirations to be a regional power became a given factor of the region's security from the 1970s onward.

Changes now affecting both the internal and external dimensions of Indonesia's foreign policy suggest that this blandness is being consciously traded for a more distinctive diplomatic profile. Indonesia may, in fact, be entering a fourth stage of its diplomatic history—once more in the active mode. The source of this new, more active policy is a matter for debate. Indisputably, though, a key factor has been the stable economic growth of the latter 1980s. This period saw Indonesia weather the fall in world oil prices that almost crippled the country's hydrocarbon-dependent economy, recover, and begin to prosper. Economic success has bred confidence—a mood Suharto has now indicated that he wishes to translate into more active diplomacy. A few years ago, Suharto referred to the more responsible role he felt Indonesia could play in world affairs once development was securely under way.[4] In his August 1990 national address, Suharto argued that the stage of Indonesia's development now permitted just such a role to be prosecuted.

The external dimension of Indonesian foreign policy has also altered within the last five years. After years of diplomatic dormancy, the early 1980s saw Indonesia drawn into playing a more assertive role in ASEAN affairs. For ASEAN as a whole, the fear that Vietnam's invasion of Cambodia in late 1979 could threaten regional security enhanced the association's diplomatic engagement in international affairs. Out of this grew Jakarta's mediating role in the Cambodian conflict, and with it the confidence to address other sources of regional conflict, such as the Muslim insurgency in the southern Philippines and competing claims in the South China Sea.

A third, and perhaps more important, factor explaining Indonesia's more assertive foreign policy, given the nature of the domestic power structure, is the changing view of President Suharto himself with respect to foreign policy. It is difficult to gauge with any precision just how much foreign policy is made by the president, but given his position at the apex of the political system, he is clearly an important source of impetus, if not ideas. Moreover, if the ideas are not his own, the timing of their implementation is all his. Significantly, the more engaged Suharto has become in foreign affairs, the bigger the role his own staff from the state secretariat has begun to play—often at the expense of foreign ministry officials, who have sometimes been kept in the dark ahead of important initiatives.

Arguably, Suharto's attendance at the Non-Aligned heads of government meeting in Belgrade in September 1989 marked a significant turning point in the president's approach to foreign policy. The last time Suharto had attended a Non-Aligned meeting had been in 1970 in Zambia, where he was harangued by other Non-Aligned leaders for banning the Communist Party and becoming, in their eyes, a lackey of the West. In Belgrade, by contrast, Suharto was impressed by the number of leaders who sought him out and congratulated him on policies that had strengthened Indonesia's economy and resulted in enviable prolonged stability.[5] The closing years of the 1980s also brought Suharto international awards for some of his development programs, which also helped him lose his shyness in international forums.

Encouraged by the recognition of his achievements, Suharto shed his previous timid, almost neglectful, view of international diplomacy and embarked on a series of overseas visits to Washington, the Soviet Union, Europe, and Latin America in the following three years. By contrast, until 1989, the most significant overseas trip Suharto had made was to Eastern Europe in 1986. The leading mass daily newspaper *Kompas* reflected Suharto's new approach when it declared in a September 1989 editorial, after the Belgrade meeting, that "a new phase in Indonesian foreign policy" had begun.[6]

To some extent the sudden shift toward activism masked a degree of continuity. Although Indonesia seemed to have abandoned its torch-bearing role in the developing world in favor of wooing Western foreign capital, the foreign ministry was quietly but diligently enhancing Indonesia's profile in the Non-Aligned Movement, the Group of 77, and other South-South forums. However, without the full involvement of the leadership, these remained low-key diplomatic initiatives. Now that Suharto was more engaged, some of these initiatives began to fly. Given the timing of this shift in Suharto's approach, many political analysts concluded that the president wanted an enhanced diplomatic profile to reinforce his mandate before presidential elections in 1993. At home and abroad, Suharto was being criticized for being too conservative in his ways and out of touch with the domestic and international realities facing Indonesia. However, the extent to which Suharto needed rather than believed in an active foreign policy is less germane to the subject of this chapter than the fact that by the end of the 1980s, Suharto clearly supported and was participating in a more active Indonesian foreign policy.

If, indeed, the post-1989 period marks a new phase in Indonesian foreign policy, and a more active one at that, what impact will this have on the region? Arguably, Indonesia is considerably more important in the regional diplomatic and strategic order than the rest of ASEAN. Indonesia is the largest state in Southeast Asia, with the world's biggest Muslim population and armed forces of almost half a million men (445,000 in 1991). As Robert Tilman observed: "Indonesia's strategic location in the middle of several major sea arteries forces the country into the mainstream of international politics."[7] Indonesia's natural preeminence and strategic importance have led many in the past to question how far Indonesia could pursue a more active foreign policy before colliding with regional sensitivities and with emerging Asian powers beyond.

However, this somewhat esoteric perception of Indonesia's preeminence has not always been so evident in reality because of the New Order's policy of self-containment, most directly expressed by its commitment to ASEAN. From a perspective beyond the immediate region, Indonesia's enviable political stability under President Suharto's New Order government gave the major powers little cause to worry about threats to the strategic sea lanes Indonesia straddles. Indonesia came into the international spotlight when Suharto's predecessor Sukarno came close to delivering the country to Asia's communist bloc and threatened Western strategic interests. In the wake of the Cold War, it is perhaps even less likely that major powers will worry about Indonesia's political alignment. This suggests in a way that earlier perceptions of its preeminence were based more on fears of which of the Cold War protagonists would play the role of patron power, rather than on any intrinsic threat to the region posed by Indonesia.

The Western powers may no longer be concerned about Indonesia's becoming a communist state, but the strategic implications of a more active foreign policy are certainly significant for the country's near neighbors. So long as Indonesia's aims were focused inward, on enhancing economic and political stability, there were few concerns in the region about Indonesian foreign policy. But more worrying for some are signs that Indonesia is beginning to look at broader issues and its role in the world beyond Southeast Asia. Some would argue that this is part of a trend in Southeast Asia for close links between domestic and international political orientations to become less pronounced.[8] Growing self-confidence and lasting internal political stability have enabled governments in the region to adopt positions on the international stage that do not necessarily reflect domestic political preoccupations.

When, for example, the Indonesian government donated U.S. $10 million to the African National Congress in 1990, the gesture was accepted as a bid to burnish Non-Aligned credentials. No one inside the country raised questions about funding an organization with socialist or, worse, allegedly communist sympathies. Ironically also, in a country where long-term political prisoners have been in detention for almost as long as Nelson Mandela, Mandela's visit to Jakarta in 1990 was not considered sensitive in domestic terms at all.

But if Indonesia can now afford to articulate principles divorced from its own domestic concerns, what does this imply for the region? Does it mean that Jakarta's commitment to regionalism and the need to guard against the threat of intervention by competing big powers will continue to be valid assumptions underpinning Indonesian foreign policy?

The region's previous experience of Indonesia's articulating a more active foreign policy was not a happy one, and this perception seems to have survived the end of the Sukarno era. The fact that Malaysia and Singapore cling to the Five-Power Defense Arrangement set up after Indonesia's confrontation with Malaysia in 1963–65 suggests that suspicions of Indonesia linger. Now that Indonesia has acquired the confidence to assert itself again, how will this affect the region?

The Nationalist Dimension

To understand Indonesian foreign policy, it is important to set it in the indigenous context. Because Indonesia's independence was the product of a self-styled revolution and armed struggle, not of a negotiated transfer of sovereignty, Indonesian nationalism was by nature virulently anti-imperialistic. These strong anti-imperialist sentiments were carried over into the postindependence era by Sukarno, who adopted a political strategy that hinged partly on perpetuating the radical, activist fervor of revolution with "politics as the commander."

Driven by Sukarno's revolutionary fervor, on the diplomatic front this activism found expression at the 1955 Afro-Asia Congress in Bandung. The historic meeting, which was attended by China's Zhou Enlai, India's Nehru, and Egypt's Gamal Abdul Nasser, among others, embedded the idealistic notion of new nations shaping a new world order firmly in the Indonesian psyche. The esteem bestowed on Indonesia for hosting this event, the contemporary significance of which is easy to forget, should not be underestimated. The New Order's colorless diplomatic carapace is easily shed when it comes to reviving memories of the conference and the "Bandung spirit." The most recent celebration of the event in 1986 showed just how easily some of the old sentiments are revived.

These activist ideals have never been entirely extinguished, and although much tempered by current realities, they remain potent among Indonesia's intellectual establishment. Nationalism is a difficult term to apply to diplomacy, as all diplomacy is, almost by definition, an exercise in nationalism. But in the Indonesian case, political nationalism has injected a strong sense of purpose into foreign affairs. When he was foreign minister, Mochtar Kusumaatmadja put it this way:

> Our foreign policy is a principled one; not based on expediency, not calculated on a profit and loss basis—though of course there is something of this. But there are certain basic questions of principle where Indonesia will never yield.[9]

Yet despite the lip service paid to anticolonial activism, the emergence of the New Order after 1966 saw Indonesian diplomacy replace confrontation with accommodation; idealism gave way to pragmatism. Expressions of Indonesian nationalism turned inward to concentrate on national development. Rather than being buried, the activist ideals of the Sukarno period were set aside in favor of a low profile better suited to the domestic goals on which the New Order pinned its legitimacy. Indonesia's reliance on Western export markets and, perhaps more importantly, on Western aid rendered impractical any expression of the country's Non-Aligned identity beyond that of paying lip service to the movement's aims.

More recently, some elements of the foreign policy establishment have seen global developments as a chance to reinvigorate Indonesia's diplomatic profile.

As the economy emerged from the recession of the late 1970s and early 1980s and began to bloom, some felt that Indonesia's remarkable record of stability and growth earned it the right to assert a higher profile and revive some of the nationalist ideals of the past.

There was, however, a difference of opinion within the ruling establishment. The more cautious, but politically influential, armed forces were prone to over-exaggerating threats to stability and cautioned against striking a high profile in the region and beyond. Up until very recently, the military establishment regarded diplomacy as a means of preserving the country's internal security. This need for "national resilience" allowed little scope for diplomatic adventurism. Instead, the military insisted on open, accommodative relations with the non-communist West and maintained a high degree of suspicion of the communist bloc. Drawing heavily on their experience combating communist influence in the mid-1960s, the Indonesian military remained skeptical about the implications of global détente as it unfolded in the late 1980s:

> It may be true that in the spirit of the new detente the superpowers may be less disposed to a direct military involvement. But they could still be more indirectly involved by supplying more arms for their respective protagonists in any such conflicts. Therefore disarmament at the global level may not necessarily mean disarmament in such areas of the world as Southeast Asia.[10]

While the foreign ministry devoted time to developing Non-Aligned concepts such as the Zone of Peace, Freedom, and Neutrality (ZOPFAN), developed in the early 1970s, and more recently the Southeast Asia Nuclear Weapons-Free Zone (SEANWFZ), the military establishment was more interested in the procurement of Western military hardware. Though prone to exaggeration, the contrasting strategic concerns of the military and civilian establishments have certainly meant that many policy decisions are the product of compromises and trade-offs between the two groups.

More recently, emergence from the recession brought on by the oil crisis of the early 1980s into a period of growth and prosperity peaking in the early 1990s may have merged these differences of view. Sustained economic and political stability persuaded the military to be less concerned about the communist threat, and therefore more open to dealing with foreign powers. Involvement in the Cambodia debacle at the United Nations helped the foreign ministry acquire a taste for more active diplomacy. These two trends helped bring the military and civilian factions involved in foreign policymaking together. There was an emerging realization of Indonesia's potential as what Professor Juwono Sudharsono of the University of Indonesia refers to as a "middle-ranking power." An awkward label that is hard to define, this is probably best construed as an expression of Indonesia's confidence rather than as a comparative measure of power. For above all, Indonesia's remarkable economic progress since the mid-1980s has restored a sense of confidence to the country and encouraged many to question the timid face and low profile adopted by Indonesia toward the outside world.

Indonesia as Chairman of the Non-Aligned Movement

The fullest expression of Indonesia's new active phase of foreign policy was given when President Suharto was elected chairman of the Non-Aligned Movement in September 1991 for a five-year period. This was not the first time Indonesia had aspired to the position, but it was the first time that the diplomatic lobbying and trade-offs involved were effectively prosecuted. In fact, to most observers it seemed that the difference this time around was Suharto's commitment to assuming the higher diplomatic profile the position involved.

There were those, of course, who said that by the time Suharto opened the Non-Aligned heads of government conference in Jakarta in September 1991, the movement meant very little. The end of the Cold War, it was said, had deprived the Non-Aligned Movement of a cause; there was no more ideological alignment to abstain from. But for many Indonesians that was not the point. The NAM gave Indonesia a chance to perform on a wider stage, to show off some of the diplomatic prowess it had demonstrated in handling the Cambodia peace process. Only now Suharto as chairman had to deal with the vexing questions of peace in the Middle East and the ethnic conflict in Bosnia-Herzegovena.

These were not easy issues for Suharto and his government to tackle because of domestic sensitivities. Money for the ANC was one thing; deciding whether to give material support to the Muslim cause in Bosnia became an emotional issue because of Indonesia's Muslim identity. When the ethnic conflict in Bosnia exerted pressure on Muslim countries to throw their weight behind the beleaguered Bosnian government, Suharto would not be drawn into the fray. Indonesian diplomats explained that they feared inflaming Muslim sentiment at home. "Indonesia doesn't want to radicalize the situation because of the size of its Muslim population," commented Foreign Minister Ali Alatas in July 1993. Suharto took an even bigger risk when, soon after the 1994 Israeli–PLO peace accord, he held a brief meeting with Israel's Prime Minister Yitzhak Rabin in Jakarta. To avoid stirring up domestic sentiment, Suharto claimed the meeting was held in his capacity as chairman of the Non-Aligned Movement. Quite possibly, he also had the domestic situation in mind. By invoking his role as NAM chairman, he may have wanted to remind the increasingly vocal Islamic lobby in Indonesia that he still called the shots.

Becoming chairman of the Non-Aligned Movement gave Suharto the opportunity to reinvigorate his leadership at home and burnish his qualities as a statesman. Ironically, however, these were both qualities that many Indonesians were beginning to consider that their long-serving president lacked in the modern post–Cold War context. Unlike his energetic fellow ASEAN leader Dr. Mahathir Mohamad from Malaysia, Suharto lacked the stamina and the linguistic ability to engage world leaders in the new, more collegial style of the postsuperpower era. Having said that, it was also remarkable that Suharto, who was a late starter, managed to maintain a degree of momentum in the new wider context of Indonesian foreign policy—as indicated by the decision to hold the 1994 Asia Pacific Economic Cooperation (APEC) leaders' meeting in Indonesia.

Economic Priorities

Indonesia's new role in the Non-Aligned Movement harked back to the spirit of Bandung and the more idealistic, nationalist vein running through Indonesian foreign policy. But there were more pragmatic aspects to this new activist tendency. For there is a sense in which the political motivation that colored assertive Indonesian foreign policy in the past is now being replaced—as elsewhere in the world—by economic factors. Increasingly, Indonesia regards itself as a nascent economic power in the region. Economic reform and liberalization, which were forced on the New Order government by the oil crisis of the early 1980s, have begun to unlock the country's potential as a market, rather than simply a producer of goods for other markets. Foreign investors in the region single out Indonesia as a country of lasting economic potential partly for this reason. All this economic potential is teaching foreign policymakers the importance of the global economic system and the complex web of regional and subregional relations of which it is composed.

Added to this, the new foot soldiers of wider Indonesian interests are very likely to be her entrepreneurs and large corporations. Economic growth has had a cathartic effect on the self-esteem and financial power of the domestic private sector and given large business groups an appetite for overseas expansion. Indonesian corporate expansion in the Philippines, Singapore, and Malaysia has been evident for some years. Traditionally close ties with Hanoi have also facilitated pioneering ASEAN investment in Vietnam. (The first joint-venture commercial bank opened in Vietnam after the Hanoi government decided to liberalize the economy was Indovina Bank in 1990, which involved Bank Summa, an Indonesian private bank.) More remarkable have been limited but successful forays into U.S., European, and Australian corporate territory.

It is too early to say just how much influence Indonesia's corporate sector can bring to bear on foreign policy, but it is likely to breed pragmatism and accommodation in areas involving trade. This can be seen in two areas in which its impact has been noticeable. Trade ties between Beijing and Jakarta established in 1985 certainly helped pave the way for the normalization of relations in August 1990. President Suharto's close ties with certain Indonesian-Chinese businessmen are believed to have helped persuade him to bury the hatchet with Beijing. Certainly the fact that prominent business tycoons like Liem Sioe Long have long maintained channels of communication through business with the Chinese government must have kept the president informed of the mood in Beijing.

On a smaller scale, the close cooperation of Jakarta's politically well-connected business groups with the government has proved crucial to the acceptance of Singapore's growth triangle concept, linking the economies of Johor in Malaysia, Riau province in Indonesia, and Singapore. Businessmen also played a key role in the development of the Northern Growth Triangle, which links North Sumatra, the west coast of Malaysia, and southern Thailand. Singapore used commercial arguments to sell the Growth Triangle idea, although its ultimate strategic objective was to cement a much closer relationship with Jakarta.[11] But for Indonesia, there was also a domestic economic advantage. Allowing businessmen and regional officials the autonomy to develop their own areas helped achieve a degree of decentralization—a goal that Indonesia's unitary state system makes it politically difficult to achieve.

Overall, these changes seem to herald a new, more pragmatic style of active diplomacy—one drawing on the ideals of the past, but tempered by contemporary economic realities. Of itself, this is unlikely to produce any radical shift in policy, but to some extent the effect is noticeable in responses to new external conditions.

Indonesia and ASEAN

If the latent activism and idealism of Indonesian foreign policy are finding new expression with the rise of national self-confidence, this raises questions about Indonesia's assumed role as the linchpin of ASEAN's survival. Indonesia's commitment to ASEAN has always suggested a willingness to allow itself to be contained by ASEAN. But there are some suspicions in the region that a more confident Indonesia may want to look beyond its immediate regional setting to articulate its concerns and further its interests.

Although Indonesia has always abided by the ASEAN consensus, this does not mean that the policies adopted by ASEAN have always suited Indonesia's interests. Lower tariffs and freer intra-ASEAN trade essentially run counter to Indonesia's protectionist instincts and interests. Accommodation of the Philippines' desire—until 1991—to maintain U.S. bases on its territory meant that neither ZOPFAN nor SEANWFZ has come close to being implemented in any meaningful way. Yet while Indonesia's economy lagged behind those of its ASEAN partners, there was no alternative but to suppress these differences.

Indonesia's economic boom coincided with President Suharto's status as senior ASEAN leader becoming less ambiguous. It was a role he was careful to modulate alongside Lee Kuan Yew when the latter was prime minister of Singapore. After stepping down in November 1990, however, Lee Kuan Yew's international image became that of a statesman in the background, leaving Malaysia's Prime Minister Dr. Mahathir Mohamad as an eager contender for the intellectual leadership of ASEAN. Suharto perceived Mahathir as pretentious in this regard, and may have encouraged Indonesian diplomats to drop their guard and assert themselves more forcefully than usual at ASEAN meetings. It was largely at Indonesia's insistence that the Malaysian proposal for an East Asian Economic Group (EAEG), first floated in late 1990, was substantially reshaped and diluted in ASEAN official meetings—and eventually buried at the ASEAN summit in January 1992.[12] Malaysia was seeking full endorsement of the modified East Asian Economic Caucus (EAEC) at the summit. But Indonesia could not bring itself to agree even to a much diluted proposal, and what emerged in the final summit declaration was only agreement to study the idea further.

The basis of Jakarta's objection was less the substance of the Malaysian proposal (Indonesia had floated a similar idea in 1984, at which time Malaysia argued that it was premature) than Mahathir's failure to consult Suharto as the senior leader in ASEAN.[13] While there was much unhappiness about the way Mahathir has tested the limits of ASEAN harmony by pushing for his East Asia Economic Grouping, the aggressive manner in which Indonesia sought to undermine the concept was also deemed excessive in the ASEAN context by some—not only Malaysian—ASEAN diplomats.[14] Indonesians argued in their defense that consultation was the key to maintaining the ASEAN framework. They claimed that Thailand's proposal for an ASEAN Free Trade Area (AFTA) was more favorably received in Jakarta (despite more substantial domestic economic arguments for not supporting it) simply because Thai officials were scrupulous about consulting Indonesia before launching the proposal.

It is but a short step, however, from claiming that consultation is the glue that holds ASEAN together to demanding that Indonesia, as the largest ASEAN state, be the arbiter of what is good for ASEAN and what is not. The 1992 Singapore summit was colored by Indonesia's insistence on a variety of issues, including the view that ASEAN should not invite the major powers to accede to the Bali treaty of amity and cooperation. Singapore, with some support from Thailand and the Philippines, took the view that the association of major powers with the treaty could act as a first step toward a consultative security framework, possibly along the lines of the Conference on Security Cooperation in Europe (CSCE). Indonesia offered the contrary view that to invite the major powers to sign a treaty essentially tailored to Southeast Asian nations was to invite the threat of intervention by the big powers. Even though to some this looked like a move by Indonesia to remain the largest treaty signatory, the argument was persuasive, and Singapore's proposal was shelved.[15]

Indonesia has supported and endorsed the ASEAN Regional Forum, established in 1993, which brings together the foreign ministers of seventeen Asia-Pacific countries to discuss regional security. Although the forum includes the major regional powers—China, the United States, and Japan—it is nevertheless ASEAN-centric and ASEAN-led, which quelled Indonesian fears of being marginalized. More cogently, Indonesia's initial reluctance to be drawn into a regional security forum has been significantly eroded by growing concern about China's strategic intentions in the region.

These recent examples of Indonesia's assertiveness within ASEAN are interesting, but do not easily translate into a bid for regional leadership, nor should they suggest any weakening of Indonesia's self-imposed containment that could threaten ASEAN's credibility. Rather, they are the consequences of Indonesia's new self-confidence and the active rather than passive role in regional affairs this implies, which has resulted in some frustration with ASEAN. Nonetheless, Indonesia will always feel it has to tread carefully where ASEAN is concerned to avoid being labeled "big brother."

Indonesia and the Emerging Asian Powers

If economic confidence is breeding a more active foreign policy and assertiveness in the region, it is fair to ask how this is likely to affect attitudes toward the growing prominence of major Asian powers such as Japan and China. Traditionally, Indonesia's attitude toward external powers and the threat of their interference in the region's affairs has been considered the most reactionary. This reflex, which has its roots in the struggle for independence and was reinforced by the support China lent the Indonesian Communist Party in the mid-1960s, has been distilled over the years into a simple but somewhat nebulous vision of "regional resilience," recently conceptualized as ZOPFAN and SEANWFZ.

Yet, in spite of the rhetoric of regional resilience, Indonesia, perhaps conscious of its Non-Aligned roots, has tended to engage all those powers with interests in the region, regardless of their ideological identity. The staunchly anticommunist tenor of the New Order never interfered with its relations with Moscow, for example, which saw a marked improvement in the latter part of the 1980s. Even the freezing of ties with Beijing did not bring about a retaliatory recognition of Taiwan—implying that the freeze was never intended to be permanent.

This pattern of engagement with the communist bloc, including North Korea and (even at the height of the conflict in Cambodia) Hanoi, could be seen as a manifestation of Indonesia's commitment to the Non-Aligned movement. More accurately, though, it was a legacy of the 1955 Bandung Conference. The fact that Indonesia never seemed to lose sight of the ideals of peaceful global coexistence expressed at the Bandung Conference was also something the communist powers seized on to maintain ties with Jakarta. Significantly, in his Vladivostok speech in July 1986, in which the main outlines of new Soviet thinking toward the region were presented, Mikhail Gorbachev cited the Bandung Conference as a milestone in the evolution of global diplomacy.

Like other Southeast Asian states, Indonesia has traditionally viewed China with a mixture of fear and mistrust. But unlike Thailand and Burma, which translated an ancient tributary relationship into a modern foreign policy of appeasement, Indonesia's relations with China have been conducted on more equal terms, perhaps because of the extent to which ancient as well as recent history governs Indonesian perceptions. Indonesian diplomats often refer to the fact that the Javanese Kingdom of Majapahit in the late thirteenth century was the only regional polity at that time to successfully resist a Mongol invasion—the commander of the invasion force was sent back to China with his ears cut off.

In more recent times, suspicion of China was driven by its links with the Indonesian Communist Party. Diplomatic ties were frozen after the alleged abortive communist coup of September 1965. China is also viewed as a potential economic competitor. Just two years after normalizing ties with Beijing in 1990, the government was considering erecting trade barriers to resist the influx of cheap Chinese imports! Against this, Indonesia is the only ASEAN country without claims to islands in the South China Sea, and is distant enough from the mainland in strategic terms not to possess a front-line mentality regarding China's claims on the area.

It is worth noting that both China and the Soviet Union before its demise have treated Indonesia as an important regional power in its own right to a far greater extent than was ever demonstrated by the West. Michael Williams notes that under President Gorbachev, Moscow's wooing of Indonesia increased markedly, citing an official Soviet foreign ministry publication that in late 1989 described Indonesia as a world power.[16] China, for its part, went to remarkable lengths to accommodate Indonesia's terms for the normalization of ties in August 1990. Given that Beijing is normally obsessively fussy about having its preeminence observed, visits to Jakarta by senior Chinese leaders before Suharto's 1991 visit to Beijing must be considered a special honor. It can only be assumed that given the strong economic ties that bind most of the ASEAN region to the West, the rapidly diminishing communist bloc saw the need to woo the region using diplomatic rather than commercial charms.

Having said that, by the mid-1990s, Indonesia was among the more vocal of the ASEAN states in questioning China's intentions as a regional power. "Will China become a conventional great power which conforms to international and regional rules of the game? Or will it become a revolutionary power which acts in whatever ways it sees fit?"[17] Indonesian military strategists were concerned about China's close military ties with Burma and its hostile posture in the South China Sea. One senior Indonesian military officer explained that the military establishment's posture toward China was at variance with the foreign ministry's.

> The foreign ministry sees China as part of Northeast Asia, whereas the military establishment has always seen China as part of Southeast Asia—because history has taught us that China's assertiveness is directed Southward toward Southeast Asia.[18]

Yet by 1994 greater concern about China had seeped into foreign ministry thinking, probably because it was becoming part of a broader ASEAN concern.

It bred a new foreign policy initiative, when Foreign Minister Ali Alatas went to Burma in March 1994 to help draw the military-dominated SLORC regime closer to the ASEAN mainstream.

The United States and Japan have become, of course, key financial guarantors of the New Order. But this has not meant that Indonesia has become a client state of these two powers. Even though for the U.S. government, Suharto and the New Order represented a model of compliance with the Cold War antipathy toward communist states, this did not mean that Indonesia was prepared to become a forward base for U.S. forces. The close relationship with Washington was always tempered by a demonstrative measure of independence—in line with Non-Aligned principles. It therefore came as something of a surprise when Indonesia became a key supporter of the Asia Pacific Economic Cooperation (APEC) process. Indonesia was initially cool to the Australian-proposed grouping because of fears that it would eclipse ASEAN—and by implication Indonesia's preeminent role as the largest state in the association. So it was with mild surprise that some ASEAN diplomats noted Indonesia's firm support for the 1993 APEC leaders' meeting hosted by President Clinton in Seattle. Perhaps this was because Washington was careful to cultivate Suharto's growing attachment to his role as a global statesman by giving Indonesia the chance to host the second leaders' meeting in 1994.

The relationship with Japan has been closer, which is perhaps not surprising given that aid flows from Japan reached annual sums in excess of U.S. $2 billion by the end of the 1980s. Of all the ASEAN countries, Indonesia is perhaps the most ambivalent in its reflection on the Japanese imperial legacy. Memories of the Japanese occupation are easily clouded by the struggle for independence it helped trigger.[19] A 1988 visit to Jakarta by the senior Japanese official responsible for the defense forces left in its wake the suspicion that Indonesia would accept rather than reject offers of defense cooperation with Japan if they were politically acceptable to other ASEAN member states.[20]

One incident that appears to defy explanation was the brief closure of the Lombok Straits by the Indonesian authorities in September 1988. The action was curious, given the strategic importance of the straits for the shipping of all the major powers and Indonesia's limited naval capacity to enforce a closure over an extended period. At the time, analysts speculated that the move amounted to a demonstration, probably aimed at Japan. As to why it was felt necessary to mount this demonstration, no one seems to have a clue. One area of speculation is that economic factors—the need to pressure Tokyo into giving more aid on more favorable terms—were involved. At the time, Japan was beginning to suggest that the levels of concessionary aid Indonesia was receiving were likely to be cut in step with the improving rate of economic growth.

On the question of India's strategic potential in the region, Indonesia appears to have fallen in with the Australian defense establishment, which contends that the size of India's navy defines it as a regional power to beware of. On visits to

Australia, Indonesian defense chiefs have expressed interest in sharing data from an over-the-horizon radar system being developed in Australia, a move that can be read in terms of a shared threat perception. But given the vague and tradition-ally remote interest devoted to the subcontinent shared by all ASEAN countries, it would be wrong to suggest that Indonesia is any more inclined to view India as a threat.

For Indonesia, the dilemma seems to be how to assert its unchanged attitude toward major power involvement in the region, given the changed parameters of its dealings with those powers. Having abandoned the provocative nationalist themes of the Sukarno era, Indonesia seemed to opt for what Michael Liefer aptly describes as preference for "the least objectionable superpower to be on tap and not on top."[21] Japan's massive aid commitments to Indonesia, not to mention its preeminent volume of foreign investment in the country, suggest a tap not easily turned off.

With the world increasingly defined in multipolar terms—China, Japan, and India are all likely to emerge as regional powers as the predominant influence of the United States and the Soviet Union in the region recedes—Indonesia, along with its ASEAN partners, has been debating the security needs of the region in this new context. Yet while it is fair to say that Singapore, the Philippines, and to a lesser extent Malaysia and Thailand all favor the evolution of some form of enhanced multilateral security framework over time, Indonesia remains staunchly opposed to any security arrangement that involves the major powers. This much emerged at the 1992 ASEAN summit.

Yet while Indonesia defends regional resilience in its purest form and is committed to the establishment of ZOPFAN and SEANWFZ, it has shown no inclination to be left out of the new cooperative defense arrangements the United States is currently pursuing in the wake of its withdrawal from bases in the Philippines. Specifically, Indonesia has agreed in principle to allow U.S. naval vessels to be serviced at ship-repair facilities in Surabaya. Also likely to materi-alize is agreement to share the new air-weapon training range in South Sumatra, a facility the United States would like to see take on some of the joint training opportunities lost with the Crow Valley training range in the Philippines. Indone-sia has also shown interest in the ASEAN Regional Forum (ARF) established in Singapore in 1993. The degree of interest probably reflects the opportunity the forum offers for military and civilian officials to confer on regional security—a model well suited to Indonesia's dual military and civilian political system.

Indonesia's interest in the ARF also reflects increasing concern, especially in military circles, about the potential for Chinese aggression in Southeast Asia. Jakarta is already well apprised of Beijing's claims over disputed islands in the South China Sea, through the annual workshops on the issue sponsored by the Foreign Ministry. Lately, the military has also harbored concern about China's burgeoning relationship with Burma, which essentially grants Beijing access to the Malacca Straits via the Andaman Sea. In fact, the Indonesian military has

taken to advising the military junta in Rangoon on matters of political development in the hope that this will speed up Rangoon's integration with ASEAN.

The flexibility of Indonesia's approach to defense cooperation in the region
suggests a grasp of the realities, which allows a measured adjustment of principles. Illustrating this was one senior Indonesian naval officer, who argued recently that ZOPFAN must be adjusted to take into account the extent to which
relations with the great powers now impinge on the wider Asia-Pacific region.
To some extent this pragmatism is driven by the wide gulf between Indonesia's
Non-Aligned and neutralist ideals and its actual capacity to defend them. Under
the New Order, Indonesia's armed forces have not been equipped with a significant force-projection capability. This was certainly fortunate for Indonesia's policy of self-containment and the security of the region, but it also reflected to a
great extent the military's obsession with internal security problems. That situation, however, is changing. Indonesia, like its ASEAN neighbors, is currently
expanding its navy and air force with the acquisition of new assets, and recently
acquired thirty-nine surface ships from the defunct East German navy.

Building Bridges

While it may be premature to judge just how Indonesia's attempts to project
itself as a constructive midsized power in the region mesh with the emergence of
China, Japan, and India as new strategic players, another symptom of this sense
of regional entitlement has been an urge to mediate in regional disputes. In the
past five years, Indonesia has played the role of mediator in the Cambodian
conflict, launched an initiative to resolve conflicts in the South China Sea, and,
less realistically, offered its good offices to help resolve disputes as far away as
the Middle East and Kashmir.

One explanation of this as a diplomatic strategy is that Indonesia has felt compelled to project a constructive image in world affairs in order to allay the suspicions
of its neighbors. Emmerson argues that one factor driving Indonesia's Cambodia
policy was "Jakarta's awareness, almost never publicly acknowledged, of the ana-
logical use to which Vietnam's seizure of Cambodia could be put."[22]

But seen in the broader ASEAN perspective, another factor was Indonesia's
comparatively warm relations with Hanoi, which have deep roots in the armed
struggle for independence both countries share. Clearly, with Thailand playing
the role of a so-called front-line state and Singapore leading ASEAN's campaign at the United Nations to recognize the resistance coalition government of
Cambodia, Jakarta appeared to all concerned the most likely candidate for the
role of "honest broker."

Reflecting on the series of negotiations involving the four Cambodian factions in which Indonesia was involved between 1988 and 1991, it was not always
apparent that Indonesia stood to gain. The factions themselves were reluctant to
be drawn near a compromise, prompting some in ASEAN to scoff at Indonesia's

wasted energies. Moreover, once France and then the permanent five members of the UN security council entered the peace process, Indonesia's role appeared to be marginalized. Foreign ministry officials in Jakarta were understandably frustrated by the apparent failure to reach a settlement entirely within the regional framework they were spearheading. France's insistence that the peace process be crowned with a signing in Paris in October 1992 left a bitter taste.

Within the region, Indonesia's understandable pride in helping to resolve ASEAN's major security headache in Cambodia was somewhat dented by Thailand's late intervention in the process under the Chatichai Choonhavan government. Singapore's role was also not perceived to be all that constructive. The mild bickering over how to conduct the negotiations left some officials in Jakarta wondering if other ASEAN countries resented the profile Indonesia was acquiring as a mediator in the dispute. More realistically, Indonesia's attempts to channel its fresh diplomatic energies in a positive, constructive manner ran up against conflicting interests in the region. Thailand was encumbered with its attachment to the Khmer Rouge as a bulwark against Vietnam, while Singapore seemed to be in no hurry to normalize relations with Vietnam, perhaps out of regard for ties with China.

In another sense, Indonesia faces a contradiction between its desire to play a constructive role in the region and the less palatable aspects of its domestic security concerns. Perhaps no better picture of the contrasting faces of Indonesian diplomacy in the 1990s can be drawn than the image of Indonesian soldiers shooting into a crowd of Timorese mourners in November 1991, set against the arrival four months later of elite airborne infantry from Jakarta in Phnom Penh, this time wearing the blue berets of United Nations peacekeeping troops. The international outcry over the military's actions in East Timor, and to a lesser extent in Aceh, posed acute problems for the foreign ministry—not to mention Suharto himself—as it struggled to juggle national pride with the desire to be perceived as a responsible global player. Allegations of further human rights abuses in East Timor have accompanied what looked in early 1995 like a worsening security situation in the disputed territory.

The government's speedy response to the international community's demand for a thorough investigation into the November 12, 1991, incident in East Timor, though still considered inadequate in some quarters, did satisfy Indonesia's major donors as to its desire to act responsibly. This is perhaps more significant than it seems. In domestic circles, some felt that the government had bent too far; it had sacrificed senior military officers and brought shame to the armed forces in public. It was an indication, however, of the country's new diplomatic priorities as a regional power, and augurs well for the future.

Notes

This chapter is a revised and updated version of an article that first appeared in *Contemporary Southeast Asia* in March 1993. In preparing the original, I was greatly helped by Dr.

Chandran Jeshurun of the Institute of Southeast Asian Affairs in Singapore. I am also indebted to officials of the Indonesian foreign ministry and defense ministry in Jakarta for their valuable input.

1. Herbert Feith, "Dynamics of Guided Democracy," in *Indonesia*, ed. Ruth McVey (New Haven, CT: Yale University Press, 1963), p. 350.

2. Michael Liefer, *Indonesia's Foreign Policy* (London: Allen and Unwin, 1983), pp. 177–78.

3. Suharto, address before the People's Consultative Assembly, December 31, 1967.

4. Cited in Gordon R. Hein, "Soeharto's Foreign Policy: Second Generation Nationalism in Indonesia" (Ph.D. thesis, University of California, Berkeley, 1986).

5. Private communication with senior Indonesian foreign ministry official, October 1991.

6. *Kompas* (Jakarta), September 15, 1989.

7. Robert O. Tilman, *Southeast Asia and the Enemy Beyond* (Boulder, CO: Westview Press, 1987), p. 40.

8. Multhia Alagappa, "The Dynamics of Regional Security in Southeast Asia: Change and Continuity," *Australian Journal of International Affairs*, vol. 45, no. 1 (May 1991), p. 8.

9. Mochtar Kusumaatmadja, speech in Jakarta, Indonesia, June 13, 1988.

10. General L.B. Moerdani, speech in Singapore, November 12, 1988, in *Jakarta Post*, November 16, 1988.

11. T. Huxley, "Singapore and Malaysia: A Precarious Balance," *Pacific Review*, vol. 4, no. 3 (1991), pp. 204–13.

12. Michael R.J. Vatikiotis, "Action at Last," *Far Eastern Economic Review*, February 6, 1992, pp. 10–11.

13. Analysis based on discussions with senior ASEAN officials attending the 1992 ASEAN summit in Singapore.

14. See "Indonesia Rocks the ASEAN Boat," *Business Times* (Kuala Lumpur), January 28, 1992; and Mohammad Ariff, "Indonesia's Role as Big Brother," *Star* (Kuala Lumpur), January 25, 1992.

15. Vatikiotis, "Action at Last," pp. 10–11.

16. Michael C. Williams, "New Soviet Policy toward Southeast Asia: Reorientations and Change," *Asian Survey*, vol. 31, no. 4 (April 1991), pp. 364–77.

17. L.B. Moerdani, speech entitled "The Changing Security Environment in the Asia-Pacific Region," delivered at Fourth Defence Services Asia Conference, Kuala Lumpur, April 21, 1994.

18. Private communication with senior member of Indonesian Defense Ministry staff, Jakarta, April 1994.

19. Nigel Holloway, ed., *Japan in Asia* (Hong Kong: Far Eastern Economic Review, 1991).

20. Michael R.J. Vatikiotis, "A Military Manoeuvre," *Far Eastern Economic Review*, July 14, 1988.

21. Liefer, *Indonesia's Foreign Policy*, p. 176.

22. Donald K. Emmerson, "Power and Pancaroba: Indonesia in a Changing World of States," *International Journal*, vol. 11, no. 6 (Summer 1991).

9

From Domino to Dominant: Thailand's Security Policies in the Twenty-First Century

Danny Unger

Compared with its partners in the Association of Southeast Asian Nations (ASEAN), Thailand since the 1960s has been particularly prone to coping with security threats by embracing extraregional powers. This propensity is readily explained by Thailand's geographical location and its proximity to plausible sources of threat. Other ASEAN states' colonial legacies also may have contributed to their enhanced concern for seeming to be following nonaligned policies. Among the ASEAN states, only Singapore comes close to Thailand in its reliance on extraregional powers to assure its security.

The perceived alacrity with which Thailand has accepted offers of protection from outside the region has been a frequent source of ASEAN concerns and complaints. Today, however, Thailand is moving to diminish its security dependence on any one extraregional power and, thereby, hoping to augment its autonomy. This policy is consistent with what we would expect given the reduced level of threat now confronting Thailand.

Thailand's security environment has changed dramatically in a very short period of time. Vietnam's invasion of Cambodia in 1978 brought a powerful and hostile military force to Thailand's border for the first time since 1941. Fortunately for Thailand, this development did not coincide with the height of the domestic communist and Muslim insurgencies that since the 1960s had preoccupied Thais responsible for the kingdom's security. Nonetheless, the presence of the Vietnamese army along, and sometimes across, Thailand's Cambodian border had a major impact on Thai security thinking and helped to reorient Thai foreign policy. In particular, it led Thailand into closer security cooperation with China, previously viewed as a major threat.

Today, Vietnamese forces have left Cambodia, a new Cambodian government holds the promise of establishing stability there for the first time in a generation, and Thailand enjoys good and improving relations with all its neighbors and near neighbors, with the possible exception of Cambodia. In this new post–Cold War environment, Thai leaders are moving to diminish their dependence on China while expanding their economic and political ties with states throughout the region. The remarkable absence of threat now confronting Thailand, however, may not last far into the next century.

Three such potential threats are worth noting briefly here. Indonesia is likely to emerge as a major regional actor with significant power-projection capabilities over the next thirty years. However, geographical, historical, and institutional factors that have made ASEAN something akin to a security community suggest that Indonesia will not be a threat to major Thai interests. Further, Indonesia and Thailand compete directly over relatively few issues. Finally, Indonesian power, even as it expands, will be checked by the far greater power of China.

More likely than a threat from Indonesia would be one from Vietnam. Like Indonesia, Vietnam is likely to develop eventually into a greater economic and military power than Thailand. Thailand and Vietnam have no history of cooperative relations, and they will compete, along with China, for influence in Cambodia and Laos. Vietnam's successful integration into ASEAN would diminish such a threat. At least as likely, Thailand and Vietnam might view each other as useful instruments, albeit inadequate on their own, in contending with an increasingly dominant China.

China is likely to challenge Thai efforts to influence developments in Thailand's mainland Southeast Asian neighbors, Burma (Myanmar) and Indochina. This will be a decidedly lopsided competition in which Thailand's principal strategy will of necessity emphasize joint economic gains or, if that fails, accommodation. Thailand's relations with China would also be complicated if China and Japan emerged as major regional adversaries. Should such an environment emerge, Thailand could be expected to resist identifying its interests with either one. In a polarized environment, however, that choice might be foreclosed.

Alignment with Japan against China in such circumstances might be expected because states generally have a higher propensity to balance than to bandwagon and because China, for four reasons, probably will emerge as the greater threat to Thailand. First, China's proximity would make it less expensive for it to threaten Thai interests in a variety of ways than for Japan to do so. Second, China's proximity results in China and Thailand competing more than do Japan and Thailand. The former pairing will take on more of the attributes of a zero-sum relationship, at least on some issues of mutual concern. Third, like the United States today, Japan increasingly will come to be viewed as a relatively complacent, status-quo-oriented power without irredentist claims.[1] In addition, Thai policymakers will see Japan both as more familiar than China (in terms of its interests and modus operandi) and as a relatively pacifist, satisfied trading state. (This is likely to hold true even as, or if, Japan gradually develops increasing independent power-projection capabilities.) Fourth, over the next several decades, China will emerge as a stronger power than Japan, both economically and militarily. In sum, consistent with balance-of-threat theory, Thailand should align with Japan rather than China because of the former's greater distance and lesser capabilities, and because of Thai perceptions that Japan's aims are less aggressive.[2] This conclusion, however, draws on abstract arguments and ignores the possibility that the proximity and potency of the Chinese threat could make such a policy prohibitively dangerous. States do sometimes bandwagon.

Should Thailand perceive a significant threat to its security interests from some source other than China, however, Thailand would have to turn to China for security assurances. For the reasons cited above, China would be far more likely to lend the necessary assistance. This would be particularly true if Thailand were threatened by Vietnam. China and Vietnam, like China and Thailand, are likely to be competitors across a number of issues. This could increase China's incentives for helping Thailand resist Vietnamese threats. In addition, Japan and Vietnam may well develop a close, cooperative relationship that would lead Japan to be particularly unwilling to side with Thailand in any conflict.

The dilemmas posed to Thai policymakers by these various scenarios underscore the continued importance to Thailand of a close and cooperative security relationship with the United States. (Thailand's decision late in 1994 not to allow the United States to preposition military supplies offshore did little to foster such a relationship in the short term.) Thais, however, have relatively little ability to influence the longevity of that link. In order to develop the themes introduced above, the following sections of this chapter provide a historical overview of modern Thai foreign policy, a more detailed discussion of contemporary Thai security thinking concerning the great powers and Thailand's neighbors, and a survey of domestic developments that could threaten the achievement of Thai national interests.

Foreign Policy Flexibility

Responding to shifts in the security context, Thai elites have moved Thai foreign policy through four phases of alliance diplomacy in the postwar period. Following World War II, Thailand faced low levels of threat, to which it responded with minimal external security dependence. Over the 1950s and 1960s, Thailand faced increasingly severe threats to its security stemming from communist neighbors in China and Indochina and their support for communist insurgencies in Thailand itself. In response, Thai security policies began to shift toward a policy of concentrated security dependence. Without effective local alliance opportunities,[3] over the early 1960s Thailand increasingly committed itself to an alliance with the United States.

When the United States failed to reach its goals in Indochina and withdrew its forces from mainland Southeast Asia in the early 1970s, Thailand was left in an exposed and vulnerable position. The usefulness, as well as the credibility, of U.S. security commitments receded in the early 1970s, even as threat levels remained high. During this period, Thais no longer viewed the United States as a reliable security guarantor, and continued intimate ties threatened to become an obstacle to the forging of closer links with former adversaries. To protect Thai interests, Thai diplomats moved quickly to reduce their ties to the United States and to adjust their relations with communist neighbors. Together with Indonesia, Malaysia, the Philippines, and Singapore, Thailand moved to strengthen ASEAN (created in 1967) and called for the establishment of a nuclear-free zone in the region in 1976. These steps were aimed at securing Thai interests against communist states and avoiding involvement in conflicts among the great powers. During this brief period, Thailand was forced to rely on a variety of ad hoc diplomatic measures as a substitute for an effective balance-of-threat policy. These steps, however, failed to provide the Thais with an adequate degree of security during a period of intense internal and external turmoil.

It was the onset of the third Indochinese war that afforded Thailand another opportunity to rely on a foreign power, this time China, to secure its interests. With Vietnamese forces in Cambodia, Thai perceptions of threat grew, and, in response, Thailand turned to China. By the late 1970s, as levels of threat remained high and, indeed, increased, Thailand again turned to a policy of concentrated security dependence. Thailand is now entering a fifth stage marked by relatively diffuse external security dependence in the face of significantly reduced threats. These stages are sketched out below.

A Brief Review of Thailand's Foreign Policies

In Siam's initial encounters with the West, it was able to preserve its nominal independence. Although the imperialist powers compelled Siam to accept unequal treaties that limited its fiscal and juridical sovereignty, it remained under the direct leadership of its traditional elite. Siamese leaders, therefore, did not lose their legitimacy in the face of a nationalist anti-imperialist movement, and no significant group of Thai leaders saw the need for an effective mobilization of broad segments of the population for such a struggle. One result of this leadership continuity has been that during this century, Thailand's task has been not to create but to protect the nation.[4]

Siamese leaders' successful maintenance of their independence in the nineteenth century is particularly impressive when we consider Siam's geographical position, relatively unprotected by natural barriers to foreign forces from the east or west.[5] Siamese kings preserved Siam's nominal sovereignty in considerable part by playing off Britain against France in an arrangement that suited the interests of those powers. Nonetheless, Siam was forced to pay costs to retain its independence. Most important, Siamese leaders ceded to France and Great Britain some 40 percent of Siamese territory.[6]

Reflecting the influence of the largely British- and French-educated elite, Siam declared war on Germany in 1917 and dispatched over 1,000 troops to Europe. As a result, Siam was a charter member of the League of Nations and was able to hasten the pace of negotiations aimed at overturning the unequal treaties, a process that was not completed until 1939. Local ties to Britain and France remained strong, but they were counteracted in the 1930s by elites educated in Germany and the United States and by the rising power of Japan. Thailand was the only state to abstain from the vote in the League of Nations censuring Japan's invasion of Manchuria. Japan mediated a Franco-Thai clash in 1940 that resulted in Thailand's regaining some of the territory it had ceded earlier in the century. After being forced by Japan to allow Japanese troops passage through Thai territory, Thailand signed a formal alliance agreement with Japan at the end of 1941.

Immediately after the war, Thailand moved to establish amicable ties with all of the major powers, including China and the Soviet Union. Not facing any grave external threats, Thai elites saw no need for close external alliances. To reach agreements with France and Great Britain, Thailand was forced again to give up territories gained by those countries from Thailand but briefly lost during the war. In late 1946, Thailand became a member of the United Nations.

A strong Thai anticommunist policy emerged only after the overthrow of Prime Minister Pridi Phanomyong in 1947. As late as 1949, Thailand resisted a Philippine initiative to establish an Asian anticommunist front.[7] By the following year, however, the Thai leadership was increasingly concerned about a Chinese threat to its survival, U.S. forces in Korea were demonstrating a U.S. commitment to the region, and the United States, through the Joint U.S. Military Advisory Group, was providing substantial military aid to Thailand. Thailand aligned itself with the United States, sending 4,000 troops to Korea in 1950 and recognizing the Bao Dai regime in South Vietnam. Thailand was the first Asian country to support the United Nations Security Council resolution calling for the use of force on the Korean peninsula.[8]

In the early 1950s, Thai military leaders explicitly linked internal and external anticommunist policies. The Thais were concerned by the establishment of the United National Front of the Peoples of Vietnam, Laos, and Cambodia in 1951 and, particularly, by Vietminh incursions into Laos in 1953 and 1954.[9] Meanwhile, in 1953, China established an autonomous state for the Thai minority in Yunnan Province that Thais feared would serve as a base for Thai political exiles.

By 1954, despite U.S. unwillingness to commit itself unambiguously to the defense of Thailand against attack, Thailand was prepared to be a signatory of the Manila Pact[10] establishing the Southeast Asian Treaty Organization (SEATO). Increased U.S. economic assistance helped to sweeten the package. When, toward the end of the decade, Field Marshal Sarit Thanarat emerged dominant from a protracted struggle for power among different Thai military factions, he moved to secure Thai-U.S. relations and cut off trade with China.

Thai-U.S. military cooperation began in 1950 with the launching of an Agreement Respecting Military Assistance that provided training for Thai military officers and influenced the design of the Chulachomklao Military Academy, the breeding ground for Thailand's military elite and the factions within it. Over the next two decades, U.S. influence in Thailand steadily expanded along with U.S. economic and military assistance. Partly as a result of U.S. aid and military expenditures in the region, Thai economic growth began to speed up in the late 1950s. And U.S. military assistance also helped the Thai military to entrench its control over Thai politics. Thai commitment to anticommunism and support for U.S. policies in Southeast Asia developed gradually, but by the mid-1960s, the United States had gained a critical resource facilitating the major U.S. military commitment in support of an independent South Vietnam.[11]

The Vietnam War

The Thai leadership grew increasingly concerned about North Vietnamese power in the early 1960s. This concern manifested itself in Thai unhappiness with developments in Laos and the perceived inadequacy of the U.S. commitment to Thai security. The Thais did not favor the outcome of the 1962 Geneva Conference on Laos supporting a neutral government there. And they continued to be concerned about the Manila Pact's requirement of a unanimous vote in favor of acting to defend any of the members subject to external aggression before the treaty's provisions would come into force (a SEATO protocol brought Cambodia, Laos, and South Vietnam into association with SEATO). That same year, China began to broadcast the Voice of the People of Thailand. Faced with mounting security threats, Thai leaders became more willing to increase their security dependence on the United States.

Initially, Thailand complained about the communist threat in Laos while making overtures toward the Soviet Union on trade and cultural activities. As the crisis in Laos worsened, however, Thailand sent forces to the Thai border. This move helped to gain the attention of the United States (which, along with Australia, Britain, and New Zealand, sent troops to Thailand), and in 1962 the Rusk-Thanat accord committed the United States to act to protect Thai security without awaiting SEATO agreement. The accord also provided for the stationing of U.S. troops in Thailand. Previously, the Thai government had been pushing the fortunes of the Lao right. With this commitment to Thailand's security, the United States won Thai support for a neutralist Lao government.

In the 1963 Thai-U.S. Special Logistics Agreement, Thailand and the United States undertook to improve Thailand's transportation system, to develop a deepwater port at Satahip as a supply base for air bases in the northeast, and to establish communications and intelligence facilities in eastern Thailand. In a 1964 agreement, Thailand allowed the United States to use its territory as a base from which to bomb Vietnam. In 1965, the Diem government fell, communist forces advanced in South Vietnam, and the Thai Communist Party (officially established only in 1968) launched attacks on Thai government forces. In response, the Thai leadership sought additional support from the United States, including U.S. assistance for counterinsurgency programs. Thailand sent troops both to Laos and to Vietnam ("irregular" forces in the former case). Under a secret 1965 contingency plan, the United States committed itself to defend Thailand in the event of attack from Laos or Vietnam.

U.S. assistance to Thailand expanded rapidly. By 1969, Thailand was receiving $45 million in economic aid and $75 million in military aid, and U.S. military spending in Thailand was helping to sustain a rapid economic expansion and buildup of security infrastructure.[12] At the same time, the United States was expanding its military presence in Thailand, with 50,000 troops deployed at seven major air bases (five in the northeast, one in Bangkok, and one in the southeast).[13]

Having gained wholehearted Thai backing for U.S. policies in Vietnam, in 1968, President Lyndon Johnson halted U.S. bombing of North Vietnam. President Richard Nixon's enunciation of the Guam Doctrine in 1969 foreshadowed U.S. troop withdrawals from Southeast Asia and sparked a Thai reevaluation of its heavy security dependence on the United States. As a result, Thai foreign minister Thanat Khoman announced that Thailand would try to establish talks with China, thereby increasing its room for diplomatic maneuvering.[14] With the U.S. security guarantee becoming less reliable at a time when external threats remained forbidding, Thailand moved to use diplomacy to reduce the hostility of regional communist states. Thanat also signaled some interest in Soviet president Leonid Brezhnev's June 1969 proposal for an East Asian collective security arrangement.

With the United States rapidly withdrawing from Southeast Asia, Bangkok took the initiative in seeking gradual U.S. troop withdrawals from Thailand. These were largely completed by 1976. Bangkok also began to adjust its policies toward Vietnam, decreasing its vehement opposition to Vietnamese activities in Laos and refraining from actively supporting the Lon Nol government that overthrew Sihanouk in Cambodia. Finally, Thailand increased its emphasis on regional cooperation, largely through ASEAN, and began to explore talks with China and Vietnam.

A major reorientation in Thai security policies, however, did not come until widespread demonstrations in October 1973 ended, briefly, the Thai military's control of political power. The mid-1970s were a period of extreme uneasiness in Thailand. At the same time that the relationship with the United States was undergoing major changes, Thailand was experiencing major political and social upheavals. The local communist insurgency continued to expand. Indochina, meanwhile, was coming under communist control. Under these circumstances, Thai leaders adopted a series of ad hoc measures aimed at diminishing the threats emerging from Cambodia and Vietnam.

Faced with a succession of crises, Thailand increased its emphasis on its ties with ASEAN and moved toward establishing formal diplomatic links with China. Even before normalization of those ties in 1975, the Chinese played a role in sponsoring negotiations between Kampuchea and Thailand. These links and the antipathy evident between Kampuchea and Vietnam helped to lessen Thai fears about Vietnamese domination of all of Indochina. In August 1976, Thailand and Vietnam established diplomatic relations.

Thailand's democratic interlude ended in 1976 with a military coup, and the new government under Thanin Kraivixien adopted a hard-line anticommunist policy. Thanin, however, was overthrown the following year, and the Kriangsak Chomanan government renewed efforts aimed at reaching an accommodation with the communist regimes in Indochina. The Kriangsak government normalized relations with Kampuchea early in 1978 and opened the shared border for trade. Kriangsak's first overseas travel as prime minister was to the capitals of the other ASEAN countries. Soon thereafter, he traveled to China. In 1978, Thailand pursued discussions with the Soviet Union and proposed that ASEAN invite the Indochinese states to join in the creation of a zone of peace, freedom, and neutrality in the region (the Kuala Lumpur Declaration in 1971 had committed ASEAN to the creation of such a zone). At the same time, the Thai government was tacitly supporting both Vietnamese incursions against the Khmer Rouge and Chinese support for the Cambodian regime.[15] By this time, events were in motion that would wreck Thailand's efforts to foster regional political accommodation. China was actively seeking local friends to use against Vietnam.

The strategic context in which Thailand was forced to operate changed radically with the accentuation of conflicts among Asian communist countries in the late 1970s, culminating in the Vietnamese entry into COMECON in June 1978, the signing of the Treaty of Friendship and Cooperation with the Soviet Union in November 1978, the invasion of Kampuchea the following month, and the Chinese strike into Vietnam early the following year. In the meantime, China was able to establish diplomatic relations with the United States and strengthen its ties with Japan. For Thailand, these events called for a major readjustment in its policies. For the first time in nearly forty years, Thailand faced a hostile and powerful enemy across its border. Furthermore, the conflict was looking increasingly likely to draw in external powers. With the Vietnamese cementing their dependence on Moscow and heightening Thai feelings of insecurity, Thailand moved to bolster its ties to Beijing. At the same time, ASEAN assumed increased importance as the diplomatic vehicle for a strategy of isolating Vietnam and the Heng Samrin government in the United Nations.

The initial Thai response to the conflict in Kampuchea was to welcome any increases in U.S. assistance it could attract, to depend more on Chinese statements of support, and to assume publicly "a strict policy of neutrality between the contending forces and noninvolvement in the conflicts."[16] The ASEAN countries sought to avoid isolating Vietnam and put forward proposals that might meet Vietnamese security concerns and avoid the tight linkage that was developing between the conflict in Cambodia and the Sino-Vietnamese struggle. At the same time, Thailand acquiesced to the presence in Thailand of scores of thousands of Khmer Rouge retreating before advancing Vietnamese forces. Bolstered by increases in U.S. military support and, particularly, Chinese promises to respond to any attacks on Thailand, most Thais felt that the threat of Vietnamese attack was receding. Diplomatically, the ASEAN-orchestrated strategy, strongly supported by China and the United States, was to continue support for the Khmer resistance forces arrayed against the Heng Samrin government. In annual rituals in the United Nations, this international coalition was able to preserve the anti-Vietnamese coalition's claim to Cambodia's United Nations seat.

In October 1979, Thailand began to give sanctuary to Cambodian refugees. This policy was funded by international aid organizations. These camps served as bases for the anti-Vietnamese resistance and, at various times, invited limited Vietnamese attacks across the Cambodian border into nearby areas in Thailand.

Despite the presence of powerful Vietnamese forces on its border, Thailand's security situation looked less precarious than it had in the mid-1970s. Externally, the ASEAN states had consolidated their ties and their support for Thailand. Thailand and the United States had begun to redefine their security links, and, most critically, China was becoming Thailand's principal security guarantor. Internally, Chinese and Vietnamese efforts to influence Thai policies led to an end to external support for communist insurgencies in Thailand. By 1979, China had ceased its Voice of the People of Thailand broadcasts and was calling on Thai communists to concentrate their attacks on the Vietnamese. These factors, combined with internal weaknesses and flexible Thai government policies,[17] led the Thai communist movements to fall apart rapidly.

Without China's backing, Thailand would have had to accommodate Vietnamese control of Cambodia. And without Thailand's commitment to resist that control, ASEAN would have been prepared to accept expanded Vietnamese power, particularly if it meant a diminution in Chinese influence. Indeed, the firmness of ASEAN backing for Thailand's intransigent stand on Vietnam depended in part, most clearly in the cases of Indonesia and Malaysia, on a desire to avoid seeing Thailand draw still closer to China.

In 1980, in an effort to keep Sino-Soviet rivalry out of the region, Indonesia and Malaysia attempted briefly to revive a neutral stance for ASEAN on the Cambodian conflict. The Kuantan declaration issued by Premier Hussein Onn and President Suharto called for a settlement that recognized legitimate Vietnamese security concerns. Indonesian and Malaysian leaders hoped that a settlement would prevent China from entrenching its power in the region.

When the Vietnamese launched a major dry season offensive in late 1984 and overwhelmed most of the resistance bases along the Thai border, the ASEAN countries abandoned their earlier flirtation with more conciliatory policies and stepped up calls for military aid to the resistance forces. The Thais were concerned that the western extension of Vietnamese control would lead to more Khmer reliance on Thai supply routes to move arms to the resistance.[18] Thailand faced not only the loss of a buffer zone along its Cambodian border but increased danger of Vietnamese incursions into Thai territory. In fact, however, the success of the Vietnamese offensives had the effect of forcing the resistance to rely more completely on guerrilla tactics and helped to keep the conflict from concentrating on the Thai border.

Nonetheless, in subsequent years the Vietnamese moved beyond brief intrusions into Thai territory and began to take positions inside Thailand. For example, in early 1987, the Vietnamese occupied a hilltop well within the Thai border with Cambodia and Laos. This was in an area used by the Khmer Rouge to move arms supplies into Cambodia. Press reports indicated that Thai military efforts to expel the Vietnamese were ineffective and resulted in considerable casualties.[19]

Toward a Cambodian Settlement

The stalemate on the ground in Cambodia continued. However, just as, in the late 1970s, developments outside Southeast Asia had shattered the assumptions underlying Thai foreign policies aiming at regional political accommodation, so, in the late 1980s, fundamental changes in Moscow began to encourage the resuscitation of Thailand's more accommodating policies. President Mikhail Gorbachev's Vladivostok speech in July 1986 foreshadowed coming political shifts in the region. That same year, Thai foreign minister Siddhi Savetsila called for enhanced flexibility in Thai foreign policy and a stronger emphasis on Thai foreign economic interests.[20] In May 1988, Prime Minister Prem Tinsulanonda traveled to Moscow. Hanoi subsequently announced that, by the end of that year, it would withdraw 50,000 (half) of the troops it still had in Cambodia. In June of that year, Vietnamese foreign minister Nguyen Co Thach traveled to Bangkok, the first direct high-level contacts between the two countries on the Cambodian issue in two years.

The momentum toward peace launched by Gorbachev picked up further impetus with the election in July 1988 of Chatichai Choonhavan as Thai prime minister. Chatichai called for Thai flexibility in dealing with Indochina and spoke of the need to transform the area "from a battleground into a trading market." Meanwhile, Siddhi continued to meet with Thach during two further visits to Bangkok in the summer of that year. In January 1989, having convinced himself that the Vietnamese withdrawal from Cambodia was genuine, Siddhi traveled to Hanoi. Among his entourage were business executives from his Social Action Party.[21]

Chatichai's emphasis on Indochina's value to Thailand as a market represented a coalescence of several factors. First, of course, was the shift in underlying conditions—Soviet military withdrawal from the region and closer Soviet-Chinese ties (Vice Premier Arkhipov visited Beijing in December

1984)—suggesting the potential for a settlement of the Cambodian conflict. During 1987, high-level Thai officials visited Moscow and Soviet foreign minister Shevardnadze came to Bangkok. In January 1989, Vietnamese deputy foreign minister Dinh Nho Liem made a trip to Beijing. Meanwhile, China was improving its relations with Laos.

A second factor pushing Thai foreign policy in new directions was the improvement in relations between Laos and Thailand following a prolonged border battle between the two that began in late 1987. Closer ties to Laos increased Thai confidence that Vietnam would not be able to maintain firm control over Cambodia and Laos and that Thailand could work to increase its influence in these two countries serving as buffers between Thailand and Vietnam. Preventing Vietnamese domination over the trans-Mekong area has been a traditional Thai concern.

A third factor contributing to the shift in Thai policies under Chatichai grew out of his power base—a coalition of business interests eager to exploit Indochinese markets and resources at a time when the supply of Thailand's own natural resources was diminishing.[22] These desires were only intensified by the realization that firms from Hong Kong, Singapore, and Taiwan, among others, were getting the jump on Thai businesses in establishing themselves in Indochina.

Finally, and perhaps most important, a major boost in Thai economic growth, including significant increases in nontraditional manufactured exports, raised Thai confidence and expectations that Thailand could play a significant regional economic role.[23] Hence the popularity of the theme of Thailand emerging as a center for a regional *suwannaphum,* or Golden Land. With Thailand entertaining such aspirations, some observers feared for the durability of Thailand's commitment to the goals of the Khmer resistance forces. This issue also provoked divisions within the Thai leadership, with the foreign ministry and some military leaders concerned about the independent initiatives being launched by the prime minister and his advisers. The former group worried that Thailand was moving prematurely to reduce the pressure on Vietnam to push the Hun Sen government toward a negotiated settlement. In addition, sudden, bold initiatives by Thailand threatened the carefully nurtured consensus among ASEAN countries in their approaches to the Indochina conflict.

In January 1990, soon after the full withdrawal of Vietnamese troops from Cambodia, the five permanent members of the United Nations Security Council approved an Australian peace proposal for Cambodia. The plan called for a ceasefire, an end to outside military aid, and a comprehensive political settlement. The Hun Sen government would turn over the administration of Cambodia to a UN transitional authority, while the resistance would relinquish its hold on Cambodia's UN seat. The new plan envisioned the United Nations for the first time exercising executive authority in a member state.[24]

The participants to the Cambodian conflict finally signed the peace accords in Paris in October 1991, promising the end of a conflict that began in late

1978. Implementation of the accords was slow and difficult. The Khmer Rouge declared a boycott of the second phase of the disarmament process (cantonment, demobilization, disarmament), and in June 1992 announced that it would boycott an international conference aimed at drumming up aid for Cambodia. Nonetheless, despite repeated Khmer Rouge threats of reprisals, voter turnout for the elections held in May 1993 was surprisingly high. The United National Front for an Independent, Neutral, Peaceful and Cooperative Cambodia (Funcinpec) scored an impressive electoral victory, with the Cambodian People's Party (the State of Cambodia party) pulling enough votes to deny Funcinpec a majority. Immediately following the election, squabbling erupted between these two groups. Eventually, however, they agreed to establish a new government, and Sihanouk resumed his former position as Cambodia's monarch. The Khmer Rouge, however, remained outside the reconciliation process, and the new government in Phnom Penh was slow to establish political stability or effective administration.

Having traced the outline of the principal security challenges and threats facing Thailand over the past thirty years, I will now turn to a discussion of Thailand's contemporary relations with the major East Asian powers.

Thailand and the Extraregional Powers

Although India is rapidly building up its naval capabilities and naval presence in the Indian Ocean, it is too early to predict what impact this will have on the region generally or on Thailand specifically. In the longer run, much will depend on the course of economic reform in India and developments in politics on the subcontinent. Similarly, it is difficult to predict the future nature of Russia's regional role. Thai interest in Russia is modest given its rapidly declining influence over and support of Vietnam, its reduced military presence in the region, and its limited economic potential. One possible area for future cooperation is arms sales. Thai interest in Russia as a source of weapons systems picked up following the Malaysian purchase of MiG-29s. In 1993, the Thai army put a Russian helicopter on the short list of candidates. Ultimately, however, the army opted for one provided by Bell, its traditional U.S. supplier. In any case, for the foreseeable future, China, Japan, and the United States will be the major East Asian powers.

China

Many Thais are worried about what they perceive as excessive dependence on China. Within the military, younger officers voiced such concerns in the early 1980s. When these Young Turks failed in their coup attempt in 1981, the development of closer ties to China picked up speed.[25] The Chinese, for their part, are likely to continue to be interested in maintaining close ties with Thailand, in part as a means of pressuring Vietnam.[26] When Li Peng became Chinese premier, his first overseas trip was to Thailand in November 1988.[27] Today, Thailand and the United States invite Chinese officials to observe their joint military exercises.

With the loss of U.S. military credits in the 1980s, the Thai military developed an appetite for relatively inexpensive Chinese armaments. These purchases began in 1985. The first major items, purchased in 1987, included tanks and armored personnel carriers. The navy ordered Chinese frigates. The Thais also expressed interest in Chinese aircraft. In addition to being relatively inexpensive, Chinese arms purchases reduced Thailand's heavy dependence (close to 80 percent in the early 1980s) on U.S. weapons systems. Press accounts suggested that an additional motivation in these purchases was the large commissions made available to top military leaders by the arms brokers who arranged these deals.[28] Some observers fretted in the late 1980s that increasing Thai military purchases from China were being fueled by "common vested interests, bureaucratic and otherwise"[29] that might accelerate the trend toward rising Thai dependence on China.

Both Indonesian and Vietnamese officials criticized these purchases, particularly the decision in 1988 to establish a stockpile of Chinese armaments.[30] The Thai military saw a need for such a stockpile given the growing role Chinese weapons were assuming in the Thai arsenal. Indeed, Thai armed forces overcame shortages during the 1988 border conflict with Laos only by means of military airlifts.

More recently, the Thai military's interest in Chinese arms has declined as a result of concerns about their reliability. The Thai military has had problems with tanks breaking down and a lack of spare parts. This shift became evident about the time that General Chaovalit stepped down as supreme commander of the armed forces. The outcome of the Gulf War and the striking advantage enjoyed by more sophisticated weapons systems presumably reinforced this shift away from China as a supplier of military hardware.

In any case, rapid Chinese economic growth and China's expanding military capabilities suggest to Thai leaders that China will emerge as the region's dominant power. Today, only the United States is in a position to check rising Chinese influence. Ultimately, and particularly should the United States fail to choose that role for itself, Japan could come to play such a role. As suggested above, such a development would not be welcomed in Bangkok, although it might be seen as preferable to the absence of any significant checks whatsoever.

In the shorter term, Thai leaders are encouraging the rapid expansion of economic links with China. These involve significant growth in trade and investment flows. Some 100 Thai business officials accompanied Prime Minister Chuan Leekpai on his September 1993 trip to China. Among major new projects under way are a large investment in tourist facilities in Shenzhen and a joint oil marketing arrangement in Thailand. In other ASEAN countries, these enormous investments in China by ethnic Chinese Indonesians or Malaysians sometimes occasion raised eyebrows or worse. This has not been a sensitive issue in Thailand, however, given the near disappearance of ethnicity as a source of tension in Thai politics.

Meanwhile, Chinese leaders in Yunnan are working actively with Thailand, as well as Burma and Laos, to develop a "Golden Quadrangle" that would enable exporters in Yunnan to move goods down the Mekong River and then overland to Thai ports on the Gulf of Thailand. In July 1993, representatives of the four countries discussed this notion in Beijing. A subsequent meeting was convened in August in Chiang Rai, followed by a meeting with the Asian Development Bank in Manila.[31] These developments are consistent with Thai concerns to establish mutually beneficial economic links with China so that it will be inclined to use its growing power in ways congruent with Thai interests.

Japan

Since the late 1970s, Japan has become increasingly important to Thailand. Japan's official development assistance expanded rapidly during the 1980s, and Thailand was one of the principal recipients of that aid. Much of this was used to finance the construction of critically needed infrastructure.

Japan, along with other East Asian countries, is Thailand's principal source of foreign investment. This investment played a central role in pushing the Thai economy out of a period of slower growth in the mid-1980s and launching its export-led expansion. Japanese advisers in Thailand work with Thai officials to try to facilitate the movement of Japanese direct investment into Thailand. Since the early 1980s, officials of the two countries have been meeting on a regular basis to try to overcome a variety of economic difficulties ranging from trade imbalances to regulatory obstacles to further economic interaction. Japanese officials play advisory roles in most key economic agencies, and Japanese delegations, including state officials and representatives of Keidanren (Federation of Economic Organizations), meet with Thai officials to discuss Thai government policies and development plans.

Japan also has become increasingly important to Thailand as a source of international political support. Japan worked with the ASEAN countries and the United States in the 1980s to help ensure that the anti-Vietnamese Khmer resistance was able to maintain its UN seat. Japan also has tried to represent a variety of East Asian interests in forums such as the Group of Seven. Japan is a principal player in all regional economic groupings, public and private (with the exception, to date, of the East Asian Economic Causus), and hence its policies on issues of regionalism go a long way in determining the framework within which other countries in the region design their policies. Thai leaders view positively Japan's growing interest in fostering the development of such groupings.

In the past, Southeast Asian leaders tended to worry that any Japanese interest in a stronger political or, in particular, security role in Southeast Asia would lead to a revival of Japanese militarism. While some local leaders continue to entertain such anxieties, clearly attitudes are changing. Indicative of the extent of change in Southeast Asian perceptions of Japan is the fact that many officials in the ASEAN countries now explicitly welcome enlarged Japanese political and security roles in the region. Thailand has led the way in calling on Japan to play a greater security role. Foreign Minister Siddhi called on Japan to play a larger security role in the region, and Prime Minister Chatichai suggested that Japanese and Thai naval forces conduct joint maneuvers.[32] Japanese navy chief of staff Admiral Fumio Okabe told reporters in 1993 that the Japanese navy was considering "friendship exercises" in Southeast Asia following expressions of interest in joint drills from Indonesia, Singapore, and Thailand.[33]

Japan also has been using its economic assistance to foster closer links between Thailand and Indochinese states. The Japanese, for example, have funneled assistance to Laos through Thailand. With Japan preparing to expand its economic assistance to Vietnam, Prime Minister Miyazawa declared during a January 1993 visit to Thailand that Japan would host a conference on the "comprehensive development of Indochina" and called on Southeast Asian states to "strengthen their organic cohesion and pursue the development of the region as a whole."[34] In this, Miyazawa clearly was harking back to former prime minister Fukuda's efforts to foster cooperation between the region's capitalist and communist states in the 1970s. In addition, however, he was reflecting a strengthening Japanese propensity to promote multilateral frameworks in seeking to address problems. Thai leaders also view favorably the development of such a habit.

Indeed, it is striking to observe the degree to which Japanese and Thai interests have moved in tandem over the last century. Diplomats in the two countries are fond of noting similarities rooted in religion, monarchical institutions, absence of colonial experience, and (less frequently noted) cooperation during war. Japan proved modestly useful to Thailand in its border negotiations with France earlier in this century. Japan launched its first significant diplomatic initiatives in the postwar period, with Prime Minister Takeo Fukuda proposing in 1976 that it serve as a bridge between the ASEAN and Indochinese states. Under this scheme, high levels of Japanese economic assistance would facilitate regional reconciliation in Southeast Asia. Japan also supported Chatichai's initiatives, which served to shift the course of Thai (and ASEAN) policy toward Cambodia and Vietnam.

During the 1970s, and to a lesser degree today, Thais have been concerned about the extent of their economic dependence on, and size of their trade deficits with, Japan. These anxieties, however, will tend to diminish for both economic and security reasons. Economically, Thailand's dependence on Japan is now at or close to its highest level. Increasingly, Thai investment and trade relations with greater China and South Korea will expand. High levels of investment and trade with the United States and Western Europe also will continue. At the same time, Thai concerns about economic dependence on Japan will recede as Thais increasingly come to view Japan as a valuable counterweight to closer and perhaps militarily more threatening neighbors, including China.

The United States

While far less important to Thailand than in the past, the United States remains one of Thailand's key partners for both economic and security reasons. The United States' inadvertent role in triggering Thailand's political strife in 1992 by expressing disapproval of the prime minister designate suggested the extent of continuing U.S. influence. In 1994, U.S. denial of visas to particular Thai parliamentarians again served to set off a political fracas. The United States remains Thailand's principal supplier of weapons systems. The two countries continue to carry out annual joint military exercises and pursue a variety of joint training programs. The United States also maintains a weapons stockpile in Thailand. Thailand was the first country (in 1985) without U.S. military bases to agree to the maintenance of such a stockpile.[35] During the Gulf War, Thailand afforded the United States access to its air base at U-Tapao, and the Seventh Fleet continues to make regular visits to Thailand.[36] The Thais, like others in the region, are concerned about the durability of the post–Cold War U.S. military presence in Southeast Asia, particularly following the Filipino expulsion of the United States from military bases in 1992. In 1993, the Thai foreign ministry proposed the establishment of a bilateral forum with the United States for regular discussion of security issues.

Nonetheless, relations between the two countries are characterized less by security cooperation than in the past. Furthermore, economic tensions between the two countries have increased as the United States has become more aggressive and unilateral in pursuing its economic interests abroad and as Thailand has become a source of manufactured exports that formerly reached the U.S. market from Hong Kong, Japan, Singapore, or Taiwan. During Chatichai's tenure as prime minister, U.S. demands for stronger protection of intellectual property rights by the Thai government and disagreements concerning the appropriate policy tack to take in Cambodia increased friction in the relationship. Previously, during the Prem years, Thailand suffered the effects (depressed global prices) of U.S. government subsidies for U.S. rice exporters. Thailand has become a target of unilateral U.S. trade initiatives under the so-called Special 301 legislation that requires the executive branch to identify, threaten, and take retaliatory measures against "unfair" traders. Thai leaders, along with other ASEAN members, have been less than forceful in their support for President Clinton's proposal that the Asia Pacific Economic Cooperation group be used as a forum for trade negotiations.[37]

Nevertheless, the United States remained an important Thai backer throughout the Cambodian crisis. Successive U.S. administrations have reaffirmed the U.S. commitment to Thailand's security. And Thailand, like other countries in the region, would like to see a healthy U.S. economy that could drive global economic demand, reduce protectionist pressures in the United States, and diminish the extent of Japan's regional economic dominance. At least as important, for a variety of reasons Thai leaders would like to see the United States sustain its security commitments in Southeast and Northeast Asia. Finally, the number of elite Thais educated in the United States and the size of the Thai community in the United States may work to sustain relatively cooperative relations between Thailand and the United States.

Relations with Neighbors

In this section I discuss recent development in Thailand's relations with other Southeast Asian countries—first its communist and socialist neighbors, and then the other ASEAN states.

Mainland Southeast Asian Neighbors

Thailand enjoys, for now, a position of economic preponderance on mainland Southeast Asia. In addition, the mainland Southeast Asian states are increasingly likely to share a wariness of China's potential to limit their autonomy. At the same time, however, Thailand has traditional and ongoing conflicts with its neighbors that are likely to persist even as economic cooperation expands.

Since Burma's independence in 1948, Burmese and Thais have had a variety of conflicts. Opium-growing tribes with links to the Burmese Communist Party have been active in northern Thailand. Burmese have been concerned that Thai road building along their border would facilitate the mobility of Karen forces in Burma and that Thailand was serving as a supply route for arms going to the Karen National Union. The Thais looked upon the union with some favor, given their concern that, should it collapse, the Burmese communists were as likely as the government in Rangoon (Yangon) to replace it. The long, mountainous border between Burma and Thailand and the sprawl of groups such as the Shan across it complicate relations between the two countries.

Following elections in Burma in 1990, the subsequent declaration of martial law, and the failure of the army to accept the election's outcome, Thailand helped to diminish the extent of Burma's international pariah status. This policy of "constructive engagement" toward the State Law and Order Restoration Council (SLORC) reflected in part official Thai policy concerns as articulated by foreign ministry officials, who argued against international isolation of the military regime. Their initial success in gaining ASEAN backing for this policy was threatened as a result of Indonesian and Malaysian unhappiness with the Burmese government's harsh treatment of its Muslim minority (some 270,000 refugees are now in Bangladesh). Nonetheless, Thailand has managed to secure ASEAN and Japanese support for its Burma policy.[38] As host of the 1994

ASEAN summit, Thailand invited Burma to informally observe the inaugural meeting of the ASEAN Regional Forum.

At the same time, leading Thai military officers have been able to take advantage of Burma's financial straits to secure valuable logging and gem mining concessions inside Burma. This, however, has tended to aggravate problems between Burma and Thailand, as groups such as the Karenni have enriched themselves through the protection services they provide Thai loggers. Using these funds, the Karenni have been able to buy arms with which to resist central control from Rangoon.[39] Border conflicts that temporarily flared up in 1992 were settled in December of that year with an agreement by both sides to pull back their troops. Both China and Thailand have been pressing the Burmese government to show some flexibility and to seek a negotiated end to its civil war. For its part, the Burmese government announced in July 1993 that it would scrap Thai logging concessions at the end of that year.[40]

The Thais also are concerned about growing Chinese influence in Burma. Indeed, China has replaced Thailand as the main buyer of Burmese timber. The Chinese have become a very large supplier of arms to Burma, and PLA advisers may be serving there as well. Chinese engineers have been improving bridges and roads linking Burma and China.[41] China now has access to Burma's modest port facilities on the Indian Ocean.[42] Thais, meanwhile, have been active in advancing relations with Burma. High-level officials made visits to Burma in 1993, and agreements are in place aimed at improving road links and a possible natural gas pipeline from the Burmese coast to western Thailand. To achieve the latter aim, Thais have been pressuring the Mons and other Burmese insurgents in eastern Burma to seek a truce with the Burmese government.[43]

Thais view Burma and the three Indochinese states as natural areas in which to extend Thailand's burgeoning economic power. Indeed, Thailand has now begun in a modest way to extend "foreign cooperation" to these states. During fiscal year 1992–93, most of the approximately $8 million in aid was channeled to Indochina, aiming to "develop their market economies and strengthen their human resources."[44] Thailand is providing the financing for the Burmese contribution to the bridge over the Moei River along their joint border. Thais anticipate that infrastructure projects on Thailand's eastern seaboard and an Australia-funded bridge linking Nongkhai in Thailand with Vientiane will enable Thailand to play a role as a center of regional development and a conduit to Indochina for foreign capital and services. Indeed, with the encouragement of the Bank of Thailand, the baht is widely used throughout Burma and Indochina. Meanwhile, those countries, together with China and Thailand, are working with the Asian Development Bank to coordinate infrastructure projects aimed at facilitating use of the Mekong River as a transport link among them.[45]

When the Vietnamese withdrew from Cambodia, Thai merchants began replacing them long before the conclusion of the UN mission there. Traders were reputed to have been particularly rapacious under Thailand's military dictators (turning "liberation zones" into zones of plunder). Merchants provided Cambodian political parties with funding necessary for their electoral drives in return for timber, real estate, and banking concessions. The Khmer Rouge imported foreign workers, including many Thais, to mine gems in western Cambodia. As one Cambodian put it, "The Thai are eating off of all of our plates, and no one is strong enough to stop them." Another Cambodian complained: "We fought to get rid of Vietnamese invaders. Now we have to worry about the Thais."[46] UNTAC also has been critical of Thai operations in Cambodia.[47] These issues are particularly sensitive given Thailand's historical links with Cambodian provinces west of the Mekong.

When the Khmer Rouge withdrew from the peace process, the Cambodian Supreme National Council and the United Nations moved to isolate them through sanctions on oil supplies entering Cambodia and logging exports leaving from Khmer Rouge areas. The Thai military resisted these measures, forcing the Thai government initially to seek a grace period before complying with UN resolutions. Eventually, Thailand agreed to honor them.[48]

Elections and the formation of a new Cambodian government have not put an end to these difficulties. Cambodian leaders were incensed in September 1993 by a statement made by a Thai military leader suggesting that the new Cambodian government represented merely a faction within Cambodia—the other faction, presumably, being the Khmer Rouge. Cambodians also complained that Thailand continued to provide sanctuary to Khmer Rouge forces and even provided them with heavy arms, including tanks. By October, one rumor had Deputy Prime Minister Hun Sen thinking about taking his case against Thailand before the United Nations Security Council.[49] And many Cambodian leaders saw a Thai hand in the July 1994 coup attempt in Phnom Penh.

Relations between Laos and Thailand, meanwhile, have improved dramatically since the border battles of late 1988. The Thais have given Vientiane assurances that they will try to impede antigovernment forces using Thailand as a base area for operations in Laos, and Thailand is now extending foreign economic cooperation to Laos. The Lao and Thai central banks have concluded a cooperation agreement, and the latter is extending technical assistance to the former.[50] Many Thai academics and officials are providing Laos with advisory and training services. And Thai investment in Laos began to take off in 1993, in construction, manufacturing, and services.

Former prime minister Anand traveled to Vietnam in January 1992. Anand called on the United States to lift its embargo against Vietnam and invited Vietnamese to observe the annual Thai-U.S. Cobra Gold military exercises. Anand's visit followed by a week that of former Thai supreme commander Suchinda Kraprayoon. Two members of the Thai royal family visited Vietnam in 1992 and 1993. Other ASEAN leaders also made trips to Hanoi in 1992. Then, in October 1993, Vietnamese Communist Party chief Do Muoi and Foreign Minister Nguyen Manh Cam visited Thailand and met with the king. Leaders of the two countries discussed their respective approaches to development of the Mekong River, joint claims in the Gulf of Thailand, disputed civil aviation rights, and potential cooperation in the development of fishing industries.[51] The end of the Cambodian conflict and Vietnam's increasing interest in inviting foreign capital and expanding its foreign commercial relations promise major improvements in Thai-Vietnamese relations. In addition, both countries increasingly may share a desire to stem growing Chinese influence in the region. The sharp shift in Vietnam's domestic and foreign policies, the Thai and Vietnamese abilities to cooperate on the Cambodian and other issues, and the prospect of joint economic gains have created, at least for now, a fundamentally new Thai-Vietnamese relationship. Nonetheless, as noted above, their shared interests in Cambodia and Laos as well as a variety of fishing and other disputes could test relations in the future. This competition will become more evident once Vietnam's economy is more robust and Vietnamese firms are able to challenge Thai ones.

The Vietnamese are interested in becoming members of ASEAN. ASEAN officials, for their part, have been encouraging Vietnamese participation in ASEAN-sponsored activities in a variety of fields, including police cooperation. In July 1992, Laos and Vietnam acceded to the 1976 ASEAN Treaty of Amity and Cooperation and were invited to the ASEAN annual foreign ministers' meeting in Singapore in 1993 as observers. In 1994 Vietnam and Laos attended as observers the meeting of the ASEAN Regional Forum, and ASEAN decided, without specifying when, to accept Vietnam's application for membership. Most officials in the ASEAN countries recognize, of course, that ongoing differences between the states of Indochina and ASEAN make full integration of the former exceedingly difficult in the near future. Indeed, recent efforts to accelerate the ASEAN Free Trade Area (AFTA) suggest that the ASEAN countries have decided that they are as concerned with deepening their association as with broadening it.

As the Lao and Vietnamese economies (and, eventually, those of Burma and Cambodia as well) develop, however, the desire to integrate more fully within ASEAN may increase. Laos, in particular, which is likely to experience growing dependence on Thailand, may push for membership in a larger economic grouping as a means of multilateralizing that dependence. Laos is exceptional because of its small size, its landlocked position, the role of the Mekong, and the ethnic affinity extending across it. In the longer run, neither Cambodia nor Vietnam is likely to be so dependent.

The ASEAN Countries

In addition to its border problems to the west and east, Thailand continues to have a variety of disputes with its southern neighbor, Malaysia. The rapid decline of both the communist insurgency and the southern Thai separatist movement helped to remove those issues as occasional sources of tension between the two countries. A series of arson and other attacks in southern Thailand in August 1993, however, revived this issue, along with Thai worries that Muslim separatists were retreating across the border into Malaysia. Thais also had fishing wrangles with Malaysia, as well as with Cambodia and Vietnam. Thailand emerged as the major fishing power in the Andaman and South China seas in the 1970s. Tensions developed during the 1980s as Thai fishing fleets increasingly depleted Thai marine resources and exploited their numerical strength in other states' waters.[52] By 1986, Thailand had some 16,000 fishing vessels, with about 85 percent of its catch coming from the Gulf of Thailand. The problem was compounded by divergent understandings of which waters belonged to which state.

Malaysia and Thailand signed a treaty for joint development of the continental shelf in 1979, but in 1985, Malaysian fishing legislation led to renewed conflicts. By 1987, the two countries had established a Joint Commission for Bilateral Cooperation. Thais hope that this can serve as a model for Thai-Vietnamese cooperation on this issue. The Thai government has tried to address fishing problems by regulating expansion of Thai fishing fleets and enforcing its agreements. In fact, however, there is little evidence of Thai state capacity to enforce compliance on the part of Thai industry. Meanwhile, the government is forced to negotiate with its neighbors for the release of the hundreds of Thai vessels and crews seized for alleged violations of neighbors' waters.

Mutual Malaysian and Thai commitment to ASEAN has helped these countries to mitigate bilateral problems. Within ASEAN more broadly, however, fundamental differences in the approach to regional issues persist. These could grow significantly worse in the future. One of the principal cleavages within ASEAN has long concerned the role of external powers. All countries in the region share aspirations to keep foreign powers from meddling in the region's conflicts and thereby exacerbating them. For some, however, fears of domination by other regional states outweigh these scruples. This issue is evident with respect to Malaysia and Singapore, which continue to participate in the Five-Power Defense Agreement along with Australia, New Zealand, and the United Kingdom. Recently, Indonesian officials have made increasingly pointed statements concerning this arrangement's anachronistic character, in particular its genesis as a pact aimed at Indonesia.

Singapore, as a prosperous but tiny and trade-dependent state, is always interested in maintaining as broad a network of ties as possible. Singapore officials have suggested inviting the permanent five members of the UN Security Council to endorse the ASEAN Treaty of Amity and Cooperation. Indonesia opposes this step as inviting interference in regional affairs by foreign powers. In an effort to foster "preventive diplomacy" on issues such as Cambodia, the drug trade, and the islands in the South China Sea, the Thai foreign ministry has been pushing closer links between ASEAN and the United Nations.[53] More recently, ASEAN has launched initiatives aimed at fostering cooperation with UN agencies other than the Security Council. Singapore and Thailand have been organizing a series of workshops on ASEAN–UN Cooperation for Peace and Preventive Diplomacy.[54] The ASEAN decision in 1993 to establish an ASEAN Regional Forum is particularly significant in this regard.

Thailand is the region's principal example of conflict between the desire to promote strong regional associations on the one hand and the need for security relations with external powers on the other. This certainly reflects Thailand's geographical position and the salience of the threats Thai leaders have perceived. It may also reflect Thailand's freedom from colonial control and, as a result, greater self-confidence in dealing with foreign powers.

Since the late 1970s, Thailand's ASEAN partners have worried about Thailand's close links to China. Just as Thailand had used its "obliging helplessness"[55] in the 1960s in turning to the United States, in the late 1970s Thailand turned to China. As a front-line state in the global effort to curb the growth of the power of the Soviet Union and its allies, Thailand's security needs outweighed its interest in foiling efforts by extraregional powers to increase their influence in Southeast Asia. Thai interests in the trans-Mekong region, including close ties to Laos, and its vulnerability to attack from the east forced Thailand to seek external means of maintaining its vital interests. Paribatra suggests that traditionally Thailand has cultivated patrons from outside the region when it has found itself unable to secure the trans-Mekong area from potentially hostile forces.[56] Hence, by drawing China more closely into the region, Thailand frustrated ASEAN efforts to minimize external interference.

Indonesia and Malaysia, in particular, have tended to view Thailand rather as the French have perceived (with ambivalence) the United Kingdom's insistence on maintaining its close ties to the United States.[57] In both cases, ongoing close relations with extraregional powers threaten to undermine regional institution building. Varying threat perceptions within ASEAN have tended to exacerbate this problem. Even after Vietnam's invasion of Cambodia, Indonesians and Malaysians were as apt to see Vietnam as a necessary counterweight to Chinese power as they were to view Vietnam as a potential threat.

For practical purposes, these conflicts were generally resolved in Thailand's favor. Thailand was the front-line state, and the ASEAN countries wanted to provide it with full support, in part to minimize the extent to which Thailand would feel it had to rely on China. Indonesian and Malaysian patience paid off, as during the late 1980s, the Thai position moved closer to that of its fellow ASEAN members. Once the Thais were convinced of the genuineness of the Vietnamese commitment to withdraw forces from Cambodia (completed in October 1989), they became more sympathetic to the view that the Hun Sen government should play a key role in postsettlement Cambodia.

The Soviet Union's disintegration, Vietnam's withdrawal from Cambodia, closer Lao-Thai cooperation, and extraordinary economic growth in Thailand have transformed Thailand's security context. Thai talk of a *suwannaphum* under

Thailand's economic leadership in mainland Southeast Asia has resulted in a new set of ASEAN anxieties. As Thailand has become increasingly interested in the commercial potential of Burma and Indochina, other ASEAN members worry that this serves to weaken Thailand's commitment to strengthening the organization. Thailand, according to this view, is a continental state interested primarily in the trans-Mekong region and Burma, while the others are maritime states whose interests remain broadly dispersed. Some observers see evidence to sustain such concerns in Thailand's Seventh Five-Year Plan (1991–96), which aims to make Thailand a regional economic center, and in various Thai government regulatory adjustments, particularly in the financial and monetary areas, aimed at facilitating such a role.

Echoing concerns from the 1970s and 1980s, observers within ASEAN now fear that the economic pull exerted by emerging possibilities in the trans-Mekong region will deflect Thai energies from efforts to strengthen ASEAN. Such concerns were particularly acute during Chatichai's tenure as prime minister in the late 1980s. Indeed, ASEAN members then viewed Thailand with concern, much as Germany's fellow European Community members viewed the supposedly distracting influence that Eastern Europe exerted on German policies. These ASEAN fears receded somewhat while Anand was in office. Anand has long been associated with ASEAN and supportive of efforts to further ASEAN integration (he was the chair of the ASEAN task force that issued a set of proposals in 1983 calling for enhanced economic cooperation within the grouping). And it was during his tenure as prime minister that ASEAN committed itself to the creation of an ASEAN Free Trade Area (AFTA) under the Framework Agreement on Enhancing ASEAN Economic Cooperation. Plans originally called for lowering tariffs on manufactured goods and processed agricultural products in a staged process over a fifteen-year period, at the end of which tariffs would be within a 5 percent ceiling. When ASEAN economic ministers subsequently met in October and December 1992, they established two tracks for lowering tariffs, one over fifteen years and an accelerated track aimed at achieving reductions over seven to ten years.

These decisions apparently came in response to concern at the time about the deadlocked talks at the General Agreement on Tariffs and Trade. While this initiative is certain to face difficult hurdles in the years ahead, it is an intelligent response to the concern that foreign investment increasingly will be attracted to other regions (Eastern Europe, Latin America). The framework offers greater potential for success by allowing any two members to proceed with cuts if other members are not prepared to follow suit. While it was initially proposed in 1991 by Anand, Malaysian prime minister Mahathir Mohamad has been particularly energetic in pushing the plan, hoping for efforts to sponsor industrial complementarity schemes.

Some recent discussions of ASEAN have overplayed the gap between the interests of ASEAN peninsular and insular states. Thailand's economic interests are global. Indochina will not assume major economic importance for Thailand any time soon. Thailand's economic ties to ASEAN, however, are likely to grow considerably in the future, just as those among the East Asian newly industrializing countries accelerated beginning in the mid-1980s. In fact, investment from Japan and other East Asian countries has been pushing the process of economic integration within Southeast Asia.

In political and security terms, ASEAN has been highly successful in reducing regional tensions. ASEAN appears to be developing into a security community whose states are relatively free of the need to plan for war with one another. Nonetheless, military spending among the ASEAN states is rising rapidly, with various states seeking to acquire new military capabilities.

Reflecting geographic factors, Thailand has the largest land forces among the ASEAN countries. Thailand has some 500 tanks, about 1,000 armored personnel carriers, close to 400 pieces of towed artillery, and over 130 helicopters.[58] These figures, however, do not tell us a great deal about the capabilities of Thai forces. By and large, when called upon to perform in action, the Thai military has not been impressive. This results from problems of coordination at various levels of the armed forces.

Thailand's navy consists of some five frigates, fifty coastal patrol craft armed with assorted missile systems, and handfuls of mine warfare, amphibious, and antisubmarine warfare vessels. In terms of naval forces, Indonesia is the region's major military power. Indonesia recently has acquired additional submarines, and Malaysia has indicated interest in following the Indonesian lead.[59]

The Thai air force includes eighteen F-16s, fifty-six F-5s, eighty-six COIN aircraft, and a variety of transport aircraft and helicopters. This force appears to be broadly comparable to those of Indonesia and Singapore. Malaysia is purchasing new aircraft, both U.S. F/A-18s and Russian MiG-29s, fighter-bombers that will enable Malaysia to expand its military roles to include patrol of its coasts.[60]

Despite growing levels of defense spending in the region in the 1980s, none of the countries in Southeast Asia has the capability to carry out large military operations using air and naval forces. Vietnamese and Chinese armies and Soviet and U.S. air and naval forces have shaped the region's security environment. Today, Chinese, Indian, and Japanese naval forces are becoming more formidable, while Russian and U.S. power-projection capabilities are diminishing, albeit at radically different rates.

In the past, ASEAN has played a more important political than economic roles. While expectations for enhanced economic coordination are growing, the organization also is expanding its political and security roles. Following up on earlier Australian and Canadian suggestions, in 1991 Japan urged that the ASEAN Post-Ministerial Conference be used as a forum for the discussion of security issues. These concerns were then addressed in that forum the following year. With the Clinton administration relatively supportive of efforts to foster regional security discussions, ASEAN and Japan have continued to push for a larger ASEAN role in such talks. Together with their Post-Ministerial Conference partners, the ASEAN states met in Singapore in May 1993 to discuss regional security issues. While differences within ASEAN remained in evidence, the meeting suggested further movement in the direction of institutionalizing regional security discussions within the ASEAN Regional Forum.[61]

In order to provide for its security in the future, ASEAN could try to build on the existing network of bilateral and trilateral defense relations.[62] In the event of a major reduction in the U.S. regional military presence, ASEAN could seek a defense agreement with Australia, New Zealand, and Papua New Guinea.[63] The ASEAN states are attempting to expand their cooperation with Australia and New Zealand in securing the freedom of sea lanes of communication as well as combating growing piracy problems in the South China Sea.[64] Ultimately, as Thai army commander Suchinda Kraprayoon noted early in 1991, no ASEAN defense arrangement can substitute for a continuing U.S. military presence in the region.[65]

Among the problems still facing ASEAN are finding a means of broadening participation in its discussions without losing its influence as part of the broadening process; creating a multilateral grouping that does not afford Indonesia undue influence; and creating a stronger regional institution without sacrificing crucial external security links.

Politics and Problems in Thailand

In the final analysis, Thailand's ability to manage the challenges it faces in its relations with the great powers, as well as with its neighbors, will depend not only on the environment in which Thailand operates, but also on economic, political, and social developments in Thailand itself. In this section, I turn briefly to these issues.

The Thai military faces both operational and political problems. The former concern the military's limited efficacy. In the latter part of the 1980s, particularly during the tenure of Supreme Commander Chaovalit Yongchaiyuth, the Thai military attempted to increase its effectiveness. This initiative came in response to both budget austerity, worsened as a result of the desire to buy expensive new weapons systems, and experiences indicating the military's limited success in performing its nominal functions.[66]

Budgetary problems resulted from the significant reduction in U.S. military assistance, particularly military sales credits, as well as slow economic growth in the mid-1980s. Between 1979 and 1987, military spending declined from 21 to 18 percent of the national budget. General Chaovalit argued that Thailand could not afford to maintain a large standing army, as it represented an unacceptable drain on national resources. He hoped to reduce the force levels of some battalions, including those in the south, while mechanizing others. He also spoke about the desirability of moving toward a volunteer force and reducing the numbers of top brass (a situation in which Thailand had "more generals than tanks.")[67] In the face of entrenched military interests, Chaovalit was able to realize only some of these goals.

Force modernization, however, did produce a theoretical Thai offensive capability to complement its theoretical defensive capacities. Thai forces would have the option of responding to a Vietnamese attack from along the Cambodian border by striking east into Laos and Vietnam from northeastern Thailand. The Thai military achieved this force modernization largely through Chinese arms purchases that made possible the mechanization of divisions in northeast and central Thailand. Fortunately, the sudden changes in Vietnam's foreign policies make it likely that this alleged Thai capability will remain theoretical.

In 1990, the Thais began to indicate an interest in obtaining a helicopter carrier for the navy. Given the Russian military withdrawal from the region and closer Thai-Vietnamese relations, the motivations for the proposed purchase were unclear. One justification would be to support disaster relief work.[68] While the Thai Budget Bureau resisted the move, the military eventually prevailed.[69] Thai army general Surayudh Chulanonda announced in September 1992 that the military would reduce its spending by 25 percent over the remainder of the 1990s, with more than half of that to take place over the next five years. The largest cuts would come from the army.[70]

Following the military violence in May 1992, the king's intercession, and the June 10 reinstatement of Anand as interim prime minister, Anand removed top military officers from their positions in the military hierarchy and from the boards of various state-owned enterprises. The new defense minister, Banchob Bunnag, called on the military to stick to its professional role as a military force. The head of the air force was removed from his position as chairman of the Communications Authority of Thailand and replaced by a civilian. In August 1992, Anand demoted Army Commander General Issarapong Noonpakdi, Supreme Commander Air Force Marshal Kaset, Army Chief of Staff General Viroj Saengsanit, and Commander of the First Army Region Chainarong Noonpakdi. Anand also revoked an executive order making the supreme commander the director of Thailand's Internal Peacekeeping Force. Control of domestic conflicts now rests in the hands of the police. While the contest clearly should not be seen as settled, proponents of civilian rule and parliamentary democracy have gained the advantage over the Thai military. Meanwhile, the military has continued to maintain a dominant role in Thai foreign policy toward Burma and Indochina, despite efforts by the Chuan Leekpai government to give greater control to the foreign ministry and National Security Council (under stronger civilian guidance).

Economic Expansion

The Thai economy has consistently performed well for over three decades. Few economies can match its extended record of strong and stable growth. A major qualitative change in Thailand's economic expansion began in the 1980s as the country increased its exports of a broad variety of manufactured products and sharply reduced its long-standing dependence on exports of agricultural products. Over a five-year period, average annual real economic growth was over 10 percent. Much of this growth was stimulated by foreign direct manufacturing investment, well over half of it coming from other East Asian economies.

With economic expansion increasingly linked to foreign markets, Thailand may at first glance appear to be increasing its vulnerability. This concern, however, is misplaced. In the first place, Thailand is increasing its wealth and skills, and, hence, its capacity to respond to future shocks requiring further adjustments.[71] Further, Thailand thus far has been quite successful in diversifying its export markets and continues to seek new buyers in the Asian subcontinent, Indochina, the Middle East, and Eastern Europe. Most important, however, the spurt of economic growth, together with the tenure of the insulated technocratic Anand government, allowed Thailand to address many fundamental underlying economic and regulatory weaknesses. With these accomplished, the prospects for consistent, stable growth look very strong.

Some observers were concerned in 1992 that the political violence of May would cripple Thailand's economic growth. In retrospect, these fears appear to have been overblown. Foreign investment is in fact down somewhat, but this merely continues a trend that preceded the street clashes between soldiers and civilians. Investment is slowing in part as a result of infrastructural bottlenecks in Thailand. Japanese investment has receded from the high levels of the late 1980s. Those rates, however, were unsustainable and represented, in part, a one-time shift of productive assets prompted by the yen's sharp appreciation over the latter 1980s. In any case, investment from the East Asian newly industrializing countries is replacing that from Japan. Recent economic reforms, lower inflation, strong economic growth, and eventual improvements in physical infrastructure are likely to continue to attract high levels of foreign investment. And the latest round in the yen's appreciation is leading to more Japanese investment. Furthermore, recent Thai economic growth has been driven in considerable part by growing domestic demand and export markets within East Asia itself. Tourism in Thailand, however, suffered as a result of the 1992 political violence, AIDS, environmental problems, and a string of catastrophes in 1993 (fires and collapsing buildings) that diminished the luster of Thailand's international reputation.

On balance, and despite some significant longer-term problems, it is difficult to be pessimistic about Thailand's medium-term economic prospects. To be sure, raising the level of human capital will take longer than raising that of physical capital, the means of institutionalizing stable but meaningful political competition remain elusive, and regional and class disparities in wealth are growing in a context of rapid change and political instability. Particularly disconcerting in 1993 was the resurgence of Muslim separatist activity in the south and the sharp debates in parliament surrounding the adoption of an Islamic administrative bill. Nevertheless, Thailand enjoys many advantages in a region that has produced rapid economic growth over a long period. With China, the Indochinese countries, and perhaps India and the Philippines joining that process, Thailand can afford to make mistakes. In the next section, I note some of the potentially dangerous ones.

Emerging Problems

In addition to problems of political instability, social inequality, and inadequate labor skills, Thailand faces dangers resulting from environmental degradation, the spread of the AIDS virus, and the ongoing drug trade. In 1988, Thailand suffered major flood damage in the south caused in part by uncontrolled logging in the area. Thailand faces major problems of loss of marine resources, water pollution, the disposal of toxic substances, and high levels of air pollution in Bangkok. Power plants have poisoned waters with sulfur dioxide, and molasses spills pollute rivers.

The Anand government moved to address many of these problems, combining public awareness programs with some regulatory punch. In 1992, Anand transferred some $20 million from the country's Oil Fund (used to cushion local energy prices against sharp increases in international prices) to help fund the newly created Environment Fund.[72] In 1993, Japan approved nearly $1 billion in aid to Thailand, much of it to address environmental problems. In the area of tourism, where the interests of business and environmentalists coincide, real progress may be possible. It remains to be seen, however, how effective Thai authorities will be in regulating the behavior of decentralized, smaller industrial and service operations around the country. A 1993 conflagration that killed hundreds of workers in a Bangkok toy factory that failed to meet existing fire prevention standards and the collapse of a hotel expanded without reference to building codes serve as warnings on this score. They also arouse unease for some at the prospect of Thai nuclear power plants. The first of these is scheduled to begin operation in 2006.

While extremely difficult to estimate, the potential costs to Thailand accruing from the AIDS epidemic will be enormous—as high as $8 billion by the end of this century, according to one estimate. These will take the form of government spending, reduced employment, discouragement of investment, and a host of opportunity costs. Some estimates suggest that as many as 2 to 4 million Thais will be HIV-positive by 2000, more than half of those women.[73] Other studies suggest even more staggering levels of infection, reaching over 4 million by that time.[74] Prostitutes from Burma and Indochina working in Thailand are also helping to transmit the virus around the region. Fortunately, Thailand has launched an aggressive campaign against the disease, particularly in the area of public awareness. The royal family, Prime Minister Anand, the former head of family planning campaigns, Mechai Viravaidhya, a variety of nongovernmental organizations, and a host of others have at least helped to raise awareness of the problem in Thailand. The extent to which they are influencing causal behavior patterns is not yet clear. In any case, the epidemic has already spread widely and is certain to exact heavy economic, psychological, and social tolls.

Thailand has long had a major role in the international narcotics business. This has proved a boon to criminal organizations and to some leading government officials. About half the world's supply of opium is produced in the Burmese area of the Golden Triangle, and until recently, much of it was refined in Thailand and shipped abroad from Thai ports. In the early 1990s, however, these operations appear to be relocating, with traffic increasingly moving through Cambodia, China, and Laos. Thais may continue to exert considerable influence over the business, but it appears that less of it actually takes place in Thailand than in the past.[75] Nonetheless, drug abuse in Thailand continues to be a problem of serious concern.

Conclusion

In the past, Thailand has been able to adjust its domestic and foreign policies to meet emerging threats and opportunities. This was evident in its nineteenth-century modernization, its sympathy for national socialism in the years before World War II, its brief and intermittent adoption of parliamentary government following that war,[76] and its more recent response to regional and global economic changes in post–Cold War Asia. Thailand has successfully pursued foreign policies, both strategic and economic, that have brought its interests into line with prevailing international developments.

Thailand's combination of intermittent bureaucratic incompetence and occasional political chaos often leads observers to underestimate the society's more fundamental strengths and to attribute Thai successes to dumb luck. Kukrit Pramoj argues that a spirit watches over Thailand's destiny to ensure that it emerges largely unscathed from its various travails. Muthiah Alagappa sees in Thailand "a weak modern state," riven with deep-seated conflicts and vulnerable to domestic conflicts and external intervention.[77] In fact, however, Thailand demonstrates the ways in which a strong and cohesive society has been able to overcome, at least for a period of time, serious administrative and political deficiencies.

Some observers deride Thailand's propensity to "bend with the wind" or its "audacious inconstancy." Thailand, however, has been remarkably successful. Without an inordinate commitment of resources to its own defense, it has skillfully used external alliances to defend its political and territorial integrity. Vulnerable to land invasion and, for a period, to insurgencies, Thailand has at times increased its dependence on a single foreign security guarantor. In the past it has been able to reduce that dependence as its external environment has altered. Unlike the United States, however, China will not simply withdraw militarily from the region. Hence, China presents Thailand with a longer-term problem. Nonetheless, Thailand retains a capacity to use its ties with countries both within the region and beyond it to retain its maneuvering room in its relations with China. Japan will become increasingly important to Thailand in this role.

Notes

1. While this describes the dominant view of Japan today, historical factors and Japan's low profile, resulting in less familiarity, work to sustain anxiety about directions Japan will take in the future.

2. Stephen M. Walt, *The Origins of Alliances* (Ithaca, NY: Cornell University Press, 1987).

3. Local alliances are not necessarily preferable. While the gap in relative power may be smaller, the reciprocal obligations may be stronger. Furthermore, the interests of states in geographical proximity are more likely to conflict (although this should be less true of states without land boundaries).

4. Charles E. Morrison and Astri Suhrke, *Strategies of Survival: The Foreign Policy Dilemmas of Smaller Asian States* (New York: St. Martin's Press, 1978), p. 110.

5. Today, Thailand's land borders run for some 2,800 miles, bounded by Laos, Cambodia, Malaysia, and Burma.

6. This may have been a blessing in the long run, resulting in a more homogeneous population than would otherwise have been the case.

7. Donald E. Neuchterlein, *Thailand and the Struggle for Southeast Asia* (Ithaca, NY: Cornell University Press, 1965), p. 104, cited in Richard Doner, "Thai Foreign Policy: An Analytical Survey," manuscript, 1982.

8. Wiwat Mungkandi, paper presented at Chulalongkorn University American Studies Program and University of California, Berkeley Conference on Thai-U.S. Relations, March 25–28, 1985, p. 14.

9. Usha Mahajani, "U.S. Intervention in Laos and Its Impact on Laotian Relations with Thailand and Vietnam," in Mark W. Zacher and R. Stephen Milne, eds., *Conflict and Stability in Southeast Asia* (Garden City, NY: Anchor Books, 1974), pp. 243–44.

10. Australia, France, New Zealand, Pakistan, the Philippines, Thailand, the United Kingdom, and the United States signed the pact in September 1954. The pact commits each member to act to meet a shared military threat and calls for consultation in the event of any other threat to the territory, sovereignty, or political independence of any member.

11. Thai bases not only were relatively cheap and close to bombing targets, but helped to reduce U.S. dependence on bases in Japan. Use of the latter had increasingly helped to stimulate a major antiwar movement there.

12. Total U.S. military aid to Thailand between 1950 and 1971 came to over $1 billion, about equal to the Thai military budget during that period. Bjorn Hagelin, "Military Dependency: Thailand and the Philippines," *Journal of Peace Research,* 25: 4, 1988, p. 433.

13. U.S. facilities in Thailand included two army communication bases, two navy bases, three air force fighter bases, an air force operations base, and a strategic bomber and combat support base. Hagelin, "Military Dependency," p. 433.

14. Clark D. Neher, "The Foreign Policy of Thailand," in David Wurfel and Bruce Burton, eds. *The Political Economy of Foreign Policy in Southeast Asia* (New York: St. Martin's Press, 1990), p. 192.

15. Nayan Chanda, "The External Environment," in Wurfel and Burton, eds., *The Political Economy of Foreign Policy,* p. 64.

16. Then adviser to Prime Minister Prem Tinsulanonda, Air Chief Marshal Siddhi

Savetsila, quoted in Barry Kramer, "Thailand, A U.S. Treaty Partner, Faces Threat from Vietnam-Cambodia War and Refugee Tide," *Wall Street Journal,* January 22, 1980, p. 48.

17. Beginning in 1977, the Defense Ministry implemented a system of "total defense" as outlined in Prime Ministerial Orders 66/2523 and 65/2523. These efforts, which involved a growing military role in rural development activities, attempted to strike at the underlying socioeconomic conditions that were perceived to be fostering the communist insurgency in Thailand.

18. At its height, the Chinese and Thais are estimated to have cooperated in funneling 300 to 500 tons of materiel to the Khmer Rouge every month. M.R. Sukhumbhand Paribatra, *From Alignment to Enmity: Thailand's Evolving Relations with China* (Bangkok: Institute of Security and International Studies, Chulalongkorn University, 1987), p. 18.

19. Paisal Sricharatchanya, "Intrusive Encounters," *Far Eastern Economic Review,* April 30, 1987, p. 28; Rodney Tasker, "The Battle of Chong Bok," *Far Eastern Economic Review,* June 18, 1987, p. 19.

20. Clark D. Neher, "The Foreign Policy of Thailand," in Wurfel and Burton, eds., *The Political Economy of Foreign Policy,* pp. 193–96.

21. Paisal Sricharatchanya, "Making Up," *Far Eastern Economic Review,* January 12, 1989, p. 21.

22. This was particularly true of timber following an October 1988 ban on logging in Thailand.

23. Many Thais were also, of course, pleased to defuse the crisis to their east. This not only allowed controls on military spending, which had increased rapidly in the late 1970s and early 1980s, but also offered protection against increasing expansion of the military's economic and social roles and, hence, its dominance in Thai society. Finally, some observers were concerned that military leaders were developing a significant vested interest in the perpetuation of the conflict. See Sukhumbhand Paribatra "Stretegic Implications of the Indochina Conflict: Thai Perspectives," *Asian Affairs,* Fall 1984, pp. 40–42.

24. Michael Field and Murray Hiebert, "Regime of Last Resort," *Far Eastern Economic Review,* January 25, 1990, pp. 8–9

25. Leszek Buszynski, "Thailand: The Erosion of a Balanced Foreign Policy," *Asian Survey,* 22: 11, November 1982, p. 1049.

26. Ibid., p. 1046.

27. Leszek Buszynski, "New Aspirations and Old Constraints in Thailand's Foreign Policy," *Asian Survey,* 29: 11, November 1989, p. 1068.

28. See Tai Ming Cheung, "Officers' Commission," *Far Eastern Economic Review,* July 2, 1992, p. 13.

29. Paribatra, *From Enmity to Alignment,* p. 23.

30. The United States had previously reached agreement with Thailand on establishing a war-reserve stockpile in Thailand for use by U.S. forces.

31. "4-Country Development Zone Promoted at Peking Talks," *Bangkok Post Weekly,* July 16, 1993, p. 11; Nusara Thaitawat and Phitsanu Thepthong, "ADB Asked to Study 4-Nation Ringroad," *Bangkok Post Weekly,* August 20, 1993, p. 6.

32. Elliott Kulick and Dick Wilson, *Thailand's Turn* (New York: St. Martin's Press, 1992), p. 165.

33. *Japan Digest,* 4: 20, May 24, 1993, p. 11.

34. Paul Handley, "Japan's Clarion Call," *Far Eastern Economic Review,* January 28, 1993, pp. 10–11.

35. Eric Teo Chu Cheow, "New Omnidirectional Overtures in Thai Foreign Policy," *Asian Survey,* 26: 7, July 1986, p. 757.

36. Rodney Tasker, "Security Embrace," *Far Eastern Economic Review,* February 18, 1993, pp. 12–13.

37. *Bangkok Post Weekly*, July 30, 1993, p. 12; *Bangkok Post Weekly*, October 22, 1993, p. 13.

38. *Bangkok Post Weekly*, September 24, 1993, p. 2.

39. Bertil Lintner, "Collective Insecurity," *Far Eastern Economic Review*, December 3, 1992, pp. 22–23.

40. Bertil Lintner, "Soft Option on Hardwood," *Far Eastern Economic Review*, July 22, 1993, p. 25.

41. Marc Wrangel, "The Burma-China Connection," *Manager*, No. 53, May 1993, pp. 60–64.

42. Paul Handley, "River of Promise," *Far Eastern Economic Review*, September 16, 1993, pp. 68–70.

43. "Army Commander Pays Goodwill Visit to Burma," *Bangkok Post Weekly*, August 20, 1993, p. 6; "Government Urges Mon Rebels to Make Peace with SLORC," *Bangkok Post Weekly*, September 17, 1993, p. 6.

44. Text of speech by Foreign Minister Arsa Sarasin on "Thailand's Indochina Policy," before the Thailand Chapter of the Young Presidents' Organization in Bangkok, August 17, 1992.

45. Handley, "River of Promise."

46. *Washington Post*, May 17, 1992, p. C7; *International Herald Tribune*, August 26, 1992, p. 4; August 12, 1992, p. A23.

47. Nayan Chanda, "Strained Ties," *Far Eastern Economic Review*, December 17, 1992, pp. 26–28.

48. Ken Stier, "Log Rolling," *Far Eastern Economic Review*, January 21, 1993, pp. 15–16.

49. *Bangkok Post Weekly*, September 17, 1993, p. 6; *Bangkok Post Weekly*, October 22, 1993, p. 6; *Bangkok Post Weekly*, October 29, 1993, p. 6.

50. *The Nation*, December 18, 1992, p. B16.

51. *Bangkok Post Weekly*, October 29, 1993, p. 7.

52. This discussion is taken from Ted L. McDorman, "International Fishery Relations in the Gulf of Thailand," *Contemporary Southeast Asia*, 12: 1, June 1990, pp. 40–54.

53. Rodney Tasker, "Another Voice," *Far Eastern Economic Review*, February 25, 1993, pp. 25–26.

54. *Bangkok Post Weekly*, October 15, 1993, p. 7.

55. Buszynski, "Thailand," p. 1037.

56. Paribatra, "Strategic Implications," p. 35.

57. In fact, the Philippines and Singapore also have, or had until recently in the former case, close security links with the United States. Indeed, Indonesia and Malaysia have closer links than they generally care to advertise.

58. These figures are taken from Sheldon Simon, "Regionalization of Defense in Southeast Asia," *NBR Analysis*, vol. 3, no. 1, June 1992, p. 23.

59. Tai Ming Cheung, "Instant Navy," *Far Eastern Economic Review*, February 16, 1993, pp. 11–12.

60. Michael Vatikiotis and Melana Zyla, "Scrambled Jets," *Far Eastern Economic Review*, February 18, 1993, pp. 10–11.

61. Michael Vatikiotis, "The First Step," *Far Eastern Economic Review*, June 3, 1993, p. 18.

62. See Simon, "Regionalization of Defense in Southeast Asia," pp. 20–22; Jusuf Wanandi, "ASEAN and Security Cooperation in Southeast Asia," International Institute for Global Peace Special Report, Tokyo, March 1991. Wanandi explicitly excludes the Five-Power Defense Arrangement, which was aimed originally at Indonesia.

63. Wanandi, "ASEAN."

64. Malcolm Kennedy and Michael O'Connor, "Regional Naval Cooperation Boosted at Bali Conference," *Defender*, 10: 1, Autumn 1993.

65. Leszek Buszynski, "Southeast Asia in the Post-Cold War Era," *Asian Survey*, 32: 9, September 1992, pp. 830–47.

66. One problem concerns the lack of coordination among the military services. Real military power usually resides in army headquarters rather than in the Supreme Command. As one observer noted, "Thai army officers are semi-serious when they joke that they would rather shoot a fellow Marine than a Vietnamese invader." Tai Ming Cheung, "Unmovable Object," *Far Eastern Economic Review*, June 25, 1992, pp. 10–12.

67. Thailand has about one general for every 300–350 troops, a ratio some ten times that in most Western militaries. Many generals serve without apparent responsibilities. Tai Ming Cheung, "Unmovable Object"; Rodney Tasker, "Remodelled Army," *Far Eastern Economic Review*, May 20, 1993, p. 21.

68. Rodney Tasker, "Reaching for the Sky," *Far Eastern Economic Review*, February 22, 1990, p. 22

69. Rodney Tasker, "Order Arms," *Far Eastern Economic Review*, October 4, 1990, p. 20.

70. *International Herald Tribune*, September 28, 1992, p. 2.

71. See Albert Hirschman's discussion of the ways in which less developed economies are necessarily more vulnerable to foreign economic shocks. *National Power and the Structure of International Trade* (Berkeley: University of California Press, 1945), pp. 13–52.

72. "Environment to Play Bigger Role in Development Plan," *Thailand, Update*, Joint Public-Private Consultative Committee, August 1, 1992, p. 1.

73. Andrew Waller, "A Fight on All Fronts," *Far Eastern Economic Review*, February 13, 1992, pp. 28–35.

74. *Bangkok Post Weekly*, September 3, 1993, p. 2; *Bangkok Post Weekly*, October 15, 1993, p.2.

75. Nate Thayer, "Diverted Traffic," *Far Eastern Economic Review*, March 18, 1993, pp. 24–25.

76. Morrison and Suhrke, *Strategies of Survival*, p. 141.

77. Muthiah Alagappa, *The National Security of Developing States: Lessons From Thailand*, (Dover, MA: Auburn House Publishing, 1987), pp. 60, 237–39

10

Vietnam's Foreign Policy in the Post-Soviet Era: Coping with Vulnerability

Michael Leifer

Vietnam's foreign policy has been transformed almost beyond recognition within a relatively short span of time.[1] It has been driven by pragmatism at the expense of ideology in the interest of regime and national security. Both of these core goals were in some jeopardy by the mid-1980s and more so by the turn of the decade, with the Cold War ending and an attendant loss of external patronage. Revolutionary Vietnam had always enjoyed such patronage. The post-Soviet era has been distinguished by its conspicuous absence. For Vietnam, the central issue of foreign policy has been how to overcome an acute problem of vulnerability that had not been contemplated in April 1975 with the triumphal attainment of national unification.

Few states can match Vietnam's recent experience of falling from international grace. Lionized as a symbol of national liberation struggle, it became a virtual diplomatic pariah within only a few years of reunification. Relative isolation during the early 1980s aggravated economic distress induced by dogma and made necessary a radical reversal of domestic course in mid-decade. Concurrent changes in the pattern of global politics reinforced a vulnerable condition and impelled the change of domestic course, with signal consequences for foreign policy. With the astounding loss of Soviet patronage, Vietnam's political leadership had little alternative but to come to terms fully with a national debility that threatened its political order. A foreign policy of regional and international accommodation became the only rational choice, despite a formal attachment to ideological virtues expressed, for example, in the name of the state, the Socialist Republic of Vietnam.

An important part of Vietnam's difficulties arose from miscalculating the so-called correlation of forces in deciding to invade Cambodia in December 1978.[2] That decision reflected a strategic perspective in which the security of

Vietnam was tied closely to its ability to determine the political identity of neighboring Laos and Cambodia within an Indochinese domain. In the event, Vietnam failed to realize its strategic purpose. After more than a decade of costly military engagement, it was obliged to withdraw its forces from Cambodia and to abandon the government that it had installed in January 1979. It did so, ironically, for the very reason that had obliged the United States to withdraw from Vietnam: a loss of political will arising from domestic circumstances.

Vietnam, both as a revolutionary movement and as a state, had been instrumental in shaping the pattern of international politics in Southeast Asia for more than four decades. The Cold War provided the overall context for its role, particularly after the outbreak of hostilities in Korea in 1950. Vietnam's significance was that its potential for enforcing changes in political identity within Indochina became coupled to the prospect of far-reaching changes in the regional and global balances of power. The assumption, held above all in Washington, that a resolution of internal conflict in Indochina to communist advantage would have disturbing strategic consequences provided the rationale for a fruitless and costly military intervention.

The Communist Party of Vietnam had made a corresponding dominolike judgment. The military experience of confronting the French after the Pacific War had persuaded its leadership to incorporate all the countries of Indochina within a common strategic perspective. That perspective, expressed in a prerogative special relationship with Laos and Cambodia, became invested with an imperative quality in the late 1970s as the changing pattern of Cold War politics disinterred a historical antagonism with China.[3] Moreover, Pol Pot's Cambodia came to be regarded as China's bridgehead of aggression in Indochina, which had to be eliminated in the interest of national security.

In its confrontation with France, Vietnam's Communist Party had been able to attract material support from China, proffered out of self-interest. In its confrontation with the United States, the party had enjoyed both Chinese and Soviet material benefaction in mixed measure as well as attracting wider international backing. Against China, the Soviet Union fulfilled the critical supporting role. As Vietnam's sole external patron of any substance, it provided access to material aid and countervailing power for more than a decade. Assistance from the Soviet Union and its Eastern European bloc allies, with some help from India, proved crucial after 1979. The ultimate loss of such access with the end of the Cold War, and then the disintegration of the Soviet Union and the failure to realize a compensating normalization with the United States, substantially diminished Vietnam's capacity to shape the regional pattern of power. Moreover, with the end of the Cold War, that pattern in Indochina lost its international significance, which Vietnam had used to advantage by exploiting major power rivalries. In consequence, the ruling party in Hanoi has come full circle to the circumstances of the Geneva Conference on Indochina of 1954, when the political interests of Vietnam were compromised as a result of major power accommodation. Vietnam has been obliged to fend for itself by forging new relationships with countries that were its prime adversaries during the Cambodian intervention.

The international settlement of the Cambodian conflict in Paris in October 1991 eased Vietnam's vulnerable condition, but did not overcome it. Its government still has to cope with an intimidating China, which seemed determined to chasten Vietnam for its political impertinence since reunification and to ensure that it knew and kept its subordinate regional place. As of this writing, a long-sought countervailing normalization of relations with the United States has been frustrated because of the sustained salience in U.S. domestic politics of the issue of American servicemen missing in action (MIAs) from the Vietnam War. Hanoi's considerable cooperation in searches for remains of American servicemen enabled President Clinton to withdraw objections to lending to Vietnam by multilateral institutions in July 1993. In February 1994, he lifted a trade and investment embargo that had been imposed on the entire country with the fall of Saigon in 1975. This important step toward normalization was coupled, however, with the condition that the establishment of diplomatic relations would require further progress on the MIA issue.

Confronting Vulnerability

As indicated above, the turning point in foreign policy for Vietnam was its Cambodia war.[4] Assuming that it was possible to reconcile priorities of external security and economic doctrine because of assurances of Soviet backing, Vietnam's Politburo committed the country to a punishing and ultimately fruitless ordeal. They failed to anticipate the international coalition that mobilized against their attempt to reshape the regional balance of power. Instead of being applauded as a benefactor for having rid Cambodia of a political pestilence, Vietnam found itself denounced at the United Nations for having violated the cardinal rule of the society of states. More seriously, its ruling party failed to calculate the prospect, pace, and likely consequences of political change within the Soviet Union until it was too late.[5]

By the mid-1980s, Vietnam's Communist Party was facing a crisis of confidence and legitimacy as the long-heralded economic promise of the revolution failed to materialize. A notable expression of political dissent was the establishment in the southern part of the country in May 1986 of the Club of Resistance Fighters by disgruntled military veterans. The party's radical solution to economic distress was to jettison its centralist planning model in favor of a market-based alternative under the guidance of a new and reformist general secretary, Nguyen Van Linh. The decision of its Sixth National Congress in December 1986 to adopt a policy of *Doi Moi,* or renovation, was an attempt to cope with economic failure and its political consequences in an increasingly uncertain international environment influenced by the impact of Mikhail Gorbachev's "new political thinking." In Hanoi, there was almost certainly the initial expectation that economic reform would not only counter material decline and political alienation but also permit the sustained pursuit of external security goals in Indochina. Preserving the regime established in Cambodia by force of arms in January 1979 appeared to remain a prime objective.[6] But by the Party's Seventh National Congress, which convened in June 1991, it had become impossible to reconcile those two priorities, a judgment registered in a toned-down assertion of a special relationship with the lesser states of Indochina.[7] The overriding priority of *Doi Moi* was impeded nonetheless by the problem of Cambodia, which came between Vietnam and a desirable full access to the international economy, which its coalition adversaries could deny. Cambodia had once been represented as the key to Vietnam's national security, with its postinvasion condition described as irreversible. Vietnam's involvement there became instead a fundamental obstacle to economic recovery, which was the only way to overcome an underlying problem of regime security. A declared unconditional withdrawal of troops from Cambodia in September 1989 eased relations with adversaries but failed to bring about a transformation of Vietnam's international position. Hanoi's insistence on preserving the administration implanted in Phnom Penh and denying roles in a political settlement to the Khmer Rouge and the United Nations led to an inconclusive outcome at an international conference in Paris in July–August 1989. In the meantime, the United States remained obdurate in tying normalization to Vietnam's active cooperation in promoting a Cambodian settlement, while the Soviet Union became a rapidly declining asset. In the circumstances, Vietnam was obliged to make a critical choice between internal and external priorities in favor of the former.

That choice was expressed in Vietnam's grudging acquiescence to a settlement of the Cambodian conflict, mediated by the United Nations Security Council, that it had previously resisted.[8] The terms of that settlement included participation by the Khmer Rouge in the Supreme National Council, a symbol of Cambodia's sovereignty that had been devised to circumvent the problem of power sharing among the country's four warring factions by delegating authority to the United Nations. The world body would assume a quasi-administrative role during a transitional period before elections to choose a new government. Such provisions diminished the status of the administration in Phnom Penh that had been set up in Vietnam's interest. However much the terms of the Cambodian peace settlement were resented, economic necessity reinforced by international isolation determined Vietnam's political choice. The long-held strategic priority of a special relationship with the lesser states of Indochina had to be relinquished, at least in the case of Cambodia. That with Laos could be sustained only through looser fraternal ties because Vietnam could not fulfill the obligations of a patron.

With the end of the Cold War, Indochina has ceased to enjoy its former strategic coherence, which Vietnam inherited from France. Nonetheless, geopolitical considerations will oblige Vietnam to maintain a continuing interest in political change in both Cambodia and Laos, but with little early prospect of influencing it in either state. The more immediate practical priority of foreign policy has been to cope with a vulnerability rooted in problems of economic development.[9] Vietnam's leaders have been confronted with a choice similar to that faced by a bankrupt Indonesia in March 1966, when General Suharto assumed executive authority from President Sukarno. Indonesia chose the road of development based on a close engagement with the international capitalist economy but had the good fortune to attract the immediate support of the United States and Japan and the major international financial agencies. Indonesia was able also to take an early initiative in promoting a structure of regional reconciliation, the Association of Southeast Asian Nations (ASEAN), which could serve as a vehicle through which to influence the shape of regional order. Vietnam has not enjoyed such corresponding good fortune; it did not embark on market reforms with the full engagement in the international economy that Indonesia enjoyed, and it has still to assume membership in ASEAN. Moreover, Indonesia was not obliged to confront a major problem of national security. Vietnam, by contrast, has had to deal virtually unaided with an overshadowing and testy China, which, despite formal rapprochement, seems to want to settle an old political account in a way that leaves no doubt of the unequal nature of the bilateral relationship.

The fact of the matter is that Vietnam has ceased to count regionally in the way it once did. Foreign policy is dictated by the imperative of economic reform and employing its benefits to maintain a political monopoly for the Communist Party, which is seen as synonymous with upholding socialism and national independence. To that end, the Politburo in Hanoi has been obliged to behave in a pragmatic manner to the best of its limited ability. Regional acceptance has been encouraged by dissipation of an earlier fear of Vietnam and the specter of a reassertive China. The problem for Vietnam is that growing regional acceptance does not offer an opportunity to participate in a structure that might readily withstand China's blandishments. ASEAN has never aspired to become an alliance with a capability for projecting collective military power against a common adversary. Vietnam, with Laos, in acceding to ASEAN's Treaty of Amity and Cooperation in Southeast Asia in Manila in July 1992, took an important symbolic step toward regional rehabilitation and ultimate membership. But that act of accession did not presage an expansion of a security regime as an alternative source of external countervailing power. To that extent, Vietnam's sense of vulnerability has been mitigated but not overcome.

At issue for the government in Hanoi is how to manage changes in international relationships required by imperatives of political economy. Before discussing those problems of management, it is pertinent to comment in passing on the subject of foreign policy itself.

For any country, foreign policy is a matter of internal debate whose participants and terms depend on the nature of the political system. In the case of

Vietnam, that debate has never really reached the public domain. Moreover, Vietnam's Communist Party has enjoyed a remarkable record of concealing intramural contention and avoiding in the main the kind of political turbulence and purges that other fraternal parties have experienced. Analysis of alleged tension between pro-Soviet and pro-Chinese factions within the Politburo has never been particularly illuminating or rewarding, although it should not be discounted altogether.

During Vietnam's adjustment to the emerging post-Soviet era, there was certainly a debate about preserving the socialist model of economic development, which was won by reformers, who showed their strength with the political rehabilitation of Nguyen Van Linh in the office of Communist Party general secretary in December 1986. A more fundamental debate came to the fore at the turn of the next decade, reconciling economic reform with a forward policy in Indochina. One signal of the way in which that internal debate was resolved was the announcement at the Seventh National Congress in June 1991 of the resignation from office and from all party positions of Foreign Minister Nguyen Co Thach. Nguyen Co Thach had enjoyed a reputation as a Sinophobe, and his removal was interpreted as a necessary concession to Beijing in the interest of rapprochement on terms that could no longer be denied because of Vietnam's intrinsic vulnerability.

China's intentions have remained a matter of concern, but for the time being, vigorous debate on that dimension of foreign policy seems to have become muted. Vietnam's leaders have been obliged to come to terms with living under China's intimidating shadow without access to their accustomed countervailing power. A mitigating factor has been the assurance that the ruling party in Beijing has an undoubted interest in perpetuating a socialist regime in Hanoi, given the acute difficulties faced by its remaining fraternal partners in Pyongyang and Havana. Consequently, debate in Vietnam has been directed toward the internal political consequences of foreign economic policy. It expresses itself over the management of attendant external influences on domestic life, with concern registered in a strengthening of the state's internal security apparatus.

Managing Changing Relationships

China

Fundamental to Vietnam's predicament in foreign policy has been its strained relationship with a neighboring and overshadowing China, which since the end of 1978 has turned on the issue of Cambodia. That tormented country served as the arena of indirect conflict between former allies over the balance of power in Indochina. China was prominent among Vietnam's adversaries in insisting that its occupation be liquidated and also that its political legacy be expunged. Virtually from the outset, Vietnam's policy toward Cambodia had been to offer concessions on military withdrawal in return for being able to consolidate the position of the government that it had brought into the country almost literally in the saddlebags of its army. Its effective military withdrawal from Cambodia by the end of September 1989 failed to satisfy its Chinese adversaries. They seemed determined then that the government in Phnom Penh should be dismantled and that the Khmer Rouge should become a legitimate party to a political settlement.

The eventual political settlement to the Cambodian conflict, which was endorsed by an international conference that reconvened in Paris in October 1991, involved major concessions by Vietnam, but not a total abdication of its position. Innate weakness obliged it to tolerate the Khmer Rouge as a member of the symbolically sovereign Supreme National Council and the intervening quasi-administrative role of the United Nations Transitional Authority in Cambodia, or UNTAC, which was empowered to conduct general elections to determine the political future of the country. The incumbent government in Phnom Penh, albeit diminished in status, remained in place after UNTAC began its work in March 1992 without attracting Chinese protest. Indeed, UNTAC's failure to exercise the measure of supervision and control of key ministries required by its mandate provoked Khmer Rouge anger but not China's public displeasure.

China's reaction to the invasion of Cambodia had been to view Vietnam as a willing proxy of a menacing Soviet Union. Its limited but punitive military intervention in Vietnam in February 1979 was intended to convey a geopolitical message, which Vietnam has been obliged to take to heart in the post-Soviet era. Sino-Soviet rapprochement and the withdrawal of Soviet support from Vietnam brought about a revision of China's earlier view of the country as an oriental Cuba. In addition, the political distance from Vietnam demonstrated by the government in Phnom Penh and its deference to Prince, now King, Norodom Sihanouk further reduced Chinese concerns about the balance of power in Indochina. In mid-October 1991, just before the International Conference on Cambodia in Paris, the ruling Kampuchean People's Revolutionary Party convened an extraordinary congress, without participation by fraternal delegates, at which its name was changed to that of the Cambodian People's Party in apparent repudiation of its once-declared lineal descent from the ruling party in Hanoi. In fact, a practical compromise appeared to be accepted in Beijing whereby Vietnam relinquished control over Cambodia, while its implanted administration continued in place, with the Khmer Rouge in a legitimate but marginal role, all subject to United Nations supervision in the transitional period before national elections. The subsequent repudiation of those elections in May 1993 by the Khmer Rouge failed to attract China's support. China's government endorsed the political outcome of the election, a coalition of all Cambodian parties except the Khmer Rouge.

Whatever the misgivings of the government in Hanoi, the Paris settlement of October 1991 removed the burning issue of Cambodia from Sino-Vietnamese relations. A process of rapprochement set in train in the late 1980s appeared to culminate on November 10, 1991, with a meeting of party and state leaders in Beijing, at which agreements on trade and border cooperation were signed.[10] The meeting was represented as a high-level one rather than as a party-to-party occasion, which was symptomatic of an underlying coolness in the new relationship. Despite the apparent convergence of the interests of the two regimes, shocked by the course of events in Eastern Europe and determined to reconcile market economics with authoritarian politics, an underlying tension has remained.[11]

Problems in the relationship have arisen in acute form over territorial and maritime jurisdiction in the South China Sea. Vietnam had concealed its differences with China over competing claims to jurisdiction until after its unification, by which time China had assumed total control over the contested Paracel Islands.[12] Indeed, in 1958, Pham Van Dong, as prime minister of the Democratic Republic of Vietnam, had communicated his government's endorsement of all of China's territorial claims in the South China Sea. Vietnam's reversal of position in 1976 in contesting jurisdiction provoked strong comment in Beijing. China began to challenge Vietnam's measure of control over islands in the Spratly Archipelago in early 1988—significantly, without arousing any active Soviet response—while Vietnam's diplomatic protests fell on deaf ears.[13]

In February 1992, the Standing Committee of China's National People's Congress adopted a new law on territorial waters and their contiguous areas that reasserted long-standing claims to maritime jurisdiction in the South China Sea and beyond.[14] This maritime initiative had implications for a number of regional states in dispute with China. However, in reasserting its claims, China has acted with a measure of discrimination directed against Vietnam. Its government has taken evident care to avoid direct confrontation with Brunei, Malaysia, and the Philippines, all of which have claims to some of the Spratly Islands. The promulgation of the new maritime law was followed by the occupation of an additional reef in the Spratly Archipelago, but territories claimed by Brunei, Malaysia and the Philippines were not affected. In addition, China has appeared to be attempting to exploit American-Vietnamese alienation. In May 1992, the Chinese authorities entered into a contract with the Denver-based Crestone Energy Corporation to explore for oil and natural gas in 25,000 square kilometers of what the Vietnamese claim is the Tu Chinh bank on the country's continental shelf, but which the Chinese maintain is part of the maritime domain of the Spratly chain. A Crestone spokesman was reported as saying that China had promised the use of naval power to protect the offshore exploration.[15] China pointedly chose to conclude the agreement with Crestone during a visit to Beijing by the former general secretary of Vietnam's Communist Party, Nguyen Van Linh. It also took place in the presence of an American diplomat, albeit one of junior status.

Li Peng paid a visit to Vietnam at the end of November 1992, the first by a Chinese prime minister since that by Zhou Enlai in 1971. He made a series of conciliatory statements, stressing that both countries were engaged in socialist construction and that China would neither seek to fill any so-called regional vacuum nor seek to impose hegemony.[16] Despite the positive tone that Li Peng conveyed, the two governments were unable to reconcile any of their territorial differences. In March 1993, Nguyen Dy Nien, Vietnam's deputy foreign minister, revealed a continuing absence of progress over territorial differences despite the onset of negotiations between expert officials the previous October.[17] An agreement on basic principles for "the settlement of border territory issues" was concluded in October 1993, followed in November by the first visit to China by a Vietnamese head of state since that by Ho Chi Minh in 1959. However, President Le Duc Anh and his counterpart Jiang Zemin failed to signal any progress concerning their governments' competing claims to sovereignty. A return visit to Vietnam by President Jiang Zemin in November 1994 produced an agreement to set up a joint expert group to deal with rival claims to the Spratly Islands—without any indication of compromise on either side.

A Vietnam obliged to concentrate on economic reform has not been in any position to engage in military confrontation over territorial differences with a China that enjoys overwhelming advantages. Vietnam's military machine has fallen into disrepair and lacks in particular a naval and air force capability able to match that of China, which has begun to purchase SU-27 long-range jet fighters from Russia for probable deployment in the South China Sea from their base on Hainan Island and enhanced its naval and amphibious capability.[18] Further potential for military deployment into the South China Sea was indicated with the publication by *Yomiuri Shimbun* in August 1993 of a satellite photograph showing a Chinese airfield on Woody Island, the largest territory in the disputed Paracels group.[19]

Vietnam's armed forces leadership has been disinclined to make public China's acts of assertiveness in the South China Sea, preferring to engage in private communication through military attachés' offices. The foreign ministry in Hanoi has prevailed in the interbureaucratic squabble and has not allowed the country's case to go by default, despite its inability to advance it in any material sense. For example, in April 1993, the anniversary of national liberation was marked by Vice Premier Tran Duc Luong paying a well-publicized visit to the Spratly Islands and by a reassertion of sovereignty over both the Spratly and Paracel groups. In April 1994, Vietnam signed contracts with a consortium of American and Japanese companies led by Mobil for exploration in an adjoining westerly field within the area of China's claim to the *Tu Chinh* bank.

Contention over maritime jurisdiction has been only the most prominent of a number of issues that are symptomatic of the underlying tension in the Sino-Vietnamese relationship despite the formal reestablishment of party-to-party ties. Vietnam has been obliged to suffer Chinese interference in maritime traffic and oil drilling operations, consoling itself with the knowledge that Beijing is not out to destroy the regime in Hanoi, but only to demonstrate that regime's subordinate position. China has also intervened to limit Vietnam's burgeoning relationship with Taiwan by limiting the right of Taipei's flag carrier to fly to major cities. It has not, however, sought to constrain the scale of Taiwan investment.

China intimidates but also tolerates Vietnam. In the changed circumstances after the end of the Cold War, it would not be in China's interest to encourage the collapse of Vietnamese communist power into an Eastern European–like chaos. It suffices for the lesson of February 1979 to have been conspicuously learned—namely, that whereas France, Japan, the United States, and most recently the Soviet Union have been obliged to retreat back across the seas, China and Vietnam march together in perpetuity. On his assumption of the office of president of Vietnam in September 1992, General Le Duc Anh, a senior Politburo member, made a point of stressing publicly his government's interest in peaceful and friendly relations with China. He pointed out, "We need peaceful and friendly coexistence very much."[20] The problem for Vietnam is that it is not in a position to determine the terms of such peaceful and friendly coexistence. The fact that coexistence was used to describe the appropriate relationship is an indication of the continuing vulnerability of Vietnam in the post-Soviet era and the mixed quality of the postrapprochement ties with China. That coexistence has developed a working quality, however, is indicated by a series of agreements on economic and scientific cooperation, by a progressive opening of border crossings, and by China's being allowed to establish a consulate in Ho Chi Minh City.

The United States and Japan

Miscalculation by Vietnam in managing the relationship with the United States preceded its miscalculation over the invasion of Cambodia, which had the effect of compounding the difficulties. Vietnam has long been frustrated in its attempts to develop that relationship so as to further its economic and security interests. It has failed, above all, to communicate the conviction that it would not be to the United States' advantage in the post–Cold War era for Vietnam to remain a weak state. American reluctance to respond swiftly to Vietnamese entreaties had a bearing on the pace of rapprochement with Japan.

President Nixon had promised to heal the wounds of war after the Vietnam Peace Agreement was concluded in Paris in January 1973. However genuine his commitment, the Vietnamese government labored under a false sense of expectations in the wake of the violent unification of the country in April 1975. They actively sought reparations as a condition for normalization, which Congress would never have countenanced. By the time this condition was withdrawn, in the context of a developing second Cold War, the opportunity for an early establishment of diplomatic relations had been missed. For the Carter administration, faced with a Soviet Union in apparent violation of its obligations under détente, China offered itself as a natural strategic partner. No advantage was perceived in alienating the Chinese government through a diplomatic opening to Vietnam. Under the circumstances, only the Soviet Union could serve as a source of external countervailing power for Vietnam against a hostile China.

The Soviet Union assumed this role by entering into a treaty commitment that only served to reinforce America's hostility, especially with the invasion of Cambodia, which appeared to pose a threat to the security of Thailand. In consequence, the United States became an indirect party to reviving the notorious Khmer Rouge as a way of coercing Vietnam to liquidate its occupation and eradicate its political legacy. Under the Reagan administration, those aims were augmented by the requirement that Vietnam provide a full accounting of American servicemen missing in action during the Vietnam War. This persisting issue in American domestic politics became the fundamental obstacle to a new relationship between Washington and Hanoi. It has been pointed out that normalization of U.S.–Vietnam relations "is misleading both as a characterization of the current state of the evolving relationship and its likely status for the foreseeable future" because Vietnam "is a term that does not simply identify a sovereign state in the international system but is a label for a traumatic episode in the national experience."[21]

The United States was a party to the coalition strategy of attrition, which was intended to place unbearable strain on the society and government of Vietnam in order to resolve the Cambodian conflict. Its main impact was demonstrated through sustaining a trade and investment embargo and ensuring that Vietnam was denied access to the resources of international financial institutions. As the radical revision of Soviet foreign policy under Mikhail Gorbachev began to detach the Cambodian conflict from major power rivalries, the United States was slow to adjust its attitude toward Vietnam. The Bush administration appeared conscious of the political embarrassment that would be the consequence of the Khmer Rouge's resuming power. But it refused to contemplate accepting the Vietnamese-imposed government in Phnom Penh as a less objectionable alternative. For example, at a meeting in Brunei with ASEAN's foreign ministers in July 1989, Secretary of State James Baker argued that there was "an alternative to the teeth of the Khmer Rouge and the jaws of foreign domination." Vietnam's withdrawal of its main force units from Cambodia in September 1989 and the attendant prospect of Khmer Rouge advantage prompted only a modification of policy.

In July 1990, James Baker announced his government's willingness to enter into a dialogue with Vietnam over Cambodia, which began the following month at the United Nations in New York. The Vietnamese responded with increased cooperation in searching for remains of Americans missing in action. In January 1991, the United States was given permission to open an MIA office in Hanoi, which constituted the first official, albeit temporary, representation of any kind between the United States and the Socialist Republic of Vietnam. Greater assistance in the search for the missing in action and their remains did not induce any fundamental change in the relationship, however, to the intense frustration of the government in Hanoi. The continuity of American policy was sustained even though the earlier strategic interest in denying Vietnam's dominance in Indochina had diminished with Washington's radically revised relationship with the Soviet Union and the disappearance of any military threat to Thailand.

In April 1991, Assistant Secretary of State for East Asian Affairs Richard Solomon set out a so-called road map for normalization of relations that included a list of preconditions for Vietnam to fulfill. Apart from a full accounting for the missing in action, the Vietnamese were required to play a role in ensuring the implementation of the United Nations peace plan for Cambodia, which had been promulgated in framework form in August 1990. Full normalization could take place only after United Nations–supervised elections had been held and a new National Assembly had convened in Phnom Penh.[22] The United States had thus placed responsibility for the settlement of the Cambodian conflict on Vietnam as the price of normalization. Vietnam had in vain sought normalization as a step toward such a settlement but was not in a position to dictate terms.

The formal settlement of the Cambodian conflict in October 1991, followed closely by the end of the Soviet era, did not lead to any change in the American demands. President Bush renewed the trade and investment embargo the following September. By that time, electoral considerations were dictating his priorities, especially as the missing in action issue had demonstrated a remarkable resilience in American domestic politics. For Vietnam, there was an appalling irony in coping with the American position, which it appeared unable to modify to any significant extent. The United States had sought successfully to break the Vietnamese hold on Cambodia and yet also insisted that Vietnam be an active party to the implementation of the United Nations peace plan after its hold had been conspicuously broken. Underlying the fractured relationship was the issue of the missing in action. The Bush administration had not been convinced that its counterpart in Hanoi was being fully cooperative over the matter, and this was seemingly confirmed in October 1992 when an archive of Vietnamese photographs of Americans killed in action and other identifying artifacts were made available to the Department of Defense. Although welcomed in Washington, the initiative was interpreted as an indication of Hanoi's concern that because George Bush's electoral opponent Bill Clinton appeared to be vulnerable politically over Vietnam, he would be disinclined to move rapidly on normalization.[23] In fact, the pace of normalization was not affected. During the election campaign, Bill Clinton let it be known that the missing in action issue was the major stumbling block to improved ties. Shortly after his victory in November 1992, in a Veterans' Day speech in Little Rock, he pledged to seek a "final and full" accounting of missing or imprisoned servicemen from the Vietnam War.

In December 1992, shortly before giving up office, President Bush modified the terms of the trade and investment embargo. American companies with interests in Vietnam were permitted to enter into so-called contingency contracts that would take effect after the embargo had been lifted. To this end, they were free to open offices, to hire staff, and to engage in marketing and feasibility studies. Companies such as the Bank of America and General Electric took early advantage of this relaxation in the terms of the embargo, but they were nonetheless constrained from engaging in actual business activity by the continuing injunction. Just before President Clinton took office, the political climate for normalization improved to a degree when a Senate committee concluded a fifteen-month investigation into the fate of American servicemen missing in action in Indochina. It reported that there was no definitive evidence to prove allegations that American military personnel had been detained in Vietnam and Laos after withdrawal in 1973. It also applauded the very substantial strides toward full cooperation in the continuing search for the remains of servicemen missing in action made by the Vietnamese government.

The cautiousness of the Clinton administration in approaching the issue of normalization of relations with Vietnam was indicated in testimony given in April 1993 by incoming Assistant Secretary of State for East Asian and Pacific Affairs Winston Lord at his confirmation hearing before the Subcommittee on East Asia–Pacific of the Senate Foreign Relations Committee. In a statement remarkable for indicating a change of policy on appropriate structures for regional security, Winston Lord stressed that a major goal of American policy was still to obtain the fullest possible accounting of the missing in action as relations with Vietnam were normalized.[24] Moreover, the domestic political sensitivity of the issue was demonstrated soon afterward when a Russian-language translation of a purported report to a meeting of Vietnam's Politburo in September 1972 was unearthed in the archives of the Communist Party in Moscow. It suggested that Hanoi had concealed several hundred prisoners. The news provoked the comment from Zbigniew Brzezinski, former national security adviser to President Carter, that "the great likelihood is that the Vietnamese took hundreds of American officers out and shot them in cold blood, in a massacre like the one in the Katyn Woods."[25] Although General John Vessey, in his role as the president's special envoy to Vietnam on the missing in action question, cast doubt on the reliability of the content of the document after a visit to Hanoi, its appearance and the domestic reaction was symptomatic of the problem faced by President Clinton in moving speedily on normalization.

The episode was responsible for delaying a resumption of lending to Vietnam by the International Monetary Fund. In July 1993, however, President Clinton found it opportune to withdraw America's objections to multilateral lending by international financial institutions. His statement was qualified by the comment that the overriding purpose of American policy toward Vietnam was further progress on prisoners and the missing in action. The same month, Winston Lord led a delegation to Hanoi, where he reached agreement on establishing a quasi-diplomatic office, also justified in terms of facilitating the search for servicemen missing in action. A policy of modifying rather than removing sanctions was sustained when President Clinton renewed the embargo in September but permitted American companies to engage in projects in Vietnam financed by multilateral spending.

A president who was on record as having opposed American policy during the Vietnam War and who was known to have avoided military service was not in a position to offend the powerful MIA lobby. The political climate changed, however, in January 1994, when the Senate passed a nonbinding resolution urging that economic sanctions against Vietnam be lifted. President Clinton announced the lifting of those sanctions on February 3 but left open the issue of diplomatic relations, which was tied still to the MIAs. Progress toward that end was indicated in May 1994 when Vietnam and the United States agreed to set up liaison offices in their respective capitals.

From the perspective of the government in Hanoi, the establishment of normal relations with the United States has long been regarded as important for both economic and security reasons. Despite a strong suspicion that American policy had a punitive purpose, the government in Hanoi has been philosophical about the delay in full recognition in the knowledge that it was obliged to wait for Washington to find a politically appropriate time.[26] Moreover, the widening scope of Vietnam's international relationships meant that American political diffidence became a decreasing impediment to a strategy of economic reform. It is a matter of some irony that Vietnam has come to share with its former adversaries over Cambodia within ASEAN a common interest in the continuing engagement of the United States in regional security matters, especially since U.S. withdrawal from military bases in the Philippines was completed in November 1992. Indeed, the United States and Vietnam have become partners in an initiative in multilateral security dialogue in East Asia inspired by ASEAN in July 1993. The problem for Vietnam is that enthusiasm in Hanoi for a new relationship is matched in the United States by only a limited business, political, and academic constituency. And irrespective of a residual bitterness arising from the circumstances of America's ignominious withdrawal from Vietnam, which explains in part the resilience of the missing in action issue, the strategic interest of the United States in Vietnam has diminished considerably in the post-Soviet era. To that extent, an ultimate normalization of relations will not on its own address the underlying problem of vulnerability that confronts the government in Hanoi. That would also require America's active encouragement of and participation in a regional order in which Vietnam was made to feel a participating member.

Until the election of President Clinton, Japan had been constrained by American policy from taking an independent initiative toward Vietnam. Japanese private investors had indicated a strong interest but had been reluctant to make any wholehearted commitments until they were assured of official approval. The Japanese government had been a party to the United States' economic embargo and had been unwilling for some time to move ahead of the United States in economic relations with Hanoi. After the Paris agreement on Cambodia in October 1991, Japan began a limited program of economic assistance in support of infrastructural repair, but not the kind of substantial contribution to development sought by Vietnam. Although Japan then assumed a major responsibility for financing United Nations peacekeeping in Cambodia and took the unprecedented step of dispatching troops to participate in that undertaking, its government seemed content to await a signal from the United States before making a major economic commitment to Vietnam.

For the government in Hanoi, there did not seem any alternative but to wait patiently for Washington to give that signal, while seeking to reschedule former South Vietnam's outstanding debts to Japan in an attempt to demonstrate economic good faith. Finally, faced with the compelling economic opportunity presented by a reformist Vietnam, Tokyo's patience gave out. In early November 1992, after the presidential elections in the United States, its government ended fourteen years of suspension of economic aid with a commodity loan of U.S. $370 million for financing public works. Japanese private investment, which had lagged in seventh place with around U.S. $160 million committed, was given the green light and rose considerably, with Japan soon overtaking Singapore as Vietnam's largest trading partner.[27] In March 1993, Vo Van Kiet paid the first visit to Tokyo by a Vietnamese prime minister in two decades. Japan's Prime Minister Kiichi Miyazawa used the occasion to announce the resumption of loans for infrastructural projects and indicated a willingness to use his government's influence with the World Bank and the Asian Development Bank on Vietnam's behalf. Japan subsequently joined with France and others to pay off Vietnam's arrears to the International Monetary Fund so that it could qualify for new loans. Japan's lead, the establishment of diplomatic relations with South Korea, and the visit of President Mitterrand of France to Hanoi in February 1993 served to generate a growing international business interest, which reinforced the view that America's embargo had become increasingly anomalous. When Prime Minister Tomiichi Murayama returned Vo Van Kiet's visit in August 1994, he announced a new grant in aid of U.S. $73 million.

It should be appreciated that any satisfaction in Hanoi over Japan's initiative has not been matched, so far, by any strong expectation of or interest in Japan as a source of countervailing power for security against China. The Japan card, crudely put, would not appear to be in mind. Vietnam's interest in Japan would seem to be solely as a material partner that can contribute to economic development and in that way help to underpin the country's independence. Japan seems to be viewed with mixed feelings. The author Neil Sheehan has observed, for example, that the Japanese are regarded with suspicion, pointing out that "the real root of the animosity seemed to lie in a perception of Japan as a new China threatening Vietnam's independence with economic power."[28] Vietnamese expectations remain directed, ironically, at the United States. Sheehan maintains that "with the United States no longer a threat, the Vietnamese see an American diplomatic and business presence as a political counterpoise to China and an economic counterpoise to Japan."[29] There could be no better example of pragmatic classical balance-of-power calculation.

Russia

The outcome of the abortive coup in Moscow in August 1991 was traumatic and salutary for the ruling party in Hanoi. The speed with which the Communist

Party of the Soviet Union was banned and then the Soviet Union itself was dissolved was breathtaking, and the problem of adjustment cannot be exaggerated. In the wake of the disappearance of the Soviet Union, the relationship between Hanoi and Moscow can only be described as residual and not helped by an outstanding debt of U.S. $14 billion. The sudden loss of around U.S. $1 billion a year in nonmilitary aid and subsidies was quite devastating, while trade with former Soviet bloc countries, already on a hard currency basis, slumped considerably. Although there is still a vestigial Russian naval presence in Cam Ranh Bay, it has long ceased to have any relevance for Vietnam's security. A far more significant factor bearing on the relationship has been the scale of Russian arms sales to China, which has caused concern throughout Southeast Asia. The residual relationship has been maintained, nonetheless. For example, Deputy Prime Minister Yuriy Yarov visited Hanoi in May 1993 for a second meeting of the joint commission on economic, commercial, scientific, and technical cooperation. He promised continued support for the Hoa Binh hydroelectric project and for joint ventures in oil and gas.

An additional unprecedented problem for the government in Hanoi has been posed by the change of political identity in Moscow. In July 1992, much to the annoyance and frustration of the ruling party in Hanoi, an independent short-wave radio station in Moscow began broadcasting to listeners in Vietnam the virtues of democracy and the names of political prisoners. Demands that Radio Irina, as the station was known because of its Vietnamese-speaking announcer Irina Zisman, be closed down in the interest of good relations were met with the response that Russian law did not permit it.[30] This episode is symptomatic of the transformation of ties, which in turn points up Vietnam's underlying vulnerability. The furor that arose in early 1993 over the unearthing in the archives of the Communist Party of a document by Lt. Gen. Tran Van Dang about American prisoners generated a new tension in the residual relationship. The suspension of broadcasts by Radio Irina in June may have been an act of appeasement, but the station was heard subsequently on a different frequency under the call sign of Radio Hope. Relations between Hanoi and Moscow were restored in June 1994 when Vo Van Kiet signed a friendship treaty with his Russian counterpart, Viktor Chernomyrdin, replacing that signed between Vietnam and the Soviet Union in 1978. The new treaty and related cooperation agreements enabled continued Russian naval access to Cam Ranh Bay.

In Hanoi, Vietnam under communist rule had always been represented proudly as an outpost of a wider socialist commonwealth from which both material and ideological sustenance had been drawn. For Vietnam, the post-Soviet era has required a profound adjustment to a fundamentally different environment. Concrete evidence of that adjustment has been Vietnam's acquiescence to the Paris agreement on Cambodia on terms set by its adversaries in coalition and its engagement in a totally new structure of external relationships.

Association of Southeast Asian Nations

Miscalculation has also been the hallmark of Vietnam's dealings with ASEAN, which, on its formation in August 1967, was perceived and represented in Hanoi as an insidious vehicle for the prosecution of American interests. After reunification, Vietnam challenged the Association's Zone of Peace prescription for regional order and was successful in excluding it from the final communiqué of the Non-Aligned summit in Colombo in August 1976. It was also disdainful of acceding to the Treaty of Amity and Cooperation concluded by the ASEAN heads of government at their first summit in Bali the previous February. As a code of conduct for regional relations, the treaty, made open to all countries in Southeast Asia, was intended as a political bridge to the revolutionary states of Indochina. At the time, however, Vietnam was in a triumphalist mood and made public its interest in replacing ASEAN with a more appropriate regional body. For example, at the end of 1977, Prime Minister Pham Van Dong was asked, "What kind of relations are you going to establish with ASEAN?" He replied, "The policy of setting up such military blocs as ASEAN in Southeast Asia has failed and passed forever. The relationship of friendship and cooperation among countries of this region must be established on a new basis, in a new spirit."[31]

During the course of the Cambodian conflict, ASEAN assumed a vigorous diplomatic role in challenging Vietnam's occupation, especially within the United Nations. That role was not assumed without intramural difficulty because of Indonesia's concern, in particular, that it had been drawn into a politically unhygienic coalition with China against a natural security partner with whom it had shared the experience of confronting colonialism. Vietnam sought to play on such common feeling to undermine the united front against it. In the late 1980s, Indonesia was persuaded to sponsor a regional structure of negotiations that excluded China in order to overcome the diplomatic impasse over Cambodia. The initiative came to nothing, and the United Nations Security Council assumed the prime role in promoting a political settlement of the Cambodian conflict to which all ASEAN states were obliged to defer. The evident diplomatic marginality of the association did not diminish Vietnam's interest in cultivating a new relationship with it as part of an attempt to establish countervailing international ties to compensate for the loss of Soviet patronage and to cope with China's intimidation.

Individual members of ASEAN had begun to soften their attitudes to Vietnam in the late 1980s, especially after Thailand's Prime Minister Chatichai Choonhavan had declared his intention, on taking office in August 1988, of turning Indochina from a battlefield into a trading market. Indonesia had long adopted an accommodating attitude toward Vietnam, and President Suharto visited Hanoi in November 1990, well in advance of the Cambodian settlement in Paris but significantly after his first visit to China. Shortly after that settlement in October 1991, Vietnam's prime minister, Vo Van Kiet, embarked on a tour of

Indonesia, Singapore, and Thailand. Thailand and Singapore had been the most hard-line among ASEAN states in insisting that Vietnam evacuate Cambodia and play a constructive role in helping to remove the political legacy of its invasion. The willingness of the three governments to permit the first visit of a Vietnamese prime minister since the invasion of Cambodia represented a diplomatic break-through in exploring an opportunity to develop countervailing relationships to that reestablished on sufferance with China. Significantly, the tour of the three ASEAN states was undertaken just before Vo Van Kiet's first visit to Beijing as prime minister. Visits by Vo Van Kiet to the other three member states of ASEAN took place during February 1992. Acts of reciprocation included visits by Thailand's Prime Minister Anand Panyarachun in January 1992 and by Malaysia's Prime Minister Dr. Mahathir Mohamad in the following April. An even more important indication of the fundamental change in the tone of rela-tionships with ASEAN states was the willingness of Singapore's senior minister and former prime minister, Lee Kuan Yew, to travel to Hanoi and Ho Chi Minh City in April 1992 to advise on economic management.[32] At the meeting of ASEAN's foreign ministers in July 1994 in Bangkok, it was agreed to admit Vietnam to membership of the association at their next annual meeting in Brunei in July 1995.

A new relationship with ASEAN was important to Vietnam in part because of the opportunity it provided for attracting trade and investment. The government in Hanoi had become very conscious of the remarkable economic progress of most of ASEAN'S members, in contrast to Vietnam's backwardness. There was an evident urgency to make up for lost time as well as to demonstrate Vietnam's new priorities to the United States and Japan through regional economic cooperation. One import-ant indication of the way in which the relationship with individual ASEAN states has been transformed has been the wide-scale expansion of air services between Hanoi, Ho Chi Minh City, and regional capitals. In the main, ASEAN has given cautious encouragement to Vietnam since the conclusion of the Cambodian settlement in October 1991. For example, in January 1992, its heads of government meeting in Singapore granted the request of Vietnam and Laos to accede to the Treaty of Amity and Cooperation, which they had derided some sixteen years before. In July 1992, formal accession took place in Manila at the annual conference of the ASEAN foreign ministers, which gave both Vietnam and Laos observer status at such annual occasions. Full membership in ASEAN would seem to be only a matter of time, with its timing affected in part by Vietnam's ability to come to terms with the corporate culture of the association. In the meantime, bilateral links between Vietnam and members of the association have been strengthening, especially through trade and investment. For example, Singapore, whose former foreign minister Wong Kan Seng visited Hanoi in October 1992, had been the country's largest trading partner, with an annual exchange of goods valued at more than U.S. $1 billion until it was overtaken by Japan in 1993. It opened a consulate in Ho Chi Minh City shortly after establishing an embassy in Hanoi.

Vietnam's presence in Manila in July 1992 with its diplomatic begging bowl extended is a matter of some historical irony in the light of its past derision of ASEAN. Nonetheless, Hanoi's expectations for its new relationship with the association—in terms of access to an effective source of regional countervailing power—cannot be high. ASEAN has never aspired to the status of an alliance; its members have never shared a common strategic perspective, especially toward China. Its role as a security organization has always been confined to conflict avoidance and management among member governments and to corporate diplomatic initiatives beyond its walls. In Manila, in July 1992, its foreign ministers issued a declaration on the South China Sea that called on contending claimants to settle their disputes peacefully. That declaration met with Vietnam's evident approval and some reserve on China's part, but, whatever its merits, it did not indicate the emergence of a new security regime from which Vietnam could draw major comfort. That said, the government in Hanoi has joined, with keen interest, in ASEAN's attempt, with conspicuous Japanese and American involvement, to explore the prospect of a wider multilateral structure of security dialogue to underpin a post–Cold War regional order. In July 1993 in Singapore, Foreign Minister Nguyen Manh Cam participated for a second time as an observer at the annual meeting of the ASEAN foreign ministers. More important, he attended the concurrent inaugural dinner meeting of an eighteen-member embryonic multilateral Asian security dialogue named the ASEAN Regional Forum (ARF) as well as its first working session in Bangkok in July 1994.

Vietnam's newfound relationship with ASEAN undoubtedly makes a contribution to regional order.[33] At issue is the extent to which such access helps Vietnam to overcome its condition of vulnerability. The answer must be: only up to a point, to the extent that China, in particular, exercises restraint because of its interest in cultivating the economically flourishing states of Southeast Asia. Special relationships within ASEAN, for example, with Indonesia and Malaysia, based on a corresponding regional outlook can only have limited relevance to Vietnam's major problems because those states can play only a limited role on their own. Moreover, Vietnam is engaged in disputes with both of them over maritime jurisdiction in the South China Sea. An agreement was signed with Malaysia in June 1993 on joint exploration and exploitation in disputed waters in their continental shelves, but it took many years to negotiate. Differences with Indonesia over the continental shelf have still to be resolved.

The End of Indochina

In managing new relationships, Vietnam's most difficult adjustment has been coming to terms with the end of Indochina as a coherent strategic concept, which it was once able to impose on the rest of the region. The view of Indochina as a single theater was forged in the heat of national liberation struggle and then expressed after unification in 1975 in the concept of a special relationship. That special relationship was registered in treaties of Friendship and Cooperation with Laos in July 1977 and of Peace, Friendship, and Cooperation with Cambodia in February 1979. In the case of Cambodia, it was asserted and reiterated after Vietnam's invasion and occupation that the situation there was irreversible. This position proved to be untenable, as demonstrated by the terms of the Paris agreement of October 1991, which Vietnam had no alternative but to endorse. Whereas Vietnam was once in a position to define its Indochinese strategic domain, that capability no longer exists. The concept of Indochina has lost the coherence that it enjoyed during the Cold War, now that Vietnam is unable to reach out across common borders. The outcome of the May 1993 elections held in Cambodia under UNTAC's auspices has been welcomed to the extent that the coalition government has included the former ruling party in Phnom Penh and has excluded the Khmer Rouge. The truth of the matter, however, is that Cambodia has been prized from Vietnam's grasp, and a deep tension based on cultural differences and historical experience is expected to shape an uncertain future relationship. Indeed, the government in Hanoi has been obliged to suffer Khmer Rouge killings of Vietnamese settlers across a common border in the knowledge that renewed intervention would jeopardize the whole course of national policy. It is of significance that when Vietnam's prime minister, Do Muoi, received the president of Cambodia's National Assembly, Chea Sim, in March 1994, he paid tribute to "the traditional friendly and neighborly relations between the two peoples," discarding past rhetoric.

In the case of Laos, the fraternal relationship forged in the interest of security and ideology still exists, but without its former intensity. Vietnamese troops, which had been deployed there since the end of the Pacific War, were withdrawn in 1988, and the government in Vientiane has begun actively to explore alternative relationships, while claiming legitimacy for its monopoly of power on the same ideological basis as its counterpart in Hanoi. Laos has followed the example of Vietnam in economic reform but cannot look to it for substantial material support. Vietnam has been obliged to tolerate Laos's development of particular relationships with Thailand and China because it can no longer play the role of political patron to a neighboring country that once seemed little more than one of its provinces. Vietnam once defined its security in terms of political homogeneity within Indochina. It is no longer in a position to do this and will have to be content with governments in Phnom Penh and Vientiane that seek to fashion their own political identities.

Overcoming Vulnerability

Vietnam has emerged quite rapidly from a virtual pariah condition since the international resolution of the Cambodian conflict. That conflict brought to a head in particular a deterioration in relations between Vietnam and China, which had been precipitated by Hanoi's sense of betrayal at the nature and terms of

Sino-American rapprochement in the early 1970s. The erstwhile Sino-Vietnamese alliance had been forged out of expediency in order to cope with a common threat from the United States. As such, it constituted a deviation from a historical pattern. Vietnam's prevailing experience has been one of resistance to and struggle with a one-time suzerain power whose Confucian culture it shared but against which it had long defined its national identity. Indeed, a formal and grudging relationship of deference to China had been broken only with the intervention of French colonialism in the latter part of the nineteenth century. Ho Chi Minh expressed authentic national priorities when, after the end of the Pacific War, he indicated his preference for the return of the French as a less objectionable alternative to the continued presence north of the sixteenth parallel of the rapacious army of General Chiang Kai-shek, which had been charged with taking the surrender of occupying Japanese forces. The antagonism with China, which came to a head over Cambodia and which was marked by a clash of arms, returned the relationship to one characteristic of past centuries. Moreover, during that conflict, China was able to exploit a conjunction of global and regional interests to Vietnam's disadvantage, which became acute when countervailing Soviet patronage was lost.

In the post-Soviet era, Vietnam no longer faces the problem of international isolation because of its disengagement from conflict in Cambodia. The relationship with China remains the most problematic, however, because of the intrinsic mistrust and inequality that distinguishes it and the two countries' immutable close proximity. At the end of the 1970s, China embarked with success on a program of economic modernization, which has been sustained through close engagement with the international economy, despite the bloodletting in Tiananmen Square in June 1989. Moreover, the end of the Cold War, with its evident effect on America's strategic perspective and deployments in East Asia, and the breakup of the Soviet Union have permitted the People's Republic a measure of latitude in regional affairs that is quite unprecedented since its establishment in 1949. Success in economic modernization has enabled China to embark on a military buildup that has enhanced its potential for force projection beyond its mainland into the South China Sea.[34] That buildup, however, justified in terms of replacing aging equipment, has been taking place at a time when China is not subject to any apparent external threat. Vietnam, in contrast, is not capable of matching China's growing military strength. Its budget cannot provide for corresponding modernization, let alone adequate provision for spare parts for its antiquated Soviet equipment. Opportunity has arisen for access to countervailing regional relationships, but access to countervailing power is another matter.

Under the circumstances, Vietnam has little alternative but to concentrate its efforts on rebuilding its economy as the most effective way to cope with vulnerability. Although perturbed by the fragile condition of the Cambodian peace process, the government in Hanoi has avoided any initiative that might appear to reinstate it as a party to the continuing conflict. There has been strong public condemnation of Khmer Rouge killings of Vietnamese residents in Cambodia, with corresponding pleas to the United Nations to take action to protect them. But in April 1993, at a dinner in Tokyo given by Japan's prime minister, Kiichi Miyazawa, Prime Minister Vo Van Kiet provided an unequivocal assurance that "Vietnam does not intend to again dispatch its army to Cambodia."[35] A resumption of power by the Khmer Rouge and a return to the situation of the late 1970s in which their forces engaged in murderous violations across the common border would create a problem of different order. However, the public remarks made in May 1993 by Vice Minister of Foreign Affairs Le Mai are also worth noting. He reiterated: "I resolutely emphasize that we will not walk into this trap. Vietnam will not repeat its Cambodian intervention in any circumstances."[36]

Vietnam's current options in foreign policy are limited, and a realistic single-minded attention has been given to economic priorities. That policy has not been without its domestic political risks. Market economics has revived the importance of Ho Chi Minh City, which has reverted to being Saigon in everything but name and could become a locus of power rivaling Hanoi. The easing of regulations that was required for economic liberalization has brought with it demands for political reform, with agitation growing among Buddhist monks, whose dissent has taken the form of periodic demonstrations. The ruling party has responded by tightening the apparatus of repression and has been unresponsive to appeals from human rights organizations. There is no doubt that there is a smoldering crisis of ideological confidence and authority within the Communist Party of Vietnam which is subject to a declining membership but is adamantly opposed to relaxing the reins of political control. Domestic stability, with obvious implications for foreign relations, has not been subject, so far, to even moderate disturbance. There have been no signs of the kind of challenge to political order experienced by the government in Beijing in June 1989. For the time being, the Communist Party as the only political organization holds on to its monopoly of power without great additional effort. Nonetheless, the underlying situation, distinguished by the momentum of economic activity, contains within it the seeds of fundamental political change, which deeply troubles a Politburo that has no alternative but to continue along the road of reform chosen in 1986.

Given the abrupt withdrawal of Soviet bloc benefaction, the progress of economic reform has been remarkable, despite a continuation of loss-making state enterprises, an antiquated bureaucracy, an inadequate legal system, and burgeoning corruption. Growth rates of around 8 percent GDP were registered in 1992 and 1993 and were close to 9 percent in 1994. Galloping inflation has been brought under control, and the value of the dong, which has long been freely convertible, has been strengthened and stabilized. Underpinning the economy have been exports of oil and rice, with Vietnam having gone in a short space of time from a rice deficit country to the third largest exporter in the world, behind the United States and Thailand. Until February 1994, trade and investment had been hampered by the American embargo. Nonetheless, Vietnam had been able to generate a modest trade surplus of around U.S. $70 million in 1992, its first for decades, which was succeeded by a deficit of U.S. $300 million in 1993. A liberal foreign investment law, in operation since the late 1980s, has attracted major capital flows from Hong Kong, Taiwan, and South Korea in particular, and more recently from Japan, with overall commitments of U.S. $10.9 billion made by the end of 1994. Significantly, the Primal Corporation of Brunei, with royal family backing, has indicated interest in large-scale investment in oil and natural gas exploration. Vietnam's target is to double living standards from an average per capita income of around U.S. $200 by the turn of the century. Prime Minister Vo Van Kiet informed the National Assembly in December 1992 that the country required an additional infusion of U.S. $40 billion to achieve this goal. The key to successful economic development is the repair and rehabilitation of the country's infrastructure, which has begun to be undertaken. But this priority can be fully addressed only with the active cooperation of the international financial institutions, which resumed lending in the latter part of 1993.

That cooperation was held up because of American objections. In the circumstances, Vietnam had no alternative but to wait patiently for a change in American position determined by domestic political considerations. Correspondingly, Vietnam has enjoyed limited scope for foreign policy initiatives beyond an expansion of ties, which have been actively sought. Long-standing fraternal ties with North Korea were not allowed to obstruct the establishment of diplomatic relations with South Korea, while the presence of a Palestinian diplomatic mission in Hanoi did not prevent matching relations with Israel. It is not without significance that both states enjoy a special link with the United States. In 1993, Prime Minister Vo Van Kiet visited Australia and New Zealand and then France, Germany, Britain, and Belgium, and a residual association with India was cultivated as both countries engaged in corresponding economic reform.

An assiduous courting of ASEAN governments has been maintained in the hope of demonstrating a growing convergence based on corresponding models of developmental authoritarianism and finding a welcome place in a regional network of international standing. On his return from the annual meeting of ASEAN's foreign ministers held in Singapore in July 1993, Nguyen Manh Cam indicated a regional receptiveness to Vietnam's early membership in the association.

Within ASEAN, the most problematic of relationships is likely to be that with Thailand, with which Vietnam has had a long-standing rivalry for influence over the trans-Mekong region that reached a flash point over Cambodia. In the late 1980s, Thailand began to engage in a forward economic policy within mainland Southeast Asia that reflected a newfound confidence based on developmental performance. That policy, expressed in the concept of a "Golden Peninsula," suggested hegemonic aspirations that caused concern in Hanoi. Thai investment has been welcomed along with that of other ASEAN countries, but Vietnam is not likely to tolerate being treated as a source of raw materials for Thai exploitation in the way that Burma and Cambodia have been abused. Correspondingly, there is no enthusiasm for Thailand's playing the role of exclusive economic interlocutor. Thai economic penetration of Cambodia and Laos must also be a matter of concern, but there are no direct countervailing economic measures available, especially in Cambodia, where the Vietnamese presence generates hostility. Thailand poses a problem for Vietnam, but it will be addressed by permitting a share of economic access within an extensive network of relationships.

Vietnam is not expected to be a disruptive factor in regional order in the remaining years of the twentieth century. It was once depicted with alarm as the Prussia of Southeast Asia, but it is no longer in a position to challenge the national sovereignty of its neighbors, and it has been evidently reluctant to engage in a clash of arms with China in response to encroachments in the Spratly Islands or its continental shelf. Vietnam's strategic vulnerability suggests that a better analogy now would be to think of it as the Finland of the region (recalling the way that Nordic state was overshadowed by the Soviet Union). With a population of around 70 million that is still rising, Vietnam is a weak state that is more likely to be influenced by the regional pattern of power than the other way around. Its ruling party, which associates its own survival with provision for national welfare, in much the same way as the ruling party in China does, is driven by the imperative of development, for which there is only one economic model in the post-Soviet era. Foreign policy has become primarily a matter of serving this necessary goal, which requires a welcoming open door to all those who can help in the development process. Accordingly, any discussion of Vietnam's wider regional interests and ambitions can only be somewhat academic. For the time being, its foreign policy begins and ends at home, with development the overriding imperative in the cause of underpinning national independence.

It has been indicated above that debate over foreign policy would seem to have been muted by the constricting circumstances in which Vietnam has been placed in the post-Soviet era. Those circumstances are made up in particular of having China as a foreboding neighbor against whom a welcoming ASEAN, an opportunistic Japan, and a reluctant United States do not provide an alternative to a pragmatic accommodation. A policy debate would certainly revive should China again become actively assertive in the Spratly Islands or should the Khmer Rouge resume power in Cambodia. It would become most acute should a realignment occur between a Khmer Rouge–dominated Cambodia and a China still led by the political generation that sought to teach Vietnam a lesson. The restoration of that worst-case prospect—namely, Vietnam appearing to be squeezed in a strategic vice, which was the situation in 1978—does not seem at all likely in the different circumstances of the post-Soviet era. There is, of course, no certainty about its external environment, but the sights of Vietnam's foreign policy have been lowered in a realistic adjustment to a transformation in national circumstances. The overriding imperative is national economic recovery and development in the interest of a conservative political stability. That domestic priority shapes the future direction of Vietnam's foreign policy and, if sustained, can only be of positive benefit to regional order.

Notes

1. For indications of that transformation, see the report by Foreign Minister Nguyen Manh Cam to the National Assembly on December 11, 1991, in British Broadcasting Service (BBC), *Summary of World Broadcasts (SWB)*, FE/1259, pp. B/3–4, and the address to that body by the general secretary of Vietnam's Communist Party, Do Muoi, on September 19, 1992, in BBC, *SWB*, FE/1493, p. B/7. See also, "Ho Chi Minh's Thought—The Foundation of Vietnam's Foreign Policy," *Vietnam Courier* (Hanoi), no. 31 (May 1992).

2. It merits noting that in January 1979, Ha Van Lau, Vietnam's permanent representative to the United Nations, informed his Singaporean colleague: "In two weeks, the world will have forgotten the Kampuchean problem." Quoted in Kishore Mahbubani "The Kampuchean Problem: A Southeast Asian Perception," *Foreign Affairs*, Winter 1983/84, p. 410.

3. For a Vietnamese view, see *The Truth about Vietnam-China Relations over the Last Thirty Years* (Hanoi: Ministry of Foreign Affairs, 1979). See also Robert S. Ross, *The Indochina Tangle: China's Vietnam Policy 1975–1979* (New York: Columbia University Press, 1988); Anne Gilks, *The Breakdown of the Sino-Vietnamese Alliance, 1970–1979* (Berkeley, CA: Institute of East Asian Studies, University of California, 1992).

4. An excellent summary of the changing course of Vietnam's foreign policy may be found in Michael C. Williams, *Vietnam at the Crossroads* (London: Pinter Publishers for The Royal Institute of International Affairs, 1992), chap. 5. See also Michael Leifer and John Phipps, *Vietnam and Doi Moi: Domestic and International Dimensions of Reform,* Discussion Paper No. 35 (London: The Royal Institute of International Affairs, 1991).

5. See Leszek Buszynski, *Gorbachev and Southeast Asia* (London: Routledge, 1992).

6. The Political Report of the Sixth National Congress in December 1986 affirmed that consolidating and developing Vietnam's special relationship with Laos and Cambodia was "a sacred duty and a task of strategic importance to the vital interests of independence, freedom and socialism in our own country and on the Indochinese peninsula as a whole." BBC, *SWB*, FE/8447, pp. C1/11.

7. The Political Report of the Seventh National Congress in June 1991 stated, "We will ceaselessly consolidate and develop the special relationship of solidarity and friendship between our party and people and the fraternal parties of Laos and Cambodia." BBC, *SWB*, FE/1109, pp. C1/11.

8. The full terms of the Cambodian settlement may be found in *Agreement on a Comprehensive Settlement of the Cambodia Conflict,* October 23, 1991, Cm 1786 (London: HMSO, December 1991).

9. For a discussion of those problems, see Borje Llunggren, ed., *The Challenge of Reform in Indochina* (Cambridge, MA: Harvard Institute for International Development, 1993).

10. For the terms of the Sino-Vietnamese communiqué, see BBC, *SWB*, FE/122, pp. A3/1–2. See also Martin Gainsborough, "Vietnam: A Turbulent Normalization with China," *The World Today,* November 1992.

11. A succinct account of Vietnam's difficulties with China may be found in Carlyle A. Thayer, "Vietnam: Coping with China," in *Southeast Asian Affairs 1994* (Singapore: Institute of Southeast Asian Studies, 1994).

12. For the background to Sino-Vietnamese differences over maritime jurisdiction, see Lo Chi-kin, *China's Policy toward Territorial Disputes—The Case of the South China Sea Islands* (London: Routledge, 1989).

13. Vietnam's position on both the Paracel and Spratly Islands may be found in *The Hoang Sa and Truong Sa Archipelagoes and International Law* (Hanoi: Ministry of Foreign Affairs, 1988). For an account of China's role, see John W. Garver, "China's Push Through the South China Sea: The Interaction of Bureaucratic and National Interests," *The China Quarterly,* no. 132 (December 1992).

14. For the text, see BBC, *SWB,* FE/1316, pp. C1/1–2.

15. *The New York Times,* June 18, 1992. See also the justification of Crestone's position in a letter by its chairman and president, Randall C. Thompson, to the *Far Eastern Economic Review,* November 5, 1992. Crestone announced that it had begun exploration in April 1994. See *International Herald Tribune,* April 21, 1994.

16. For the text of the joint communiqué, see BBC, *SWB,* FE/1557, pp. A2/1–2.

17. In an interview with Michael Richardson, in *International Herald Tribune,* March 15, 1993.

18. See the report in *International Herald Tribune,* August 24, 1992, and also David Shambaugh "In Shanghai's Busy Shipyards, a Warning about Chinese Might," Ibid., January 15, 1993.

19. See *International Herald Tribune,* August 5, 1993.

20. BBC, *SWB,* FE/1501, pp. A2/7.

21. See David W.P. Elliot, "U.S.–Vietnam Relations: The Past, the Present, and the Future," in Dick Clark, ed., *The American–Vietnamese Dialogue* (Queenstown, MD: The Aspen Institute, 1993), p. 45.

22. The terms of the so-called road map may be found in the *International Herald Tribune,* April 11, 1991.

23. See *The New York Times,* November 1, 1992.

24. "Confirmation Hearing of Winston Lord to be Assistant Secretary of State for East Asia and Pacific Affairs," before the Senate Foreign Relations Committee, Dirksen Senate Office Building, March 31, 1993.

25. *Associated Press,* Washington, D.C., April 13, 1993. See also the report in *Far Eastern Economic Review,* May 6, 1993.

26. See the remarks of Prime Minister Vo Van Kiet in an interview with Sarah Sargent in the *International Herald Tribune,* April 12, 1993.

27. For background to Japan's policy toward Vietnam, see Tadashi Saito, "Japan's Initiative Regarding Vietnam," *Japan's Economic Institute Report* (Washington, D.C.), April 30, 1993.

28. Neil Sheehan, *Two Cities: Hanoi and Saigon* (London: Jonathan Cape, 1992), p. 46.

29. Ibid., p.47.

30. See *Far Eastern Economic Review,* October 1, 1992.

31. See *Far Eastern Economic Review,* January 13, 1978.

32. For Lee Kuan Yew's views on Vietnam's economic prospects, see the interview in *The Asian Wall Street Journal Weekly,* July 13, 1992.

33. See Michael Leifer, "Indochina and ASEAN: Seeking a New Balance," *Contemporary Southeast Asia,* December 1993.

34. For a report of American intelligence calculations of China's military expenditure, see *International Herald Tribune,* July 31–August 1, 1993.

35. *Kyodo News Service,* April 25, 1993, in BBC, *SWB,* FE/1648, pp. A1/2.

36. BBC, *SWB,* FE/1690, pp. A2/3.

Part IV:
Toward a New
Regional Order

11

Political Transformation of Communist States: Impact on the International Order in East Asia

Herbert J. Ellison

The appearance of reform leadership in China and Russia, the dominant communist powers of East Asia, was the major factor in the sweeping transformation of regional international relations from the 1970s onward. In both countries, the reform leaders rejected much of the outlook and practice of the past, and undertook new domestic and international policies. Their actions first modified and then virtually eliminated the international order inherited from the years of the Cold War and the Sino-Soviet conflict.

The question today is what sort of new order is replacing the old, and what will be the role of the communist-ruled (or, in the Russian case, formerly communist-ruled) states. The view of the present paper is that in the future, as in the past, the answer will depend greatly on internal political and economic changes that are under way in Russia and China, and to a lesser degree in Vietnam and North Korea. The purpose of the following pages is to explore those changes and the way they have affected regional international relations in the past and are likely to affect them in the future.

The essay begins with a brief review of the transformation of the regional order since the beginning of Chinese reform in the 1970s, then focuses on domestic change and its impact on the foreign policy of the four countries. The concluding section forecasts the ways in which alternative patterns of future political development are likely to affect international relations.

The Great Transformation

The reshaping of the East Asian international order started with the Chinese opening to Japan and the United States in the 1970s. What began as a diplomatic effort to end China's isolation and to win support in the ongoing conflict with the Soviet Union became a far more significant process with the reform of the Chinese economy in the late 1970s and 1980s. The impressive growth of the economy that resulted, supported by large-scale foreign trade and investment, created a powerful new role for China, which simultaneously reentered world diplomacy and the world economy.

Russia's progress along the same path began in the mid-1980s, and had different results. The new Soviet foreign and security policy of the Gorbachev era put an end both to the Sino-Soviet conflict and to the Cold War. Negotiations on the conflicts between China and the Soviet Union—Afghanistan, Cambodia, border claims, and Soviet troop deployments along the Chinese border—led to a major reconciliation in 1989. Meanwhile, the combination of U.S.-Soviet arms agreements, and the abandonment of the Soviet hold on Eastern Europe brought a rapid end to the U.S.-Soviet confrontation that had been the centerpiece of world politics for half a century, in Asia as elsewhere. One result was to open the way for constructive cooperation among the major regional powers—the United States, Japan, China, and the Soviet Union/Russia—on the formidable conflicts in Korea and Indochina.

The scope of the resulting transformation of the international system is indeed impressive. The domination by the military power of the United States and the Soviet Union has been replaced by a more balanced four-power system, with the regional power of the Soviet Union drastically reduced and the United States beginning a reduction of its regional arms deployments in the wake of extensive arms reduction agreements with Moscow. Meanwhile, both China and Japan have increased their expenditures on arms, assuming power roles proportionate to their location and their economic power.

For the smaller states, the changes are equally important. South Korea, long a major focus of the hostility of both Moscow and Beijing, has become a major economic partner of both, while North Korea has lost its ability to exploit differences between Moscow and Beijing to its own advantage, and has also lost its main sources of economic and military aid. It may retain China's verbal support for reunification, but that means peaceful reunification on mutually agreeable terms. North Korea is now compelled to seek economic support from Japan and to enter negotiations with Seoul, but its leaders show a grim determination to replace lost patrons with an independent nuclear weapons capacity.

Vietnam also quickly felt the impact of the new era. Once the Gorbachev policies hastened Sino-Soviet reconciliation, it was pressed by Moscow to surrender its position in Cambodia, and then, under Yeltsin's leadership, the Russians withdrew their bases from Vietnam and eliminated the huge economic subsidies that had sustained the feeble Vietnamese economy. Seeking the path of economic recovery, Vietnam, like China before it, was quick to see the need for reconciliation with the United States and the pursuit of economic ties with capitalist states. Like North Korea, it is now very much on its own. Proletarian internationalism has fallen victim to revision, or abandonment, of traditional communist ideology. Instead of proletarian solidarity, the slogan appears to be *sauve qui peut.*

Another important change has been the release of Moscow's control over Mongolia and the Soviet Central Asian republics. These changes have greatly transformed the Soviet geopolitical relationship with East Asia, and especially with China, with which the joint border has been reduced by more than half and whose relationship with Tibet and Xinjiang is challenged by the dismantling of the Soviet multinational state.

Where from Here?

For the United States and its Asian allies, the pressing question today is, where from here? North Korea's loss of support from China and Russia, and the endorsement by both of peaceful North–South dialogue and cooperation, seems to reduce the need for U.S. troops in South Korea, especially in view of the economic and military strength of the South and the evident economic weakness of the North. Yet the continued pursuit of nuclear weapons by the North—and its resistance to effective outside inspection—remains a major problem for the region, especially for South Korea and Japan. Meanwhile, the large arms reductions negotiated between the United States and the Russians, together with the increasingly close cooperation between Moscow and Washington on regional and global security questions, have greatly altered the context of U.S.-Japanese security cooperation. Yet here too the new situation has not brought Russian concessions on the islands issue, and the recent rightward shift in Russian politics, with strong nationalist and militarist overtones, has renewed concerns in Japan.

It is symptomatic of the changed American perceptions of current East Asian international relations that American discussion of security questions has been substantially displaced by discussion of trade, economic development, and social change. Political and economic change in Russia and China, and U.S.-Soviet arms reductions, have combined with domestic economic problems to create powerful pressures in the United States for reduction of arms expenditures, even as changes in Russian and Chinese international behavior reduce the perceived need for them. Meanwhile, challenges to American economic interests are increasingly seen as both an economic and a security issue, perhaps more important today than issues of military security conventionally defined.

While understandable, this is in fact too narrow a view of the enormous changes under way today in the international order in East Asia. These changes have indeed transformed the policy challenges, but they have not reduced them to economic issues alone. They have not eliminated security issues from the agenda, or eliminated all of the ideological conflicts that divide the major actors in the region.

The best way to capture the central issues today is to begin by looking closely at the two major actors, China and Russia, whose past policies were the main source of the two major conflicts that divided the region (Sino-Soviet and East–West). Clearly it is changes in these two countries, and, derivatively, in their main regional communist clients, Vietnam and North Korea, that have generated the movement toward a new international order in East Asia. The purpose of the following pages is to assess those internal changes and their implications for the future of the East Asian international order, beginning with China.

Domestic Reform and the Chinese Role in Asia

China's reform process is unique among those of communist states in three major ways: the length of time—now seventeen years—that it has been under way, the primary leadership of Deng Xiaoping through the entire process, and its impressive success. The rapid improvement of agricultural production and food supplies in the first stage was followed by speedy expansion and modernization of the urban economy, including services, manufacturing, transportation, and financial institutions, and the rapid expansion of exports. These achievements combined with success in agriculture to achieve unprecedented high growth rates and increases in per capita GDP.

The scope and pace of Chinese economic reform were bound to place stress on the political system. The control of the economy, and hence the power of the central governmental apparatus, was steadily reduced by the expanding economic role of independent peasants, traders, and manufacturers that came with the rapid expansion of the private economy. The process became even more pronounced as local party officials became active in private economic enterprise, developing ties and commitments that eroded their loyalty to their political superiors.

Still greater stress was generated by the process of opening up culturally and intellectually to the outside world. The enormous increase in the number of students, scholars, technicians, and economic operatives going to other parts of Asia, Europe, and North America inevitably brought with it, especially in the case of students, a desire for democratic political reform that was unacceptable to the Communist Party leaders. That desire was greatly strengthened by the strong political reform emphasis of the Gorbachev era. Hence the confrontation with the Democracy Movement in the spring of 1989, and the tragedy of Tiananmen Square in June. For conservative party leaders, concern about the domestic political opposition was increased by the evidence of sympathy in their own ranks—notably Zhao Ziyang—for the students' demands.

The anxiety of the Chinese party leaders was enormously increased by the events in Eastern Europe and Russia during the succeeding two years, as is evident from both private and public statements.[1] They were horrified by the collapse of Communist Party power in Eastern Europe in 1989 and in the Soviet Union in 1991. For these events they blamed Mikhail Gorbachev, the man who had lectured them during his May 1989 visit to Beijing on the virtues of combining political reform, perestroika-style, with economic reform.[2] In the view of the Chinese leaders, his policies had brought the destruction of communist power from Berlin to Vladivostok, and economic collapse and political anarchy in much of that vast domain.

The immediate threat to their own power, and to political stability in their country, was clear enough. It explains the harsh political repression during 1989 and 1990. Fear of the advancing tide of anticommunist revolution, which had spread from Eastern Europe to Russia, and to Russia's Inner Asian dependencies, was a major factor in Chinese policy. The official rhetoric about defense of socialism—unconvincing in a party leadership whose impressive economic reforms were building a capitalist economy—did little to obscure the main purpose: the defense of the existing structure of political power.

Unlike Gorbachev and the Eastern European reformers of the 1980s, the Chinese leaders had a full appreciation of the fragility of their political power, and reacted immediately to perceived threats to it. The course of events in Yeltsin's Russia has confirmed that understanding and given them greater confidence in the correctness of their course. So has the impressive success of their ongoing economic reform and the positive reception of their reform policy by their own people.

Yet the dynamic of successful economic reforms, to which the government remains committed and to which Deng Xiaoping has repeatedly renewed and broadened the commitment, creates its own problems. Domestically, the private sector of the economy, rural and urban, continues to gain strength, expanding the wealth and numbers of social groups that have no lasting commitment to the ruling group. The legitimacy of the regime is based on its ability to maintain political stability and to continue successful economic reform. Its solid achievements in both areas surely explain some of the present weakness of the democratic movement. Moreover, the economic problems of the republics of the former Soviet Union today tend to discredit the idea of democracy in China, while the Chinese model of reform, including the authoritarian political system that applies it, has enjoyed growing prestige in Russia.[3]

In the longer run, Chinese economic reform will doubtless erode the structure of Communist Party power. Recognition of this fact was clear in arguments among the leaders throughout 1991 and in Prime Minister Li Peng's March 25, 1993, presentation to parliament of the eighth five-year economic development plan, with its cautious expansion of private enterprise and repeated warnings about retention of party control.

In its effort to use the existing authoritarian power structure to direct and manage economic development, China is often compared to the fast-growing capitalist economies of the East Asian periphery, from South Korea to Singapore. The bulk of the economic modernization there was conducted by one-party authoritarian regimes, and the process of democratization followed the economic and social transformation. Yet however impressive the economic changes in China since the late 1970s, it has a very long way to go before it matches the present levels of per capita wealth, and of urbanization, in Taiwan or South Korea.[4]

This difference could be taken to mean that the Chinese leaders will have a longer grace period before confronting broad-based and powerful political opposition and irresistible pressures for democratization from below. But China is also very different from less numerous and more homogeneous societies like Taiwan and South Korea. It is more varied socially and economically, and the fast-developing southern and coastal provinces have already demonstrated independence on economic and political issues, suggesting independent regional power that, over time, could threaten not just the monopoly power of the party but the power of the central government under any political leadership.

Another important question for the future will be the ability of the Chinese leadership to maintain the progress and success of the economic reform. In the past the intervention of Deng Xiaoping has been crucial to keeping the reform on track, and this was evident once again in the October 1992 Party Congress.[5] At each stage of the reform's advance there has been conservative resistance, and that resistance was greatly strengthened by the political anxiety that followed Tiananmen. The momentum of successful reforms and the vast scale of the irreversible privatization of the economy argue for confidence in continuing reform. But the evidence is that resistance to change builds up periodically in the party leadership, especially in response to fears of political instability. In the past Mao has broken the logjam. His demise could well shift the balance against reform.

Another problem has been the archaic financial system inherited from the old regime, whose operation in the first half of 1993 precipitated a serious financial crisis. With the money supply rising nearly 50 percent over the level of a year earlier and the trade account in deficit, the yuan fell in value by 23 percent during June and urban retail prices were rising at the rate of 20 percent a year. The problems were traceable to the central bank, which controlled 85 percent of financial assets and channeled the majority of them to state-owned industrial firms, most of which lose money.[6] The state had managed this arrangement for nearly fifteen years, thanks to the rapid growth of the financial assets of firms and individuals, and the ability of the state to market its liabilities at positive interest rates.

It is now clear that the subsidies to state-owned firms have been largely responsible for the heavy real deficit in the state budget, about 10 percent of GDP. Until this major structural weakness is corrected, China continues to be vulnerable to destructive levels of inflation. And the change is not easy, since the government continues to depend, as it did before the reform process began in 1978, on the revenues from state-owned enterprises. Their competitive weakness in the new economic setting has caused a relentless decline of state revenues as a share of GDP and encouraged the government's inflationary fiscal policy.

It is interesting to compare the Soviet experience. Economic reform under Gorbachev and Yeltsin has been gravely weakened by the powerful and pervasive institutions, rural and urban, of the socialist economy, which were far stronger and more developed than those that existed in prereform China. The power and the attitudes of the managerial elite of the old system, and the vested interests of the socialist economic structures that they control, create a formidable barrier to change, even with a reformist government that is firmly committed to a comprehensive privatization and marketization program. Moreover, although the Soviet Union is more urbanized and highly educated, China has made much wider use over a longer time of foreign educational facilities, and has had a large flow abroad of its economic specialists and managers. This advantage has been expanded by its ties with Hong Kong and Taiwan, contributing to the creation of an economically and politically sophisticated elite that has proven highly adaptable to reform needs.

Chinese party leaders argue that the party dictatorship is essential to unity, stability, and order in China, and that without it there would be disorder and disintegration. A strong case can be made for this position. Even someone unsympathetic to communist rule would have to concede that there are no adequate social groups or political structures available to replace the apparatus of party power. A case can also be made, however, that the party leadership can validate its claim to power only by continuing and broadening the reform process and by maintaining the momentum of economic growth.

In the past, the fulfillment of that condition has been largely the achievement of Deng Xiaoping. There was no equivalent economic reform leader in Russia until Yeltsin, and by that time the party's power had been substantially dismantled. The Soviet party, when in power, failed to produce a major economic reform, which was in fact a major reason for its loss of power. Certainly the disintegration of central governmental power in Russia that came with the dismantling of party power has been a formidable obstacle to the achievement of Yeltsin's reform objectives. But when he dismantled the party apparatus after the failed August 1991 coup, the central political power was already gravely weakened, and the record confirmed his claim that the party had been mainly a barrier to effective economic reform.

If the Soviet and Eastern European political experience of recent years teaches any lesson, it is that transition from a communist dictatorship to an effective democratic political system is an incredibly complex and uncertain process. It has been most successful in the smaller, ethnically cohesive countries of Central Europe where there were substantial autonomous political and economic groupings to which responsibility and leadership could pass from the Communist Party and its bureaucracy. Without these, the result has typically been restoration of communist rule under another name, often with severe economic and social dislocation. Western critics of the Chinese leadership must acknowledge this conundrum, whatever their views of Chinese policy.

Domestic Policy and Foreign Policy in China

Chinese foreign policy statements resemble those of the Soviet leadership in the Brezhnev years. A recent policy commentary notes that "one cold war has ended—two cold wars have begun," and defines the two new cold wars as, first, that between capitalist and (the surviving) communist countries, and second, the conflicts within the Western alliance. It notes that the "confrontation between the two systems and the two ideologies is still fierce," and elaborates ways in which the conflicts within the Western alliance can be turned to China's advantage.[7]

This is, of course, a traditional communist view of a world dominated by the struggle between the capitalist and socialist systems. One is reminded, however, of official pronouncements on Chinese economic policy, which speak of socialism while the actual policy is to build capitalism. The equivalent in foreign policy is to begin with an image of global confrontation between socialism and capitalism and then proceed to policies for extending Chinese economic power, territory, and political influence. In sum, foreign policy appears to have little to do with communism and much to do with Chinese economic growth and territorial expansion. The motivating elements appear to be a mix of very practical state interests and Chinese nationalism.

The translation of such a policy into specifics is quite straightforward. Diplomatic relations are no longer a tool of communist ideological or revolutionary politics. One can ignore former Palestinian (PLO), African, and North Korean clients in favor of diplomatic relations with Israel, South Africa, and South Korea. The changes clearly bring far greater political and economic advantage. The same is true of the abandonment of Iraq, a former Chinese client, in the Gulf War. The interests of the new international Chinese economy dictated that China support the Western powers, and so it did.[8] Even in response to American human rights pressures, China, after protesting that the American demands constituted interference in Chinese internal affairs, was prepared to make changes in order to satisfy its vital American trading partner—or at least it was until Secretary Christopher's visit in March 1994, when very strong resistance appeared.

What Chinese policymakers are doing in such matters is, in both political and moral terms, precisely what other states do as well. They are pursuing their national interest as they understand it. The difficulty has come, and will probably come increasingly in the future, when the pursuit of the national interest is defined in irredentist or expansionist terms. The most prominent territorial claims of China are Hong Kong and Taiwan; one is scheduled for absorption, and the issue of contention is the self-government rights of its citizens, and the other is perceived by China as her rightful territory, but by many of its citizens as a separate nation.

Other territorial claims include the islands of the South China Sea—chiefly the Paracels and Spratlys. It is also possible that China will renew her claim to territories in the Himalayas presently owned by India, and even renew the claim to special rights over Mongolia. Finally, China will undoubtedly take a great interest in the future of the newly independent former Soviet republics in Central Asia, many of whose peoples are closely related to the indigenous population of China's Xinjiang.

A state of China's impressive size, with an army 3 million strong, with nuclear warheads and a fast-growing military budget, is bound to be a concern to its weaker neighbors. For the United States, Japan, and Russia, the question is whether China will be a peaceful and cooperative neighbor, refraining from using force to press its territorial claims and cooperating with the other states to maintain peace and order. The evidence of Chinese behavior since the reform era began is mixed, but generally encouraging. The evidence of growing military power, more assertive nationalism, and a fast-growing and increasingly powerful economy are signs that the neighbors should be attentive.

A major question that should be posed by foreign observers of Chinese foreign policy is when and where the Chinese leadership might be inclined to use coercion, including military coercion, to achieve irredentist or other expansionist goals. One thinks mainly of Taiwan, where Beijing recently put pressure upon France in an effort to halt the sale of Mirage jets to Taipei. Clearly Beijing does not wish to have a Taiwan capable of defending itself militarily against pressures from the mainland. As China presumably does not fear a Taiwan invasion, its current policy suggests that it sees military pressure upon Taiwan on the issue of unification as a serious policy option. A powerfully armed Taiwan could obviously resist such pressures more effectively.

The growth of Chinese power would seem to justify such a view. And China could be encouraged to act boldly by major recent changes in the regional international context: the collapse of Russian power, the steady reduction in U.S. military forces and bases, the close Chinese ties with South Korea, the reduced effectiveness of American-Japanese security cooperation.[9] To these changes encouraging a more assertive Chinese policy could be added another that looks increasingly serious since the Russian elections of December 1993: the increased pressure of nationalist political leaders on foreign policy in Russia. These leaders have advocated a vigorous restoration of Russian influence in the former Soviet Central Asian republics. Such a policy could be competitive with the growing Chinese economic influence in the region, and therefore a source of conflict. It is equally possible that friendly Chinese and Russian regimes would find it possible to divide spheres of power regionally.

In sum, there are serious reasons to believe that the current degree of political change in China does not guarantee that country's integration into a peaceful consortium of states sharing a common conception of international order. The erosion of traditional communist ideology is extensive. As in Russia under Gorbachev, commitment to "proletarian internationalism," whether interpreted as support of Third World communist revolution or support of fellow Asian communist regimes, has ended. But the leadership's commitment to irredentist and other territorial claims remains, together with a world view that retains a strong prejudice against the capitalist democracies.[10]

Such domestic attitudes remain a considerable obstacle to the organization of effective regional security cooperation, and could be a threat to regional peace in the event that Chinese leaders chose to use force in pursuit of territorial claims. Moreover, a serious reckoning of the regional international system should take into account China's potential leverage within the regional state system. Neither of the Koreas is likely to challenge Chinese ambitions, nor is Vietnam. And Russia, eager to restore its great-power role in the region, could well be inclined to divide regional spheres of influence with China, meanwhile expanding weapons sales and weapons technology transfer along with broader economic cooperation. Located as they are, the new Central Asian states could as easily be the object of power deals as of conflict between their giant neighbors. Concerned with nationalist insurgency in Xinjiang, China could find such a policy attractive. And there is a serious possibility that in a regional crisis created by a Chinese expansionist initiative, it would be Japan and the United States that found themselves isolated, not China.

Russia in the New Order in East Asia

The transformation of the political and economic life of Russia that has occurred since the failed coup of August 1991 and the dismantling of the Soviet Union in December of that year is still under way. A summary of the major changes that make up that transformation is an essential background to discussion of the changing role of Russia in Asia.

There are three major endings that define the enormous changes under Yeltsin: the end of communist rule, the end of the command socialist economy, and the end of the empire. All three have great importance for Russia's role in the new international order in East Asia.

The repudiation of communist rule and the dismantling of the traditional organization and power of the Communist Party marked a major shift in the attitude of the Russian leadership toward the Asian communist states. Gorbachev had favored reform communist leaders and both economic and political reform policies. But he continued to believe in a community of socialist states, even as he pursued a much more pragmatic and accommodating policy toward capitalist states. He maintained generous economic aid to an economically beleaguered Vietnam, and he urged the Chinese to add political reform to their impressive accomplishments in economic reform.

Yeltsin's policy was initially defined in strongly pro-Western terms—to "rejoin the company of civilized states." The language expressed a total repudiation of communist power and the communist legacy.[11] It reaffirmed and extended Gorbachev's new evenhandedness in relations with communist and noncommunist states, but replaced his communist ideological bias with one that favored the democratic capitalist states. Yeltsin quickly abandoned the last remnants of adversarial relations with the Western powers in favor of full partnership with them.

Even in the brief period of its application, this policy has had enormous repercussions. It has greatly accelerated agreements on arms reduction and completed the dismantling of the Cold War in Asia as in Europe. It has challenged the United States, Japan, and South Korea to review the basis of the East Asian security system that was designed for the Cold War era, stimulating the rethinking of U.S.-South Korean and U.S.-Japanese security arrangements. It has greatly accelerated the pursuit of new relationships with Taiwan, Japan, and South Korea, and it has ended all relations, including especially economic aid and arms aid, based on a perception of a "socialist community" with North Korea and Vietnam.

Yeltsin's anticommunism was at first a source of tension in relations with China, but as Chinese leaders recovered from the shock of the failure of the August 1991 coup, whose purposes they had favored, and of Yeltsin's aggressive attacks on the Communist Party, they found the new regime increasingly acceptable. It was not, as they first feared, filled with democratic militants who would join American critics of China's human rights record. Its leaders admired China's economic reform record, and were quick to see mutual advantages in deals on trade, technology, and arms. Moreover, if Yeltsin assured the West that the Cold War was ended, he assured the Chinese, at least equally emphatically, that Russia had abandoned its imperial mission in East Asia. The severance of economic aid to Vietnam and the closing of Russian bases there, the end of military ties with North Korea, and the emancipation of the republics of Central Asia offered the Chinese at least as much assurance as had been given to the United States and its Asian allies that a new day had dawned and a new regional international order could be built.

China's response to the dismantling of the Soviet Union revealed the great importance it attached to the Taiwan issue. Beijing's position on the China-Taiwan relationship was made a part of all communiqués and declarations establishing diplomatic relations with the successor states and defining the principles of future relations. And the extensive visits and agreements did much to consolidate relations. Negotiations with Russia reached a climax with the visit of President Yeltsin to Beijing, December 17–19, 1992, which brought the signing of more than twenty agreements and a joint declaration in which Russia and China were described as "friendly states." During the political crises of 1993, the Chinese maintained complete detachment, stressing that the problems were Russia's internal affair.[12]

Like Gorbachev, Yeltsin had as his key aim to accomplish the integration of Russia (then the Soviet Union) into the East Asian economy. In contrast to his predecessor, he believed that the conversion of the Russian economy into a private property–based market economy was the essential prerequisite to that task, for Asia as for other parts of the world, and the conversion of economic institutions and policy began in January 1992, immediately after the dismantling of the Soviet Union.

The conversion from socialist to capitalist economy has been the most difficult and problematic of Yeltsin's policies.[13] Elimination of the Communist Party removed only the first barrier to the process. The state-owned and state-managed economy, rural and urban, was the most highly developed in the communist world, and the reform process began with its formidable structure intact and its leadership firmly opposed to the reform scheme of Yeltsin and his colleagues.

The course of the Yeltsin economic reform was marked by sustained political conflict. Under his leadership, Deputy Prime Minister Yegor Gaidar, appointed in November 1991, led the reform effort through 1992, though opposition pressure in the parliament brought the appointment of three representatives of the "industrial lobby" (Viktor Chernomyrdin, Georgii Khizha, and Vladimir Shumeiko) as deputy prime ministers in the summer of 1992. Yeltsin relinquished his prime ministership, naming Gaidar as prime minister. Shock therapy (a stringent fiscal and monetary policy combined with broad price liberalization) was abandoned, though a large-scale privatization program was initiated for real estate and economic enterprises.

Parliamentary pressure led to the replacement of Gaidar with the conservative Chernomyrdin in December, but the naming of Boris Fedorov as deputy prime minister in charge of economic and financial policy signaled continuation of reform. However, mounting opposition from industrial and agricultural lobbies and an increasingly serious confrontation with the parliament led to the appointment of two additional conservative officials as deputy prime ministers and slowed the reform process. Even Yeltsin's impressive success in the April 1993 referendum, which endorsed both his leadership and his reform policies, was not translated into revival of reform because of the crisis in relations with the parliament.

Throughout the reform process of 1992 and 1993 (until September), the opposition sabotaged the program of macroeconomic stabilization, refused to legalize private property in land, and obstructed or distorted the privatization of state-owned enterprise. Meanwhile, the Central Bank, responsible to the parliament, frustrated efforts to control inflation by expanding credits to state enterprises. The constitution inherited from the Gorbachev era, based essentially on the Soviet constitution of 1977, produced a conservative, antireform majority in the parliament, and frustrated the Yeltsin reform program and efforts to replace the old political structure with a new one by constitutional reform.

From the beginning of 1993 through the storming of the White House by Russian armed forces on October 4, the central issue between Yeltsin and the parliamentary leader, Ruslan Khasbulatov, was precisely the question of constitutional reform—and thus of political power in the new Russian state. Convinced that the existing constitutional system doomed his reform program to stalemate or collapse, Yeltsin had challenged the parliamentary leadership with a proposal for a national constitutional referendum. He compromised with Khasbulatov by agreeing on February 18 to a special session of the Congress of People's Deputies, with which he intended to negotiate a new constitutional agreement, but made it clear that his minimum requirements would be governmental control of economic policy and of the Central Bank, whose lax monetary policy threatened hyperinflation. During the next few weeks, relations between the president and the Congress deteriorated rapidly. The president's proposals for a new constitutional system with strong presidential power, elimination of the Congress of People's Deputies in favor of a directly elected legislature, and the fashioning of a new constitution by a new constitutional assembly, rather than by the existing Congress, were met by a counterattack of Congress actions stripping the president of most of the powers granted him in late 1991.

This process was challenged by Yeltsin in a television address to the nation on March 22 in which he threatened the use of his decree power to break the legislative opposition. The compromise that ensued provided for a referendum on April 26. The referendum was undoubtedly a moral victory for Yeltsin, since the voters supported both his presidency and his economic reform policy, while expressing clear dissatisfaction with the parliament by strongly supporting early elections for a new parliament. However, since the latter did not represent a majority of the electorate, Yeltsin was denied his main hope: a new, popularly elected parliament.

Yeltsin's victory in the referendum was more moral than substantial. Though he was urged by many of the democratic leaders to mount an offensive against the parliamentary leadership and against his own obstreperous vice president, Alexander Rutskoi, and to press economic reform much more aggressively, he proceeded cautiously with economic reform. His attention was concentrated on his plan for constitutional change, and he convened, on June 7, a Constitutional Assembly to review and approve a constitutional plan on which a special commission had worked for some months.

The clash with Khasbulatov at the opening session of the assembly and the systematic attack of the parliament on the government's privatization program and budgetary controls during July and August confirmed the irreconcilability of the positions of the parliamentary leadership and the president on all major aspects of reform. Seeking to subordinate the president to the parliament, Khasbulatov had encouraged legislation reducing presidential powers. He now sought to carry that process much further, and combined it with efforts to build support in the armed forces by promises of increased financial support. By August the Khasbulatov "creeping coup," as it was styled by Yeltsin supporters, seemed ready to become more aggressive as Khasbulatov formed close ties with ultranationalist leaders against Yeltsin.

Yeltsin's counter to these actions—the dissolution of the parliament on September 23 and the announcement of new elections, was followed by armed seizure of government buildings and appeals for popular resistance to the government, a process that ended with the use of security forces by the president, on October 3 and 4, to remove Khasbulatov, Rutskoi, and their followers from the parliament building by armed force, including bombardment of the White House.[14]

Following his triumph over Khasbulatov and Rutskoi, Yeltsin made good on his commitment to free national parliamentary elections on December 12, successfully submitting his new constitution for approval by the voters at the same time. By the end of 1993, both the balance of political forces and the political structure had been greatly altered, suggesting the beginning of a new period in Russian political life. Meanwhile, the economic reform program was vigorously renewed under the leadership of Boris Fedorov, the finance minister.

Certainly the new constitutional structure, for which Yeltsin had worked patiently for two years, created the legal foundations for a much more effective governmental system, including a very strong presidency, a bicameral legislature, and a constitutional court to arbitrate disputes. The unworkable Soviet-era constitution had been replaced by a functional constitutional structure.

The election results, on the other hand, reflected attitudes and problems in Russian life that would greatly complicate Yeltsin's efforts to continue his transformation of the Russian economy, to build a new Russian statehood within existing borders while maintaining peaceful relations with the "near abroad," and generally to harmonize Russia's international policies with those of the Western democracies. The reform parties that supported the main direction of his policies made a much weaker electoral showing than expected, while the ultranationalists (chiefly Vladimir Zhirinovsky's Liberal Democratic Party) and their allies in the Communist and Agrarian parties showed impressive strength.

The new government formed at the beginning of 1994, led by Viktor Chernomyrdin and dominated by conservatives, was the result of Yeltsin's conclusion that the election results had expressed strong popular dissatisfaction with the economic reform and indicated the need to slow the reform process and ease the strain. His efforts to retain Gaidar and Fedorov in the government failed, since they regarded themselves as marginalized by the weight of conservative appointments.

In many important respects the course of Russian policy in early 1994 had taken a strong conservative and nationalist turn. A major expansion of loans to state farms and industrial enterprises, and expensive plans for expansion of the ruble zone to broaden economic ties of other former Soviet republics with Russia, suggested abandonment of previous efforts to achieve macroeconomic stabilization and to reduce the claims on government resources of loss-making state enterprises. The resigning reformers warned of imminent hyperinflation.

The postelection changes seemed also to reinforce a shift in foreign policy, already evident for several months, toward a more independent policy in relations with the West and a more assertive policy toward the states of the former Soviet Union. The former was evident in the Soviet role in Bosnia, including rejection of the NATO plan for air strikes, and the latter in the Russian claim of extraterritorial privileges in former Soviet republics for protection of resident Russians and the use of Russian armed forces in Moldova, Georgia, and Tadzhikistan. Some of these policy trends were supported by the draft of a new military doctrine that appeared for discussion in November 1993.[15]

With a formerly liberal foreign minister, Andrei Kozyrev, taking an increasingly nationalist line in foreign policy, the leading reformers leaving the government, and the lower house of the parliament dominated by a majority of nationalists and communists and their supporters, some critics claimed that the overthrow of communism in Russia had led to a new system in which the old party *nomenklatura*, peddling aggressive nationalism rather than communism, dominated the new political structure and, by a perversion of the process of privatization, now enjoyed something akin to ownership of the main economic enterprises of the nation.[16] The prospect seemed especially worrying because of the loss of effective civilian control of the military, for while the central military apparatus supported Yeltsin in October 1993, elements of the renegade Fourteenth Army in the Trans-Dniester region joined the insurgency against the government.[17]

There was, however, much evidence against such a pessimistic analysis. First, the communist–nationalist power in the new parliament (Federal Assembly) was concentrated in the lower house, the State Duma, and even there the reform parties had about a third of the seats and a significant number of the key committees. The upper house (Council of the Federation) had a reform majority. Moreover, Yeltsin achieved his objective of creating a strong presidency with the passage of the new constitution. He had legislative initiative, control of budgets, and veto power over parliamentary legislation. And although his choice of government leaders, reflecting the election results, was conservative, the leadership was still committed to development of the market economy and to continuing privatization.

The conservative leaders have argued, in the debates with the radical reformers, that it is impossible to cease abruptly all support of state industries and farms, since they employ the great majority of the population. Such a policy would create massive unemployment and generate severe social and political instability.[18] Radical reformers counter that only "shock treatment"—general liberalization of prices and an end of subsidies to state enterprises, combined with a program of strict fiscal and monetary controls—can bridge the chasm between a socialist and a capitalist economy. And their critics respond in turn that in a country with widespread production monopolies, lacking private property, private production, and a developed system of private trade and finance, a rapid transition to a new order by largely monetary policy measures is not feasible.

The clash between opposing policies made a shambles of the reformers' efforts to achieve macroeconomic stabilization. Parliament continued to allocate money to finance the vast structure of state enterprise, using the Central Bank, which it controlled, to issue currency to meet revenue deficits. The heavy monetization of public debt created high inflation, combined with severe production declines and massive capital flight to foreign banks and other financial repositories. And the chaotic economic environment, combined with the decline of state power, fostered widespread crime, including organized protection rackets, corruption of the economic ministries and economic managers, and the inflation-induced impoverishment of much of the population.

Such conditions greatly complicated the economic transition and created dangerous social instability and conflict. However chaotically, though, the expansion of the private economy continued. In some respects the decline of central power that accompanied the political feuding in Moscow helped reformist regional governments, as in the regions of Nizhni Novgorod, Yaroslavl, and St. Petersburg, to carry forward highly effective privatizing reforms within their regions. The challenge to the central government leadership taking over in early 1994 was to control inflation, restore public order, and provide an environment in which private economic investment, domestic and foreign, could succeed. Chinese practice had combined public subsidies for state enterprises with the creation of conditions favorable for the flourishing of private enterprise, but only by the sustained pursuit of macroeconomic stability.

For much of the first year (1994) of operation under the new constitution, the prospects for the Russian transition seemed to improve. In the economy, inflation declined steadily during the year, dropping from over 20 percent per month in January to about 5 percent in August. The first stage of privatization, by a voucher system, was completed in June, and a second phase, which opened broad new opportunities for both foreign and domestic purchase of shares in the newly privatized industries, opened in July. But fiscal stability was short-lived, thanks to increasing budgetary deficits, which brought the sudden collapse of the ruble in October. Efforts to deal with the monetary crisis and control the expanded inflation that followed were frustrated by the budgetary impact of the military action in Chechnya beginning in December.

Thus the first three years of Russia's postcommunist era were a bumpy ride, and in early 1995 events seemed to have taken a very negative turn: rising government deficits and renewed inflation, an intractable war in Chechnya, a break between the president and democratic leaders, and government policy increasingly dominated by a small clique made up of the leaders of the Security Council, the defense and security ministries, and the president's cronies. As often before, much of the commentary, domestic and foreign, predicted the demise of Russian democracy and the collapse of the bold effort at economic transformation.

These powerful negative developments should, however, be placed in a broader context. During the preceding three years the Soviet empire had been peacefully dismantled, Russia had made the transition from communist dictatorship to constitutional democracy with a free press, and the Russian economy had shifted from a command to a market system with a vast expansion of private ownership and at least half of the nation's goods and services privately produced.

If, within that new structure of institutions and power, there remained a large and powerful segment of the political leadership still committed to authoritarian rule and the restoration of empire, it was also true that its efforts would be powerfully constrained by the vast changes in institutions and outlook in recent years. The imperatives of the new economic system, of a free press and a powerful democratic opposition, could not be long ignored.

The foreign policy of the Yeltsin era has been no less controversial than the program of economic reform. A firm supporter of the sovereignty of the republics of the USSR during his opposition to Gorbachev, Yeltsin had been the most powerful supporter of the ill-fated Union Treaty, which conservative communist opponents sought to block by their failed coup in August 1991. Their action precipitated the collapse of the center and thus the disintegration of the federal system, leading to the formal dismantling of the USSR on December 25, 1991.

Yeltsin was blamed for the dissolution of the Soviet Union by a very broad group of the Russian political leadership, including many former allies, such as his own vice president, Alexander Rutskoi, and the head of the parliament, Ruslan Khasbulatov. Communists and nationalists alike refused to accept his argument that following the Ukrainian vote for independence on December 1, it was no longer possible to hold the USSR together except by violence. They also rejected his argument that Russia must accept the boundaries of the Soviet-era Russian Republic as those of the new Russian state, leaving the other successor states to do the same, but seeking through a loose affiliation within the Commonwealth of Independent States to maintain common structures for security and economic cooperation.

For some of Yeltsin's critics it was impossible to accept the end of Russia's imperial legacy. While reconciled to the loss of Eastern Europe, they could not accept as well the loss of the "inner empire," for centuries part of the Russian domain. But even for those who accepted a diminished Russian territory, the boundaries of the Russian Federation, drawn by communist rulers concerned with ideological rather than national-territorial issues, were unacceptable. Those boundaries excluded 26 million ethnic Russians, a large proportion of them inhabiting contiguous territories in the West and in Central Asia—some 17 million in Ukraine and Kazakhstan alone. The new Russia therefore embarked upon independent statehood with many of her political leaders rejecting the existing territorial limits of that statehood.

This enormous political problem is in many ways the key to all others. Russian irredentism has been powerfully exploited by both the nationalist and the communist parties. It has also had a special appeal to the military, particularly that group deployed in former Soviet republics, among whom the bitter feelings about the end of Soviet power run deep. Frustrated nationalist sentiments inspire denunciations of countrymen presumed to have betrayed the Russian imperial legacy, and hostility is directed by such groups at the West, particularly the United States, which is assumed to have conspired in the destruction of the Soviet state.

Given this mentality, the hostile attacks on the Russian reformers express predictable themes. In foreign policy it is the primacy of the "near abroad." The more moderate version, a version increasingly adopted by democratic leaders, including the foreign minister and president, stresses the need to monitor the condition of Russians left outside Russian borders and to seek closer economic and security cooperation with other successor states. The militant form raises constant claims of mistreatment of Russians in the near abroad and argues for reconstitution of something like the old Soviet state. The latter group usually argues as well for an authoritarian state structure and a statist economy. Its mood is emphatically antidemocratic, and its foreign policy is imperialist and nationalist.

The strength of the nationalists and communists in the December 1993 elections was reflected in the restructured Chernomyrdin government and its policies, and has been increasingly apparent in subsequent Russian foreign policy. It has brought increased conflict with Europe and the United States over Bosnia and the eastward expansion of NATO, and a more aggressive policy in relations with the newly independent states on Russia's borders.

The most serious and dangerous manifestation of the new nationalist influence was the military action against the separatist leadership in Chechnya in December 1994. Although it was, in the strict sense, a domestic action taken against an illegal separatist movement within the Russian Federation, the manner of its handling reflects the increased influence on the president of militant nationalists hostile to the claims of small nations inside as well as outside the Russian Federation. How it would affect the future influence of extreme nationalists upon both domestic and foreign policy was still unclear, but the divisions it created among military leaders and between the president and democratic leaders, the stunning evidence it offered of military confusion and incompetence, and the enormous devastation it brought to Chechnya suggest that the action could well be a major setback for the nationalist leaders. But its political and economic consequences were bound to provide a serious test of the young Russian democracy.

North Korea: The Holdout

For the smaller communist states of East Asia, the events of recent years have also brought abundant political change, though less than in China and far less than in Russia. North Korea has clearly been the most rigid in its rejection of change. Its leaders had watched with increasing concern the early progress of the Gorbachev reforms and of events in Eastern Europe, but real full shock came in 1989–91: the Eastern European revolutions of 1989 (and the absorption of the DDR by the Federal Republic a year later), the establishment of Soviet–South

Korean diplomatic relations in September 1990, and the failed coup of August 1991, followed by the suppression of the Soviet Communist Party. China's recognition of South Korea in 1992 merely completed the process.

The reunification of Germany, with the DDR acknowledged as a complete failure, worthy only of absorption and restructuring by the GDR, implied an unnerving comparison with the DPRK–ROK relationship. The recognition of South Korea by Moscow was regarded as total betrayal by a fellow communist state. And the coming to power of Yeltsin, with his avowedly anticommunist policies, completed the horror. Nearly a year before the coup there was open hostility between the Soviet Union and North Korea.

The political response of the North Korean leaders to these events was to reaffirm their determination to defend the "last Eastern outpost of socialism." Both China and the Soviet Union had urged reform on Pyongyang for many months, but with no results. Kim Il Song, controlling the government through the Central People's Committee and the National Defense Commission, rejected all advice, domestic and foreign, to consider reform. Reports of opposition demonstrations and official criticisms of older intellectuals who were still infected with "petty bourgeois individualism" and young intellectuals who "have not experienced severe trials under imperialist and capitalist exploitation" suggested restlessness in intellectual circles. Increased police surveillance, the recall of students from Eastern Europe, repressive measures against Soviet citizens in Pyongyang, and reports of riots and tearing down of portraits of Kim Il Song were some of the danger signs.

The most dangerous indications were those that illustrated the deterioration of the economy. The North Korean economy had grown increasingly slowly in the late 1980s, and probably had begun to decline by 1990. At that point a severe blow came: the cancellation of subsidized ($5 per barrel) Russian oil and the notification that beginning in 1991 all imports from the Soviet Union (57 percent of the North Korean total) must be paid for in hard currency—by a government with a growing foreign debt, scant foreign currency earnings, and virtually no foreign credit. By this point North Korea's only real friend was Cuba, and its only European diplomatic tie Albania.

By late 1990 the government was urging the population to eat two meals a day, usually consisting of rice and kimchi. And a year later it was reported that the diet remained meager, with rationing universal; that one-third of the factories were closed for lack of energy and raw materials; and that the cities were darkened at night to conserve electricity.[19]

The hard-line response of the North Korean leadership to pressures for reform, both domestic and foreign, remained quite consistent. Nonetheless, as Russian and Chinese economic support waned, North Korea turned first to Japan, establishing diplomatic relations in September 1990, and then to the United States, conducting diplomatic exchanges through the American legation in Beijing. Dialogues with South Korean representatives, strongly pressed by China, were held periodically, though without significant progress in the form of solid agreements. Both South Korea and the United States pressed particularly strongly for the right of the International Atomic Energy Association (IAEA) to send representatives to North Korea to investigate nuclear facilities and check on nuclear weapons development. Following the establishment of diplomatic relations between Seoul and Beijing in August 1992, Chinese leaders endorsed the efforts of President Roh Tae Wu of South Korea to secure a North Korean guarantee to halt development of nuclear weapons.[20]

American initiatives were crucial in subsequent efforts to achieve a specific control agreement. On October 21, 1994 the North Koreans signed an agreement to shut down its nuclear reactors, suspend its reprocessing program, and dismantle the reactors over a ten-year period. In exchange, the United States agreed to finance replacement of the reactors, at a cost of $4 billion, with new light-water reactors, the spent fuel from which would be less easily converted into weapons-grade plutonium. During the following months, however, the agreement was threatened by Pyongyang's opposition to the plan for manufacture of the reactors in South Korea.

Vietnam: The Late Arrival

From the end of the Vietnam War to the collapse of communism in Eastern Europe and the Soviet Union, the Vietnamese government's record of management of the nation's domestic and international interests was one of almost uninterrupted failure.

The doctrinaire communism of Hanoi rejected the path of reform pursued in China and, like North Korea, pressed forward with grandiose plans for socialist reconstruction, chief among them the building of a national system of socialist agro-complexes. Food continued to be scarce, economic growth was abysmally small, and only the heavy infusion of Soviet aid kept the economy from collapse. Meanwhile, the long and exhausting commitment to the Vietnamese-imposed regime in Cambodia had brought a tremendous economic drain together with international political isolation and a continuing cold war with China.

Vietnamese domestic politics were increasingly affected by trends in Soviet domestic and international policy during the second half of the 1980s. Gorbachev's advocacy of glasnost' and perestroika brought these words into the Vietnamese official vocabulary, and the Sixth Congress of December 1986 repudiated the failed economic policies of the previous decade. During the following five years, however, there was more talk than action on economic reform. Meanwhile, Soviet pressure to accommodate Chinese demands on Cambodia brought Vietnamese military withdrawal and international negotiation of a settlement of the civil war.

The events of 1989–91 in Eastern Europe and the Soviet Union were, for Vietnam as for other Asian communist states, a profoundly challenging period. Vietnam emulated the others in rejecting any compromise of the principle of party dictatorship. When party leader Tran Xuan Bach published an article titled "On the Road to Renovation," implying that a multiparty system might work better, he was summarily expelled from the party.[21] The action could not stop growing criticism of the party or erosion of the system of social controls it applied to maintain its control. Plenary sessions of the Central Committee during the year, convened with a sense of urgency, discussed measures for preventing an Eastern European–style disaster in Vietnam, but these discussions were couched almost entirely in terms of strengthening discipline within the party.

Official analysis of the failure of European communism stressed, as its main cause, the abandonment of ideological orthodoxy, particularly the leading role of the party and proletarian internationalism. But it noted as well the decline of popular faith in the party and Leninism, and the role of bureaucratic and economic failures, in this process. "Imperialist conspiracy" was assigned a role in the disaster, but next to the long list of party failures its importance seemed minor.

With this background it is not surprising that the Seventh Party Congress in June 1991 reaffirmed the party dictatorship. Party leader Nguyen Van Linh insisted that "in the present condition of our country, it is not objectively necessary to establish a political mechanism of pluralism and multiparty government."[22] The view was shared by the new party leader named at the congress, Do Muoi, a political conservative, but one who had earlier supported economic reform based on economic incentives to producers. Moreover, his successor as prime minister, Vo Van Kiet, had long been a proponent of economic reform.

The expanded commitment to economic reform was undertaken under difficult conditions, greatly aggravated by the economic and political dislocation in the Soviet Union. The Soviets failed to make promised deliveries of fertilizer and oil in 1990, and notified Vietnam in January 1991 that they would require cash payment for goods formerly given as aid. The loss of Soviet economic support led Do Muoi to seek economic support from the United States. Relations had improved since the Vietnamese had allowed the establishment of a U.S. office in Hanoi in April 1991 to supervise the search for missing soldiers. And with the signing of a Cambodian peace agreement on October 21, Secretary of State Baker announced American willingness to undertake talks on establishment of normal diplomatic relations. Still, the United States continued its refusal to endorse IMF or World Bank aid for Vietnam, cutting that country off from one of the most important sources of foreign aid.

The new reform leadership undertook, from the summer of 1991, a series of new reform initiatives that focused on the expansion of investment. Vietnam's investment rate as a proportion of GDP was about a fourth that of China. The loss-making state industries drained rather than expanded the investment resources of the country, and the government tax collections were barely more than 5 percent of the GDP, so that foreign aid and investment were desperately needed.[23] Yet these required effective commercial laws, government control of the budget deficit to limit inflation, and the confidence of potential foreign investors that the government would give firm, continuing support to private investment.

Clearly some foreign investors were convinced that Vietnam offered important opportunities. During 1991 and 1992, a number of Hong Kong, French, and Japanese investors explored possibilities and extended investment credits. Japanese interests have shown a particular interest in the Dao Hung (Big Bear) oilfield discovered by Mobil during the Vietnam War and still awaiting development. Overall, foreign investment has shown a steady upward movement, from $590 million in 1990 to almost $2 billion in 1992, and at the end of the year Vietnamese leaders were optimistic about an end to the American embargo on trade and investment, as President Bush authorized the opening of offices and the signing of contracts by American companies.[24] Not until the end of the first year of the Clinton administration, in early 1994, however, did the United States agree to end its Vietnam embargo and upgrade its diplomatic ties.

Compared to China, Vietnam has only begun the process of economic reform. It starts, as did China, from a level of real poverty—a per capita GDP of roughly $200, contrasted with a figure of $1,468 for neighboring Thailand.[25] Yet Vietnam also has significant advantages, among them a relatively high educational level of its population: 88 percent are literate, and 72 percent of children complete secondary school.

Another important advantage that Vietnam has is that the South shows great promise of rapid economic development. It has had a much shorter period of communist rule than the North, and it has a tradition of private production and trade, both rural and urban, that can respond quickly to favorable government policy. Ho Chi Minh City (Saigon) shows already the signs of a new era of private enterprise in many spheres, even in education.

The impact of the economic reform in Vietnam upon politics and foreign policy is clearly far more limited than in China, but more advanced than in North Korea. Leadership changes since 1986, and even more since 1991, have given support to reform, bringing to power a new set of leaders with greater understanding of the need for reform and greater flexibility in the design of reform measures. Political and ideological barriers have been much reduced, permitting not only a new receptivity to market-oriented economic reform, but also a new willingness to seek friendly contacts with capitalist states. As in China, the insistence upon retaining socialism means mainly that the Communist Party will continue to insist on its political monopoly. Even in this matter, however, the supporting argument is pragmatic rather than ideological—that the party provides a firm and stable political system, which is required for successful economic reform.

There is, of course, another side to this argument, which is surely not lost on the public: that if the party is not successful in economic reform, its claim to power can be challenged. As is evident from the much-increased cooperativeness of Vietnamese leaders in foreign relations, the internal economic pressures upon them make them eager to settle differences with their neighbors and with the international community more broadly, and willing to adapt to the requirements of foreign investors.

As in China and North Korea, the retention of a Communist Party dictatorship gives a small clique formidable power to define the nation's foreign policy. In contrast to China, however, the present stage of economic development in Vietnam, and the much smaller size and power of the country, assure that it will play a mainly defensive international role. The militant revolutionary nationalist ideology that made Vietnam a threat to its neighbors has mostly eroded, and Vietnam's relative economic position has greatly weakened. The party controls a state apparatus whose control over the national economy will weaken as the socialist system is dismantled. Already the central government secures a pitifully small share of national income as taxes, and the new private economy that is developing is building new, independent owners and entrepreneurs, and many new and substantially autonomous regional economic centers. As in China, the era of free markets and private enterprise contributes more to the power of society than to that of the state.

Where from Communism?

Communism has collapsed in Europe and is fading in Asia. The question is what will replace it, for the outcome will determine the kind of foreign policy that the Asian communist states pursue, and therefore the peacefulness of their integration into the international community. Zbigniew Brzezinski argued several years ago, in *The Grand Failure*, that the traditional communist system was destined to move either "to pluralist democracy or to some form of nationalistic authoritarianism."[26] He argued further that "the problem is likely to become intellectually the most interesting and politically the most central issue" of our time.[27]

The transformation of communist states is indeed the central political issue of our time, the most important cases being those of Russia and China. But the Brzezinski alternatives—pluralist democracy or nationalist authoritarianism—need some clarification and refinement, especially in view of developments since he wrote. Among the states under review here, only in Russia has the Communist Party surrendered power to a noncommunist political leadership dedicated to building a pluralist democracy, and both the political and economic foundations of that system remain weak and the outcome of the political change uncertain. But the political change that has occurred in Russia since the beginning of the Gorbachev era is wholly absent in North Korea, just beginning in Vietnam, and somewhat more advanced in China. At best, the development of a system of pluralist democracy from Asian communism is a very long-term prospect.

In the interim, the process of change in China and Vietnam has brought a gradual transition from totalitarian to authoritarian communist rule. Any effort to predict the future policy of these governments requires the kind of assessment undertaken in this essay of the forms and direction of this process, and the social and economic changes supporting it.

The term "authoritarian nationalism" used by Brzezinski needs clarification. The weakening of communist power in every case has permitted the reemergence of long-suppressed political currents, including nationalism, with or without the actual end of communist power. But the renewed influence of nationalism upon political programs has taken many forms, some supportive and some opposed to authoritarian politics. It is useful, therefore, to review the varieties of nationalist politics that have appeared with the decline of communism, and their relationship to other political currents.

In multinational communist states such as Russia, Yugoslavia, and China, the decline of communist power, and of the legitimacy of "proletarian internationalism," has been marked by competition between the nationalist claims of the ruling center and those of subject nations. In the Russian case, the nationalisms of both Eastern Europe and national republics within the Soviet Union ultimately prevailed over the policy of the center, bringing finally the peaceful dismantling of the Soviet Union. But that process was possible only after an anticommunist and democratic nationalist leadership had prevailed in the Russian Republic and supported the claims to sovereignty of the other nations of the Soviet Union.

There remain strong—currently increasingly strong—communist and nationalist groups within Russia that advocate both political authoritarianism and the rebuilding of a multinational empire comprising much of the territory of the former Soviet Union. It is no coincidence that these groups are also the most outspoken in endorsing the Chinese model of authoritarian government and statist economic policy. At present, however, they do not control the Russian government.

Clearly the power balance between the Chinese leadership in Beijing and the much smaller subject nations of Inner Asia is unlikely to permit an outcome of the struggle between competing nationalisms like that in Russia. Using a mix of nationalist and socialist slogans, the present Chinese leadership affirms the territorial integrity of the existing state, as well as the irredentist claims of its predecessors. Vietnam, on the other hand, was compelled to abandon its imperialist gains and ambitions, both by the nationalist resistance of the Cambodians, supported by China, and by the termination of the support of its Russian patron. The still totalitarian communism of North Korea, meanwhile, has not allowed the open emergence of any genuinely independent nationalist political expression, while official nationalism focuses upon the mission of reunification.

For the future development of democracy, Russia has enormous advantages over China, North Korea, and Vietnam: greater wealth, natural resources, urbanization, education, and general level of economic development, as well as greater emancipation from the political and cultural controls of the Leninist state. China has greater political stability and a long experience of successful economic reform and expansion, but virtually no development of formal democratic institutions. It has been argued, however, that in China, "as local levels of government gain greater power vis-à-vis higher levels of government, their decisionmaking process is becoming increasingly autonomous of the central leadership."[28]

Politically and culturally, Russia is poised for the transition to pluralist democracy, with the communist power monopoly replaced by a popularly elected president and parliament, a new structure of political parties, a free press, and an increasingly free educational system. The main threat to the process is the challenge of antidemocratic communists and nationalists, whose triumph would favor authoritarian government, a statist economic system, a strong military power, and an irredentist foreign policy. The threat has been increased by setbacks in the process of conversion of the socialist economy and by the protracted struggle over a new constitutional order.

Russia is unique among the current and former communist states of Asia in the scope of its political transformation and its progress toward democracy. The process of transition from the old order has been turbulent and uncertain. The deep division over the course of economic reform was exacerbated by an equally fundamental disagreement on the structure of the new political order. The window-dressing constitution inherited from the communist era lacked a functional division of powers, and political life was a constant struggle between president and parliament until the parliament was dissolved and a new constitution with a clear division of powers, and a very strong presidency, was installed by popular vote. The change has not removed the very large policy differences separating reform and conservative forces, or eliminated the fact that many of the latter are hostile to democracy on principle. But it has provided a functional democratic constitutional structure within which policy differences can be arbitrated by defined and workable constitutional rules. The rest will depend on the wisdom and skill of the political leadership.

An Overview and Comparison

What is most impressive about the Russian political transformation under Gorbachev and Yeltsin is the repeated success of the democratic forces: in the parliamentary elections of 1989 and 1990, in the election of Yeltsin to the Russian presidency and the defeat of the attempted coup in 1991, in the peaceful dismantling of the Soviet Union at the end of that year, in the victory over a second coup attempt by conservative parliamentary leaders between July and October 1993, and in the successful vote on the new constitution in December. The minority position of the radical reformers after the December elections was less important than the fact that they, together with moderate reformers, had effective control of the executive and legislative branches of government.[29] By the end of 1994, however, the rightward swing of the policies of the president, especially in the wake of the October ruble crisis and the December military action in Chechnya, indicated a significant change of political power and policy.

The most promising future scenario in Russia would be one in which it overcame its current grave transitional economic problems and consolidated its democratic gains within the new constitutional order. The main threats to such a development are three: the failure of economic reform; entanglement, under growing pressure from ultranationalist political leaders, in efforts to recover power in former Soviet territories (as opposed to constructive expansion of economic and security cooperation with the now independent states); and a substantial further increase in political support for antidemocratic nationalists and communists. The policies of the latter are strongly anti-Western, and should their power increase and one of their leaders gain the presidency (as in the 1996 elections), the course of Russian political change would be fundamentally altered. At present, even among pro-Western political leaders there is pressure for a more independent and assertive Russian foreign policy, but there is little doubt that a successful Russian democracy would, long term, be friendly to the West. At present, unfortunately, both the economic and the political foundations of the new democracy remain very vulnerable.

Meanwhile, China, though much poorer and less developed, has managed to combine political stability and economic reform into a highly effective program. Its leadership has abandoned much of communist ideology, although it retains considerable hostility to capitalism and the democratic states, even as it seeks in every way to use their institutions, their investment capital, and their markets for its economic development plans. And it combines a Communist Party dictatorship whose effective power has been much reduced with a highly successful policy of economic development whose main expansion is in the private sector. The prospects for democracy in China rest chiefly on continuing stability, economic growth, and the expansion of education and of political and cultural pluralism.[30]

There is no present Chinese or Vietnamese equivalent for the Gorbachev-era policy of actively dismantling party power by transferring it to the soviet, or state apparatus, a process completed with the ending of Communist Party leadership under Yeltsin. In China, as in Vietnam and North Korea, the leadership continues to affirm the party's power monopoly. But Chinese economic policy has greatly reduced that by diminishing the scope of public ownership and management of the national economy, and by joining the global economy. Though the party retains the levers of central power, it must now recognize the fast-growing wealth and power of private farmers, merchants, manufacturers, and investors, and accept that both its political and its economic policies are constrained by growing dependence upon access to global markets. Extensive privatization of the economy has also greatly expanded the wealth and independence of the regions, especially the south and the coastal areas, where the authority of the central party leadership is increasingly tenuous, while the center's share of the GNP continues to decline.

The most promising future scenario for China would combine the maintenance of political stability and economic modernization with growing cultural and intellectual freedom and political participation. The regime would be encouraged by its complex international economic dependence to pursue a peaceful and cooperative foreign policy, while internal social and economic change prepared the way for dismantling authoritarian rule. The process could certainly be retarded or reversed by a regime grown increasingly restrictive and oppressive either from ideological resentment of the changes unleashed by its economic reform and growing outside influence, or fearful of losing power, or both. It could also be thrown off course, with very negative results, by pursuit of an expansionist foreign policy that brought international conflict.

The future course of the North Korean and Vietnamese transitions will be chiefly the result of internal choices, but will also be influenced by the Russian and Chinese examples. The much smaller size of their populations and their power makes them less influential in the future of East Asia, but their importance should not be understated. North Korean political change will play a vital role in the future of the South, determining the character of North–South relations and the future prospects of unification. A positive policy of internal reform and constructive cooperation with the South could have a decisive influence on the future of the nation that is the strategic centerpiece of the international system in Northeast Asia. Regrettably, both seem remote prospects at present. And as Vietnam has a similarly vital place in Southeast Asia, the success of its transition will be a major influence on the future of that region. If its authoritarian political system permits, as in China, an aggressive economic reform, it may build the foundations for political reform in the process. The recent opening to the world economy, combined with the lifting of the American embargo and the opening of diplomatic relations with the United States, is a promising beginning of that process.

In conclusion, it may be useful to summarize the positive changes in the Asian communist states in recent years: the abandonment, by all except North Korea, of the traditions of communist revolution and implacable ideological hostility toward the industrial democracies; the normalization, to varying degrees, of concepts of international relations and of discourse on questions of security; the reintegration into the world economy, together with economic privatization, expansion, and international economic interdependence; the dismantling or erosion of the power of ruling communist parties; and the gradual building of the social and economic foundations of civil society.

All of these trends are encouraging for the future. But as noted repeatedly in the preceding pages, there is a great deal of variety in the process of transition from the old order to the new, and the possibilities for both economic and political instability are still disturbingly large in the two major powers and very dangerous in the unreformed case, North Korea. With the two major powers, the growth of nationalism virtually guarantees an increasingly assertive foreign policy and is likely to encourage expansionist policies, especially those based on irredentist claims. Thus all of the positive gains of recent years, promising and encouraging as they are, must be qualified in various ways by taking note of countervailing negative trends and possibilities. Only one thing is certain: The impact of communism's decline upon the politics of Asia is as important and pervasive as the impact of its original victories. It has opened up a new era in the history of East Asia and the world.

Notes

1. A March 1990 memorandum to high-level cadres of the CPC Central Committee was indicative of the mood of the leadership—namely, a sense that China was gravely threatened by the anticommunist revolutions in Eastern Europe, and deep hostility toward the Soviet leadership for their "errors." *Cheng Ming,* Hong Kong, No. 150 (April 1, 1990), pp. 6–8. *Foreign Broadcast Information Service/PRC,* April 3, 1990.

2. *Foreign Broadcast Information Service, Soviet Union,* May 17, 1989, p. 8.

3. Nicholas Kristof made much of this point in an article on Chinese foreign policy, quoting a senior Chinese foreign policy official, who said:

> If chaos continues and prices rise, then that will help the Chinese government because the last thing people here want is chaos. But if there is a quick turnaround in Russia, and production increases and living standards rise, then people here will say they want to make the leap as well.

Nicholas D. Kristof, "As China Looks at World Order, It Detects New Struggles Emerging," *New York Times,* April 21, 1992, p. A1.

4. The per capita GNP of China increased from $300 in 1978 to $400 in 1992. Ray S. Cline, ed., *China and Pacific Rim Letter,* vol. 4, no. 8, p. 2.

5. "Deng's New Hope," *The Economist,* Oct. 24, 1991, p. 36.

6. "China's Financial Fix," *The Economist,* July 10, 1993, pp. 69–70.

7. Nicholas D. Kristof, "As China Looks at World Order, It Detects New Struggles Emerging," *New York Times,* April 21, 1992, p. A1.

8. A recent study of China's policy during the Gulf War summarizes Chinese motivation as follows:

> It seems that China's agreement to cooperate with the other major powers derived not merely from its desire to manipulate the Gulf crisis in order to rehabilitate its image and lift the sanctions; it also reflected a genuine anxiety about international instability and particularly the damage it might do to international economic relations, and thus to China's modernization drive.

Yitzhak Shichor, "China and the Gulf Crisis: Escape from Predicaments," *Problems of Communism,* November–December 1991, p. 85.

9. It is interesting that the Chinese foreign policy document quoted by Nicholas Kristof (note 3 above) makes specific mention of the importance of exploiting U.S.-Japanese differences.

10. A very interesting recent analysis of the evolution of the nationalities policy of the CCP since the 1930s, combined with a careful analysis of the calculations of the Chinese leadership about Tibet and Xinjiang today, is provided in Thomas Heberer, "Droht dem chinesischen Reich der Zerfall?" *Berichte des Bundesinstituts für ostwissenschaftliche und*

internationale Studien, no. 45 (1991). Heberer argues that "no change in policy towards the national minorities would be possible without the fundamental democratization of China" (p. 52).

11. Just as one had begun to absorb the changes in Soviet foreign policy, a new set of changes emerged abruptly under Yeltsin. A very thoughtful and informed assessment of the changes in their early stage is provided by Vernon V. Aspaturian, "Farewell to Soviet Foreign Policy," *Problems of Communism,* November–December 1991, pp. 53–62. The initial aim of policy change was to eliminate entirely the communist ideological element of policy, and its main thrust was very strongly pro-Western, with remarkable proposals for quite radical disarmament, for joining NATO, etc. In the course of the first year, however, a lively foreign policy debate developed that went beyond simple repudiation of communist policy and an unqualifiedly pro-Western stance to reexamination of Russia's pre-Bolshevik legacy of international relations, an exploration of national interests, and a particularly intense study of Russia's Eurasian and Asian position and policy. With a conservative and nationalist political revival, there was also much challenge to Yeltsin's dismantling of the Soviet Union. These developments are discussed in Alexander Rahr, "'Atlanticists' versus 'Eurasians' in Russian Foreign Policy," *RFE/RL Research Report,* vol. 1, no. 22 (May 29, 1992), pp. 17–22; Suzanne Crow, "Russia Debates Its National Interests," *RFE/RL Research Report,* vol. 1, no. 28 (July 10, 1992), pp. 43–46; and Jeff Checkel, "Russian Foreign Policy: Back to the Future?" *RFE/RL Research Report,* vol. 1, no. 41 (October 16, 1992).

12. Gudrun Wacker, "Die VR China und die Nachfolgestaaten der Sowjetunion. Teil I: Der Zerfall der UdSSR und die Beziehungen zur Russischen Föderation," *Berichte des Bundesinstituts für ostwissenschaftliche und internationale Studien,* no. 49 (1993), pp. 37–38.

13. For a very thoughtful evaluation of the midyear achievements and problems of the Yeltsin economic reform, see Michael Ellmann, "Shock Therapy in Russia: Failure or Partial Success?" *RFE/RL Research Report,* vol. 1, no. 34 (August 28, 1992), pp. 48–61. And in the same issue, Erik Whitlock, "Midyear Update of Economic Indicators." The opening up of Russia to the international economy, evaluated toward the end of the first year of Yeltsin's leadership, is provided in Erik Whitlock, "Russia's Progress toward an Open Economy," *RFE/RL Research Report,* vol. 1, no. 47 (November 27, 1992), pp. 35–40.

14. For a careful analysis of the evidence for the view that Yeltsin was responding to a planned coup by Khasbulatov and his ultranationalist allies, see Alexander Rahr, "The October Revolt: Mass Unrest or Putsch?" *RFE/RL Research Report,* vol. 2, no. 44 (November 5, 1993).

15. See Stephen Foye, "Updating Russian Civil-Military Relations," *RFE/RL Research Report,* vol. 2, no. 46 (November 19, 1993).

16. This view is expressed by Yuri N. Afanasyev in "Reform Is Dead," *Foreign Affairs,* vol. 73, no. 2 (March/April 1994), pp. 21–27.

17. See Vladimir Socor, "Dniester Involvement in the Moscow Rebellion," *RFE/RL Research Report,* vol. 2, no. 46 (November 19, 1993), pp. 25–32.

18. It is interesting and relevant that Nicholas Kristof writes of China that "the government still has not dared to expose much of the huge state sector (accounting for about half of industrial production) to the cruelty of market forces, and when it does it could face strikes and revolts by disgruntled workers." "The Rise of China," *Foreign Affairs,* vol. 72, no. 5 (November/December 1993), p. 60.

19. Nicholas D. Kristof, "A Stalinist's Paradise in Korea Flounders," *New York Times,* November 17, 1991, p. 4.

20. James Sterngold, "Seoul Gets Some Diplomatic Backing in China," *New York Times,* September 30, 1992, p. A5.

21. Richard F. Staar, ed., *1991 Yearbook on International Communist Affairs* (Stanford, CA: Hoover Institution Press, 1991), p. 242.

22. Philip Shenon, "Vietnam Party Vows to Maintain Absolute Power," *New York Times,* June 25, 1991, p. A3.

23. One report suggested that the figure for investment in Vietnam was 5.2 percent of GDP in 1991. *The Economist,* December 14, 1991, p. 38.

24. "More Investment in Vietnam," *New York Times,* January 1, 1993, p. C3.

25. *The Economist,* December 14, 1991, p. 38.

26. Zbigniew Brzezinski, *The Grand Failure: The Birth and Death of Communism in the Twentieth Century* (New York: Scribner, 1989), p. 252.

27. Ibid., p. 253.

28. Suzanne Ogden, "The Changing Content of China's Democratic Socialist Institutions," *In Depth: A Journal for Values and Public Policy,* vol. 3, no. 1 (Winter 1993), p. 252.

29. For a very thoughtful brief review of the division of political power in the new constitutional order in early 1994 by an outstanding analyst, see Alexander Rahr, "The Future of Russian Reforms," *RFE/RL Research Report,* vol. 3, no. 5 (February 4, 1994), pp. 7–11.

30. I have not attempted a systematic look at China's democratization prospects in this chapter, but I would like to take note of two very stimulating articles on this issue (and the larger issue of political change in Asia) published in the final issues of *Problems of Communism.* These are Vivienne Shue, "China: Transition Postponed?" *Problems of Communism,* vol. 41, nos. 1–2 (January–April 1992), pp. 157–168; and Martin King Whyte, "Prospects for Democratization in China," *Problems of Communism,* vol. 41, no. 3 (May–June 1992), pp. 58–70. Professor Whyte provides a very thorough inventory of the historical and contemporary factors favoring and disfavoring the development of a Chinese democracy, drawing very cautious conclusions on the positive side of the balance. Professor Shue contends that "transition away from state socialism cannot be assumed necessarily, or even very probably, to eventuate in the establishment of liberal democratic capitalism." She stresses that in East Asian cultures, "capitalism has most often managed to thrive . . . only in symbiosis with strong, even authoritarian states" (loc. cit., p. 158). This reader was puzzled by the implicit assumption that democratic states are not strong states. Surely there are many examples of exceedingly sturdy and durable democratic states.

12

International Order and Organization in the Asia-Pacific Region

Harry Harding

From Singapore to Washington and from Tokyo to Canberra, officials, scholars, and policy analysts are discussing the future of international relations in the Asia-Pacific region. They are debating the impact of the collapse of the Soviet Union, the growing diplomatic assertiveness of Japan, the apparent strategic retrenchment of the United States, and the economic resurgence of China. They are asking whether the end of the Cold War and the rise of economic interdependence will lead to greater stability, or whether they will simply produce new tension and conflict. They are pondering the prospects for economic integration in the region and the desirability of multilateral security mechanisms. At root, all these questions involve different aspects of the same fundamental issue: the nature of the evolving international order in the Asia-Pacific region.

An international order can be defined as the pattern of interaction among states and the societies they govern during a particular period of time. International orders vary along three principal dimensions. The first involves the variables familiar to students of the realist tradition in the study of international politics: the number of major powers, their relative strength and dynamism, their ambitions and intentions in international affairs, and their patterns of rivalry and alliance. An analysis along this dimension would ask whether the distribution of power is such that an international order is unipolar, bipolar, or multipolar. It would also inquire whether the relationship among the major nations should be characterized as a concert of powers, a balance of powers, or a confrontation between contending blocs. Today, the relative decline of the United States and Russia, the rise of China and Japan, and the emergence of influential subregional actors such as South Korea, Vietnam, Thailand, and Indonesia inevitably raise questions about this dimension of international order in the Asia-Pacific region.

The liberal tradition in international studies emphasizes a second dimension

325

of analysis. It focuses on the degree of economic and cultural interdependence among the societies in an international system: the degree to which their citizens trade with one another, visit one another, study in one another's universities, and invest in one another's economies. An analysis in this tradition would explore whether interdependence among societies is growing or declining. It would also examine whether interdependence is helping to mediate past conflicts by giving societies a greater stake in a stable relationship, or whether it is generating new tensions as societies come into greater contact with one another. The increasing flows of goods, technology, people, and capital among the societies of the Asia-Pacific region over the past several decades indicates that interdependence in the region is rapidly increasing, but the implications for international order remain uncertain.

Finally, a third dimension of variation concerns the degree to which an international order is institutionalized. At a minimum, the regularities inherent in a particular international order can be inferred by analysts, as well as by skillful statesmen, simply by observing the interactions of states and societies. But on many occasions, these patterns can also be made more explicit. Governments can embody their relationships with other states in formal strategic alliances and economic partnerships, whether bilateral or multilateral. They can create international regimes by codifying some of the norms and principles of the international order into binding agreements.[1] They can also establish international organizations to share information, monitor conduct, interpret rules, and even serve as forums for international legislation. The discussion of cooperative security and economic integration now occurring in the Asia-Pacific region addresses this third aspect of international order: whether tensions can be reduced, problems resolved, and opportunities seized through the creation of multilateral institutions.

This chapter is a chronological survey of the international order in the Asia-Pacific region since World War II, with particular focus on the evolution of the multilateral institutions in the region. It is organized around four critical turning points: some relatively discrete events, others longer-term evolutionary processes. The historical stages demarcated by these turning points overlap to a degree. But they are sufficiently distinct chronologically and analytically to warrant separate discussion.

The first of these turning points was the emergence of the United States and the Soviet Union as the centers of a new bipolar international system at the end of World War II. The two superpowers built rival international regimes to govern the commercial and security relationships within their respective blocs. Although primarily focused upon Europe, this effort found echoes in the Asia-Pacific region as well. As we will see, however, bipolarity was always substantially looser in Asia than in Europe.

The second key development was the successive adoption of export-oriented strategies of economic development by the major governments of the region in the 1960s and 1970s. These strategies bound the Asian economies more closely first to their major overseas market, the United States, and then increasingly to one another. They also produced a growing interest in creating mechanisms for reducing barriers to trade and investment, in resolving the tensions that economic interaction invariably creates, and thus in forming multilateral regional economic institutions. Given the diversity of the major Asian economies and their lack of experience with multilateral organization, during this phase it proved feasible only to create unofficial and informal organizations to discuss these economic issues.

The third turning point involved the end of Asia's principal cold wars, most importantly those dividing the Soviet Union from the United States and China from the Soviet Union. This dual rapprochement, which occurred primarily between 1985 and 1991, had fundamental implications for order in the Asia-Pacific region, as in the global system more generally. It permitted, and even encouraged, the amelioration of relations among countries previously linked to rival powers. It enabled the creation of new international institutions for regulating or resolving international conflict, and it led to the inclusion of both the Soviet Union and China in the regimes governing commercial and security relationships.

Finally, the fourth major trend has been the rise of new centers of economic and military power in Asia—not only China and Japan, but also South Korea, Taiwan, Vietnam, and the various members of the Association of Southeast Asian Nations (ASEAN). Together with Russia and the United States, these regional powers have competing economic interests, and in some cases have territorial conflicts, overlapping spheres of influence, and historical rivalries. This has spurred consideration of the ways in which new multilateral economic and security arrangements—new forums for discussion, new regimes, and new international organizations—could help resolve or manage potential conflicts over security and economic interests.

A review of the evolution of the international order in the Asia-Pacific region during these four periods leads to several conclusions. First, there have been daunting obstacles to multilateral organization in the region. The nations of the area vary significantly in their size, level of development, political system, culture, and ethnic mix. They have diverse historical experiences, and they often view one another with considerable mistrust. The boundaries of the region are vague; there is no consensus as to whether it should include South Asia, the Pacific Coast countries of Latin America, or even Canada and the United States. Consequently, Asia has been slower than Europe to develop regional institutions, in either the economic or the security sphere. But growing economic interdependence, the end of Asia's cold wars, and the growing strategic complexity of the region have given much greater impetus to institution building. In particular, the Asia-Pacific region has seen two important organizational breakthroughs in recent years. The Asia Pacific Economic Cooperation (APEC) forum, formed in 1989, is the first official regionwide organization intended to discuss trade, investment, and other economic issues. In the security realm, the comparable innovation was the addition of strategic questions to the agenda of ASEAN's

Post-Ministerial Conference (ASEAN-PMC) in 1992, and the subsequent decision to create a separate ASEAN Regional Forum on security (ARF) in 1994.

Nonetheless, the obstacles to creating regional institutions are still readily apparent. Despite these two breakthroughs in the official sphere, there are far more channels for informal and unofficial dialogue than there are formal intergovernmental organizations. Institution building has proceeded considerably farther at the subregional level than at the regionwide level. Both APEC and ARF are struggling to reach agreements on their agendas. It is by no means certain that either institution will be able to develop rules or norms that will be binding on its members. Looking ahead, therefore, while it is virtually certain that the international order in the Asia-Pacific region will be multipolar, it is not clear whether it will develop the degree of institutionalization that can guarantee its stability.

The Era of Loose Bipolarity

Within a few years after the end of World War II, the international order took on the semblance of a bipolar system centering on the Soviet Union and the United States. The two superpowers were engaged in a global rivalry for strategic advantage. Each of them organized friendly nations into military alliances and economic groupings that they controlled. The nuclear standoff made it highly unlikely that either of the two superpowers would ever launch a direct attack on the other, but they did employ a combination of offensive and defensive strategies to extend and maintain their influence elsewhere. Although there was fairly extensive diplomatic, economic, and cultural interaction within each bloc, the two camps had relatively little contact with each other, each one fearing that economic and cultural ties might strengthen its rival while subverting itself.

The Asia-Pacific region was in some ways a prime example of the bipolar nature of the Cold War world. Like Europe, East Asia was divided into two blocs centering on Moscow and Washington. The Soviet Union linked itself to the other communist states in the region: China, North Korea, Mongolia, and North Vietnam. The United States, in turn, sought to forge economic partnerships and military alliances with some of the major noncommunist countries in the region, notably Japan, South Korea, Taiwan, the Philippines, Australia, and New Zealand. Just as in Europe, the rivalry between the two blocs was reflected in both ideological antagonism and strategic confrontation. Furthermore, as in Europe, the economic, cultural, and political interactions between these two blocs remained limited. America's allies had trade and investment relations primarily with the West; whereas the members of the communist bloc had economic ties largely with one another.

Indeed, the degree of mutual isolation was, if anything, even greater in Asia than in Europe. Although the United States and its European allies maintained diplomatic relations with the Soviet Union throughout the Cold War, neither

Washington nor Tokyo established normal diplomatic ties with Beijing until the 1970s. The United States maintained a full economic embargo against China through the 1950s and 1960s, and continued one against North Korea and North Vietnam into the 1990s. In addition, Washington had diplomatic relations with neither Pyongyang or Hanoi.

However, despite the high level of mutual estrangement, for most of this period the bipolar system was significantly looser in Asia than it was in Europe. For one thing, the level of confrontation between the two superpowers was lower in the Asia-Pacific region than in Europe. Until the intensification of the Sino-Soviet dispute in the late 1960s and the military buildup undertaken by Leonid Brezhnev in the 1970s, the Soviet Union deployed relatively few advanced forces in East Asia. Moreover, at no point did the United States and the Soviet Union have forces directly arrayed against one another, as they did along the central front in Europe. Thus, the prospects for a direct clash between the military forces of the two superpowers were significantly lower in Asia than in Europe.

But this simply increased the chances for proxy conflicts: clashes between the superpowers' allies, or between one superpower and the ally of another. In contrast with Europe, which remained peaceful throughout the Cold War era, there were two major wars in East Asia during the same period: one in Korea, the other in Vietnam. In addition, there was a chronic series of crises in the Taiwan Strait, which could well have exploded into a third regional conflict between the United States and China. And, even after the United States withdrew from Vietnam, there were still armed clashes in Indochina; one between Vietnam and Cambodia in 1978 led to an all-out Chinese invasion of Vietnam the following year.

Another difference between the Cold War's two principal theaters was that bipolarity was far less encompassing in Asia than in Europe. In Europe, only a small number of relatively unimportant nations (Sweden, Switzerland, Austria, and arguably Yugoslavia) maintained their neutrality vis-à-vis both major blocs. In Asia, in contrast, the unaligned nations, such as Indonesia and India, played a much more significant role. In striking contrast with Europe, the most important multilateral organization in Asia—ASEAN—was not linked with either superpower, but was independent of both of them. Indeed, ASEAN's principal objective in the late 1960s and early 1970s was to turn all of Southeast Asia into a "zone of peace, freedom, and neutrality," withdrawing it, in effect, from the bipolar competition between the two superpowers.

Moreover, in a display of fluidity unknown in Europe, one of Asia's major powers shifted its position in the regional order three times in the course of the Cold War. The civil war in China ended the alignment between the Nationalist government and the United States that had been formed in World War II, and replaced it with an alliance between the new communist government and the Soviet Union. By the end of the 1950s, however, Beijing had become disenchanted with both Moscow's foreign policy and its domestic model of development, abandoned its alignment with the Kremlin, and assumed a role as a major independent actor. The Sino-Soviet split sparked a major military buildup on both sides of the border, and led to sharp clashes between the two countries in the late 1960s and early 1970s. With its security in doubt, China again turned to the United States for support. The Nixon visit of 1972, followed by the full normalization of Sino-American relations at the end of 1978, created another alignment between China and the United States, this time directed against the Soviet Union rather than Japan.

Finally, the level of institution building was also significantly lower in Asia than in Europe. The diversity of the region, and the mistrust among many regional powers, made it extremely difficult for either the United States or the Soviet Union to organize its followers into a multilateral military alliance. The Soviet Union was unable to create an Asian equivalent of the Warsaw Pact to counter either the United States or China. The United States and its allies did create a few multilateral security arrangements in the Asia-Pacific region, notably ANZUS (linking the United States, Australia, and New Zealand), SEATO (linking Thailand and the Philippines to the ANZUS powers, Britain, and France), and the Five-Power Defense Arrangement (linking Britain, Australia, and New Zealand to Malaysia and Singapore). But these were significantly less organized and coherent than NATO, and covered proportionately far less of the region.[2] None of America's allies in Northeast Asia—Japan, South Korea, or Taiwan—was ever brought into a multilateral alliance. And periodic proposals to create a regionwide security organization equivalent to NATO, whether directed against China or the Soviet Union, fell on deaf ears.

In the area of multilateral economic cooperation, too, Asia lagged far behind Europe. The Soviet Union tried to extend the Council on Mutual Economic Assistance (originally known as COMECON) into Asia, but North Korea and China steadfastly and consistently refused to join, seeking to maintain their independence from the Kremlin's central planning apparatus. Only Mongolia was a member of COMECON from an early stage, and Hanoi joined only with the solidification of the Soviet–Vietnamese alliance in the late 1970s.

Nor did the capitalist countries of Asia form anything remotely resembling the Iron and Steel Community, the Common Market, or the other precursors of today's European Union. To be sure, there was the Asian Development Bank (ADB), organized in the mid-1960s, but the ADB did not address trade or investment problems, or serve as a forum for the coordination of macroeconomic policy. A second grouping of East Asian capitalist economies formed in the mid-1960s, ASPAC, proved both unproductive and short-lived.[3] The lower level of economic development of most of the capitalist economies of East Asia precluded the need for multilateral economic organization in the region, as did the fact that at this stage most of these economies directed their trade toward the United States, rather than toward one another.

There were, however, other forms of international organization in Asia that were more effective. There was an extensive network of bilateral alliances and partnerships radiating out from Moscow, from Washington, and later from Beijing. The Soviet Union had military links to China (until the early 1960s), North Korea, Mongolia, North Vietnam, and eventually India. The United States had defense arrangements with Japan, South Korea, Taiwan, South Vietnam, the Philippines, Thailand, Australia, and New Zealand. After its break with the Soviet Union, China forged tacit or overt military alliances with North Korea, North Vietnam, and Pakistan, and engaged in limited forms of military cooperation with the United States. Indeed, as the bilateral confrontation between Moscow and Washington extended to Asia in the 1970s and early 1980s, many of these alliances became considerably more active than before.

Furthermore, even though there were few regional multilateral organizations, many of the Asia-Pacific nations were members of multilateral institutions on the global level. The Communist parties of the region were members of the Comintern and its successors, at least until the Sino-Soviet dispute destroyed the unity of the international communist movement in the 1960s. Most of the capitalist economies of Asia were members of the World Bank, the International Monetary Fund, and the General Agreement on Tariffs and Trade. But even here, the degree of integration was less in Asia than in Europe, since no Asian communist country was a member of the United Nations until Mongolia joined the world body in the early 1960s. China and Vietnam joined the United Nations only in the 1970s, and North Korea only in the early 1990s.

In sum, the bipolar system of the Cold War was simultaneously less encompassing, more fluid, and even more belligerent in Asia than in Europe. It was also much less extensively organized. There were few effective multilateral alliances in either camp. Nor were there any economic institutions even remotely comparable to those that were created in Eastern and Western Europe. The diversity of the region and the lower levels of economic development that characterized it in the late 1940s and early 1950s were significant barriers to the creation of an institutionalized international order.

Growing Economic Interdependence

Beginning in the early 1960s, the Asia-Pacific region was characterized by growing economic interdependence, at least among the market economies centering on the United States. One after another, Taiwan, South Korea, Singapore, Malaysia, Thailand, Indonesia, and the Philippines adopted similar strategies of economic development, all patterned after the one pioneered by Japan in the 1950s. These neomercantilist strategies involved an unusual combination of export orientation and import substitution. On the one hand, the Asian economies erected both tariff and nontariff barriers to exclude many foreign goods from their markets. On the other, they used a variety of mechanisms, ranging from undervalued currencies to infrastructural development to subsidies, to encourage the production of goods for export. For the Asian economies, the result was the best of both worlds: their governments developed efficient industries by encouraging them to compete in foreign markets, and yet continued to protect them from foreign competition in the domestic marketplace.

As the Asian economies grew, the pattern of their commercial interactions changed apace. In the early postwar years, many Asia-Pacific economies, particularly the United States, had continued to trade largely with Europe. But trade within the region grew faster than world trade as a whole, with the result that by the early 1980s, the Asian-Pacific economies were conducting 60 percent of their total trade with one another—an intensity of interaction greater than that enjoyed by their European counterparts.[4]

At first, the flow of trade and investment was primarily across the Pacific: the United States was the major source of foreign direct investment and advanced technology, provided the largest single export market for most Asian nations, and ultimately became a significant importer of capital as well. Gradually, however, Japan joined the United States as a center of growth for the region, supplying the region with increasing amounts of machinery and purchasing vast quantities of raw materials. By the late 1980s, it had surpassed the United States as the main source of capital, but not as a major market for Asian manufactured goods.

Moreover, as trade and capital flows increased, the balance of trade began to shift substantially. The United States, which had once enjoyed a surplus in its trade account with the Asian economies, went sharply into deficit. Japan, in contrast, continued to run substantial surpluses, not only with the United States, but also with most of its other trading partners in the Asia-Pacific region, except those from which it imported large amounts of raw materials. These imbalances became increasingly unacceptable politically in the United States, and the American government responded by negotiating a series of arrangements with its Asian trading partners to restrict their exports of such goods as textiles, televisions, and automobiles. Thus, as economic interdependence increased, tensions among the major trading nations in the region also mounted.

With both interdependence and conflict increasing, there was a perceived need to create better multilateral mechanisms for dealing with economic issues. Economists across the region argued that government-to-government dialogue could identify areas for cooperation among state corporations and agencies, and could reduce the barriers to trade and investment by private business interests. Negotiations could also manage the disputes being created by growing economic interaction and interdependence within the Asia-Pacific region. In other words, multilateral institutions were regarded as a suitable response to the complex blend of common and divergent interests that characterized intraregional economic relations.

In addition, from a remarkably early stage, the process of multilateral economic cooperation in the Asia-Pacific region was viewed as a necessary complement, or even counterweight, to international economic institutions based elsewhere. As one report put it, "global institutions and mechanisms" such as GATT could "no longer provide an adequate framework for dealing with the Pacific economy." This was because they were believed to be dominated by "established Atlantic and European interests" that were headed toward acceptance of managed trade, and would therefore not provide "positive encouragement to the accommodation of trade growth" that was being generated by Asia's export-oriented economies.[5] Furthermore, it was felt that some kind of Pacific Community would be needed as a counterweight to the continuing progress of economic integration in Western Europe.[6]

Alongside these acknowledged objectives, there were also some important ulterior motives at work. In the United States, many prominent Asianists, primarily in the academic and policy communities, were looking for a way to keep the United States engaged in Asia in the aftermath of the Vietnam War. Embedding the United States in a new network of Asian economic institutions, it was felt, might do just that, somewhat like the way in which American involvement in NATO kept the United States engaged in Europe. In addition, some also argued that multilateral institutions would provide a more effective—and less confrontational—way of addressing the mounting American trade deficit with Japan. Since many other nations in the region had a common interest in promoting their exports to Japan, the United States could join with them in seeking greater access to Japanese markets.

In Tokyo, too, there was an interest in multilateral economic cooperation that went beyond what government was willing to state publicly. Japan had long viewed Asia as its natural economic partner, providing it with raw materials in exchange for Japanese capital equipment and consumer goods. This kind of economic partnership was particularly attractive given the sluggish growth in much of the rest of the Third World and the prospects for diminished Japanese access to both European and American markets. Negotiated reductions of trade and investment barriers would greatly facilitate the economic integration of Japan and its Asian neighbors. Moreover, if the yen were accepted as the reserve currency of an Asian economic bloc, Japanese banks, traders, and investors would all realize substantial benefits.

One significant, if indirect, step toward the creation of multilateral economic institutions in Asia was the further integration of Japan, the region's most advanced economy, into global economic organizations. Tokyo became a member of the OECD in 1964, where it could participate in discussions of trade liberalization, investment practices, and foreign aid. Even more important, Japan was included in the emerging mechanisms for coordinating macroeconomic policy. It was involved in the discussions among financial ministers on the increasingly contentious issue of international monetary policy: the Group of Ten in 1961, the Group of Five in the early 1970s, and the Group of Seven (the G-7) beginning with the first economic summit in 1975.

But there were also proposals to create multilateral organizations to promote trade and investment specifically in the Asia-Pacific region. Perhaps the first was a recommendation for a Pacific Free Trade Area, put forward by two Japanese scholars, Kiyoshi Kojima and Hiroshi Kurimoto, in 1965. As the name implies, the proposal would have eliminated all tariffs on intraregional trade, and would have significantly reduced nontariff barriers as well. A somewhat less visionary proposal was presented in two separate reports in 1979, one by the Japanese analyst (and later foreign minister) Saburo Okita, the other by Hugh Patrick (then of Yale University) and Peter Drysdale (of Australian National University), for the creation of a multilateral regional economic organization, termed by some the Organization of Pacific Trade and Development (OPTAD). Rather than working toward a free-trade area, such an organization was intended to have the less ambitious but more realistic objective of drafting codes of conduct to promote trade, investment, and foreign aid, and providing mechanisms for resolving regional trade disputes.[7]

These early proposals encountered a number of objections and obstacles that prevented their immediate adoption. One of the most important was the question of membership. Given the gaps between planned and market economies, it was impossible to conceive of an organization that would have universal membership. Accordingly, the Patrick-Drysdale plan would have granted membership to the market-oriented economies in the region: five developed economies (the United States, Japan, Canada, Australia, and New Zealand), six developing economies (South Korea and the five ASEAN nations), and one bloc of island nations (Papua New Guinea and the South Pacific islands), with Hong Kong and Taiwan admitted as observers. Even if membership were restricted to market-oriented economies, however, the gap between developed and developing countries introduced a basic conflict of interest that obstructed the realization of such a proposal.

The ulterior motives—real or imagined—of the two largest economies in the region were a second obstacle to the acceptance of these early proposals. It was assumed that either Japan or the United States (or, in some accounts, the two nations in collusion) would dominate such a multilateral organization. Many in ASEAN, for example, worried that the United States would attempt to impose a political agenda on the process, so as to turn what was intended to be an economic organization into a multilateral alignment against the Soviet Union. Others feared that the American interest in a Pacific economic organization was intended to undermine ASEAN, split its members from the other developing countries in the region, and foster economic dependence on the United States. Those who were not concerned about American intentions worried about the Japanese: there was a widespread perception in Asia that Tokyo would attempt to dominate a multilateral economic organization as its economic power gradually rivaled that of the United States.[8]

Relatedly, there was a widespread perception that the formation of such a multilateral economic mechanism in Asia would erode other organizations.

Some Americans feared that Japan's membership in a Pacific Community would replace the alliance with the United States as the cornerstone of Japanese foreign policy. Many leaders of ASEAN saw OPTAD as competitive with their own organization. Foreshadowing the arguments about regional trading arrangements in the late 1980s and early 1990s, many policymakers and analysts committed to free trade warned that the creation of a multilateral economic organization in Asia would undermine progress toward global liberalization, especially given the perceived lack of commitment by many Asian governments to the principles of free trade. In short, organization building was seen as a zero-sum game, in which the creation of any new institution would inevitably weaken others.

Although it therefore proved impossible to form a formal intergovernmental regional economic organization in the 1960s and 1970s, other forms of institutions did begin to emerge during this period.[9] One set of organizations was subregional in scope. The first such initiative was the formation of a free-trade area comprising Australia and New Zealand in 1966. Even here, however, the idea of the complete elimination of tariff and nontariff barriers proved too ambitious, and in 1983 the entity adopted the more ambiguous, but presumably more realistic, name of the Closer Economic Relationship. A similar entity, the South Pacific Forum, was created in 1971 as an outgrowth of some narrower subregional arrangements focused on specific economic sectors. Rather than becoming a free-trade area, however, the South Pacific Forum evolved into a multinational lobby to advance its members' interests in protecting their fisheries, halting nuclear testing, and preventing the transit of naval vessels armed with nuclear weapons.[10]

In addition, although originally formed for political reasons, ASEAN began to develop an economic dimension in the 1970s, albeit one that had only modest accomplishments at the time. ASEAN promoted cooperative investment projects linking several of its member nations and launched a multinational program on human resource development. It also negotiated some tariff reductions for intraregional commerce, but primarily for goods that were not heavily traded, or else that only one country in ASEAN produced and exported.[11]

There were also consultations between ASEAN and its major trading partners on economic issues. In 1977, Japan, Australia, and New Zealand were invited to engage in dialogue with their ASEAN counterparts after the annual meeting of ASEAN ministers. In 1984, this process was expanded and formalized. Thereafter, the meetings, known as the ASEAN Post-Ministerial Conference (ASEAN-PMC), involved representatives from five industrial nations in the Pacific (the United States, Japan, Canada, Australia, and New Zealand), and from the European Community. South Korea was later added to the ASEAN-PMC as the sixth Asia-Pacific dialogue partner.

Another alternative to a formal regionwide economic organization was the process of informal dialogue, with participation by well-connected scholars, policy analysts, businesspeople, and government officials from most of the countries of the Asia-Pacific region. The first of these unofficial organizations was the Pacific Basin Economic Council (PBEC), formed in 1967 by representatives of major multinational corporations headquartered in the Asia-Pacific region. Previously, consideration of a Pacific Community had been the preserve of scholars, although some had official connections. PBEC's contribution was to move discussion of multilateral economic cooperation from the seminar room into the boardroom. PBEC tapped the business community for its membership, and thus helped to create a powerful lobby that could bring the need for regional economic cooperation to the attention of reluctant governments. PBEC's second contribution—still quite controversial—was to broaden its geographic scope to include the southeastern rim of the Pacific. From an early stage, membership in PBEC was extended to corporations from Mexico and Chile, as well as to those headquartered in North America and Asia.

A second unofficial organization formed during this period was the Pacific Trade and Development Conference (abbreviated first as PAFTAD, and then as PACTAD). When it first met in 1968, PACTAD was intended as a forum for academic economists from market economies, some of whom were closely connected with their governments, to discuss the proposals for a Pacific free-trade area. The discussion soon revealed, however, that the concept of a regional free-trade area was impractical under the circumstances. As a result, PACTAD began to develop somewhat less ambitious proposals, including development, trade, investment, technology transfer, coordinated structural adjustment, and the terms of trade for natural resources. Another PACTAD innovation, later adopted by other organizations, was to invite qualified government officials to participate in the discussions in their private capacities. This helped blur the gap between purely unofficial meetings, which most countries in the region were pleased to support, and purely official conferences, which most governments still regarded as premature.

Finally, the most important of the unofficial economic organizations in the Asia-Pacific region, the Pacific Economic Cooperation Council (PECC), was formed in 1980. PECC borrowed some of the innovations of both PBEC and PACTAD, both of which it admitted as institutional members. From PACTAD, it adopted the procedure by which government officials could attend meetings in their private capacities. PECC created a tripartite membership structure in which each national delegation was composed of representatives from the academic, business, and governmental communities. Like PBEC, PECC ultimately granted membership to representatives from Latin American nations, including Chile, Mexico, and Peru. But it went even further, offering membership to China and observer status to Russia, and including both Hong Kong and Taiwan as full-fledged members as well. And finally, PECC added many of PACTAD's topics to its own agenda, creating subcommittees to deal with such issues as trade in manufactures, energy and mineral resources, agriculture and renewable resources, capital flows and finance, and investment and technology transfer.

In short, increasing interdependence in the Asia-Pacific region produced a growing interest in multilateral institutions, at least in the economic sphere. At this stage, however, the diversity of circumstances and interests of the major nations still precluded the creation of formal institutions. Still, there was significant progress toward creating what Robert Scalapino called "soft regionalism": the organization of unofficial and quasi-official dialogue on economic issues, and the creation or strengthening of subregional institutions.[12] Equally important for the longer term, "soft regionalism" began to produce ideas about formal multilateral organization that would become steadily more influential in the years ahead.[13]

The End of the Cold Wars in Asia

By the early 1980s, Asia was plagued with not just one cold war, but several. There was both the global competition between the Soviet Union and the United States and the more localized conflict between the Soviet Union and China. Indeed, both these disputes intensified in the 1970s. To engage in its confrontation with China and the United States, the Soviet Union greatly increased its military deployments in Asia, both conventional and nuclear. It also strengthened its alignments with India and Vietnam, and encouraged Hanoi to invade Cambodia at the end of 1978, ostensibly to rid the country of the Khmer Rouge. The rise of Soviet power and ambition, in turn, led to the rapid growth of U.S. military spending, the bolstering of the Japanese-American alliance, growing strategic cooperation between Beijing and Washington, and the creation of a tacit alignment of ASEAN, Japan, China, and the United States against the Vietnamese intervention in Cambodia.

There were also two other cold wars in Asia, resulting from the division of China and Korea in the late 1940s. Although armed conflict in the Taiwan Strait had basically ended, Beijing and Taipei maintained their uneasy stalemate, with virtually no economic, cultural, or political contacts between them. The situation along the demilitarized zone in Korea was even more tense. North Korea continued a steady buildup of conventional forces, deployed in offensive positions. It also engaged in acts of terrorism abroad, targeting the South Korean cabinet during a state visit to Burma and South Korean civilian airliners flying over the Indian Ocean. Nor were there any significant commercial or humanitarian ties between North and South Korea.

Two interrelated developments in the region's communist states greatly eased the cold wars in Asia, and brought several of them to an end. One was the growing interest in the region in market-oriented, outward-looking programs of economic reform; the other, the communist states' gradual adoption of more accommodative foreign policies, not only to reduce the burdens of military preparations, but also to maximize their access to markets, capital, and technology abroad. Both these trends stemmed from a common calculation: the economic dynamism of the Asia-Pacific region was so great that those who remained isolated from it would be doomed to a strategically subordinate position, whereas engaging in more extensive economic interaction with the region demanded significant adjustments in both foreign and domestic policy.

Albeit for somewhat different reasons and to different degrees, these two trends spread across communist Asia, from China to the Soviet Union and from Mongolia to Vietnam. As already noted, China began to adjust its foreign policy in the early 1970s, largely to break free of its self-imposed isolation and to find partners with which to counter the expansion of Soviet influence. Later in the same decade, exhausted by the turmoil of the Cultural Revolution and liberated by the death of Mao Zedong, Chinese leaders concluded that the only way to restore their flagging legitimacy and rehabilitate their inefficient economy was to launch a program of economic reform. This encouraged a further expansion of China's international ties, as Beijing sought to improve relations with its neighbors so that it could minimize defense expenditures, concentrate its resources on domestic economic development, and maximize its access to capital and markets abroad.

Where China lagged behind some of the other communist states was in the area of political transformation. To be sure, there was a relaxation of totalitarian controls over society, a step that Chinese leaders understood to be a prerequisite for developing a market-oriented economy. But the mechanisms for the articulation of public opinion and the aggregation of the demands of various interests remained woefully underdeveloped. Moreover, although it somewhat restored the party's tarnished authority, rapid economic change produced tensions of its own. The Tiananmen crisis of 1989 demonstrated the explosive potential of a situation in which urban society had gained the power to speak but not the right to be heard.

By the mid-1980s, the Soviet Union had also concluded that it could no longer afford the cost of its confrontation with both China and the United States. Under Mikhail Gorbachev, the Kremlin reduced or eliminated the obstacles to an improvement of relations with Washington and Beijing. Gorbachev announced the withdrawal of Soviet forces from Afghanistan, the cessation of Soviet support for the Vietnamese intervention in Cambodia, and the unilateral reduction of Soviet forces in the Far East. He agreed with the United States to eliminate all intermediate-range nuclear missiles, including those stationed in Asia. Gorbachev's visit to Beijing in May 1989, although overshadowed by the antigovernment demonstrations in Tiananmen Square occurring at the same time, marked the end of the confrontation between China and the Soviet Union. The Soviet leader's series of summits with Ronald Reagan and George Bush effectively ended the Cold War between the Soviet Union and the United States.

At about the same time, the Soviet leader also launched a program of domestic reform under the twin slogans of glasnost' and perestroika. Here, in contrast to China, political change far outstripped economic reform. Gorbachev fell from power, the Soviet Union collapsed, and the successor Russian Federation moved rapidly if unsteadily in the direction of more democratic institutions. Conversely, ill-conceived and poorly implemented attempts at a comprehensive restructuring of the economy led, at least in the short run, to a collapse of production, rampant inflation, a devalued currency, and a surge in crime and corruption.

By the end of the decade, the transformation of foreign and domestic policy had spread to Vietnam and Mongolia. Faced with an unwinnable war in Cambodia and the withdrawal of Soviet support, Hanoi decided to withdraw its troops and reestablish friendly relations with all its neighbors. It also launched a program of domestic transformation remarkably similar to that of China: gradual but effective economic reform, coupled with much slower and reluctant steps toward political change. The consequences were also comparable: a surge in exports and a boost in production, but uncertainty as to whether political institutions would evolve fast enough to manage the contradictions that would be produced by rapid social transformation.

If the Vietnamese experience resembled China's, developments in Mongolia were comparable to those in the Soviet Union. As Soviet aid declined, Mongolia also experimented with rapid and comprehensive economic reform, but experienced a decline in output even more dire than that in the Soviet Union. As the Soviet Union attenuated its alliance with Mongolia, Ulan Bator also rapidly adjusted its foreign policy to establish or renew ties with China, Japan, South Korea, and the United States. From its former position as Moscow's closest ally in East Asia, Mongolia became, in essence, a neutral state, reliant for its security on the good will of its neighbors.

The one exception to these twin trends was North Korea. Although Pyongyang made a nominal decision to open its economy to foreign trade and investment, it remained more committed than any other Asian communist state to clinging to its totalitarian political system and its centrally planned economy. Under pressure from China and the Soviet Union—and in the awareness that neither Beijing nor Moscow would veto South Korean participation in the United Nations if Seoul applied for membership alone—Pyongyang reluctantly agreed to join the United Nations. Under similar pressure, it also reluctantly consented to subject its nuclear program to international inspection. But North Korea did not become a member of the principal international economic organizations or of the various regimes intended to control the spread of nonconventional weapons. It remained the region's sole "outlier": the only nation that did not accept the broad outlines of the emerging international order in the Asia-Pacific region.

The end of Asia's cold wars sent ripples across the region. Nations that had been members of one adversarial bloc were now free—or were actually forced— to seek a reduction of tensions with members of the other. Thus, the rapprochement between China and the Soviet Union led to similar rapprochements between China and India, China and Vietnam, and China and Mongolia. The end of the cold war between China and the United States made it possible for both South

Korea and Taiwan to improve their ties with Beijing. And the improvement of relations between the United States and the Soviet Union made possible the improvement of relations between South Korea and the Soviet Union, between Mongolia and the United States, and between the United States and Vietnam.

At the same time, many of the security arrangements created during the Cold War decayed or collapsed. Those centering on the former Soviet Union (such as those linking Moscow to Hanoi, Pyongyang, Ulan Bator, and New Delhi) disintegrated, leaving Moscow's erstwhile allies to find other methods for ensuring their security. Some of America's alliances in the western Pacific were also called into question: that with New Zealand because of a dispute over port calls by American nuclear-armed and nuclear-powered warships, and that with the Philippines because of Manila's decision to ask the United States to withdraw from its military bases in the country. Other elements in the U.S. alliance system—especially those with Japan and South Korea—remained intact, but were entangled in chronic disputes over burden sharing and episodic differences over the common foreign policies that the members of the alliance should pursue.

The end of the cold wars in Asia also permitted changes in the composition of international regimes and organizations in the region. For one thing, as the communist states of the region adopted new foreign and economic policies, they became suitable for membership in global economic and security regimes that they had once spurned, or that had once spurned them. Thus China ratified the Nuclear Non-Proliferation Treaty, signed the Chemical Weapons Convention, and agreed to abide by the provisions of the Missile Technology Control Regime. China and Vietnam joined the United Nations, the World Bank, the International Monetary Fund, and the Asian Development Bank. China applied for membership in GATT, with Vietnam almost certain to follow. In short, the end of the cold wars made it possible for the major international regimes, whose membership had previously been limited to the noncommunist countries in Asia, to gain almost universal membership in the region.

The reduction of tensions in Asia was also conducive to a growing interest in building cooperative economic connections among former adversaries. The best known of these is "Greater China," a complex network of relations linking Hong Kong and Taiwan to the coast of mainland China, as well as Hong Kong to Taiwan, Taiwan to Vietnam, and the Chinese entrepreneurs of Southeast Asia to mainland China. But there are other transnational economic networks as well. The Tumen River project in Northeast Asia would join Russia, China, and the two Koreas. A "Bohai Circle" links China and South Korea; a network centering on the Sea of Japan connects Japan, Russia, and the two Koreas; the "Sijori Growth Triangle" draws together Singapore, Malaysia, and Indonesia; and the Mekong River area binds Thailand, Cambodia, Laos, and China's Yunnan province.

Robert Scalapino has described these new networks of commercial activity as "natural economic territories."[14] And, indeed, their emergence has reflected the natural desire of modern entrepreneurs to create, through investment, industrial production networks that cross international borders in search of comparative advantage. As in so much of the Asian development experience, however, most of these commercial activities have received the active support of governments or international agencies. The Tumen River project, for example, obtained substantial assistance from the United Nations Development Program. Mainland China created four special economic zones directly opposite Taiwan and Hong Kong to encourage the development of what is now known as Greater China. The links between China and South Korea, and among Singapore, Malaysia, and Indonesia, also received the active encouragement of the governments in question. These may be natural economic phenomena, but they have extensive political backing.

Finally, the end of Asia's cold wars made it possible to develop subregional cooperative security regimes to deal with local crises and disputes. On the Korean peninsula, there was extensive cooperation among the four major external powers—the United States, Japan, China, and Russia—to prevent the recurrence of conflict and to encourage North Korea to adopt a more flexible and responsible policy toward the rest of the world. In Cambodia, the major powers joined ASEAN in effective cooperation to secure the withdrawal of Vietnamese forces, the disarmament of the contending Cambodian factions, and the implementation of competitive elections for a new constitutional assembly. The nations with competing claims to the islands in the South China Sea held a series of informal multilateral working meetings, at which it was recommended to avoid the use of force to pursue territorial claims and launch cooperative activities to prevent piracy and drug trafficking, to endure navigational safety, to protect marine life, and to exploit and develop the area's natural resources. Finally, Russia, China, and the Central Asian republics began negotiations to resolve their border disputes, to reduce force deployments along their frontiers, and to develop confidence-building measures to ensure that tensions remain low.

Unfortunately, less progress was made in other subregional disputes. Japan and Russia were unable to make any progress in resolving their disagreements over the Northern Territories. Japan and China did not even begin to discuss their dispute over the Senkaku (or Diaoyutai) Islands northeast of Taiwan. And, despite the rapid development of economic and cultural ties across the Taiwan Strait, Taipei and Beijing were unable to find ways of increasing their mutual security through official bilateral discussions.

Nor was it possible, as the Cold War wound down, immediately to create a formal regionwide multilateral security organization.[15] Such a proposal was first made in the late 1980s, when the Soviet Union and Australia separately suggested the creation of a Conference on Security and Cooperation in Asia (CSCA) to parallel the CSCE in Europe, and when Moscow recommended the negotiation of nuclear and conventional arms control arrangements in the Asia-Pacific region, again similar to those being discussed in Europe at the time.

These proposals for a regionwide security organization immediately aroused strong objections.[16] The Soviet proposals quite clearly embodied a biased agenda. They were presented at a time when the United States was committed to a maritime strategy against Moscow: the threat to use American naval power in the western Pacific to open a second front against the Soviet Union in the event of the initiation of hostilities along the Central European front. Virtually all of Gorbachev's specific arms control proposals were directed, in one way or another, at the U.S. maritime strategy. The limitations on naval forces in the Western Pacific, or even around the Korean peninsula, would have restricted the American ability to project naval force against the Soviet Far East. The creation of a nuclear-free zone in the Indian Ocean potentially would have denied transit rights to American nuclear-armed ships. Similarly, the call for a nuclear-free zone on the Korean peninsula was viewed at the time as an attempt to prevent the United States and South Korea from using a nuclear deterrent to overcome North Korea's tremendous advantage in conventional weapons.

Aside from the bias inherent in the initial Soviet proposals, there were also other objections to the idea of multilateral cooperative security in Asia. The first, and most basic, was the concern that the strategic situation in Asia was so complex, and the level of interaction among some of the governments in the region so low, that cooperative security mechanisms comparable to the CSCE would be doomed to failure. The multipolar character of the strategic situation in the region, for example, would arguably complicate the negotiation of any arms control or confidence-building measures. The absence of formal diplomatic relations between several pairs of major actors (mainland China and Taiwan, North and South Korea, North Korea and either Japan or the United States, the United States and Vietnam) also made an official dialogue difficult. Furthermore, there was little precedent in Asia for a multilateral discussion of security issues.

Thus, not surprisingly, the Soviet proposals for naval arms control and for nuclear-free zones in Asia were dismissed out of hand by both Japan and the United States in the late 1980s. The Soviet and Australian proposals for an official multilateral dialogue on Asian security issues were also rejected— Moscow's bluntly, Canberra's somewhat more gently—on the grounds that such a forum would be dominated by a fruitless discussion of the one-sided Soviet arms control proposals. But although these proposals proved impractical at the time, in retrospect they all played important functions. They significantly stretched the limits of academic debate and official discussion, facilitating the introduction of more viable forms of organization immediately, and possibly laying the groundwork for the creation of regionwide cooperative security measures later on.

More progress was made in launching unofficial multilateral discussions of security matters. In the late 1980s, following the abortive proposals from the Soviet Union and Australia for a CSCA, there emerged a number of informal dialogues on security in the Asia-Pacific region, roughly the equivalent of the early academic dialogues on economic cooperation sponsored by PACTAD. Among the most important of these were conferences organized by American organizations such as the University of California, the Asia Society, the Pacific Forum, and the United Nations Association of the United States. On the other side of the Pacific, similar meetings were arranged by a variety of Asian organizations, including a series sponsored by the Mongolian Academy of Sciences and another, known as the Asia-Pacific Roundtable, conducted by the Institute of Strategic and International Studies of Malaysia.

Subsequently, there were also two important efforts to create, in the security sphere, the equivalent of the PECC: an organization that would include not only scholars and policy analysts but also government officials, at least in their private capacity. In 1990, the Canadian foreign minister proposed a dialogue on cooperative security in the northern Pacific, with participants from Canada, the United States, Japan, the two Koreas, Russia, and China. This North Pacific Cooperative Security Dialogue (NPCSD) involved a program of academic research and conferences, attended by policy planners from the foreign ministries of the seven countries. The NPCSD held a series of workshops and conferences between 1991 and 1993, until a new administration in Ottawa seemed to lose interest in the program.

In 1993, an even broader organization was created: the Council for Security Cooperation in the Asia Pacific (CSCAP). This organization is modeled even more closely aafter the PECC than was the NPCSD. It comprises national delegations, each of which includes not only scholars and policy analysts, but also government officials paraticipating in their private capacities. The original sponsors of CSCAP included research institutes from ten countries: Australia, Canada, Indonesia, Japan, South Korea, Malaysia, the Philippines, Singapore, Thailand, and the United Stataes. Membership is open to all countries and territories in the region, and both New Zealand and North Korea have subsequently been added to the list of participants. Unfortunately, China has balked at membership in CSCAP, objecting to the organization's interest in including participants from Taiwan.

Together, these developments amounted to a significant change in the international order in the Asia-Pacific region. The ideological differences between communist and noncommunist countries were largely eliminated, with only North Korea sticking to the totalitarian framework of the past. The adversarial quality of most relationships eased, as nations sought the economic and strategic benefits of improved relations with their neighbors. And the mutual isolation that was so characteristic of the bipolar system—the absence of normal commercial, cultural, and even diplomatic ties—was ended by the explosion of such relations throughout the region. This permitted the inauguration of informal cooperative security arrangements at both the regional and subregional levels, although not yet the creation of a formal multilateral security organization.

The Uncertainties of Multinodality

According to conventional wisdom, the international order of the Asia-Pacific region is undergoing a transformation from the bipolarity of the Cold War era to a more multipolar system. This assessment is half correct. It is true that economic dynamism is producing a larger number of independent and influential actors in the region, far more than a bipolar or even a tripolar model would allow. On the other hand, rather than being mutually isolated and mutually antagonistic, as the term "polarity" implies, the major actors of the Asia-Pacific region are highly interdependent economically and culturally, for almost all of them realize that to choose autarky is to opt for a permanently inferior position. As interdependence increases, societies become so intertwined that the flexibility of alignment inherent in a traditional multipolar system becomes highly constrained. Moreover, there are so many centers of economic and military power that hegemony becomes virtually impossible, even though conflict and competition continue.

As I have suggested elsewhere, the emerging international order in the Asia-Pacific region might therefore be better described as a multinodal system, rather than as a multipolar one.[17] But by whatever term it is known, developments in the region are generating significant new uncertainties in both the economic and the strategic realms. These uncertainties, in turn, are proving an important stimulus for the creation of new international regimes and organizations.

One of the most important developments in the Asia-Pacific region in the past decade has been the dramatic changes in the relative power of the major actors. One superpower, the Soviet Union, has collapsed altogether. Its successor state in East Asia, the Russian Federation, has significantly less military and economic power than its predecessor, as a result of military retrenchment and economic recession. Equally important, Moscow's will to exercise influence in the Asia-Pacific region seems significantly reduced, as the result of its preoccupation with domestic reform, with its relations with other former Soviet republics, and with its ties to Europe and the United States.

The power of the United States has also declined, although not as precipitously as that of the former Soviet Union. Although the gradual retrenchment of American military power in the region can be justified given the collapse of America's main adversary, it is nonetheless perceived in Asia as a reflection of a reduction in America's political will and material resources. Indeed, the relative decline of the economic power of the United States is a major factor in regional perceptions of America. The slow rate of economic growth, low rates of saving and investment, chronic budget and trade deficits, the depreciation of the dollar, sluggish overseas investment, cuts in the foreign aid program, and the reduction of U.S. forward deployments—all these suggest to many Asian observers that the United States is no longer the dominant economic power it once was. Equally important is the erosion of America's normative power as a result of decades of unchecked violence, socioeconomic inequality, and drug abuse.

Conversely, other actors in the Asia-Pacific region are experiencing sharp increases in national power. Despite some reverses in recent years, Japan is now regarded as a rival to the United States in terms of economic power. The flow of official economic assistance and of foreign direct investment from Japan to the rest of the region is greater than that from the United States. In technology, Japan has surpassed the United States in some areas, and has caught up in others. Militarily, Japan now has one of the most sophisticated armed forces in the region, and has shown a growing willingness to deploy it in international peacekeeping operations abroad. Diplomatically, Tokyo is taking more initiatives on regional and global issues, sometimes in directions not totally consistent with the preferences of the United States.

China, too, is rapidly rising. Sustained growth, averaging around 10 percent per year over the last fifteen years, is increasing the nation's economic resources. Recalculations of the size of China's economy on the basis of purchasing power parity have suggested that China's gross national product is perhaps three times larger than previously believed, rivaling that of Japan. Given the outward orientation of the economy, China is increasingly being regarded in part as an attractive opportunity for trade and investment, but also as an increasingly worrisome economic competitor. Recent increases in China's military budget, together with official suggestions that China is seeking various kinds of force projection capabilities, are causing alarm elsewhere in the region.

Still other nations are gaining in power and influence. The "four little dragons"—South Korea, Hong Kong, Singapore, and Taiwan—are transforming their economies by developing more advanced technology, shifting their labor-intensive manufacturing operations abroad, and creating more sophisticated financial and commercial services. Malaysia and Thailand are taking their place as the next group of newly industrial economies (NIEs) in East Asia. Vietnam, with 70 million people, and Indonesia, with almost 200 million people, will become increasingly important actors in the region as their rate of economic growth accelerates.

At the same time as the relative power of the nations of East Asia is being transformed, their economic interdependence is also increasing. Countries that once exported primarily to the United States and Japan are now exporting more to one another, as economic dynamism throughout the region is producing new markets for their products. The flow of direct foreign investment is becoming more complex. Singapore, Taiwan, Hong Kong, and South Korea are joining the United States and Japan as important sources of foreign investment for the developing economies in the region, as entrepreneurs seek lower-cost production bases as wages increase and currencies appreciate at home. Even China has begun to export capital in the region, particularly to Hong Kong and parts of Southeast Asia.

The emergence of a multinodal system in the Asia-Pacific region is producing significant uncertainties, both strategic and economic. Economically, interde-

pendence is continuing to generate competition and conflict as well as cooperation, just as it did in the 1960s and 1970s. Domestic industries in many countries
are petitioning their governments for protection against foreign competition. At
the same time, however, export-oriented industries are pressing their governments to help them gain freer access to markets abroad. Governments are increasingly preoccupied with the bilateral balance of payments with their trading
partners, and with preserving a competitive advantage vis-à-vis potential rivals.

These economic tensions are exacerbated by mutual suspicions of the intentions of the governments of key economies. Throughout the region, there is
concern that the declining competitiveness of the United States and its shrinking
relative economic power will lead it to abandon a commitment to free trade in
favor of some form of economic protectionism. Conversely, there is growing
resentment in the United States of what is perceived as Asian neomercantilism: a
desire to take advantage of relatively open access to American markets, while at
the same time maintaining barriers to imports and investment from abroad.

Strategically, too, there are uncertainties. There are a variety of subregional
disputes that could still give rise to armed conflict. These include not only the
three conflicts that are the legacy of the Cold War—those on the Korean peninsula, in the Taiwan Strait, and in Indochina—but also a variety of territorial
disputes both on land and at sea. On land, there are disputes between China and
Russia, China and the Central Asian republics, China and India, and China and
Vietnam. At sea, China and Japan, Russia and Japan, China and South Korea,
and China and a number of Southeast Asian countries have competing claims
either to islands off the coasts of East Asia or to the resources of the seabed.
Although, as noted above, the end of the Cold War has yielded some progress in
constructing cooperative security mechanisms to address these issues, none of
them has been fully resolved.

In addition, there is growing concern about the emergence of unconventional
threats to national security, many of which are the product of the growing economic interaction and interdependence in the area. These include piracy, drug
smuggling, terrorism, and other forms of transnational criminal activity. They
also include threats to the regional environment, such as pollution, climatic
change, and excessive fishing. Threats to these nations' access to essential economic commodities is another grounds for apprehension, as is the uncontrolled
flow of refugees across national frontiers that might be occasioned by natural
disaster, war, poverty, or political repression.

Finally, there remain widespread suspicions about the longer-term intentions
of major powers, particularly Japan, Russia, and China. Although none appears
at present to pose a fundamental challenge to the status quo, there is still concern
that all three nations may retain the desire to establish some degree of hegemony
in Asia. There is also an acute awareness that unresolved territorial issues, overlapping spheres of influence, and the existence of ethnic minorities that span
international borders could give rise to conflict between these major powers.

Moreover, the domestic situation in all three countries remains to some degree uncertain, with Asian analysts pointing to the rise of militarism in Japan, nationalism in China, and revanchism in Russia as troubling possibilities.

These mutual suspicions are being translated into what many observers regard as the beginnings of a regional arms race.[18] The Gulf War of 1991 demonstrated the extent to which the arsenals of most Asian countries are technologically inferior, at least relative to the state-of-the-art weapons fielded by the Americans. And, at the same time, Asia's economic prosperity is giving governments the resources to spend on acquiring more modern weaponry, a demand that arms merchants in the United States, Europe, and Russia, facing shrinking domestic markets, are all too pleased to meet. At present, the arms race is primarily conventional, but China's program to modernize its nuclear arsenal and North Korea's program to acquire one could give it a nuclear dimension as well.

These uncertainties have been exacerbated by qualms about the vitality of global economic and security institutions. Although ultimately successful, the protracted negotiations during the Uruguay Round of GATT called into question the preservation of an open global trading system that can continue to absorb the output of Asia's export-oriented economies. The emergence of the EC in Europe and NAFTA in North America is producing concern that the global trading system is being undermined by regional groupings that may be open to their own members but relatively closed to outsiders.

Strategic uncertainties are being intensified by the absence of global institutions that could provide a degree of confidence and security. Although the United Nations seems to be more active than ever before, its peacekeeping forces have been defied in regional conflicts in Bosnia, Somalia, and Haiti, and as yet have proven relatively ineffective. Many traditional alliances are in disarray, as the end of the Cold War removed their common enemy and the shifts in relative power upset the distribution of responsibility within them.

These developments have led to an increasing interest in the formation of new regional regimes and organizations to supplement the existing regional and global institutions whose viability is now in question. The purpose of these new institutions would be to provide greater mutual confidence by creating forums for discussing disagreements, establishing rules of conduct, and even developing sanctions for noncompliance. They would also be intended to draw in nations such as China, Vietnam, Mongolia, and eventually North Korea that are not yet fully integrated into economic and security relationships in the area. As a result, the Asia-Pacific region, which had relatively few regionwide multilateral institutions in the Cold War era, is now seeing unprecedented efforts to create new economic and security regimes and organizations.

One of these has been the creation of a free-trade area within ASEAN. Although ASEAN primarily focused on political and strategic objectives during its early years, it has increasingly directed its attention to economic matters. In January 1992, ASEAN created the ASEAN Free-Trade Area (AFTA), which involves the elimination of tariffs on intraregional trade over a fifteen-year period. The primary aim is to attract more foreign investment by promising that a foreign venture in any one ASEAN country will be able to export its output on a duty-free basis to all other members of ASEAN—a market totaling more than 300 million people. Unfortunately, progress in implementing AFTA has been slow, with the four largest members of ASEAN drawing up long lists of goods that they intend to exclude from tariff reductions.[19]

There has also been progress toward creating formal economic organizations at the regional level. In 1990, Malaysia proposed the creation of an East Asian Economic Group (EAEG), presumably to promote economic cooperation among its members, to counter the formation of the EC and NAFTA, and to lobby for Asian interests in the Uruguay Round of the GATT negotiations. The Malaysian proposal was immediately controversial, for it excluded both the United States and Australia. To bar the United States was economically irrational, since it would have created an unnecessary and costly obstacle between the members of the EAEG and the country that was the region's largest single export market. Furthermore, excluding the United States and Australia was also politically insensitive, since it implied that the EAEG was intended only for countries with populations that were ethnically Asian, not for nations whose peoples were largely of Caucasian extraction.

As a result, Malaysia's proposal for an EAEG (later renamed the EAEC, or East Asian Economic Caucus) has been largely set aside. One of its purposes, the facilitation of economic cooperation within Southeast Asia, has been met by the creation of the ASEAN Free-Trade Area, mentioned above. Its other purposes are being promoted by the Asia Pacific Economic Cooperation (APEC) forum. This organization was formed in 1989 under Australian leadership and with active Japanese support. The familiar reservations of the members of ASEAN— that a regionwide economic entity would reduce the vitality and prestige of their own organization—were assuaged by giving the ASEAN Secretariat a key role in arranging the earliest APEC meetings and by holding those initial meetings in conjunction with the ASEAN ministerial sessions. The Australian government also emphasized that APEC would take its decisions through consultation and consensus, another attempt to relieve the concerns of the Southeast Asian nations that a regionwide organization would be dominated by the United States and Japan. The major American reservations about the EAEG were also skillfully addressed by Canberra: from the beginning, APEC included the United States and Canada among its members, and was explicitly committed to the principles of free trade.

At about the same time, there was a similar breakthrough toward the creation of an official regionwide security organization. In 1992, the members of ASEAN agreed to use their annual Post-Ministerial Conference to address security matters as well as economics. Moreover, participation in this aspect of the ASEAN-PMC was expanded to include Vietnam, which had just acquired observer status in ASEAN, and China and Russia, which were invited to participate as guests. Two years later in 1994, this security dialogue was expanded and formalized to become the ASEAN Regional Forum, or ARF.

This breakthrough was attributable to several factors. The collapse of the Soviet Union ended the earlier concern that official multilateral dialogue would be dominated by the presentation of one-sided and unacceptable Soviet proposals for naval arms control in the western Pacific. Although Moscow continued to present similar proposals for consideration, the improvement in relations between Russia and the United States, and to a lesser degree between Russia and Japan, made a formal multilateral dialogue more acceptable to Tokyo and Washington than had been true in earlier years.

The sponsorship of the initiative also made a considerable difference. The previous proposals for multilateral dialogue had come from the Soviet Union, Australia, and Canada. Gorbachev's proposals could be easily rejected on the grounds that they were one-sided and unacceptable. The Australian and Canadian proposals could be ignored because they were sponsored by governments that did not carry much weight in the region. But a proposal from ASEAN, the region's most important regional grouping, could not be disregarded or dismissed. Thus, Tokyo and Washington both agreed to participate in a meeting that they might well have avoided had it been conducted under other auspices.

Finally, the need for a multilateral security dialogue was more widely acknowledged in 1992 than it had been in the late 1980s. The rapid implosion of Russian military power in the region, the more gradual retrenchment of American forces, and the withdrawal of the United States from its air and naval bases in the Philippines were regarded as potentially destabilizing. Also unsettling to some in the region were new developments in Japanese and Chinese defense doctrine: Tokyo's decision to contribute troops to United Nations peacekeeping operations and Beijing's commitment to acquire force projection capabilities, including the purchase of advanced weapons from the former Soviet Union. The prospect of a renewed arms race in the region increased the attractiveness of multilateral security dialogue as a potential preventive measure.

Although the formation of APEC and of ARF can be regarded as significant breakthroughs in the creation of regional order, much work must be done before either of them can become a fully effective organization. One outstanding issue is the question of membership. The founding members of APEC were the same as the founding members of PECC: the members of ASEAN (now including Brunei, as well as Indonesia, Thailand, Malaysia, the Philippines, and Singapore), the United States, Japan, Canada, Australia, New Zealand, and South Korea. In 1991, thanks to intensive diplomatic efforts by Seoul, membership was extended to the three Chinese economies—mainland China, Hong Kong, and Taiwan—with Taiwan entering APEC under the name Chinese Taipei. In 1993, membership was arranged for Papua New Guinea, Mexico, and Chile as well. But the question of offering membership to other Asian economies, including

Russia, Mongolia, North Korea, the countries of Indochina, and the island nations of the South Pacific, has not yet been resolved. Nor has the issue of membership for Latin American countries been fully addressed, although by agreeing to membership for Mexico and Chile, APEC has strongly implied that others will be considered as well. Indeed, at its Seattle meeting in 1993, APEC deferred such knotty questions by announcing a three-year moratorium on the consideration of new applications for membership.

ARF also has to grapple with questions of participation. Other than the members and observers of ASEAN, only the regular dialogue partners in the ASEAN-PMC, plus Russia and China, have been invited to join the process; India, Mongolia, Taiwan, and North Korea have not been included. If ARF is to address security issues throughout the region, the representation of nations from Northeast and South Asia must be increased. Alternatively, if ARF is to restrict itself to a consideration of security in Southeast Asia, as presently seems more feasible, then corresponding mechanisms for security dialogue in Northeast and South Asia should be created.

Even more important, the issue of agenda must also be resolved. In neither APEC nor ARF is there yet any full agreement on how ambitious the organization's focus and objectives should be. ARF will have to determine the relative priorities to be assigned to the various security problems in the region: the remaining subregional disputes, the emerging unconventional threats to national security, and the possibility of a regionwide arms race. It will also have to decide whether to content itself with general discussions of various regional and subregional security problems, or whether it can begin to establish binding norms of international conduct. Such norms might include requirements that governments provide more complete information about their defense budgets, national security doctrines, and military deployments and exercises. They might also include even more stringent norms that would regulate deployments and arms transfers in ways that would preclude a regional arms race.

APEC has had similar problems. Some Asian countries have advocated a relatively conservative agenda for the organization: the exchange of information on patterns of trade, investment, and technology transfer, and cooperative projects in fields such as tourism, energy, environment, and infrastructural developments. Some in the United States have proposed that APEC negotiate a reduction of the barriers to trade and investment in the region, going beyond whatever agreements are reached in the final stages of the Uruguay Round of GATT and ultimately aiming at the construction of an Asia-Pacific free-trade agreement. Some in Japan and Australia have taken a middle position, advocating the harmonization of regulations involving foreign investment, customs procedures, product standards, and professional qualifications. The APEC meeting in Bogor, Indonesia, in 1994 endorsed the objective of achieving free trade in the region by the year 2020, without raising barriers to trade with other parts of the world. Subsequent meetings, however, are expected to be more contentious, as the members debate the concrete meaning of these two vague concepts, "free trade" and "open regionalism," to which APEC is now committed. They will also have to determine the relative pace and priority to be assigned to trade liberalization, development cooperation, and trade and investment facilitation, which remain potentially competitive items on the APEC agenda.[20]

In sum, the diversity of interests and outlooks is still a major obstacle to building multilateral organizations in the Asia-Pacific region. Countries will continue to act unilaterally in pursuit of their objectives, and to engage in bilateral negotiations with individual counterparts on issues of common concern. Nevertheless, there is a growing consensus that multilateral institutions are necessary to manage the complexity of interdependence and the uncertainty produced by the decline of the two superpowers.

Conclusion

Although the Asia-Pacific region had relatively low levels of multilateral organization throughout the Cold War era, it has now embarked on the path of institution building. Essentially, three factors have, in tandem, contributed to this development. The first has been the end of most of Asia's cold wars and the willingness of almost all of Asia's communist governments to begin economic reform, reduce tensions with former adversaries, and develop commercial relations with as many of their neighbors as possible. This trend has made it possible for the communist states of the region to join global international organizations, for more countries to construct informal cooperative mechanisms to address subregional security problems, and for the regional economies to form economic linkages across what had previously been unsurmountable political and ideological divides.

The second trend reshaping the international order in the Asia-Pacific region has been growing economic interdependence. This has increased the interest in forming regional regimes to govern and regulate economic activity, especially given the fact that the vitality and durability of global economic institutions such as GATT are now in doubt. It has also increased the need to deal with some of the unconventional security problems—from emigration to environmental protection—that are linked to growing economic dynamism and interaction. In comparison with Europe, however, it is notable that institution building in the Asia-Pacific region has followed economic interdependence rather than leading it.

Finally, the third factor at work is the growing complexity of the balance of power in the region. The collapse of the Soviet Union, the relative decline of the United States, and the rise of regional powers such as Japan and China are producing doubt about the stability of the region. This uncertainty is being exacerbated by the weakening of some of the alliances that once provided security for some of the weaker states in the area. At a time when the two superpowers can no longer offer the same security guarantees as in the past, there is a greater interest in creating multilateral security mechanisms to perform the same task. Moreover, the nearly universal interest in economic development and commercial interaction gives greater hope about the viability of such mechanisms.

The gradual shift of the international order in the Asia-Pacific region from bipolarity to multinodality has therefore increased the prospects for the creation of multilateral regimes and institutions in both the economic and security realms. But the process has been gradual, obstructed by the remaining elements of diversity and mistrust in the area. Asia has not seen the early emergence of formal regionwide multilateral organizations. Instead, it has experimented first with unofficial dialogues and subregional approaches, so as to gain experience and mutual confidence that can be applied to official regional institutions.

The creation of regional security regimes has lagged considerably behind the formation of economic institutions. The first multilateral scholarly dialogue on economic matters, PACTAD, was convened in 1968, whereas the first academic discussions of security issues took place only in the mid-1980s. The breakthrough in creating an official regionwide economic institution, APEC, took place in 1989, whereas it took three more years for a similar development to occur in the security realm. Understandably, it took the countries of the region much longer to acknowledge common security interests than to recognize compatible economic objectives. Once it began, however, the process of creating multilateral security institutions in Asia has moved much more rapidly than that of organizing the region economically. It took two decades to move from the creation of PBEC to the organization of APEC, whereas it required less than ten years to proceed from the first unofficial security dialogues to the agreement to discuss strategic issues in the ASEAN-PMC.

Despite the preliminary progress in building regional institutions, the work remains incomplete. Neither APEC nor ARF has achieved universal membership throughout the Asia-Pacific region. The two institutions remain discussion forums, sometimes with small secretariats, but with few concrete accomplishments, or even full agreement on an agenda. In this sense, the process of creating an institutionalized international order in Asia is still far behind that in Europe.

Looking ahead, there are several scenarios for order and organization in the Asia-Pacific region. In theory, powerful global institutions, such as GATT and the United Nations Security Council, could obviate the need for regional organization. But the world is too complex to be governed from a single center. Regional organization will remain essential; the issue is how coherent and effective those institutions will be.

One possibility is that the region could move rather steadily toward the creation of effective institutions, with APEC removing barriers to trade and investment and with ARF evolving into a Conference on Security Cooperation in Asia that could provide greater confidence in security arrangements. Although such a development is conceivable in the long run, the remaining differences in national interests and perceptions make it unlikely in the shorter term. The prospects for such institutions could be increased, however, if global institutions seem to be weakening, especially if GATT proves ineffective in halting the spread of protectionism, or if the United States announces a gradual reduction in its forces deployed in forward positions in the Pacific. Such developments might stimulate Asian governments to build regional institutions to fill the gap.

At the other extreme, it is conceivable that the efforts at institution building will fail virtually completely and that the region will fall back on the traditional remedies of self-help that are predicted by realist theories of international relations. In economics, there could be a rising tide of protectionism, mercantilism, and managed trade. In security matters, there could be an accelerated arms race, accompanied by the creation of either short-term alignments or longer-term alliances to counter perceived threats. Such developments would not necessarily produce open conflict, either military or economic, but they would make for a much more inefficient and costly international order in the region.

The most likely outcome is for a continuation of recent trends toward partial institutionalization. In both security and economic matters, the region could witness the emergence of multiple overlapping organizations—some regionwide, some subregional; some formal, others unofficial. These organizations would have partial success in setting and enforcing rules of conduct, in resolving or managing conflicts, and in providing greater predictability. But they would not completely stop nations from relying on unilateral measures and bilateral negotiations to pursue their economic and strategic objectives.

It is remarkable how small a role the United States government initially played in the creation of multilateral institutions in the Asia-Pacific region. Almost all of the initiatives came from other quarters. Proposals for multilateral security dialogues were put forward by the former Soviet Union, Australia, and Canada, whereas the idea of a formal regional economic organization came primarily from Japan, Australia, and Southeast Asia. To the extent that Americans took the lead in advocating economic and security cooperation, they were primarily from the academic or business communities, rather than from government. During the Reagan and Bush administrations, Washington's official position was either obstructive (as in the case of security cooperation) or passive (as in the case of economic organization).[21]

Fortunately, the Clinton administration has been considerably more enthusiastic about institution building in Asia. Indeed, the concept of a "New Pacific Community" has been the cornerstone of American policy in the region ever since the new administration took office in 1993. Accordingly, the U.S. attitude toward both types of multilateral organization has moved one step forward: from obstructive to passive on multilateral security dialogue, and from passive to positive on regional economic dooperation.

Further, American leadership will be a key to shaping the future. If the U.S. government plays an active but realistic role in creating multilateral organizations, the prospects for institutionalization will be greatly enhanced. If, on the other hand, Washington disengages from Asia, disdains the need for institution building, or attempts to impose agendas that are unacceptable to its Asian partners, then the possibility of creating a stable international order in the Asia-Pacific region will be considerably reduced.

Notes

1. On international regimes, see Stephen D. Krasner (ed.), *International Regimes* (Ithaca, NY: Cornell University Press, 1983); Oran R. Young, "International Regimes: Toward a New Theory of Institutions," *World Politics,* 39:1 (October 1986), pp. 104–22; Stephan Haggard and Beth A. Simmons, "Theories of International Regimes," *International Organization,* 41:3 (Summer 1987), pp. 491–517; and John Gerard Ruggie, "Multilateralism: The Anatomy of an Institution," *International Organization,* 46:3 (Summer 1992), pp. 561–98.

2. On the relative weakness of SEATO, see Leszek Buszynski, *SEATO: The Failure of an Alliance Strategy* (Singapore: Singapore University Press, 1983). SEATO as an organization was actually disbanded in 1977, although the Manila Treaty that created it technically remains in force.

3. On ASPAC, see Norman D. Palmer, *The New Regionalism in Asia and the Pacific* (Lexington, MA: Lexington Books, 1991); and Walt W. Rostow, *The United States and the Regional Organization of Asia and the Pacific, 1965–1985* (Austin: University of Texas Press, 1986).

4. Peter Drysdale, *International Economic Pluralism: Economic Policy in East Asia and the Pacific* (New York: Columbia University Press, 1988), pp. 60–63. Drysdale shows that the intensity of intraregional trade was the result more of geographic proximity and the relative absence of barriers than of inherent economic complementarities.

5. Hugh Patrick and Peter Drysdale, *An Asian-Pacific Regional Economic Organization: An Exploratory Concept Paper,* prepared for the Senate Committee on Foreign Relations by the Congressional Research Service, Library of Congress (Washington, DC: U.S. Government Printing Office, July 1979), p. 13.

6. For evidence that this argument was being made as early as the late 1960s, see Donald Crone, "The Politics of Emerging Pacific Cooperation," *Pacific Affairs,* 65:1 (Spring 1992), p. 69.

7. Okita laid out his views to an American audience in "The Pacific Community Idea," in "Three Dialogues with Saburo Okita," Occasional Paper No. 1 (Washington, DC: East Asia Program, The Wilson Center, December 1979). The Patrick-Drysdale proposal is in Patrick and Drysdale, *An Asian-Pacific Regional Economic Organization.*

8. For a summary of the reservations, see Obaid ul Haq, "The Pacific Basin Community: Problems and Prospects," in Robert Downen and Bruce Dickson (eds.), *The Emerging Pacific Community: A Regional Perspective* (Boulder, CO: Westview Press, 1984), pp. 40–41; and Patrick and Drysdale, *An Asian-Pacific Regional Economic Organization.*

9. For early reviews of the evolution of economic cooperation in the Asia-Pacific region, see R. Sean Randolph, "Pacific Overtures," *Foreign Policy,* no. 57 (Winter 1984–85), pp. 128–42; Palitha T.B. Kohona, "The Evolving Concept of a Pacific Basin Community," *Asian Survey,* 26:4 (April 1986), pp. 399–419; and Thomas J. Timmons, "The Pacific Community: Evolution of an Idea," Asian Studies Center Backgrounder No. 62 (Washington, DC: The Heritage Foundation, May 1987). For more recent overviews, see Drysdale, *International Economic Pluralism,* chap. 8; Palmer, *The New Regionalism in Asia and the Pacific;* and Crone, "The Politics of Emerging Pacific Cooperation."

10. On multilateral organization in the southwest Pacific subregion, see Palmer, *The New Regionalism in Asia and the Pacific,* chap. 6.

11. On ASEAN's limited achievements in the economic realm, see *The Economist,* October 24, 1992, p. 35.

12. For Scalapino's views see, *inter alia,* his *Major Power Relations in Northeast Asia,* Asian Agenda Report No. 9 (Lanham, MD, and New York: University Press of America and the Asia Society, 1987), p. 7. He applied the term "soft regionalism" to the process of institutionalization in Northeast Asia in the 1980s, but it could appropriately be applied to the region as a whole as well.

13. On the importance of ideas in international relations, see Judith Goldstein and Robert O. Keohane (eds.), *Ideas and Foreign Policy: Beliefs, Institutions, and Political Change* (Ithaca, NY: Cornell University Press, 1993).

14. Robert A. Scalapino, *The Last Leninists: The Uncertain Future of Asia's Communist States* (Washington, DC: Center for Strategic and International Studies, 1992). p. 20.

15. This discussion of proposals for security organization in the Asia-Pacific region draws heavily on the work of Canadian scholars and officials who have monitored the process from an early stage. See, for example, Paul Evans, "Emerging Patterns in Asia Pacific Security: The Search for a Regional Framework," paper presented to the Fifth Asia Pacific Roundtable, Kuala Lumpur, June 1991; Stewart Henderson, "Canada and Asia Pacific Security: The North Pacific Cooperative Security Dialogue: Recent Trends," Working Paper No. 1 (Toronto: North Pacific Cooperative Security Dialogue Research Programme, York University, January 1992); Douglas M. Johnston, "Anticipating Instability in the Asia-Pacific Region," *Washington Quarterly,* 15:3 (Summer 1992), pp. 103–12; and Peggy Mason, "Asia Pacific Security Forums: Rationale and Options: Canadian Views," paper presented to the Sixth Asia Pacific Roundtable, Kuala Lumpur, June 1992.

16. Many of these reservations were sympathetically summarized in Richard Fisher, "Why Asia Is Not Ready for Arms Control," Asian Studies Center Backgrounder No. 113 (Washington, DC: The Heritage Foundation, May 1991).

17. See my "Yataiquyudi xin shidai: zong liangji dao duozhongxin" [The New Era in the Asia-Pacific Region: From Bipolarity to Multinodality], in Yuan Ming (ed.), *Kua shijidi tiaozhan: zhongguo guoji guanxi xuekedi fazhan* [Facing the Challenge of a New Century: The Development of International Relations Studies in China] (Chongqing: Chongqing Publishing House, 1993), pp. 145–68.

18. See, for example, Michael T. Klare, "The Next Great Arms Race," *Foreign Affairs,* 72:3 (Summer 1993), pp. 136–52.

19. *South China Morning Post,* July 22, 1993, Business Section, p. 10.

20. Two useful compendia of divergent views on APEC are *Awashima Forum: Regional Integration and the Asia-Pacific Economy* (Tokyo: Japan Institute of International Affairs, 1993); and Richard J. Ellings (ed.), *Americans Speak to APEC: Building a New Order with Asia,* NBR Analysis, vol. 4, no. 4 (Seattle: National Bureau of Asian Research, November 1993). See also Jimmy Wheeler and Rosemary Pugh Piper, "APEC: Looking for a Leading Role in Asia's Future," Hudson Briefing Paper No. 144 (Indianapolis, IN: The Hudson Institute, September 1992).

21. One exception to this generalization was the Reagan administration's appointment of Richard Fairbanks to serve as U.S. ambassador-at-large for Pacific Basin affairs in the mid-1980s. As Donald Crone points out, this step can be regarded as a symbol of a growing official interest in creating an official regional economic organization. See Crone, "The Politics of Emerging Pacific Cooperation"; and Randolph, "Pacific Overtures."

Index